New Perspectives on

W9-CEA-497

MICROSOFT®
WORD 2000

Introductory

BEVERLY B. ZIMMERMAN
Brigham Young University

S. SCOTT ZIMMERMAN
Brigham Young University

ANN SHAFFER

APPROVED COURSEWARE

COURSE
TECHNOLOGY

Thomson Learning™

ONE MAIN STREET, CAMBRIDGE, MA 02142

New Perspectives on Microsoft Word 2000—Introductory is published by Course Technology.

Senior Editor	Donna Gridley
Senior Product Manager	Rachel Crapser
Developmental Editors	Ann Shaffer/Robin Romer
Acquisitions Editor	Christine Burmeister
Product Manager	Catherine Donaldson
Associate Product Manager	Karen Shortill
Editorial Assistant	Melissa Dezotell
Production Editor	Daphne Barbas
Text Designer	Meral Dabcovich
Cover Art Designer	Douglas Goodman

© 1999 by Course Technology, a division of Thomson Learning.

For more information contact:

Course Technology
One Main Street
Cambridge, MA 02142
Or find us on the World Wide Web at: http://www.course.com

For permission to use material from this text or product, contact us by
Web: www.thomsonrights.com
Phone: 1-800-730-2214
Fax: 1-800-730-2215

Trademarks

Disclaimer

ISBN 0-7600-6993-X

Printed in the United States of America

2 3 4 5 6 7 8 9 10 BM 04 03 02 01 00

PREFACE

The New Perspectives Series

About New Perspectives

Course Technology's **New Perspectives Series** is an integrated system of instruction that combines text and technology products to teach computer concepts, the Internet, and microcomputer applications. Users consistently praise this series for innovative pedagogy, use of interactive technology, creativity, accuracy, and supportive and engaging style.

How is the New Perspectives Series different from other series?

The **New Perspectives Series** distinguishes itself by **innovative technology**, from the renowned Course Labs to the state-of-the-art multimedia that is integrated with our Concepts texts. Other distinguishing features include **sound instructional design, proven pedagogy**, and **consistent quality**. Each tutorial has students learn features in the context of solving a realistic case problem rather than simply learning a laundry list of features. With the **New Perspectives Series**, instructors report that students have a complete, integrative learning experience that stays with them. They credit this high retention and competency to the fact that this series incorporates critical thinking and problem-solving with computer skills mastery. In addition, we work hard to ensure accuracy by using a multi-step quality assurance process during all stages of development. Instructors focus on teaching and students spend more time learning.

Choose the coverage that's right for you

New Perspectives applications books are available in the following categories:

Brief
2-4 tutorials

Brief: approximately 150 pages long, two to four "Level I" tutorials, teaches basic application skills.

Introductory
6 or 7 tutorials, or Brief + 2 or 3 more tutorials

Introductory: approximately 300 pages long, four to seven tutorials, goes beyond the basic skills. These books often build out of the Brief book, adding two or three additional "Level II" tutorials. The book you are holding is an Introductory book.

Comprehensive
Introductory + 4 or 5 more tutorials. Includes Brief Windows tutorials and Additional Cases

Comprehensive: approximately 600 pages long, eight to twelve tutorials, all tutorials included in the Introductory text plus higher-level "Level III" topics. Also includes two Windows tutorials and three or four fully developed Additional Cases.

Advanced
Quick Review of basics + in-depth, high-level coverage

Advanced: approximately 600 pages long, covers topics similar to those in the Comprehensive books, but offers the highest-level coverage in the series. Advanced books assume students already know the basics, and therefore go into more depth at a more accelerated rate than the Comprehensive titles. Advanced books are ideal for a second, more technical course.

Office
Office suite components + integration + Internet

Office: approximately 800 pages long, covers all components of the Office suite as well as integrating the individual software packages with one another and the Internet.

Custom Editions

Choose from any of the above to build your own Custom Editions or CourseKits

Custom Books: The New Perspectives Series offers you two ways to customize a New Perspectives text to fit your course exactly: *CourseKits*™ are two or more texts shrink-wrapped together and offer significant price discounts. *Custom Editions*® offer you flexibility in designing your concepts, Internet, and applications courses. You can build your own book by ordering a combination of topics bound together to cover only the subjects you want. There is no minimum order and books are spiral bound. Contact your Course Technology sales representative for more information.

What course is this book appropriate for?

New Perspectives on Microsoft Word 2000—Introductory can be used in any course in which you want students to learn some of the most important topics of Word 2000, including creating styles, outlines, tables, and tables of contents, creating form letters and mailing labels, and integrating Word with other programs and with the World Wide Web. It is particularly recommended for a short-semester course on Microsoft Word 2000. This book assumes that students have learned basic Windows navigation and file management skills from Course Technology's *New Perspectives on Microsoft Windows 95—Brief,* or the equivalent book for Windows 98 or NT.

What is the Microsoft Office User Specialist Program?

The Microsoft Office User Specialist Program provides an industry-recognized standard for measuring an individual's mastery of an Office application. Passing one or more MOUS Program certification exam helps your students demonstrate their proficiency to prospective employers and gives them a competitive edge in the job marketplace. Course Technology offers a growing number of Microsoft-approved products that cover all of the required objectives for the MOUS Program exams. For a complete listing of Course Technology titles that you can use to help your students get certified, visit our Web sit at **www.course.com**.

New Perspectives on Microsoft Word 2000—Introductory has been approved by Microsoft as courseware for the Microsoft Office User Specialist (MOUS) Program. After completing the tutorials and exercises in this book, students may be prepared to take the MOUS exam for Microsoft Word 2000. For more information about certification, please visit the MOUS program site at **www.mous.net**.

Proven Pedagogy

CASE

Tutorial Case Each tutorial begins with a problem presented in a case that is meaningful to students. The case turns the task of learning how to use an application into a problem-solving process.

45-minute Sessions Each tutorial is divided into sessions that can be completed in about 45 minutes to an hour. Sessions allow instructors to more accurately allocate time in their syllabus, and students to better manage their own study time.

1.
2.
3.

Step-by-Step Methodology We make sure students can differentiate between what they are to do and what they are to read. Through numbered steps – clearly identified by a gray shaded background – students are constantly guided in solving the case problem. In addition, the numerous screen shots with callouts direct students' attention to what they should look at on the screen.

TROUBLE?

TROUBLE? Paragraphs These paragraphs anticipate the mistakes or problems that students may have and help them continue with the tutorial.

Tutorial **Tips** |—

Tutorial Tips Page This page, following the Table of Contents, offers students suggestions on how to effectively plan their study and lab time, what to do when they make a mistake, how to use the Reference Windows, MOUS grids, Quick Checks, and other features of the New Perspectives Series.

Read

"Read This Before You Begin" Page Located opposite the first tutorial's opening page for each level of the text, the Read This Before You Begin Page helps introduce technology into the classroom. Technical considerations and assumptions about software are listed to save time and eliminate unnecessary aggravation. Notes about the Student Disks help instructors and students get the right files in the right places, so students get started on the right foot.

Quick Check Questions Each session concludes with meaningful, conceptual Quick Check questions that test students' understanding of what they learned in the session. Answers to the Quick Check questions are provided at the end of each tutorial.

RW

Reference Windows Reference Windows are succinct summaries of the most important tasks covered in a tutorial and they preview actions students will perform in the steps to follow.

TASK REFERENCE

Task Reference Located as a table at the end of the book, the Task Reference contains a summary of how to perform common tasks using the most efficient method, as well as references to pages where the task is discussed in more detail.

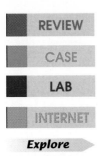

End-of-Tutorial Review Assignments, Case Problems, Internet Assignments, and Lab Assignments Review Assignments provide students with additional hands-on practice of the skills they learned in the tutorial using the same case presented in the tutorial. These Assignments are followed by three to four Case Problems that have approximately the same scope as the tutorial case but use a different scenario. In addition, some of the Review Assignments or Case Problems may include Exploration Exercises that challenge students encourage them to explore the capabilities of the program they are using, and/or further extend their knowledge. Finally, if a Course Lab accompanies a tutorial, Lab Assignments are included after the Case Problems.

File Finder Chart This chart, located in the back of the book, visually explains how a student should set up their data disk, what files should go in what folders, and what they'll be saving the files as in the course of their work.

MOUS Certification Chart In the back of the book, you'll find a chart that lists all the skills for the Microsoft Office User Specialist Exam on Word 2000. With page numbers referencing where these skills are covered in this text and where students get hands-on practice in completing the skills, the chart can be used as an excellent study guide in preparing for the Word MOUS exam.

The Instructor's Resource Kit for this title contains:

- Electronic Instructor's Manual
- Data Files
- Solution Files
- Course Labs
- Course Test Manager Testbank
- Course Test Manager Engine
- Figure Files

These teaching tools come on CD-ROM. If you don't have access to a CD-ROM drive, contact your Course Technology customer service representative for more information.

The New Perspectives Supplements Package

Electronic Instructor's Manual. Our Instructor's Manuals include tutorial overviews and outlines, technical notes, lecture notes, solutions, and Extra Case Problems. Many instructors use the Extra Case Problems for performance-based exams or extra credit projects. The Instructor's Manual is available as an electronic file, which you can get from the Instructor Resource Kit (IRK) CD-ROM or download it from **www.course.com**.

Data Files Data Files contain all of the data that students will use to complete the tutorials, Review Assignments, and Case Problems. A Readme file includes instructions for using the files. See the "Read This Before You Begin" page or the "File Finder" chart for more information on Data Files.

Solution Files Solution Files contain every file students are asked to create or modify in the tutorials, Review Assignments, Case Problems, and Extra Case Problems. A Help file on the Instructor's Resource Kit includes information for using the Solution Files.

Course Labs: Concepts Come to Life These highly interactive computer-based learning activities bring concepts to life with illustrations, animations, digital images, and simulations. The Labs guide students step-by-step, present them with Quick Check questions, let them explore on their own, test their comprehension, and provide printed feedback. Lab icons at the beginning of the tutorial and in the tutorial margins indicate when a topic has a corresponding Lab. Lab Assignments are included at the end of each relevant tutorial. The Labs available with this book and the tutorials in which they appear are:

Tutorial 1   Tutorial 7

Figure Files Many figures in the text are provided on the IRK CD-ROM to help illustrate key topics or concepts. Instructors can create traditional overhead transparencies by printing the figure files. Or they can create electronic slide shows by using the figures in a presentation program such as PowerPoint.

Course Test Manager: Testing and Practice at the Computer or on Paper Course Test Manager is cutting-edge, Windows-based testing software that helps instructors design and administer practice tests and actual examinations. Course Test Manager can automatically grade the tests students take at the computer and can generate statistical information on individual as well as group performance.

Online Companions: Dedicated to Keeping You and Your Students Up-To-Date Visit our faculty sites and student sites on the World Wide Web at **www.course.com**. Here instructors can browse this text's password-protected Faculty Online Companion to obtain an online Instructor's Manual, Solution Files, Student Files, and more. Students can also access this text's Student Online Companion, which contains Student files and all the links that the students will need to complete their tutorial assignments.

More innovative technology

Course CBT

Enhance your students' Office 2000 classroom learning experience with self-paced computer-based training on CD-ROM. Course CBT engages students with interactive multimedia and hands-on simulations that reinforce and complement the concepts and skills covered in the textbook. All the content is aligned with the MOUS (Microsoft Office User Specialist) program, making it a great preparation tool for the certification exams. Course CBT also includes extensive pre- and post-assessments that test students' mastery of skills. These pre- and post-assessments automatically generate a "custom learning path" through the course that highlights only the topics students need help with.

Course Assessment

How well do your students really know Microsoft Office? Course Assessment is a performance-based testing program that measures students' proficiency in Microsoft Office 2000. Previously known as SAM, Course Assessment is available for Office 2000 in either a live or simulated environment. You can use Course Assessment to place students into or out of courses, monitor their performance throughout a course, and help prepare them for the MOUS certification exams.

WebCT

WebCT is a tool used to create Web-based educational environments and also uses WWW browsers as the interface for the course-building environment. The site is hosted on your school campus, allowing complete control over the information. WebCT has its own internal communication system, offering internal e-mail, a Bulletin Board, and a Chat room.

Course Technology offers pre-existing supplemental information to help in your WebCT class creation, such as a suggested Syllabus, Lecture Notes, Figures in the Book/ Course Presenter, Student Downloads, and Test Banks in which you can schedule an exam, create reports, and more.

Acknowledgments

Sincere thanks to the reviewers for their excellent feedback: Janet Sheppard, Collin County Community College; Mary Dobranski, College of St. Mary; and Tony Gabriel, Computer Learning Center. Thanks also go out to John Bosco, Quality Assurance Project Leader, and Nicole Ashton, John Freitas, Alex White, and Jeff Schwartz, QA testers, for verifying the technical accuracy of every step.

Many thanks to all the smart, friendly, helpful folks at Course Technology, including Melissa Dezotell, for managing the review process so smoothly, Karen Shortill, for her expertise on the supplements, and Catherine Donaldson, for all her contributions. In particular, thanks to Rachel Crapser, senior product manager, for steering us through the rough waters of the Office 2000 beta with so much professionalism and good cheer. Thanks to Robin Romer, development editor, for her encouraging phone calls and expert editing. Thank you to Daphne Barbas, production editor, for magically transforming the manuscript into a published book.

Ann Shaffer, S. Scott Zimmerman, & Beverly Zimmerman

I also owe a great debt to Beverly and Scott Zimmerman, writers and teachers extraordinaire, for giving me the opportunity to be a part of their team. And special thanks to Lois Sachtjen, for being such a kind and helpful friend.

Ann Shaffer

TABLE OF CONTENTS

Tutorial 3   WD 3.01

Creating a Multiple-Page Report
Writing a Recommendation Report for AgriTechnology

Tutorial 4 — WD 4.01

Desktop Publishing a Newsletter

Creating a Newsletter for FastFad Manufacturing Company

Tutorial 5 — WD 5.03

Creating Styles, Outlines, Tables, and Tables of Contents

Writing a Business Plan for EstimaTech

Tutorial 6   WD 6.01

Creating Form Letters and Mailing Labels

Writing a Sales Letter for The Pet Shoppe

Reference Window List

Tutorial Tips

These tutorials will help you learn about Microsoft Word 2000. The tutorials are designed to be worked through at a computer. Each tutorial is divided into sessions. Watch for the session headings, such as Session 1.1 and Session 1.2. Each session is designed to be completed in about 45 minutes, but take as much time as you need. It's also a good idea to take a break between sessions.

To use the tutorials effectively, read the following questions and answers before you begin.

Where do I start?
Each tutorial begins with a case, which sets the scene for the tutorial and gives you background information to help you understand what you will be doing. Read the case before you go to the lab. In the lab, begin with the first session of a tutorial.

How do I know what to do on the computer?
Each session contains steps that you will perform on the computer to learn how to use Microsoft Word 2000. Read the text that introduces each series of steps. The steps you need to do at a computer are numbered and are set against a shaded background. Read each step carefully and completely before you try it.

How do I know if I did the step correctly?
As you work, compare your computer screen with the corresponding figure in the tutorial. Don't worry if your screen display is somewhat different from the figure. The important parts of the screen display are labeled in each figure. Check to make sure these parts are on your screen.

What if I make a mistake?
Don't worry about making mistakes—they are part of the learning process. Paragraphs labeled "TROUBLE?" identify common problems and explain how to get back on track. Follow the steps in a TROUBLE? paragraph only if you are having the problem described. If you run into other problems:

- Carefully consider the current state of your system, the position of the pointer, and any messages on the screen.

- Complete the sentence, "Now I want to…" Be specific, because identifying your goal will help you rethink the steps you need to take to reach that goal.

- If you are working on a particular piece of software, consult the Help system.

- If the suggestions above don't solve your problem, consult your technical support person for assistance.

How do I use the Reference Windows?
Reference Windows summarize the procedures you will learn in the tutorial steps. Do not complete the actions in the Reference Windows when you are working through the tutorial. Instead, refer to the Reference Windows while you are working on the assignments at the end of the tutorial.

How can I test my understanding of the material I learned in the tutorial?
At the end of each session, you can answer the Quick Check questions. The answers for the Quick Checks are at the end of that tutorial.

After you have completed the entire tutorial, you should complete the Review Assignments and Case Problems. They are carefully structured so that you will review what you have learned and then apply your knowledge to new situations.

What if I can't remember how to do something?
You should refer to the Task Reference at the end of the book; it summarizes how to accomplish tasks using the most efficient method.

Before you begin the tutorials, you should know the basics about your computer's operating system. You should also know how to use the menus, dialog boxes, Help system, and My Computer.

How can I prepare for MOUS Certification?
The Microsoft Office User Specialist (MOUS) logo on the cover of this book indicates that Microsoft has approved it as a study guide for the Word 2000 MOUS exam. At the back of this text, you'll see a chart that outlines the specific Microsoft certification skills for Word 2000 that are covered in the tutorials. You'll need to learn these skills if you're interested in taking a MOUS exam. If you decide to take a MOUS exam, or if you just want to study a specific skill, this chart will give you an easy reference to the page number on which the skill is covered. To learn more about the MOUS certification program refer to the preface in the front of the book or go to **www.mous.net**.

Now that you've read the Tutorial Tips, you are ready to begin.

New Perspectives on

MICROSOFT®
WORD® 2000

Read This Before You Begin

To the Student

Data Disks

To complete the Level I tutorials, Review Assignments, and Case Problems, you need 1 Data Disk. Your instructor will either provide you with this Data Disk or ask you to make your own.

If you are making your own Data Disk, you will need 1 blank, formatted high-density disk. You will need to copy a set of folders from a file server or standalone computer or the Web onto your disks. Your instructor will tell you which computer, drive letter, and folders contain the files you need. You could also download the files by going to www.course.com, clicking Data Disk Files, and following the instructions on the screen.

The following shows you which folders go on your disk, so that you will have enough disk space to complete all the tutorials, Review Assignments, and Case Problems:

Data Disk 1

Write this on the disk label:
Data Disk 1: Word 2000 Tutorials 1-4

Put these folders on the disk:
Tutorial.01, Tutorial.02, Tutorial.03, Tutorial.04

When you begin each tutorial, be sure you are using the correct Data Disk. Refer to the "File Finder" Chart at the back of this text for more detailed information on which files are used in which tutorials. See the inside front cover of this book for more information on Student Disk files, or ask your instructor or technical support person for assistance.

Course Labs

The Word Level I tutorials feature an interactive Course Lab to help you understand word processing concepts. There are Lab Assignments at the end of Tutorial 1 that relate to this Lab.

To start a Lab, click the **Start** button on the Windows taskbar, point to **Programs**, point to **Course Labs**, point to **New Perspectives Course Labs**, and click the name of the Lab you want to use.

Using Your Own Computer

If you are going to work through this book using your own computer, you need:

- ■ **Computer System** Microsoft Windows 95, 98, NT, or higher must be installed on your computer. This book assumes a typical installation of Microsoft Word.

- ■ **Data Disk** You will not be able to complete the tutorials or exercises in this book using your own computer until you have your Data Disk.

- ■ **Course Labs** See your instructor or technical support person to obtain the Course Lab software for use on your own computer.

Visit Our World Wide Web Site

Additional materials designed especially for you are available on the World Wide Web. Go to http://www.course.com.

To the Instructor

The Data Files and Course Labs are available on the Instructor's Resource Kit for this title. Follow the instructions in the Help file on the CD-ROM to install the programs to your network or standalone computer. For information on creating Data Disks or the Course Labs, see the "To the Student" section above.

You are granted a license to copy the Data Files and Course Labs to any computer or computer network used by students who have purchased this book.

In this tutorial you will:

- Start and exit Word

- Identify the components of the Word window

- Choose commands using the toolbars and menus

- Create and edit a document

- Enter the date with AutoComplete

- Correct spelling errors with AutoCorrect

- Scroll through a document

- Save, preview, and print a document

- Record properties for a document

- Use the Word Help system to get help

LAB

Word Processing

CREATING A DOCUMENT

Writing a Business Letter for Crossroads

CASE

Crossroads

Karen Liu is executive director of Crossroads, a small, nonprofit organization in Tacoma, Washington. Crossroads distributes business clothing to low-income clients who are returning to the job market or starting new careers. To make potential clients in the community more aware of their services, Crossroads reserves an exhibit booth each year at a local job fair sponsored by the Tacoma Chamber of Commerce. Crossroads needs to find out the date and location of this year's fair, as well as some other logistical information, before reserving a booth. Karen asks you to write a letter requesting this information from the Tacoma Chamber of Commerce.

In this tutorial you will create Karen's letter using Microsoft Word 2000, a popular word-processing program. Before you begin typing the letter, you will learn to start the Word program, identify and use the elements of the Word screen, and adjust some Word settings. Next you will create a new Word document, type the text of the Crossroads letter, save the letter, and then print the letter for Karen. In the process of entering the text, you'll learn several ways of correcting typing errors. You'll also find out how to use the Word Help system, which allows you to quickly find answers to your questions about the program.

SESSION 1.1

In this session you will learn how to start Word, how to identify and use the parts of the Word screen, and how to adjust some Word settings. With the skills you learn in this session, you'll be prepared to use Word to create a variety of documents, such as letters, reports, and memos.

Four Steps to a Professional Document

Word helps you produce quality work in minimal time. Not only can you type a document in Word, you can quickly make revisions and corrections, adjust margins and spacing, create columns and tables, and add graphics to your documents. The most efficient way to produce a document is to follow these four steps: (1) planning and creating, (2) editing, (3) formatting, and (4) printing.

In the long run, *planning* saves time and effort. First, you should determine what you want to say. State your purpose clearly and include enough information to achieve that purpose without overwhelming or boring your reader. Be sure to *organize* your ideas logically. Also, decide how you want your document to look. In this case, your letter to the Tacoma Chamber of Commerce will take the form of a standard business letter. Karen has given you a handwritten note with all her questions for the Tacoma Chamber of Commerce, as shown in Figure 1-1.

Figure 1-1	KAREN'S QUESTIONS ABOUT THE JOB FAIR

Please write the Tacoma Chamber of Commerce and find out the following:

What are the location and dates for this year's job fair?

Is a map of the exhibit area available? What size booths are available and how can we reserve a booth?

Who do we contact about what physical facilities are available at each booth?

Send the letter to the Chamber's president. The address is 210 Shoreline Vista, Suite 1103, Tacoma WA 98402.

After you've planned your document, you can go ahead and *create* it using Word. The next step, *editing*, consists of reading the document you've created, then correcting your errors, and, finally, adding or deleting text to make the document easy to read.

Once your document is error-free, you can *format* it to make it visually appealing. Formatting features, such as white space (blank areas of a page), line spacing, boldface, and italics can help make your document easier to read. *Printing* is the final phase in creating an effective document. In this tutorial, you will preview your document before you spend time and resources to print it.

Starting **Word**

Before you can apply these four steps to produce a letter in Word, you need to start Word and learn about the general organization of the Word screen. You'll do that now.

To start Microsoft Word:

1. Make sure Windows is running on your computer and the Windows desktop appears on your screen.

2. Click the **Start** button on the taskbar to display the Start menu, and then point to **Programs** to display the Programs menu.

3. Point to **Microsoft Word** on the Programs menu. See Figure 1-2.

| Figure 1-2 | STARTING MICROSOFT WORD |

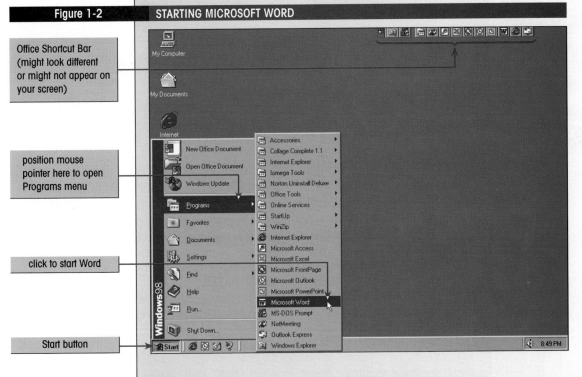

Office Shortcut Bar (might look different or might not appear on your screen)

position mouse pointer here to open Programs menu

click to start Word

Start button

TROUBLE? Don't worry if your screen differs slightly from Figure 1-2. Although the figures in this book were created while running Windows 98 in its default settings, these operating systems share the same basic user interface. Microsoft Word should run equally well using Windows 95, Windows 98 in Web style, Windows NT, or Windows 2000.

TROUBLE? If you don't see the Microsoft Word option on the Programs menu, ask your instructor or technical support person for help.

TROUBLE? If the Office Shortcut Bar appears on your screen, your system is set up to display it. Because the Office Shortcut Bar is not required to complete these tutorials, it has been omitted from the remaining figures in this text. You can close it or simply ignore it.

4. Click **Microsoft Word**. After a short pause, the Microsoft Word copyright information appears in a message box and remains on the screen until the Word program window, containing a blank Word document, is displayed. See Figure 1-3.

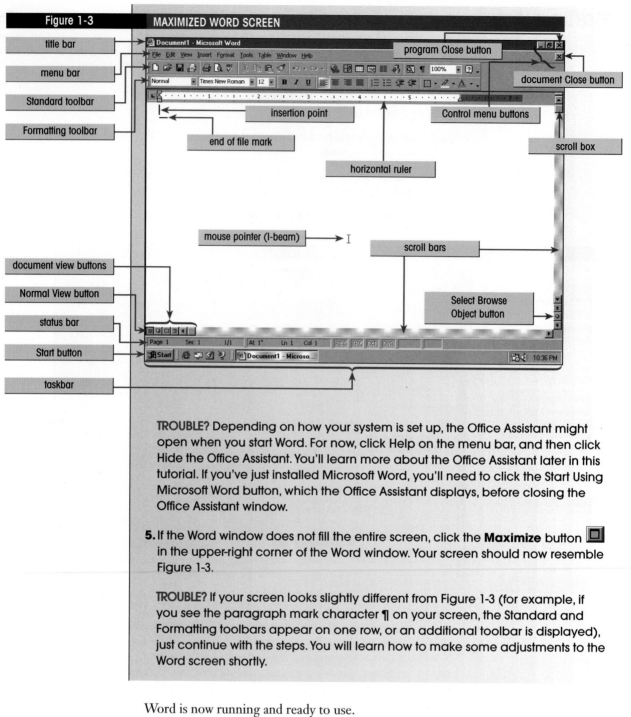

Figure 1-3   MAXIMIZED WORD SCREEN

TROUBLE? Depending on how your system is set up, the Office Assistant might open when you start Word. For now, click Help on the menu bar, and then click Hide the Office Assistant. You'll learn more about the Office Assistant later in this tutorial. If you've just installed Microsoft Word, you'll need to click the Start Using Microsoft Word button, which the Office Assistant displays, before closing the Office Assistant window.

5. If the Word window does not fill the entire screen, click the **Maximize** button in the upper-right corner of the Word window. Your screen should now resemble Figure 1-3.

TROUBLE? If your screen looks slightly different from Figure 1-3 (for example, if you see the paragraph mark character ¶ on your screen, the Standard and Formatting toolbars appear on one row, or an additional toolbar is displayed), just continue with the steps. You will learn how to make some adjustments to the Word screen shortly.

Word is now running and ready to use.

Viewing the Word Screen

The Word screen is made up of a number of elements, each of which is described in Figure 1-4. You are already familiar with some of these elements, such as the menu bar, title bar, and status bar, because they are common to all Windows screens.

If at any time you would like to check the name of a Word toolbar button, just position the mouse pointer over the button without clicking. A **ScreenTip**, a small yellow box with the name of the button, will appear.

Figure 1-4	DESCRIPTION OF WORD SCREEN ELEMENTS
SCREEN ELEMENT	**DESCRIPTION**
Control menu buttons	Size and close the Word window and the document
Document Close button	Closes the open document when only one document is open
Document view buttons	Switch the document between four different views: normal view, Web layout view, print layout view, and outline view
Document window	Area where you enter text and graphics
End-of-file mark	Indicates the end of the document
Formatting toolbar	Contains buttons to activate common font and paragraph formatting commands
Horizontal ruler	Adjusts margins, tabs, and column widths; vertical ruler appears in print layout view
Insertion point	Indicates location where characters will be inserted or deleted
Menu bar	Contains lists or menus of all the Word commands. When you first display a menu, you see a short list of the most frequently used commands. To see the full list of commands in the menu, you can either click the menu and then wait a few seconds for the remaining commands to appear or click the menu and then click or point to the downward-facing double-arrow at the bottom of the menu.
Mouse pointer	Changes shape depending on its location on the screen (i.e., I-beam pointer in text area; arrow in nontext areas)
Program Close button	Closes the current document if more than one document is open. Closes Word if one or no document is open.
Scroll bars	Shifts text vertically and horizontally on the screen so you can see different parts of the document
Scroll box	Helps you move quickly to other pages of your document
Select Browse Object button	Displays buttons that allow you to move quickly through the document
Standard toolbar	Contains buttons to activate frequently used commands
Start button	Starts a program, opens a document, provides quick access to Windows Help
Status bar	Provides information regarding the location of the insertion point
Taskbar	Shows programs that are running and allows you to switch quickly from one program to another
Title bar	Identifies the current application (i.e., Microsoft Word); shows the filename of the current document

Keep in mind that the commands on the menu bars initially display the commands that are used most frequently on your particular computer. When you leave the menu displayed for a few seconds or point to the double-arrow, a more complete list of commands appears. Throughout these tutorials, point to the double-arrow if you do not see the command you need.

Checking the Screen Before You Begin Each Tutorial

Word provides a set of standard settings, called **default settings**, that are appropriate for most documents. However, the setup of your Word document might have different default settings from those shown in the figures. This often happens when you share a computer and another user changes the appearance of the Word screen. The rest of this section explains what your screen should look like and how to make it match those in the tutorials.

Setting the Document View to Normal

You can view your document in one of four ways—normal, Web layout, print layout, or outline. **Web layout view** and **outline view** are designed for special situations that you don't need to worry about now. You will, however, learn more about **print layout view**—which allows you to see a page's design and format—in later tutorials. You will use **normal view,** which allows you to see more of the document, for this tutorial. Depending on the document view selected by the last person who used Word, you might need to change the document back to normal view.

To make sure the document window is in normal view:

1. Click the **Normal View** button ▤ to the left of the horizontal scroll bar. See Figure 1-5. If your document window was not in normal view, it changes to normal view now. The Normal View button looks pressed in to indicate that it is selected.

Figure 1-5	CHANGING TO NORMAL VIEW

Web Layout button

Normal View button

status bar

Print Layout button

Outline View button

Normal View

Sec 1   1/1   At 1"   Ln 1   Col 1   REC TRK EXT OVR

Start   Document1 - Microso...   4:14 PM

Displaying the Toolbars and Ruler

These tutorials frequently use the Standard toolbar and the Formatting toolbar to help you work more efficiently. Each time you start Word, check to make sure both toolbars appear on your screen, with the Standard toolbar on top of the Formatting toolbar. Depending on the settings specified by the last person to use your computer, you may not see both toolbars, or your toolbars may appear all on one row, rather than one on top of another. You also may see additional toolbars, such as the Drawing toolbar.

If either toolbar is missing, or if other toolbars are displayed, perform the next steps.

To display or hide a toolbar:

1. Position the pointer over any visible toolbar and click the right mouse button. A shortcut menu appears. The menu lists all available toolbars and displays a check mark next to those currently displayed.

2. If the Standard or Formatting toolbar is not visible, click its name on the shortcut menu to place a check mark next to it. If any toolbars besides the Formatting and Standard toolbars have check marks, click each one to remove the check mark and hide the toolbar. Only the Standard and Formatting toolbars should be visible, as shown in Figure 1-6.

Figure 1-6	TWO TOOLBARS ON ONE ROW

Document1 - Microsoft Word

File Edit View Insert Format Tools Table Window Help

Times New Roman   12   B I U

Standard toolbar

Formatting toolbar

If the toolbars appear on one row, as in Figure 1-6, perform the next steps to move the Formatting toolbar below the Standard toolbar.

To move the Formatting toolbar:

1. Click **Tools** on the menu bar, and then click **Customize**. The Cu: box opens.

   TROUBLE? If you don't see the Customize command on the Tools me the double-arrow, as explained earlier in this tutorial, to display the fu commands.

2. Click the **Options** tab, and then click the **Standard and Formatting toolbars share one row** check box to remove the check.

3. Click **Close**. The Customize dialog box closes. The toolbars on your screen should now match those in Figure 1-3.

As you complete these tutorials, the ruler also should be visible to help you place items precisely.

To display the ruler:

1. Click **View** on the menu bar, and then point to the double-arrow at the bottom of the menu to display the hidden menu commands.

2. If "Ruler" does not have a check mark next to it, then click **Ruler**.

Setting the Font and Font Size

A **font** is a set of characters that has a certain design, shape, and appearance. Each font has a name, such as Courier, Times New Roman, or Arial. The **font size** is the actual height of a character, measured in points, where one point equals 1/72 of an inch in height. You'll learn more about fonts and font sizes later, but for now simply keep in mind that most of the documents you create will use the Times New Roman font in a font size of 12 points. Word usually uses a default (or predefined) setting of Times New Roman 12 point in new documents, but someone else might have changed the setting after Word was installed on your computer. You can see your computer's current settings in the Font list box, and the Font Size list box, in the Formatting toolbar, as shown in Figure 1-7.

Figure 1-7	DEFAULT FONT AND FONT SIZE SETTINGS

default font

default font size

If your font setting is not Times New Roman 12 point, you should change the default setting now. You'll use the menu bar to choose the desired commands.

To change the default font and font size:

1. Click **Format** on the menu bar, and then click **Font** to open the Font dialog box. If necessary, click the Font tab. See Figure 1-8.

| Figure 1-8 | FONT DIALOG BOX |

use this font

use this point size

click to make selected font settings the defaults

2. In the Font text box, click **Times New Roman**.

3. In the Size list box, click **12** to change the font to 12 point.

4. Click the **Default** button to make Times New Roman and 12 point the default settings. Word displays a message asking you to verify that you want to make 12-point Times New Roman the default font.

5. Click the **Yes** button.

Displaying Nonprinting Characters

Nonprinting characters are symbols that can be displayed on the screen but that do not show up when you print your document. You can display them when you are working on the appearance, or **format**, of your document. For example, one nonprinting character marks the end of a paragraph (¶), and another marks the space between words (•). It's sometimes helpful to display nonprinting characters so you can see whether you've typed an extra space, ended a paragraph, typed spaces instead of tabs, and so on. Generally, in these tutorials, you will display nonprinting characters only when you are formatting a document. You'll display them now, though, so you can use them as guides when typing your first letter.

To display nonprinting characters:

1. Click the Show/Hide ¶ button ¶ on the Standard toolbar. A paragraph mark (¶) appears at the top of the document window. See Figure 1-9.

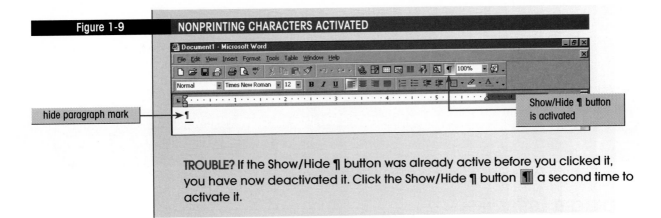

Figure 1-9	NONPRINTING CHARACTERS ACTIVATED

hide paragraph mark

Show/Hide ¶ button is activated

TROUBLE? If the Show/Hide ¶ button was already active before you clicked it, you have now deactivated it. Click the Show/Hide ¶ button ¶ a second time to activate it.

To make sure your screen always matches the figures in these tutorials, remember to complete the checklist in Figure 1-10 each time you sit down at the computer.

Figure 1-10	WORD SCREEN SESSION CHECKLIST

SCREEN ELEMENT	SETTING	CHECK
Document view	Normal view	☐
Word window	Maximized	☐
Standard toolbar	Displayed, below the menu bar	☐
Formatting toolbar	Displayed, below the Standard toolbar	☐
Other toolbars	Hidden	☐
Nonprinting characters	Hidden	☐
Font	Times New Roman	☐
Point size	12 point	☐
Ruler	Displayed	☐

Now that you have planned a document, opened the Word program, identified screen elements, and adjusted settings, you are ready to create a new document. In the next session, you will create Karen's letter to the Tacoma Chamber of Commerce.

Session 1.1 QUICK CHECK

1. In your own words, list and describe the steps in creating a document.

2. How do you start Word from the Windows desktop?

3. Define each of the following in your own words:

   a. nonprinting characters
   b. document view buttons
   c. font size
   d. default settings

4. How do you change the default font size?

5. How do you display or hide the Formatting toolbar?

6. How do you change the document view to normal view?

SESSION 1.2

In this session you will create a one-page document using Word. You'll correct errors and scroll through your document. You'll also name, save, preview, and print the document, and learn how to use the Word Help system.

Typing a Letter

You're ready to type Karen's letter to the Tacoma Chamber of Commerce. Figure 1-11 shows the completed letter printed on the company letterhead. You'll begin by opening a new blank page (in case you accidentally typed something in the current page). Then you'll move the insertion point to about 2½ inches from the top margin of the paper to allow space for the Crossroads letterhead.

Figure 1-11   JOB FAIR LETTER

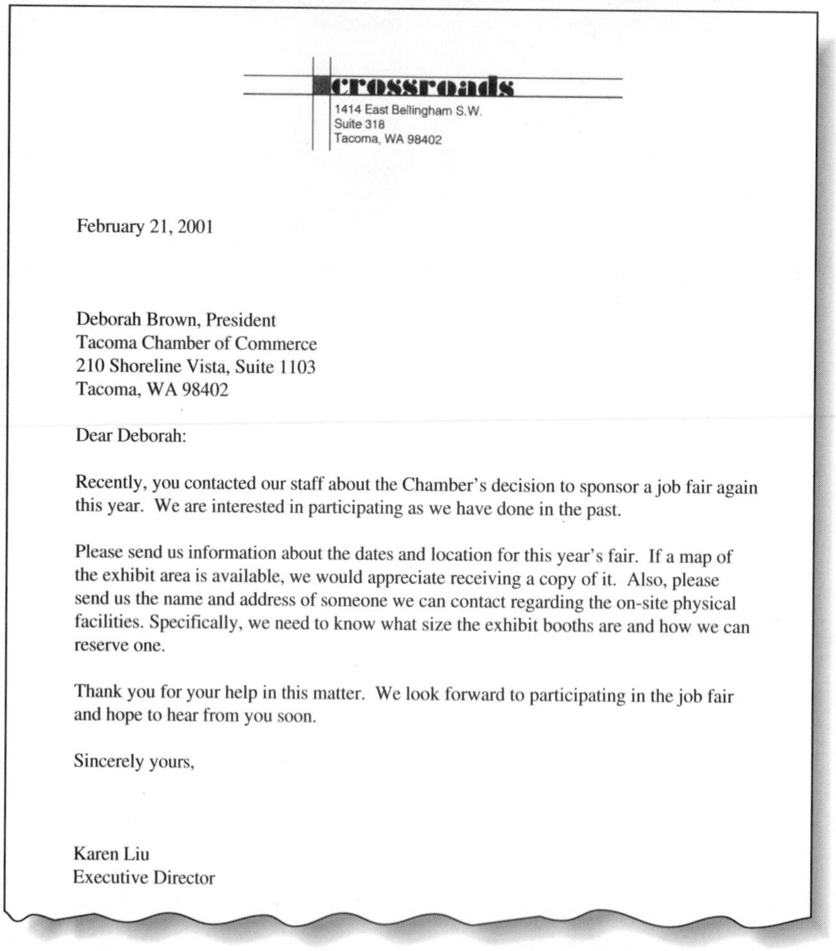

crossroads
1414 East Bellingham S.W.
Suite 318
Tacoma, WA 98402

February 21, 2001

Deborah Brown, President
Tacoma Chamber of Commerce
210 Shoreline Vista, Suite 1103
Tacoma, WA 98402

Dear Deborah:

Recently, you contacted our staff about the Chamber's decision to sponsor a job fair again this year. We are interested in participating as we have done in the past.

Please send us information about the dates and location for this year's fair. If a map of the exhibit area is available, we would appreciate receiving a copy of it. Also, please send us the name and address of someone we can contact regarding the on-site physical facilities. Specifically, we need to know what size the exhibit booths are and how we can reserve one.

Thank you for your help in this matter. We look forward to participating in the job fair and hope to hear from you soon.

Sincerely yours,

Karen Liu
Executive Director

To open a new document:

1. If you took a break after the last session, make sure the Word program is running, that nonprinting characters are displayed, and that the font settings in the Formatting toolbar are set to 12-point Times New Roman. Also verify that the toolbars and the ruler are properly displayed.

2. Click the **New Blank Document** button 🗋 on the Standard toolbar to open a fresh document.

   If you have the taskbar displayed at the bottom of your screen, you see an additional button for the new document. If you wanted to switch back to Document1, you could simply click its button on the taskbar. Notice that the new document has only one set of Control menu buttons. When two or more documents are open, you click the Close button in the upper-right corner of the title bar to close that document. When only one document is open, you can click the Close Window button in the upper-right corner of the menu bar to close the document and leave Word open, or you can click the Close button in the upper-right corner of the title bar to close the document and exit Word.

3. Press the **Enter** key eight times. Each time you press the Enter key, a nonprinting paragraph mark appears. In the status bar (at the bottom of the document window), you should see the setting "At 2.5"," indicating that the insertion point is approximately 2½ inches from the top of the page. Another setting in the status bar should read "Ln 9," indicating the insertion point is in line 9 of the document. Note that your settings may be slightly different. See Figure 1-12.

Figure 1-12	DOCUMENT WINDOW AFTER INSERTING BLANK LINES

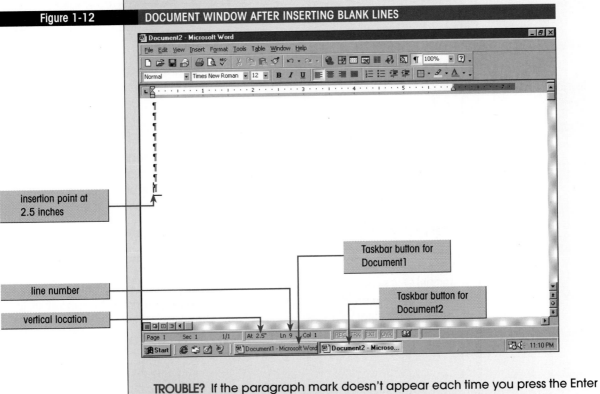

insertion point at 2.5 inches

line number

vertical location

Taskbar button for Document1

Taskbar button for Document2

TROUBLE? If the paragraph mark doesn't appear each time you press the Enter key, the nonprinting characters might be hidden. To show the nonprinting characters, click the Show/Hide ¶ button on the Standard toolbar, as described earlier in this tutorial.

> **TROUBLE?** If you pressed the Enter key too many times, press the Backspace key to delete each extra line and paragraph mark. If you're on line 9 but the "At" number is not 2.5", don't worry. Different monitors produce slightly different measurements when you press the Enter key.

Using **AutoCompleteTips**

Now you're ready to type the date. You'll take advantage of Word's **AutoComplete** feature, which automatically types dates and other regularly used words and text for you.

To insert the date using an AutoComplete tip:

1. Type **Febr** (the first four letters of February). An AutoComplete tip appears above the line, as shown in Figure 1-13. If you wanted to type something other than February, you would simply continue typing to complete the word. In this case, though, you want to accept the AutoComplete tip, so you will press the Enter key in the next step.

Figure 1-13	AUTOCOMPLETE TIP

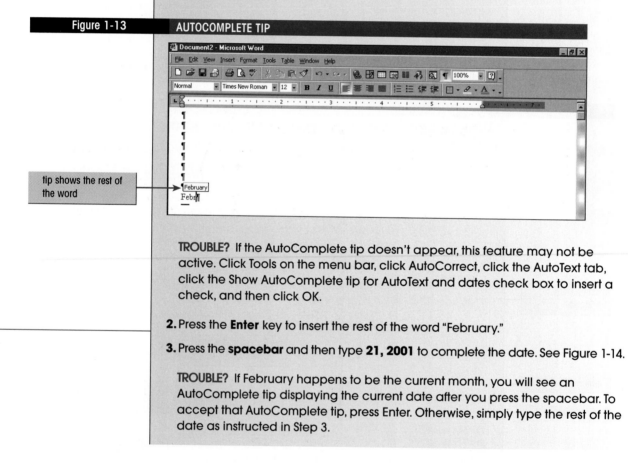

tip shows the rest of the word

> **TROUBLE?** If the AutoComplete tip doesn't appear, this feature may not be active. Click Tools on the menu bar, click AutoCorrect, click the AutoText tab, click the Show AutoComplete tip for AutoText and dates check box to insert a check, and then click OK.

2. Press the **Enter** key to insert the rest of the word "February."

3. Press the **spacebar** and then type **21, 2001** to complete the date. See Figure 1-14.

> **TROUBLE?** If February happens to be the current month, you will see an AutoComplete tip displaying the current date after you press the spacebar. To accept that AutoComplete tip, press Enter. Otherwise, simply type the rest of the date as instructed in Step 3.

Figure 1-14	DATE ENTERED IN THE DOCUMENT

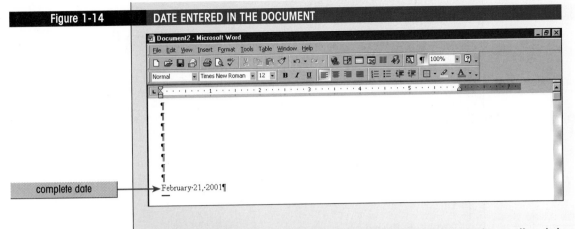

complete date ───────→ February·21,·2001¶

4. Press the **Enter** key four times to insert three blank lines between the date and the inside address. The status bar now should display "Ln13."

Next, you'll enter the inside address shown on Karen's note.

Entering Text

You'll enter the inside address by typing it. If you type a wrong character, simply press the Backspace key to delete the mistake and then retype it.

To type the inside address:

1. Type **Deborah Brown, President** and then press the **Enter** key. As you type, the nonprinting character (•) appears between words to indicate a space.

TROUBLE? If a wavy red or green line appears beneath a word, check to make sure you typed the text correctly. If you did not, use the Backspace key to remove the error, and then retype the text correctly.

2. Type the following text, pressing the **Enter** key after each line to enter the inside address:

Tacoma Chamber of Commerce
210 Shoreline Vista, Suite 1103
Tacoma, WA 98402

3. Press the **Enter** key again to add a blank line between the inside address and the salutation.

4. Type **Dear Deborah:** and press the **Enter** key twice to double space between the salutation and the body of the letter. When you press the Enter key the first time, the Office Assistant might appear, asking if you would like help writing your letter. Depending on the settings on your computer, you might see a different Office Assistant than the one shown in Figure 1-15.

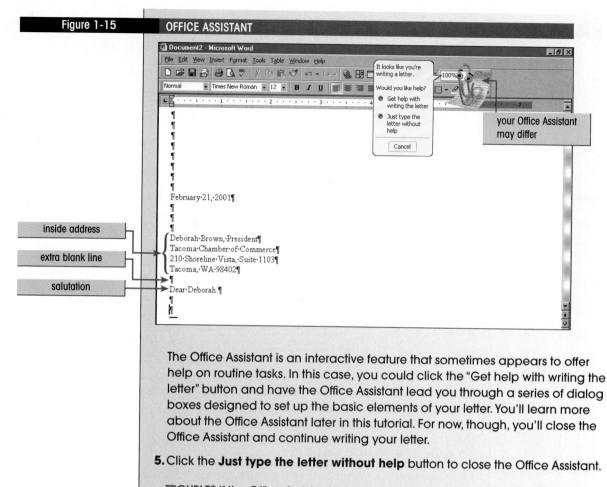

The Office Assistant is an interactive feature that sometimes appears to offer help on routine tasks. In this case, you could click the "Get help with writing the letter" button and have the Office Assistant lead you through a series of dialog boxes designed to set up the basic elements of your letter. You'll learn more about the Office Assistant later in this tutorial. For now, though, you'll close the Office Assistant and continue writing your letter.

5. Click the **Just type the letter without help** button to close the Office Assistant.

TROUBLE? If the Office Assistant remains open, right-click the Office Assistant, and then click Hide to close it.

You have completed the date, the inside address, and the salutation of Karen's letter, using a standard business letter format. You're ready to complete the letter. Before you do, however, you should save what you have typed so far.

Saving a Document for the First Time

The letter on which you are working is stored only in the computer's memory, not on a disk. If you were to exit Word, turn off your computer, or experience an accidental power failure, the part of Karen's letter that you just typed would be lost. You should get in the habit of frequently saving your document to a disk.

The first time you save a document, you need to name it. The name you use is usually referred to as the **filename**. To make it easy for you to keep track of the various documents stored on your computer, or 3½-inch disk, or Zip disk, it's important to use names that accurately describe their contents. For example, if you use a generic name such as "Letter" for this particular document, you won't be able to differentiate it from other letters in the future. Instead, you should use a more descriptive name, such as Tacoma Job Fair Letter.

<u>Saving a Document for the First Time</u>
- Click the Save button on the Standard toolbar (or click File on the menu bar, and then click Save).
- If necessary, change the folder and drive information.
- In the File name text box, type the filename.
- Click the Save button (or press the Enter key).

After you name your document, Word automatically appends the .doc filename extension to identify the file as a Microsoft Word document. However, depending on how Windows is set up on your computer, you might not actually see the .doc extension. These tutorials assume that filename extensions are hidden.

To save the document:

1. Place your Data Disk in the appropriate disk drive.

   TROUBLE? If you don't have a Data Disk, you need to get one before you can proceed. Your instructor or technical support person will either give you one or ask you to make your own by following the instructions on the "Read This Before You Begin" page at the beginning of this tutorial. See your instructor or technical support person for more information.

2. Click the **Save** button 🖫 on the Standard toolbar. The Save As dialog box opens. See Figure 1-16. Note that Word suggests using the first few characters of the letter ("February 21") as the filename. You will replace the suggested filename with something more descriptive.

Figure 1-16	SAVE AS DIALOG BOX

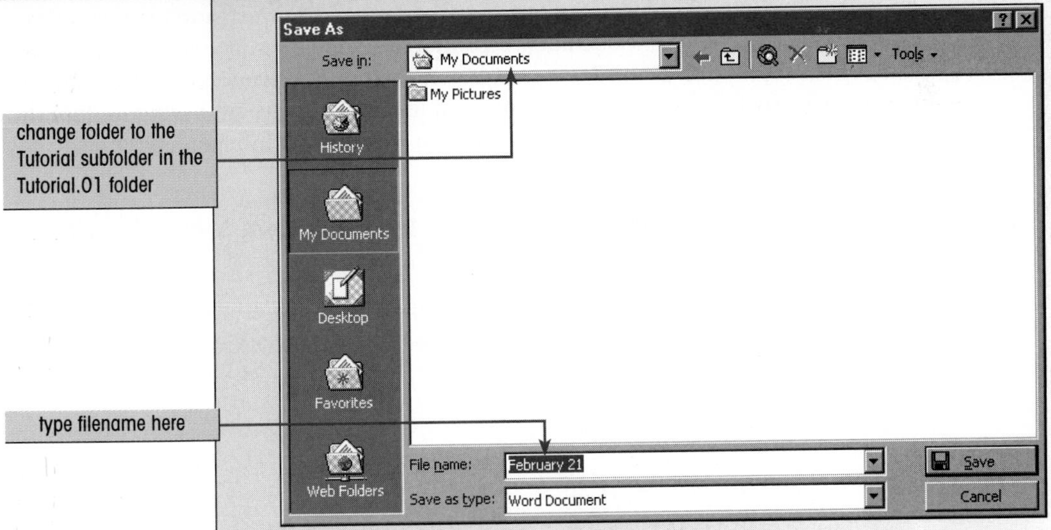

change folder to the Tutorial subfolder in the Tutorial.01 folder

type filename here

Save As

Save in: My Documents

My Pictures

File name: February 21

Save as type: Word Document

3. Type **Tacoma Job Fair Letter** in the File name text box.

4. Click the **Save in** list arrow, click the drive containing your Data Disk, double-click the **Tutorial.01** folder, then double-click the **Tutorial** folder. The Tutorial folder is now open and ready for you to save the document. See Figure 1-17.

Figure 1-17	SAVE AS DIALOG BOX WITH TUTORIAL FOLDER OPEN

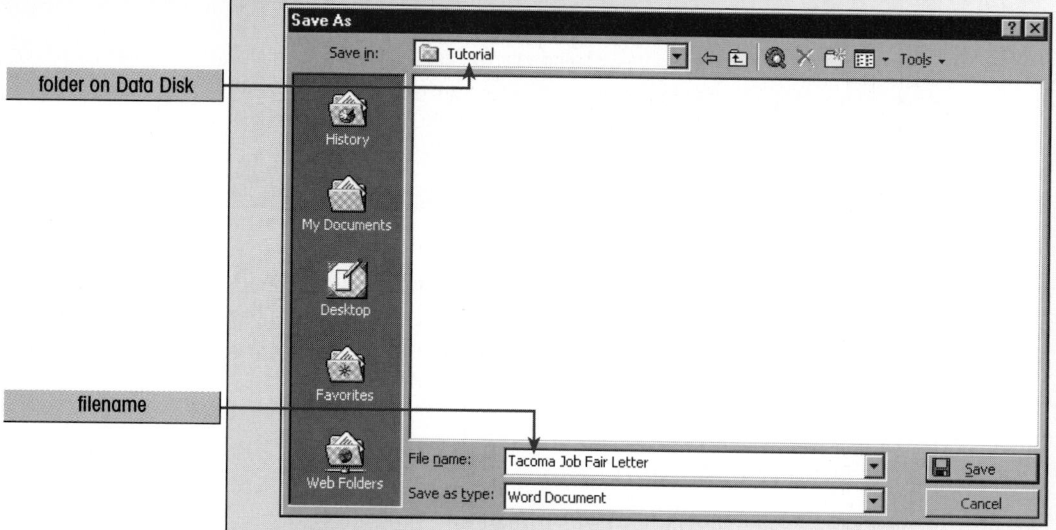

folder on Data Disk

filename

TROUBLE? If Word automatically adds the .doc extension to your filename, then your computer is configured to show filename extensions. Just continue with the tutorial.

5. Click the **Save** button in the Save As dialog box. The dialog box closes, and you return to the document window. The name of your file appears in the title bar.

Adding **Properties to a Document**

After you save a document, you should record some descriptive information in a special dialog box known as the document's **properties page**. The information that you record here is known, collectively, as a document's **properties**. For example, you might include your name and a description of the document. Later, you or one of your co-workers can review the document's properties for a quick summary of its purpose, without having to skim the entire document. You'll look at the properties page for the Tacoma Job Fair Letter next.

> ### To view the properties page for the Tacoma Job Fair Letter document:
>
> 1. Click **File** on the menu bar, click **Properties**, and then, if necessary, click the **Summary** tab. The Tacoma Job Fair Letter Properties dialog box opens, as shown in Figure 1-18.

Figure 1-18   **PROPERTIES PAGE FOR THE ACTIVE DOCUMENT**

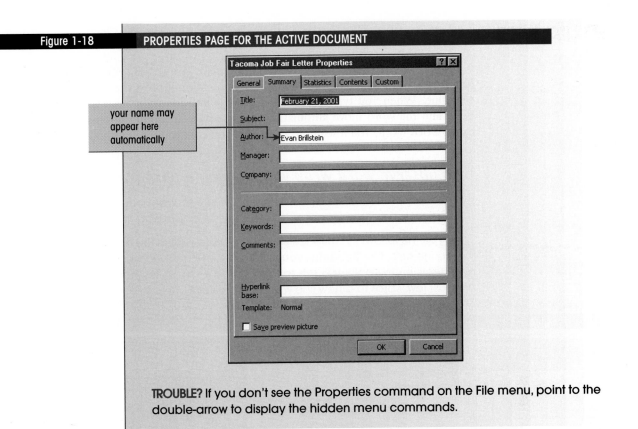

your name may
appear here
automatically

TROUBLE? If you don't see the Properties command on the File menu, point to the double-arrow to display the hidden menu commands.

This dialog box takes its name from the active document (in this case, "Tacoma Job Fair Letter"). Depending on how your computer is set up, the Author text box already may contain your name or the name of the registered owner of your copy of Word. In addition, the Title text box may contain the document's first line of text, "February 21, 2001." Because you already have assigned a descriptive name to this file ("Tacoma Job Fair Letter"), there's no reason to include a title here. You can delete this title and then enter relevant information in the appropriate text boxes. The Comments text box is a good place to record useful notes about the document, such as its purpose.

To edit the contents of the properties page:

1. Verify that the text in the Title text box is highlighted, and then press the **Delete** key.

2. Press the **Tab** key twice. The insertion point moves to the Author text box.

3. If necessary, type your name in the Author text box.

4. Click the Comments text box, and then type **A letter requesting information on the job fair.**

5. Click **OK**. The Tacoma Job Fair Letter dialog box closes, and the document's new properties are saved.

It's good practice to add information to a document's properties page right after you save the document for the first time. You will find such information useful once you have accumulated a number of Word documents and want to organize them. You can use the properties to find documents quickly. As you will see in the Review Assignments at the end of this tutorial, you can view a document's properties page without actually opening the document.

Word Wrap

Now that you have saved your document and its properties, you're ready to complete Karen's letter. As you type the body of the letter, do not press the Enter key at the end of each line. When you type a word that extends into the right margin, both the insertion point and the word move automatically to the next line. This automatic line breaking is called **word wrap**. You'll see how word wrap works as you type the body of Karen's letter.

To observe word wrap while typing a paragraph:

1. Make sure the insertion point is at Ln 20 Col 1 (according to the settings in the status bar). If it's not, move it to that location by pressing the arrow keys.

2. Type the following sentence slowly and watch when the insertion point jumps to the next line: **Recently, you contacted our staff about the Chamber's decision to sponsor a job fair again this year.** Notice how Word moves the last few words to a new line when the previous one is full. See Figure 1-19.

Figure 1-19	WORD WRAPPING TEXT

beginning of first paragraph

word wrapped to a new line

¶
Dear·Deborah:¶
¶
Recently,·you·contacted·our·staff·about·the·Chamber's·decision·to·sponsor·a·job·fair·
again·this·year.¶

end of line after word wrap

Page 1   Sec 1   1/1   At 4.8"   Ln 21   Col 17   REC TRK EXT OVR

TROUBLE? If your screen does not match Figure 1-19 exactly, don't be concerned. The Times New Roman font can have varying letter widths and produce slightly different measurements on different monitors. As a result, the word or letter at which word wrap occurred in your document and the status bar values might be different from that shown in Figure 1-19. Continue with Step 3. If you see any other AutoComplete tips as you type, ignore them.

3. Press the **spacebar** twice, and type **We are interested in participating as we have done in the past.** This completes the first paragraph of the letter.

4. Press the **Enter** key to end the first paragraph, and then press the **Enter** key again to double space between the first and second paragraphs.

Scrolling a Document

After you finish the last set of steps, the insertion point will be at or near the bottom of your document window. It might seem that no room is left in the document window to type the rest of Karen's letter. However, as you continue to add text at the end of your document, the text that you typed earlier will **scroll** (or shift up) and disappear from the top of the document window. You'll see how scrolling works as you enter the final text of Karen's letter.

To observe scrolling while you're entering text:

1. Make sure the insertion point is at the bottom of the screen, to the left of the second paragraph mark in the body of the letter.

TROUBLE? If you are using a very large monitor, your insertion point may still be some distance from the bottom of the screen. In that case, you may not be able to perform the scrolling steps that follow. Simply read the steps to familiarize yourself with the process of scrolling. You'll scroll longer documents later.

2. Type the second paragraph, as shown in Figure 1-20, and then press the **Enter** key twice to insert a blank line. Notice that as you type the paragraph, the top of the letter scrolls off the top of the document window. Don't worry if you make a mistake in your typing. You'll learn a number of ways to correct errors in the next section.

TROUBLE? If you have difficulty reading the text in Figure 1-20, refer back to Figure 1-11.

| Figure 1-20 | TOP OF THE LETTER SCROLLED OFF THE SCREEN |

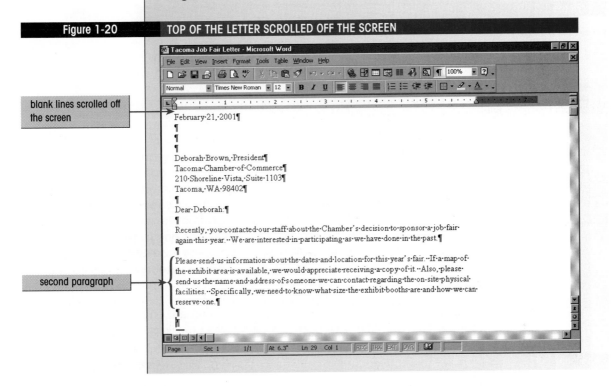

blank lines scrolled off the screen

second paragraph

Correcting Errors

Have you made any typing mistakes yet? If so, don't worry. The advantage of using a word processor is that you can correct mistakes quickly and efficiently. Word provides several ways to correct errors when you're entering text.

If you discover a typing error as soon as you make it, you can press the Backspace key to erase the characters and spaces to the left of the insertion point one at a time. Backspacing will erase both printing and nonprinting characters. After you erase the error, you can type the correct characters.

Word also provides a feature, called **AutoCorrect**, that checks for errors in your document as you type and automatically corrects common typing errors, such as "adn" for "and." If the spelling of a particular word differs from its spelling in the Word electronic dictionary, or if a word isn't in the dictionary at all (for example, a person's name), a wavy *red* line appears beneath the word. A wavy red line also appears if you type duplicate words (such as "the the"). If you accidentally type an extra space between words or make a grammatical error (such as typing "He walk to the store." instead of "He walks to the store."), a wavy *green* line appears beneath the error. You'll see how AutoCorrect works when you intentionally make typing errors.

To correct common typing errors:

1. Carefully and slowly type the following sentence exactly as it is shown, including the spelling errors and the extra space between the last two words: **Word corects teh commen typing misTakes you make.** Press the **Enter** key when you are finished typing. Notice that as you press the spacebar after the word "commen," a wavy red line appears beneath it, indicating that the word might be misspelled. Notice also that when you pressed the spacebar after the words "corects," "teh," and "misTakes," Word automatically corrected the spelling. After you pressed the Enter key, a wavy green line appeared under the last two words, alerting you to the extra space. See Figure 1-21.

Figure 1-21	DOCUMENT WINDOW SHOWING TYPING ERRORS

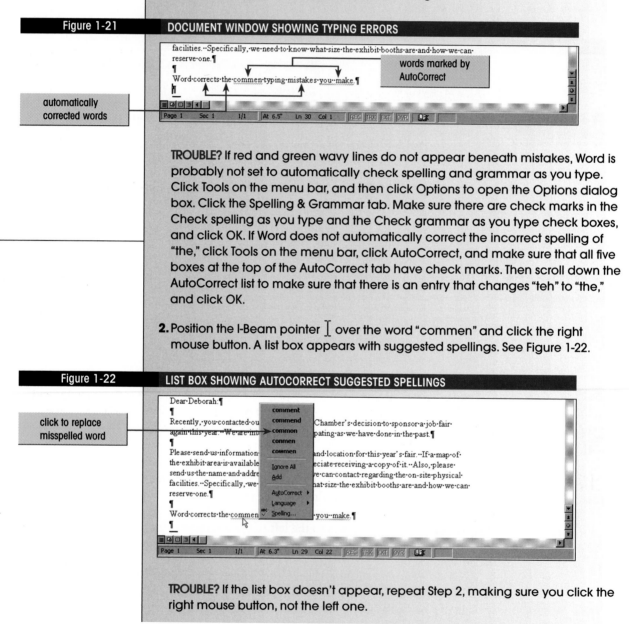

TROUBLE? If red and green wavy lines do not appear beneath mistakes, Word is probably not set to automatically check spelling and grammar as you type. Click Tools on the menu bar, and then click Options to open the Options dialog box. Click the Spelling & Grammar tab. Make sure there are check marks in the Check spelling as you type and the Check grammar as you type check boxes, and click OK. If Word does not automatically correct the incorrect spelling of "the," click Tools on the menu bar, click AutoCorrect, and make sure that all five boxes at the top of the AutoCorrect tab have check marks. Then scroll down the AutoCorrect list to make sure that there is an entry that changes "teh" to "the," and click OK.

2. Position the I-Beam pointer ⌶ over the word "commen" and click the right mouse button. A list box appears with suggested spellings. See Figure 1-22.

Figure 1-22	LIST BOX SHOWING AUTOCORRECT SUGGESTED SPELLINGS

TROUBLE? If the list box doesn't appear, repeat Step 2, making sure you click the right mouse button, not the left one.

3. Click **common** in the list box. The list box disappears, and the correct spelling appears in your document. Notice that the wavy red line disappears after you correct the error.

4. Click to the right of the letter "u" in the word "you." Press the **Delete** key to delete the extra space.

You can see how quick and easy it is to correct common typing errors with AutoCorrect. Remember, however, that there is no substitute for your own eyes. You should thoroughly proofread each document you create, keeping in mind that AutoCorrect will not catch words that are spelled correctly, but used improperly (such as "your" for "you're"). Proofread your document now, and use AutoCorrect or the Backspace or Delete keys to correct any mistakes.

Before you continue typing Karen's letter, you'll need to delete your practice sentence.

To delete the practice sentence:

1. Click between the period and the paragraph mark at the end of the sentence.

2. Press and hold the **Backspace** key until the entire sentence is deleted. Then press the **Delete** key to delete the extra paragraph mark.

3. Make sure the insertion point is in line 29. There should be one nonprinting paragraph mark between the second paragraph and the paragraph you will type next.

Finishing **the Letter**

You're ready to complete the rest of the letter. As you type, you can use any of the techniques you learned in the previous section to correct mistakes.

To complete the letter:

1. Type the final paragraph of the body of the letter, as shown in Figure 1-23, and then press the **Enter** key twice. Accept or ignore AutoComplete tips as necessary. Unless you have a very large monitor, the date and, possibly, part of the inside address scroll off the top of the document window completely.

Figure 1-23	FINAL PARAGRAPH

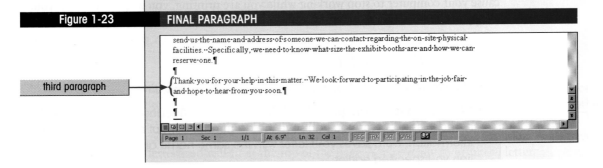

third paragraph

send·us·the·name·and·address·of·someone·we·can·contact·regarding·the·on-site·physical· facilities.··Specifically,·we·need·to·know·what·size·the·exhibit·booths·are·and·how·we·can· reserve·one.¶

Thank·you·for·your·help·in·this·matter.··We·look·forward·to·participating·in·the·job·fair· and·hope·to·hear·from·you·soon.¶

Page 1   Sec 1   1/1   At 6.9"   Ln 32   Col 1   REC TRK EXT OVR

When printing a document, you have two choices. You can use the Print command on the File menu, which opens the Print dialog box in which you can adjust some printer settings. Also, you can use the Print button on the Standard toolbar, which simply prints the document using default settings, without displaying a dialog box. In each session of these tutorials, the first time you print from a shared computer, you should check the settings in the Print dialog box and make sure the number of copies is set to one. After that, you can use the Print button.

To print a document:

1. Make sure your printer is turned on and contains paper.

2. Click **File** on the menu bar, and then click **Print**. The Print dialog box opens. See Figure 1-26.

Figure 1-26   **PRINT DIALOG BOX**

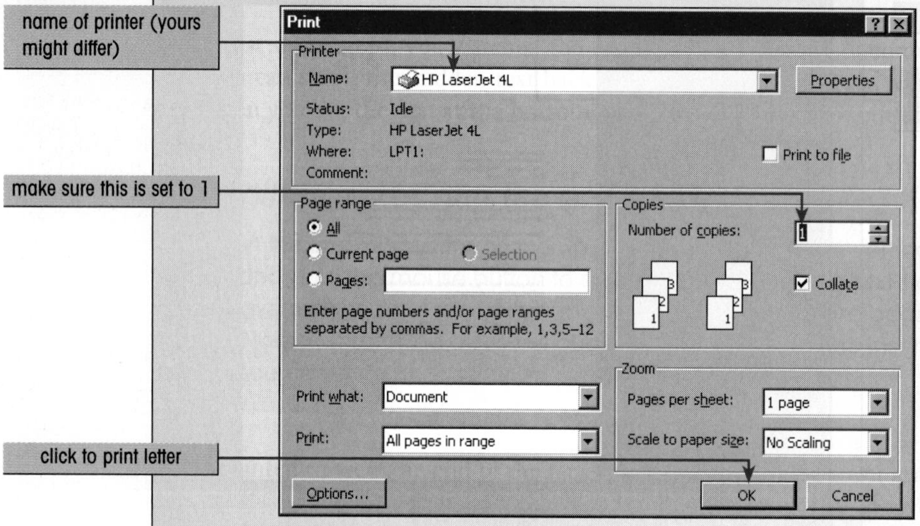

name of printer (yours might differ)

make sure this is set to 1

click to print letter

---

3. Verify that your settings match those in Figure 1-26. In particular, make sure the number of copies is set to 1. Also make sure the Printer section of the dialog box shows the correct printer. If you're not sure what the correct printer is, check with your instructor or technical support person.

   TROUBLE? If the Print dialog box shows the wrong printer, click the Printer Name list arrow, and then select the correct printer from the list of available printers.

4. Click the **OK** button to print Karen's letter. A printer icon 🖨 appears at the far right of the taskbar to indicate that your document is being sent to the printer.

Your printed letter should look similar to Figure 1-11 but without the Crossroads letterhead. The word wraps, or line breaks, might not appear in the same places on your letter because the size and spacing of characters vary slightly from one printer to the next.

Karen also needs an envelope to mail her letter in. Printing an envelope is easy in Word. You'll have a chance to try it in the Review Assignments at the end of this tutorial. If you wanted to find out how to print an envelope yourself, you could use the Word Help system.

Getting **Help**

The Word Help system provides quick access to information about commands, features, and screen elements.

The **What's This?** command on the Help menu provides context-sensitive Help information. When you choose this command, the pointer changes to the Help pointer ⃗?, which you can then use to click any object or option on the screen, including menu commands, to see a description of the item.

You've already encountered another form of help, the animated Office Assistant. The **Office Assistant** is an interactive guide to finding information on Microsoft Word. As you learned earlier in this tutorial, the Office Assistant sometimes opens automatically to help you with routine tasks. You also can ask the Office Assistant a direction question, and it will search the Help system to find an answer in plain English. The Office Assistant is a context-sensitive tool, which means that it is designed to offer information related to your current task. If you simply want to look up some information in Word's Help system, as you would in an Encyclopedia, you can use the Index and Contents tabs. You will learn how to use the Office Assistant as well as to display the Index and Contents tabs in the following steps.

REFERENCE   WINDOW   **RW**

Getting Help from the Office Assistant

- Click the Microsoft Word Help button on the Standard toolbar (or click Help on the menu bar and then click Microsoft Word Help).
- Type your question, and then click the Search button.
- Click a topic from the list of topics displayed.
- Read the information in the Microsoft Word Help window. For more information, click the relevant underlined text.
- To display the Index or Contents tab, click the Show button in the Microsoft Word Help window. Click the Hide button to hide these tabs.
- To close the Microsoft Word Help window, click its Close button.
- To hide the Office Assistant, click Help on the menu bar, and then click Hide the Office Assistant.

You'll use the Office Assistant now to learn how to print an envelope.

To use the Office Assistant to learn how to print an envelope:

1. Click the **Microsoft Word Help** button 🔲 on the Standard toolbar. The Office Assistant opens, offering help on topics related to the task you most recently performed (if any), and asking what you'd like to do. The Office Assistant shown in Figure 1-27 takes the form of an animated paperclip, but your Office Assistant may differ.

Figure 1-27
OFFICE ASSISTANT

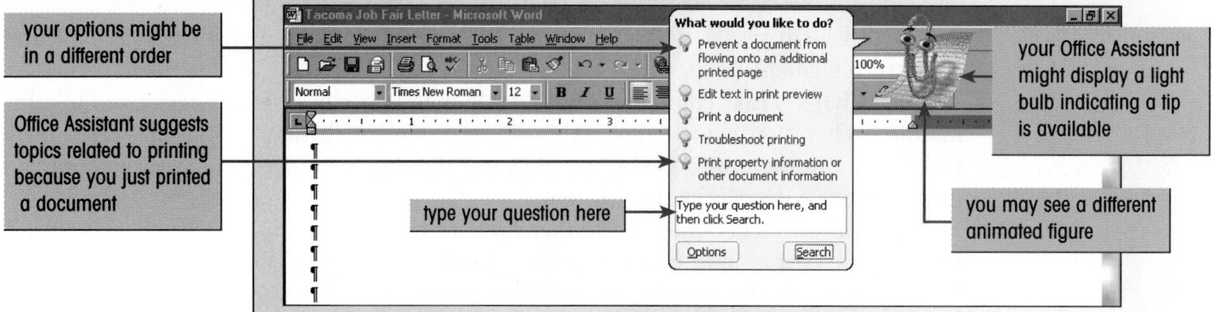

your options might be in a different order

Office Assistant suggests topics related to printing because you just printed a document

type your question here

your Office Assistant might display a light bulb indicating a tip is available

you may see a different animated figure

2. Type **How do I print an envelope?** and then click the **Search** button. The Office Assistant window shows topics related to envelopes.

TROUBLE? If you do not see a space to type a question, click the Help with something else option button, and then continue with Step 2.

3. Click **Create and print envelopes.** The Microsoft Word Help window opens next to or on top of the Word window, with even more specific topics related to printing envelopes.

4. Click **Create and print an envelope.** The Microsoft Word Help window displays the precise steps involved in printing an envelope. See Figure 1-28. To scroll through the steps, drag the vertical scroll bar. Note that within a Help window, you can click on underlined text to display more information.

Figure 1-28
STEPS FOR PRINTING AN ENVELOPE

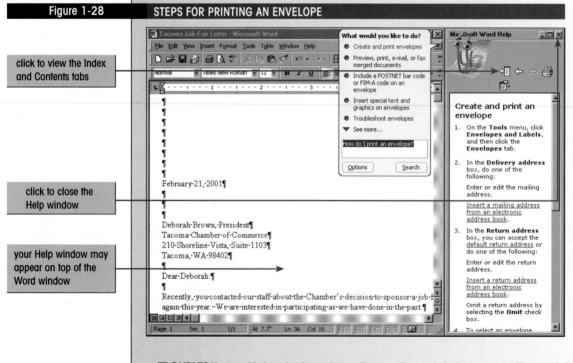

click to view the Index and Contents tabs

click to close the Help window

your Help window may appear on top of the Word window

TROUBLE? If your Help window doesn't exactly match the one in Figure 1-28, just continue with these steps. You will learn how to display and hide additional tabs of the Help Window shortly.

5. Click the **Show** button ![icon]. Additional Help window tabs appear, as in Figure 1-29. The most useful of these are the Contents tab (where you can search by general topics) and the Index tab (where you can look up a specific entry). You will have a chance to practice using these tabs in the Review Assignments at the end of this tutorial.

Figure 1-29	ADDITIONAL HELP TABS

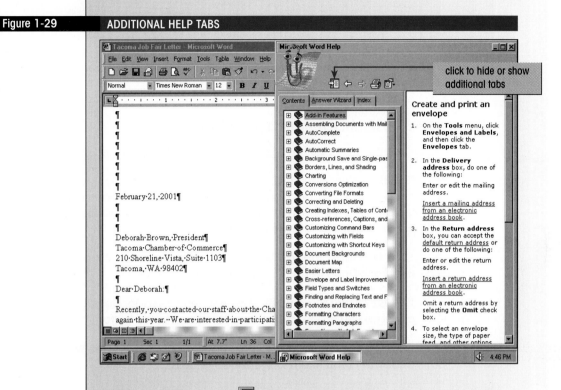

6. Click the **Hide** button ![icon] to return the Help window to its original size.

7. Click the **Close** button ![X] on the Microsoft Word Help window. The Microsoft Word Help window closes, and the Word program window fills the screen again.

8. Click **Help** on the menu bar, and then click **Hide the Office Assistant**. The animated Office Assistant disappears.

TROUBLE? If the Office Assistant asks if you want to hide it permanently, choose the "No just hide me" option.

Some Help windows have different formats than those you've just seen. However, they all provide the information you need to complete any task in Word.

Exiting Word

You have now finished typing and printing the letter to the Tacoma Chamber of Commerce, and you are ready to **exit**, or quit, Word. When you exit Word, you close both the document and the program window.

REFERENCE WINDOW   **RW**

Exiting Word
- Click the Close button for each open document (or click File on the menu bar, and then click Exit).
- If you're prompted to save changes to the document, click the Yes button; then, if necessary, type a document name and click the Save button.

Because you've completed the first draft of Karen's letter, you can close the document window and exit Word now.

To close documents and exit Word:

1. Click the **Close** button ⊠ in the title bar to close the letter.

   TROUBLE? If you see a dialog box with the message "Do you want to save the changes you made to Tacoma Job Fair Letter?," you have made changes to the document since the last time you saved it. Click the Yes button to save the current version and close it.

2. Click the **Close Window** button ⊠ on the right side of the menu bar to close the blank Document1.

   TROUBLE? If you see a dialog box with the message "Do you want to save the changes you made to Document1?," click the No button.

3. Click the **Close** button ⊠ in the upper-right corner of the Word window. Word closes, and you return to the Windows desktop.

You give the letter for the Tacoma Chamber of Commerce to Karen for her to review. Now that you have created and saved your letter, you are ready to learn about editing and formatting a document in the next tutorial.

Session 1.2 QUICK CHECK

1. Explain how to save a document for the first time.

2. What is the advantage of recording information about a document in its Properties dialog box?

3. Explain how word wrap works in a Word document.

4. What is the Office Assistant, and how do you use it?

5. In your own words, define each of the following:

   a. scrolling
   b. AutoComplete
   c. AutoCorrect
   d. print preview

6. Describe two methods for exiting Word.

REVIEW ASSIGNMENTS

Karen received a response from the Tacoma Chamber of Commerce containing the information she requested about the job fair, and Crossroads has firmed up its plans to participate as an exhibitor. Karen must now staff the booth with Crossroads employees for each day of the five-day fair. She sends a memo to employees asking them to commit to two dates. Create the memo shown in Figure 1-30 by completing the following:

1. If necessary, start Word and make sure your Data Disk is in the appropriate disk drive, and then check your screen to make sure your settings match those in the tutorials.

2. If the Office Assistant is open, hide it by using the appropriate command on the Help menu.

3. Click the New Blank Document button on the Standard toolbar to display a new document.

4. Press the Enter key six times to insert approximately 2 inches of space before the memo headings.

5. Press the Caps Lock key, and then type "MEMORANDUM" (without the quotation marks) in capital letters.

6. Press the Enter key twice, type "TO:" (without the quotation marks), press the Caps Lock key to turn off capitalization, press the Tab key three times, and then type "Crossroads Staff Members" (without the quotation marks).

7. Press the Enter key twice, type "FROM:" (without the quotation marks), press the Tab key twice, and then type your name. Throughout the rest of this exercise, use the Caps Lock Key as necessary to turn capitalization on and off.

Explore

8. Press the Enter key twice, type "DATE:" (without the quotation marks), press the Tab key three times. Insert today's date from your computer clock by clicking Insert on the menu bar, clicking Date and Time, clicking the date format that corresponds to June 16, 2001, and then clicking OK.

9. Continue typing the rest of the memo exactly as shown in Figure 1-30, including any misspellings and extra words. Notice how Word automatically corrects some misspellings. (You will have a chance to practice correcting the remaining errors later.) Press the Tab key twice after "SUBJECT:" to align the memo heading evenly. Include two blank lines between the Subject line and the body of the memo.

Figure 1-30   **SAMPLE MEMO**

MEMORANDUM

TO: Crossroads Staff Members

FROM: Karen Liu

DATE: June 16, 2001

SUBJECT: Dates for 2001 Job Fair

The the 2001 Job Fair sponsored by the Tacoma Chamber of Commerce will be held
October 20-25, 2001,from 11:00 a.m. to 5:00 p.m.. This fiar provvides us with an
oportunity to inform Tacoma residents about our services. Previously, we have each spent
two days helping at the exhibet. Please let me know which days you would prefer this
year. I would like this information by tomorrow.

Thanks for your help.

10. Save your work as **Job Fair Reminder Memo** in the Review folder for Tutorial 1.

11. Click File on the menu bar, and then click Properties. Delete the existing title for the document, verify that your name appears in the Author text box, and type a brief description of the document in the Comments text box. Click OK to close the document's properties page.

12. Correct the misspelled words, indicated by the wavy red lines. If the correct version of a word does not appear in the list box, press the Escape key to close the list, and then make the correction yourself. To ignore an AutoCorrect suggestion, click Ignore All. Then correct any grammatical or other errors indicated by wavy green lines. Use the Backspace key to delete any extra words or spaces.

13. Scroll to the beginning of the memo. Click at the beginning of the first line and insert room for the letterhead by pressing the Enter key until MEMORANDUM is at line 12.

14. Save your most recent changes.

Explore 15. Use the What's This? feature to learn about the Word Count command on the Tools menu. Click Help on the menu bar, and then click What's This? Click Tools on the menu bar, click Word Count, and then read the text box. When you are finished, click the text box to close it.

16. Preview and print the memo.

17. Use the Office Assistant to open a Microsoft Word Help menu with the steps necessary for printing an address on an envelope.

ore 18. With the Help window open on one side of the screen, and the Word window open on the other, follow the instructions for printing an envelope. (Check with your instructor or technical support person to make sure you can print envelopes. If not, print on an 8½ x 11-inch sheet of paper.) To place the Help and Word windows side by side, right-click the taskbar and then click Tile Windows Vertically. When you are done, right-click the taskbar and then click Undo Tile.

Explore ▶ 19. With the Help window open, click the Show button, if necessary, to display the additional Help tabs. Click the Index tab, type "Help" (without the quotation marks) and then click the Search button. View the topics related to Word's Help system in the Choose a topic list box. Click any topic in the right-hand window to read more about it. Next, click the Contents tab, review the main topics on that tab, and then click any plus sign to display subtopics. Click a subtopic to display additional topics in the right-hand window, then click one of those topics to display even more information. Continue to explore the Contents and Index tabs. When you are finished, close the Microsoft Word Help window. Hide the Office Assistant.

20. Close the document without saving your most recent changes.

21. Click the Open button on the Standard toolbar.

Explore ▶ 22. Verify that the Review folder for Tutorial 1 is displayed in the Look in list box, right-click the Job Fair Reminder Memo, and then click Properties in the shortcut menu. Review the document's properties page. You can use this technique to find out about the contents of a document quickly, without opening the document. Click OK to close the document's properties page, and then click Cancel to close the Open dialog box.

23. Close any open documents.

CASE PROBLEMS

Case 1. Letter to Confirm a Conference Date As catering director for the Madison Convention and Visitors Bureau, you are responsible for managing food service at the convention center. The Southern Wisconsin chapter of the National Purchasing Management Association has requested a written confirmation of a daily breakfast buffet during its annual convention scheduled for July 6-10, 2001.

Create the letter using the skills you learned in the tutorial. Remember to include today's date, the inside address, the salutation, the date of the reservation, the complimentary close, and your name and title. If the instructions show quotation marks around text you type, do not include the quotation marks in your letter. To complete the letter, do the following:

1. If necessary, start Word, make sure your Data Disk is in the appropriate disk drive, and check your screen to make sure your settings match those in the tutorials.

2. Open a new, blank document and press the Enter key until the insertion point is positioned about 2 inches from the top of the page. (Remember that you can see the exact position of the insertion point, in inches, in the status bar.)

Explore ▶ 3. Begin typing today's date. If an AutoComplete tip appears to finish the month, press Enter to accept it. Press the spacebar. If another AutoComplete tip appears with the rest of the date, press Enter to accept it. Otherwise, continue typing the date.

4. Press the Enter key six times after the date, and, using the proper business letter format, type the inside address: "Charles Quade, 222 Sydney Street, Whitewater, WI 57332."

5. Double space after the inside address (that is, press the Enter key twice), type the salutation "Dear Mr. Quade:," and then double space again. If the Office Assistant opens, click Cancel to close it.

6. Write one paragraph confirming the daily breakfast buffets for July 6-10, 2001.

7. Double space and type the complimentary close "Sincerely," (include the comma).

8. Press the Enter key four times to leave room for the signature, and then type your name and title.

9. Save the letter as **Confirmation Letter** in the Cases folder for Tutorial 1.

10. Use the document's properties page to record your name and a brief summary of the document.

11. Reread your letter carefully, and correct any errors.

12. Save any new changes.

13. Preview and print the letter.

14. Close the document.

Case 2. Letter to Request Information about a "Climbing High" Franchise You are the manager of the UpTown Sports Mall and are interested in obtaining a franchise for "Climbing High," an indoor rock-climbing venture marketed by Ultimate Sports, Inc. After reading an advertisement for the franchise, you decide to write for more information.

Create the letter by doing the following:

1. If necessary, start Word, make sure your Data Disk is in the appropriate disk drive, and check your screen to make sure your settings match those in the tutorials.

2. Open a new blank document, and press the Enter key until the insertion point is positioned about 2 inches from the top of the page. (Remember that you can see the exact position of the insertion point, in inches, in the status bar.)

3. Use AutoComplete (as described in Step 3 of the previous case project) to type today's date at the insertion point.

4. Press the Enter key six times after the date, and, using the proper business letter format, type the inside address: "Ultimate Sports, Inc., 2124 Martin Luther King Jr. Avenue, Rockton, CO 80911."

5. Insert a blank line after the inside address, type the salutation "Dear Franchise Manager:," and then insert another blank line.

6. Type the first paragraph as follows: "I'd like some information about the Climbing High indoor rock-climbing franchise. As manager of UpTown Sports Mall, a large sporting goods store, I've had success with similar programs, including both bungee jumping and snowboarding franchises."(Do not include the quotation marks.)

7. Save your work as **Rock Climbing Request Letter** in the Cases folder for Tutorial 1.

8. Use the document's properties page to record your name and a brief summary of the document.

Explore ▷

9. Insert one blank line, and type the following: "Please answer the following questions:". Then press the Enter key, and type these questions on separate lines: "How much does your franchise cost?" "Does the price include the cost for installing the 30-foot simulated rock wall illustrated in your advertisement?" "Does the price include the cost for purchasing the ropes and harnesses?" Open the Office Assistant, type the question, "How can I add bullets to lists?," click the Search button, and then click the "Add bullets to lists" topic. In the Microsoft Word Help window, click the "Add bullets or numbering" subtopic, and then follow the instructions to insert a bullet in front of each question in the document. Close the Office Assistant and the Microsoft Word Help window when you are finished.

10. Correct any typing errors indicated by wavy lines. (*Hint:* Because "UpTown" is spelled correctly, click Ignore All on the shortcut menu to remove the wavy red line under the word "UpTown" and prevent Word from marking the word as a misspelling.)

11. Insert another blank line at the end of the letter, and type the complimentary close "Sincerely," (include the comma).

12. Press the Enter key four times to leave room for the signature, and type your full name and title. Then press the Enter key and type "UpTown Sports Mall." Notice that UpTown is not marked as a spelling error this time.

13. Save the letter with changes.

14. Preview the letter using the Print Preview button.

15. Print the letter.

16. Close the document.

Case 3. **Memo of Congratulations** Judy Davidoff is owner, founder, and president of Blossoms Unlimited, a chain of garden stores. She was recently honored by the Southern Council of Organic Gardeners for her series of free public seminars on organic vegetable gardening. Also, she was named businesswoman of the year by the Georgia Women's Business Network. Do the following:

1. If necessary, start Word, make sure your Data Disk is in the appropriate disk drive, and check your screen to make sure your settings match those in the tutorials.

2. Write a brief memo congratulating Judy on receiving these awards. Remember to use the four-part planning process. You should plan the content, organization, and style of the memo, and use a standard memo format similar to the one shown in Figure 1-30.

3. Save the document as **Awards Memo** in the Cases folder for Tutorial 1.

4. Use the document's properties page to record your name and a brief summary of the document.

5. Preview and print the memo.

6. Close the document.

Explore

Case 4. **Writing a Personal Letter with the Letter Template** Word provides templates— that is, models with predefined formatting—to help you create documents quickly and effectively. For example, the Letter template helps you create letters with professional-looking letterheads and with various letter formats. Do the following:

1. If necessary, start Word, make sure your Data Disk is in the appropriate disk drive, and check your screen to make sure your settings match those in the tutorials.

2. Click File on the menu bar, and then click New. The New dialog box opens.

3. Click the Letters & Faxes tab, click Elegant Letter, and then click the OK button. A letter template opens, as shown in Figure 1-31, containing generic, placeholder text that you can replace with your own information.

Figure 1-31   ELEGANT LETTER TEMPLATE

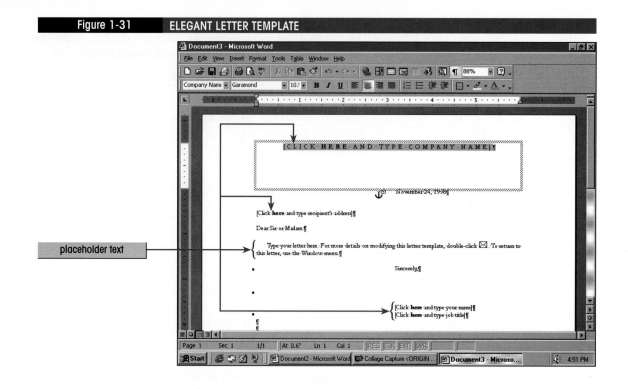

placeholder text

4. Click the line "CLICK HERE AND TYPE COMPANY NAME" (at the top of the document), and type the name of your school or company.

5. Click the line "Click here and type recipient's address," and type a real or fictitious name and address.

6. Delete the placeholder text in the body of the letter, and replace it with a sentence or two explaining that you're using the Word letter template to create this letter.

7. At the end of the letter, replace the placeholder text with your name and job title.

8. At the bottom of the page, replace the placeholder text with your address, phone number, and fax number. (Use fictious information if you prefer.)

9. Save the letter as **My Template Letter** (in the Cases folder for Tutorial 1), and then print it.

10. Use the document's properties page to record your name and a brief summary of the document.

11. Close the document.

Word
Processing

LAB ASSIGNMENTS

The New Perspectives Labs are designed to help you master some of the key computer concepts and skills presented in each chapter of the text. If you are using your school's lab computers, your instructor or technical support person should have installed the Labs software for you. If you want to use the Labs on your home computer, ask your instructor for the appropriate software. See the Read This Before You Begin page for more information on installing and starting the Lab.

Each Lab has two parts: Steps and Explore. Use Steps first to learn and review concepts. Read the information on each page and do the numbered steps. As you work through the Lab, you will be asked to answer Quick Check questions about what you have learned. At the end of the Lab, you will see a Summary Report of your answers to the Quick Checks. If your instructor wants you to turn in this Summary Report, click the Print button on the Summary Report screen.

When you have completed the Steps, you can click the Explore button to complete the Lab Assignments. You also can use Explore to practice the skills you learned and to explore concepts on your own.

Word Processing Word-processing software is the most popular computerized productivity tool. In this Lab, you will learn how word-processing software works. When you have completed this Lab, you should be able to apply the general concepts you learned to any word-processing package you use at home, at work, or in your school lab.

1. Click the Steps button to learn how word-processing software works. As you proceed through the Steps, answer all of the Quick Check questions that appear. After you complete the Steps, you will see a Quick Check Summary Report. Follow the instructions on the screen to print this report.

2. Click the Explore button to begin. Click File, then click Open to display the Open dialog box. Click the file **Timber.tex**, then press the Enter key to open the letter to Northern Timber Company. Make the following modifications to the letter, then print it. You do not need to save the letter.

   a. In the first and last lines of the letter, change "Jason Kidder" to your name.
   b. Change the date to today's date.
   c. The second paragraph begins "Your proposal did not include…". Move this paragraph so it is the last paragraph in the text of the letter.
   d. Change the cost of a permanent bridge to $20,000.
   e. Spell check the letter.

3. In Explore, open the file **Stars.tex**. Make the following modifications to the document, then print it. You do not need to save the document.

   a. Center and boldface the title.
   b. Change the title font to size-16 Arial.
   c. Boldface the DATE, SHOWER, and LOCATION.
   d. Move the January 2-3 line to the top of the list.
   e. Double space the entire document.

4. In Explore, compose a one-page double-spaced letter to your parents or to a friend. Make sure you date the letter and check your spelling. Print the letter and sign it. You do not need to save your letter.

INTERNET ASSIGNMENTS

The purpose of the Internet Assignments is to challenge you to find information on the Internet that you can use to create effective documents. The actual assignments are updated and maintained on the Course Technology Web site. Log on to the Internet and use your Web browser to go to the Student Online Companion to accompany this text at **www.course.com/NewPerspectives/office2000**. Click the Word link, and then click the link for Tutorial 1.

QUICK | CHECK ANSWERS

Session 1.1

1. (1) Plan the content, purpose, organization, and look of your document. (2) Create and then edit the document. (3) Format the document to make it visually appealing. (4) Preview and then print the document.

2. Click the Start button, point to Programs, and then click Microsoft Word.

3. **a.** symbols you can display on-screen but that don't print

   b. buttons to the left of the horizontal status bar that switch the document to normal view, Web layout view, print layout view, or outline view

   c. actual height of a character measured in points

   d. standard settings

4. Click Format on the menu bar, click Font, select the font size in the Size list box, click the Default button, and then click Yes.

5. Right-click a toolbar, and then click Formatting on the shortcut menu.

6. Click the Normal View button.

Session 1.2

1. Click the Save button on the Standard toolbar, switch to the drive and folder where you want to save the document, enter a filename in the File name text box, and then click the Save button.

2. Anyone can determine the document's purpose without having to open the document and skim it.

3. When you type a word that extends into the right margin, Word moves that word and the insertion point to the next line.

4. An interactive guide to finding information about Word; click the Microsoft Word Help button on the Standard toolbar, type your question and click Search, click the help topic you want to read.

5. **a.** as you type, text shifts out of view

   b. typing dates and other regularly used words and text for you

   c. checks for spelling and grammar errors as you type and fixes common typing errors automatically

   d. shows how the document will look when printed

6. Click the Close button in the upper-right corner of the screen; click File on the menu bar and then click Exit.

In this tutorial you will:

- Open, rename, and save a previously saved document

- Check spelling and grammar

- Move the insertion point around the document

- Select and delete text

- Reverse edits using the Undo and Redo commands

- Move text within the document

- Find and replace text

- Change margins, line spacing, alignment, and paragraph indents

- Copy formatting with the Format Painter

- Emphasize points with bullets, numbering, boldface, underlining, and italics

- Change fonts and adjust font sizes

EDITING AND FORMATTING A DOCUMENT

Preparing an Annuity Plan Description for Right-Hand Solutions

CASE

Right-Hand Solutions

Reginald Thomson is a contract specialist for Right-Hand Solutions, a company that provides small businesses with financial and administrative services. Right-Hand Solutions contracts with independent insurance companies to prepare insurance plans and investment opportunities for these small businesses. Brandi Paxman, vice president of administrative services, asked Reginald to plan and write a document that describes the tax-deferred annuity plan for their clients' employee handbooks. Now that Brandi has commented on and corrected the draft, Reginald asks you to make the necessary changes and print the document.

In this tutorial, you will edit the annuity plan description according to Brandi's comments. You will open a draft of the annuity plan, resave it, and delete a phrase. You will check the plan's grammar and spelling, and then move text using two different methods. Also, you will find and replace one version of the company name with another.

Next, you will change the overall look of the document by changing margins and line spacing, indenting and justifying paragraphs, and copying formatting from one paragraph to another. You'll create a bulleted list to emphasize the types of financial needs the annuity plan will cover and a numbered list for the conditions under which employees can receive funds. Then you'll make the title more prominent by centering it, changing its font, and enlarging it. You'll italicize the questions within the plan to set them off from the rest of the text and underline an added note about how to get further information to give it emphasis. Finally, you will print a copy of the plan.

SESSION 2.1

In In this session you will learn how to use the Spelling and Grammar checker to correct any errors in your document. Then you will edit Reginald's document by deleting words and moving text. Finally, you'll find and replace text throughout the document.

Opening the Document

Brandi's editing marks and notes on the first draft are shown in Figure 2-1. You'll begin by opening the first draft of the description, which has the filename Annuity.

| Figure 2-1 | DRAFT OF ANNUITY PLAN SHOWING BRANDI'S EDITS (PAGE 1) |

Figure 2-1   DRAFT OF ANNUITY PLAN SHOWING BRANDI'S EDITS (PAGE 2)

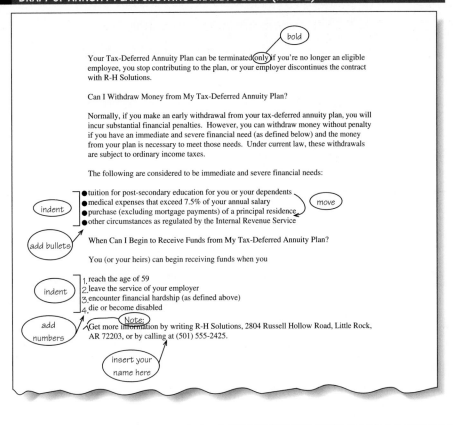

To open the document:

1. Place your Data Disk into the appropriate disk drive.

2. Start Word as usual.

3. Click the **Open** button 📂 on the Standard toolbar to display the Open dialog box, shown in Figure 2-2.

Figure 2-2   THE OPEN DIALOG BOX

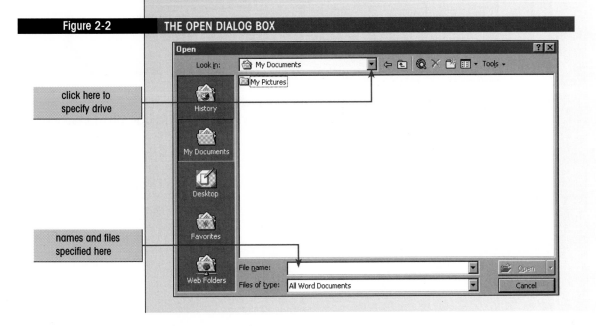

4. Click the **Look in** list arrow. The list of drives and files appears.

5. Click the drive that contains your Data Disk.

6. Double-click the **Tutorial.02** folder, then double-click the **Tutorial** folder.

7. Click **Annuity** to select the file, if necessary.

TROUBLE? If you see "Annuity.doc" in the folder, Windows might be configured to display filename extensions. Click Annuity.doc and continue with Step 8. If you can't find the file with or without the filename extension, make sure you're looking in the Tutorial subfolder within the Tutorial.02 folder on the drive that contains your Data Disk, and check to make sure the Files of type text box displays All Word Documents or All Files. If you still can't locate the file, ask your instructor or technical support person for help.

8. Click the **Open** button. The document opens, with the insertion point at the beginning of the document. See Figure 2-3.

| Figure 2-3 | THE OPEN DOCUMENT |

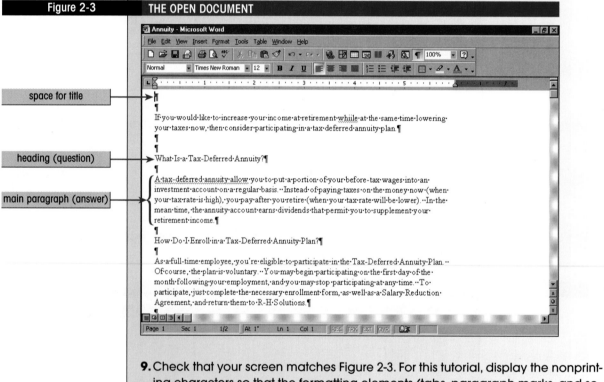

9. Check that your screen matches Figure 2-3. For this tutorial, display the nonprinting characters so that the formatting elements (tabs, paragraph marks, and so forth) are visible and easier to change.

Now that you've opened the document, you can save it with a new name.

Renaming the Document

To avoid altering the original file, Annuity, you will save the document using the filename RHS Annuity Plan. Saving the document with another filename creates a copy of the file and leaves the original file unchanged in case you want to work through the tutorial again.

> ### To save the document with a new name:
>
> 1. Click **File** on the menu bar, and then click **Save As**. The Save As dialog box opens with the current filename highlighted in the File name text box. You could type an entirely new filename, or you could edit the current one. In the next step, practice editing a filename.
>
> 2. Click to the left of "Annuity" in the File name text box, type **RHS**, and then press the **spacebar**. Press the → key to move the insertion point to the right of the letter "y" in "Annuity," press the **spacebar**, and then type **Plan**. The filename changes to RHS Annuity Plan.
>
> 3. Click the **Save** button to save the document with the new filename.

Now you're ready to begin working with the document. First, you will check it for spelling and grammatical errors.

Using the Spelling and Grammar Checker

When typing a document, you can check for spelling and grammatical errors simply by looking for words underlined in red (for spelling errors) or green (for grammatical errors). But when you're working on a document that someone else typed, it's a good idea to start by using the Spelling and Grammar checker. This feature checks a document word by word for a variety of spelling and grammatical errors. Among other things, the Spelling and Grammar checker can sometimes find words that, though spelled correctly, are not used properly. For example, the word "their" instead of the word "there" or "form" instead of "from."

> **REFERENCE WINDOW**   **RW**
>
> <u>Checking a Document for Spelling and Grammatical Errors</u>
> - Click at the beginning of the document, then click the Spelling and Grammar button on the Standard toolbar.
> - In the Spelling and Grammar dialog box, review any errors highlighted in color. Grammatical errors appear in green; spelling errors appear in red. Review the possible corrections in the Suggestions list box.
> - To accept a suggested correction, click it in the Suggestions list box. Then click Change to make the correction and continue searching the document for errors.
> - Click Ignore to skip this instance of the highlighted text and continue searching the document for errors.
> - Click Ignore All to skip all instances of the highlighted text and continue searching the document for errors. Click Ignore Rule to skip all instances of a particular grammatical error.
> - To type your correction directly in the document, click outside the Spelling and Grammar dialog box, make the desired correction, and then click Resume in the Spelling and Grammar dialog box.

You'll see how the Spelling and Grammar checker works as you check the annuity plan document for mistakes.

To check the annuity plan document for spelling and grammatical errors:

1. Verify that the insertion point is located at the beginning of the document, to the left of the first paragraph mark.

2. Click the **Spelling and Grammar** button [ABC✓] on the Standard toolbar. The Spelling and Grammar dialog box opens with the word "whiile" highlighted in red. The word "while" is suggested as a possible replacement. The line immediately under the title bar indicates the type of problem, in this case, "Not in Dictionary." See Figure 2-4.

Figure 2-4	SPELLING AND GRAMMAR DIALOG BOX

possible error

suggested correction

Spelling and Grammar: English (U.S.)

If·you·would·like·to·increase·your·income·at· retirement·whiile·at·the·same·time·lowering· your·taxes·now,·then·consider·participating·in·a· tax-deferred·annuity·plan.

Ignore
Ignore All
Add

Suggestions:
while

Change
Change All
AutoCorrect

☑ Check grammar

Options...   Undo   Cancel

3. Verify that "while" is highlighted in the Suggestions list box, and then click **Change**. "While" is inserted into the document. Next, the grammatical error "A tax-deferred annuity allow" is highlighted in green, with two possible corrections listed in the Suggestions box. The dialog box indicates that the problem concerns subject-verb agreement.

   TROUBLE? If you see the word "bondd" selected instead of "a tax-deferred annuity allow," your computer is not set up to check grammar. Click the Check grammar check box to insert a check, and then click Cancel to close the Spelling and Grammar dialog box. Next, click at the beginning of the document, and then repeat Step 2.

4. Click **A tax-deferred annuity allows** in the Suggestions box, if necessary, and then click **Change**. The misspelled word "bondd" is highlighted in red, with two possible replacements listed in the Suggestions list box.

5. Click **bond**, if necessary, to highlight it, and then click **Change**.

6. Click the **Ignore Rule** button to prevent the Spelling and Grammar checker from stopping at each of the remaining seven bullets in the document. You see a message indicating that the spelling and grammar check is complete. The Spelling and Grammar checker next selects the word "tuition," with the capitalized version

of the same word, "Tuition," listed in the Suggestions box. You do not want to accept the change because the highlighted word is the beginning of a bulleted list, not a sentence, and doesn't have to be capitalized.

7. Click **OK**. You return to the annuity plan document.

Although the Spelling and Grammar checker is a useful tool, remember that there is no substitute for careful proofreading. Always take the time to read through your document to check for errors the Spelling and Grammar checker might have missed. Keep in mind that Spelling and Grammar checker probably won't catch *all* instances of words that are spelled correctly but used improperly. And of course, the Spelling and Grammar checker cannot pinpoint phrases that are simply confusing or inaccurate. To produce a professional document, you must read it carefully several times, and, if necessary, ask a co-worker to read it, too.

To proofread the annuity plan document:

1. Scroll to the beginning of the document and begin proofreading.

   The first error is a missing hyphen in the phrase "tax deferred annuity plan" at the end of the first paragraph.

2. Click after the "x" in "tax," type - (a hyphen), and then press the **Delete** key to remove the space. Now the phrase is hyphenated correctly.

   The next error is the word "mean time" in the paragraph below the "What Is a Tax-Deferred Annuity?" heading. You need to delete the space.

3. Click after the letter "n" in "mean" and then press the **Delete** key.

4. Continue proofreading the document.

Once you are certain the document is free from errors, you are ready to make some more editing changes. To make all of Brandi's editing changes, you'll need to learn how to quickly move the insertion point to any location in the document.

Moving **the Insertion Point Around a Document**

The arrow keys on your keyboard, ↑, ↓, →, and ←, allow you to move the insertion point one character at a time to the left or right, or one line at a time up or down. If you want to move more than one character or one line at a time, you can point and click in other parts of a line or the document. You also can press a combination of keys to move the insertion point. As you become more experienced with Word, you'll decide which method you prefer.

To see how quickly you can move through the document, you'll use keystrokes to move the insertion point to the beginning of the second page and to the end of the document.

To move the insertion point with keystrokes:

1. Press the **Ctrl** key and hold it down while you press the **Home** key. The insertion point moves to the beginning of the document.

2. Press the **Page Down** key to move the insertion point down to the next screen.

3. Press the **Page Down** key again to move the insertion point down to the next screen.

4. Notice that the status bar indicates the location of the insertion point.

5. Press the ↓ or ↑ key to move the insertion point to the paragraph that begins "Your Tax-deferred Annuity Plan can be terminated...." The insertion point is now at the beginning of page 2. Notice the **automatic page break**, a dotted line that Word inserts automatically to mark the beginning of the new page. See Figure 2-5. As you insert and delete text or change formatting in a document, the location of the automatic page breaks in your document continually adjusts to account for the edits.

Figure 2-5	AUTOMATIC PAGE BREAK

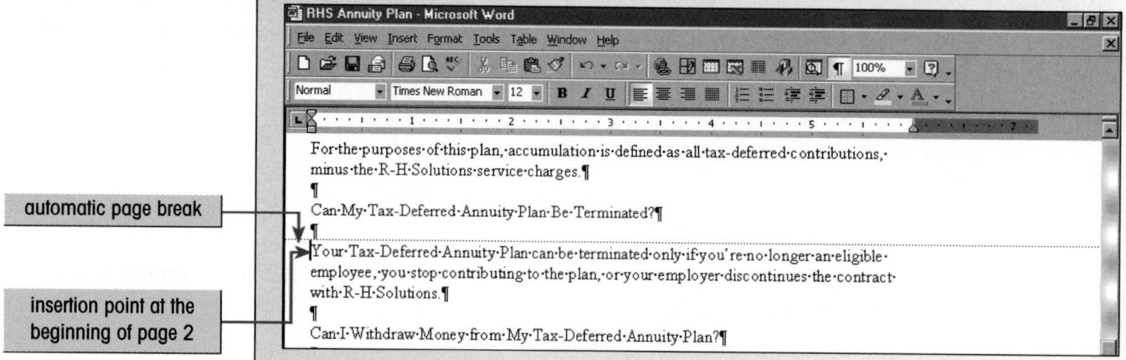

automatic page break

insertion point at the beginning of page 2

6. Press **Ctrl+End**. (That is, press and hold down the **Ctrl** key while you press the **End** key.) The insertion point moves to the end of the document.

7. Use the ← key to move the insertion point immediately before the phrase "at (501) 555-2425," and then type your name and a space.

8. Move the insertion point back to the beginning of the document.

Figure 2-6 summarizes the keystrokes you can use to move the insertion point around the document.

Figure 2-6	KEYSTROKES FOR MOVING THE INSERTION POINT
PRESS	**TO MOVE INSERTION POINT**
← or →	Left or right one character at a time
↑ or ↓	Up or down one line at a time
Ctrl+← or Ctrl+→	Left or right one word at a time
Ctrl+↑ or Ctrl+↓	Up or down one paragraph at a time
Home or End	To the beginning or to the end of the current line
Ctrl+Home or Ctrl+End	To the beginning or to the end of the document
PageUp or PageDown	To the previous screen or to the next screen
Alt+Ctrl+PageUp or Alt+Ctrl+PageDown	To the top or to the bottom of the document window

Using **Select, Then Do**

One of the most powerful editing features in Word is the "select, then do" feature. It allows you to select (or highlight) a block of text and then do something to that text, such as deleting, moving, or formatting it. You can select text using either the mouse or the keyboard; however, the mouse is usually the easier and more efficient way. With the mouse, you can quickly select a line or paragraph by clicking the **selection bar**, which is the blank space in the left margin area of the document window. Also, you can select text using various combinations of keys. Figure 2-7 summarizes methods for selecting text with the mouse and the keyboard. The notation "Ctrl+Shift" indicates that you should press and hold two keys (the Ctrl key and the Shift key) at the same time.

Figure 2-7	METHODS FOR SELECTING TEXT WITH THE MOUSE AND KEYBOARD		
TO SELECT	**MOUSE**	**KEYBOARD**	**MOUSE AND KEYBOARD**
A word	Double-click the word.	Move the insertion point to the beginning of the next word, hold down Ctrl+Shift, and then press → once.	
A line	Click in the selection bar next to the line.	Move the insertion point to the beginning of the line, hold down Ctrl+Shift, and then press → until the line is selected.	
A sentence			Press and hold down the Ctrl key, and click within the sentence.
Multiple lines	Click and drag in the selection bar next to the lines.	Move the insertion point to the beginning of the first line, hold down Ctrl+Shift, and then press → until all the lines are selected.	
A paragraph	Double-click in the selection bar next to the paragraph, or triple-click within the paragraph.	Move the insertion point to the beginning of the paragraph, hold down Ctrl+Shift, and then press ↓.	
Multiple paragraphs	Click and drag in the selection bar next to the paragraphs, or triple-click within the first paragraph and drag.	Move the insertion point to the beginning of the first paragraph, hold down Ctrl+Shift, and then press ↓ until all the paragraphs are selected.	
Entire document	Triple-click in the selection bar.	Press Ctrl+A.	Press and hold down the Ctrl key and click in the selection bar.
A block of text			Click at the beginning of the block, press and hold down the Shift key, and then click at the end of the block.

Deleting **Text**

Brandi wants you to delete the phrase "at the same time" in the first paragraph of the document. You'll use the "select, then do" feature to delete the phrase now.

To select and delete a phrase from the text:

1. Click and drag over the phrase **at the same time** located in the first line of the first paragraph. The phrase and the space following it are highlighted, as shown in Figure 2-8. Notice that dragging the pointer over the second and successive words automatically selects the entire words and the spaces following them. This makes it much easier to select words and phrases than selecting them one character at a time.

Figure 2-8	PHRASE SELECTED FOR DELETION

selected phrase

If you would like to increase your income at retirement while at the same time lowering your taxes now, then consider participating in a tax-deferred annuity plan.

2. Press the **Delete** key. The phrase disappears and the words "lowering your taxes now" move up to the same line as the deleted phrase. See Figure 2-9.

Figure 2-9	PARAGRAPH AFTER DELETING PHRASE

text wrapped back to fill space left by deleted phrase

former location of deleted phrase

If you would like to increase your income at retirement while lowering your taxes now, then consider participating in a tax-deferred annuity plan.

TROUBLE? If your screen looks slightly different than Figure 2-9, don't be concerned. The text may wrap differently on your monitor. Just make sure the phrase has been deleted.

After rereading the paragraph, Reginald decides the phrase shouldn't have been deleted after all. He checks with Brandi, and she agrees. You could retype the text, but there's an easier way to restore the phrase.

Using the Undo and Redo Commands

To undo (or reverse) the very last thing you did, simply click the **Undo button** on the Standard toolbar. If you want to reinstate your original change, the **Redo button** reverses the action of the Undo button (or redoes the undo). To undo anything more than your last action, you can click the Undo list arrow on the Standard toolbar. This list shows your most recent actions. Undo reverses the action only at its original location. You can't delete a word or phrase and then undo it at a different location.

REFERENCE WINDOW   **RW**

<u>Using Undo and Redo</u>
- Click the Undo button on the Standard toolbar to reverse your last action. Or click Edit on the menu bar, and then click Undo. Note that the exact command you see on the Edit menu will reflect your most recent action, such as "Undo Typing."
- To reverse several previous actions, click the Undo list arrow on the Standard toolbar. Click an action on the list to reverse all actions up to and including the one you click.
- To display a ScreenTip reminder of your last action, place the mouse pointer over the Undo button.
- To undo your previous actions one-by-one, in the reverse order in which you performed them, click the Undo button once for every action you want to reverse.
- If you undo an action by mistake, click the Redo button on the Standard toolbar (or click Edit on the menu bar, and then click Redo) to reverse the undo.

You decide to undo the deletion to see how the sentence reads. Rather than retyping the phrase, you will reverse the edit using the Undo button.

To undo the deletion:

1. Place the mouse pointer over the Undo button on the Standard toolbar. The label "Undo Clear" appears in a ScreenTip, indicating that your most recent action involved deleting (or clearing) text.

2. Click the **Undo** button. The phrase "at the same time" reappears in your document and is highlighted.

   TROUBLE? If the phrase doesn't reappear and something else changes in your document, you probably made another edit or change to the document (such as pressing the Backspace key) between the deletion and the undo. Click the Undo button on the Standard toolbar until the phrase reappears in your document. If a list of possible changes appears under the Undo button, you clicked the list arrow next to the Undo button rather than the Undo button itself. Click the Undo button to restore the deleted phrase and close the list box.

3. Click within the paragraph to deselect the phrase.

   As you read the sentence, you decide that it reads better without the phrase. Instead of deleting it again, you'll redo the undo. As you place the pointer over the Redo button, notice that its ScreenTip indicates the action you want to redo.

4. Place the mouse pointer over the Redo button on the Standard toolbar and observe the "Redo Clear" label.

5. Click the **Redo** button. The phrase "at the same time" disappears from your document again.

6. Click the **Save** button on the Standard toolbar to save your changes to the document.

You have edited the document by deleting the text that Brandi marked for deletion. Now, you are ready to make the rest of the edits she suggested.

Moving Text Within a Document

One of the most important uses of "select, then do" is moving text. For example, Brandi wants to reorder the four points Reginald made in the section "Can I Withdraw Money from My Tax-Deferred Annuity Plan?" on page 2 of his draft. You could reorder the list by deleting the sentence and then retyping it at the new location, but a much more efficient approach is to select and then move the sentence. Word provides several ways to move text: drag and drop, cut and paste, and copy and paste.

Dragging and Dropping Text

One way to move text within a document is called drag and drop. With **drag and drop**, you select the text you want to move, press and hold down the mouse button while you drag the selected text to a new location, and then release the mouse button.

REFERENCE WINDOW **RW**

Dragging and Dropping Text
- Select the text to be moved.
- Press and hold down the mouse button until the drag-and-drop pointer appears, and then drag the selected text to its new location.
- Use the dashed insertion point as a guide to determine the precise spot where the text will be inserted.
- Release the mouse button to drop the text at the new location.

Brandi requested a change in the order of the items in the bulleted list on page 2 of the document, so you'll use the drag-and-drop method to reorder the items. At the same time, you'll practice using the selection bar to highlight a line of text.

To move text using drag and drop:

1. Scroll through the document until you see "tuition for post-secondary education...," the first item in the list of "immediate and severe financial needs:" that begins in the middle of page 2.

2. Click in the selection bar to the left of the line beginning "tuition..." to select that line of text, including the return character. See Figure 2-10.

Figure 2-10	SELECTED TEXT TO DRAG AND DROP

selected line of text

pointer in selection bar

The·following·are·considered·to·be·immediate·and·severe·financial·needs:¶
¶
tuition·for·post-secondary·education·for·you·or·your·dependents¶
medical·expenses·that·exceed·7.5%·of·your·annual·salary¶
purchase·(excluding·mortgage·payments)·of·a·principal·residence¶
other·circumstances·as·regulated·by·the·Internal·Revenue·Service¶
¶
When·Can·I·Begin·to·Receive·Funds·from·My·Tax-Deferred·Annuity·Plan?¶
¶
You·(or·your·heirs)·can·begin·receiving·funds·when·you¶
¶
reach·the·age·of·59,¶
leave·the·service·of·your·employer¶

Page 2   Sec 1   2/2   At 3.7"   Ln 15   Col 1   REC TRK EXT OVR

3. Position the pointer over the selected text. The pointer changes from a right-facing arrow to a left-facing arrow.

4. Press and hold down the mouse button until the drag-and-drop pointer, which has a dashed insertion point, an arrow, and a small square called a move box, appears.

5. Drag the selected text down three lines until the dashed insertion point appears to the left of the word "other." Make sure you use the dashed insertion point to guide the text to its new location rather than the mouse pointer or the move box; the dashed insertion point marks the precise location of the drop. See Figure 2-11.

| Figure 2-11 | MOVING TEXT WITH DRAG-AND-DROP POINTER |

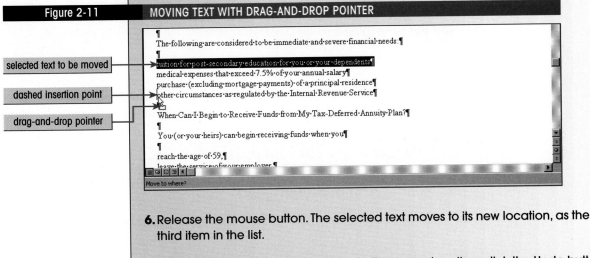

selected text to be moved

dashed insertion point

drag-and-drop pointer

6. Release the mouse button. The selected text moves to its new location, as the third item in the list.

TROUBLE? If the selected text moves to the wrong location, click the Undo button on the Standard toolbar, and then repeat Steps 3 through 6, making sure you hold the mouse button until the dashed insertion point appears in front of the word "other."

7. Deselect the highlighted text by clicking anywhere in the document window.

Dragging and dropping works well if you're moving text a short distance in a document; however, Word provides another method, called cut and paste, that works well for moving text either a short distance or beyond the current screen.

Cutting or Copying and Pasting Text

To **cut** means to remove text from the document and place it on the **Office Clipboard**, which stores up to 12 items at a time. To **paste** means to transfer a copy of the text from the Clipboard into the document at the insertion point. To perform a cut-and-paste action, you select the text you want to move, cut (or remove) it from the document, and then paste (or restore) it into the document in a new location. If you don't want to remove the text from its original location, you can copy it (rather than cutting it) and then paste the copy in a new location. This procedure is known as "copy and paste."

If you cut or copy more than one item, the Clipboard toolbar opens, making it easier for you to select which items you want to paste into the document.

REFERENCE WINDOW   RW

Cutting or Copying and Pasting Text

- Select the text you want to move.
- Click the Cut button on the Standard toolbar. (If you want to make a copy, click the Copy button instead.)
- Move the insertion point to the target location in the document.
- Click the Paste button on the Standard toolbar.
- If you have cut or copied more than one block of text, the Clipboard toolbar will open, containing one icon for each item stored on the Clipboard. To paste an item from the Clipboard toolbar into the document, click where you want the item to be inserted, and then click its icon on the Clipboard toolbar. To paste the entire contents of the Clipboard at the insertion point, click the Paste All button in the Clipboard toolbar. To erase the contents of the Clipboard, click the Clear Clipboard button on the Clipboard toolbar.

Brandi suggested moving the phrase "at any time" (in the paragraph beginning "You can change your allocation…") to a new location. You'll use cut and paste to move this phrase.

To move text using cut and paste:

1. Scroll the document up until you can see the paragraph just above the heading "How Will I Know…." on page 1.

2. Click and drag the mouse to highlight the complete phrase **at any time**. See Figure 2-12.

Figure 2-12	TEXT TO MOVE USING CUT AND PASTE

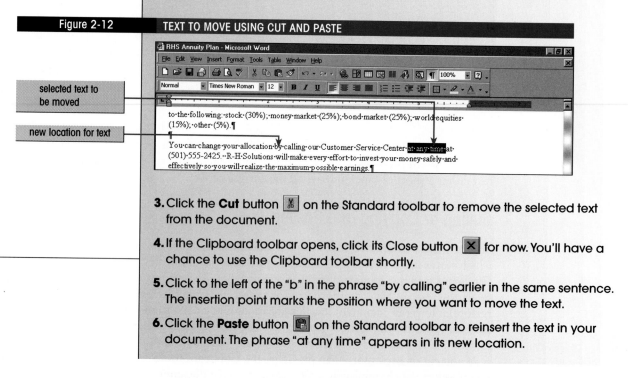

selected text to be moved

new location for text

3. Click the **Cut** button 🔏 on the Standard toolbar to remove the selected text from the document.

4. If the Clipboard toolbar opens, click its Close button ⊠ for now. You'll have a chance to use the Clipboard toolbar shortly.

5. Click to the left of the "b" in the phrase "by calling" earlier in the same sentence. The insertion point marks the position where you want to move the text.

6. Click the **Paste** button 📋 on the Standard toolbar to reinsert the text in your document. The phrase "at any time" appears in its new location.

The copy and paste feature works much the same way as cut and paste. You can try using this technique now, as you copy the phrase "Tax-Deferred Annuity Plan" from the middle of the document and then paste it at the top of the document.

1. Scroll the document up until you can see the heading "How Do I Enroll in a Tax-Deferred Annuity Plan?" on page 1.

2. In the headings, click and drag the mouse to highlight the complete phrase "Tax-Deferred Annuity Plan."

3. Click the **Copy** button 🖹 on the Standard toolbar. The Clipboard toolbar opens, containing icons for each item currently stored on the Clipboard, as shown in Figure 2-13. The "W" on the icons indicates that the copied items contain Word text. Note that your Clipboard toolbar might contain more than two icons, depending on whether you (or another user) cut or copy text before completing this tutorial. You also may see icons for other Office programs, such as Excel.

Figure 2-13	CLIPBOARD TOOLBAR WITH CUT AND COPIED ITEMS

"W" means the item contains Word text

Clipboard (2 of 12)

you may see additional icons

icon for cut phrase

icon for copied phrase

TROUBLE? If the Office Assistant opens, hide it and continue with Step 4.

4. Place the mouse pointer over each of the icons, one at a time, until the ScreenTip "at any time" appears, indicating that this is the icon for the text you cut in the previous set of steps.

5. Place the mouse pointer over each of the icons, one at a time, until the ScreenTip "Tax-Deferred Annuity Plan" appears, indicating that this is the icon for the text you just copied.

6. Scroll up and click at the beginning of the document to move the insertion point there.

7. Click the **Tax-Deferred Annuity Plan** icon in the Clipboard toolbar. The phrase is inserted at the top of the document. Now that you are finished using the Clipboard toolbar, you will delete its contents.

8. Click the **Clear Clipboard** button 🗙 button on the Clipboard toolbar. All of the icons disappear from the Clipboard toolbar.

9. Click the **Close** button ☒ on the Clipboard toolbar. The Clipboard toolbar disappears.

Finding **and Replacing Text**

When you're working with a longer document, the quickest and easiest way to locate a particular word or phrase is to use the Find command. If you want to replace characters or a phrase with something else, you can use the Replace command, which combines the Find command with a substitution feature. The Replace command searches through a document and substitutes the text you're searching for with the replacement text you specify. As Word performs the search, it stops and highlights each occurrence of the search text and lets you determine whether to substitute the replacement text by clicking the Replace button.

If you want to substitute every occurrence of the search text with the replacement text, you can click the Replace All button. When using the Replace All button with single words, keep in mind that the search text might be found within other words. To prevent Word from making incorrect substitutions in such cases, it's a good idea to select the "Find whole words only" check box along with the Replace All button. For example, suppose you want to replace the word "figure" with illustration. Unless you select the "Find whole words only" check box, Word would replace "configure" with "conillustration."

As you search through a document, you can search from the current location of the insertion point down to the end of the document, from the insertion point up to the beginning of the document, or throughout the document.

REFERENCE WINDOW   RW

Finding and Replacing Text

- Click the Select Browse Object button on the vertical scroll bar, and then click the Find button on the Select Browse Object menu. (You also can click Edit on the menu bar, and then click either Find or Replace.)
- To find text, click the Find tab; or, to find and replace text, click the Replace tab.
- Click the More button to expand the dialog box to display additional options (including the "Find whole words only" option). If you see the Less button, the additional options are already displayed.
- In the Search list box, select Down if you want to search from the insertion point to the end of the document, select Up if you want to search from the insertion point to the beginning of the document, or select All to search the entire document.
- Type the characters you want to find in the Find what text box.
- If you are replacing text, type the replacement text in the Replace with text box.
- Click the Find Next button.
- Click the Replace button to substitute the found text with the replacement text and find the next occurrence.
- Click the Find whole words only check box, and then click the Replace All button to substitute all occurrences of the found text with the replacement text.

Brandi wants the shortened version of the company name, "R-H Solutions," to be spelled out as "Right-Hand Solutions" every time it appears in the text.

To replace "R-H Solutions" with "Right-Hand Solutions:"

1. Click the **Select Browse Object** button 🔘 near the bottom of the vertical scroll bar.

2. Click the **Find** button 🔍 on the Select Browse Object menu. The Find and Replace dialog box appears.

3. Click the **Replace** tab.

4. If necessary, click the **More** button to display the additional search options.

5. If necessary, click the **Search** list arrow, and then click **All**.

6. Click the **Find what** text box, type **R-H Solutions**, press the **Tab** key, and then type **Right-Hand Solutions** in the Replace with text box. Note that because the search text is made up of more than one word, the "Find whole words only" option is unnecessary and is therefore unavailable. See Figure 2-14.

Figure 2-14   FIND AND REPLACE DIALOG BOX

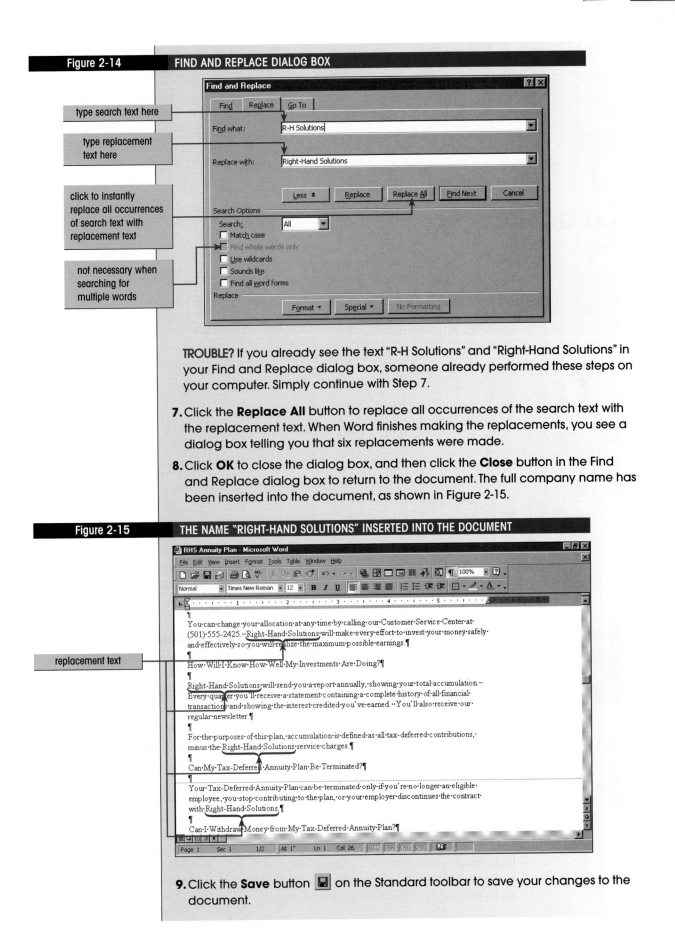

type search text here

type replacement text here

click to instantly replace all occurrences of search text with replacement text

not necessary when searching for multiple words

TROUBLE? If you already see the text "R-H Solutions" and "Right-Hand Solutions" in your Find and Replace dialog box, someone already performed these steps on your computer. Simply continue with Step 7.

7. Click the **Replace All** button to replace all occurrences of the search text with the replacement text. When Word finishes making the replacements, you see a dialog box telling you that six replacements were made.

8. Click **OK** to close the dialog box, and then click the **Close** button in the Find and Replace dialog box to return to the document. The full company name has been inserted into the document, as shown in Figure 2-15.

Figure 2-15   THE NAME "RIGHT-HAND SOLUTIONS" INSERTED INTO THE DOCUMENT

replacement text

9. Click the **Save** button 🖫 on the Standard toolbar to save your changes to the document.

You can also search for and replace formatting, such as bold, and special characters, such as paragraph marks, in the Find and Replace dialog box. Click in the Find what text box or the Replace with text box, enter any text if necessary, click the Format button, click Font to open the Font dialog box, and then select the formatting you want to find or replace. Complete the search or replace as usual.

You have completed the content changes Brandi suggested, but she has some other changes that will improve the plan's appearance. In the next session, you'll enhance the annuity plan by changing the width, spacing, and alignment of text.

Session 2.1 QUICK CHECK

1. Explain how to open a document and save a copy of it with a new name.

2. Which key(s) do you press to move the insertion point to the following places:
   a. down one line
   b. end of the document
   c. to the next screen

3. Describe the "select, then do" feature.

4. Define the following terms in your own words:
   a. selection bar
   b. Redo button
   c. drag and drop

5. Explain how to select a single word. Explain how to select a complete paragraph.

6. Describe a situation in which you would use the Undo button and then the Redo button.

7. True or False: You can use the Redo command to restore deleted text at a new location in your document.

8. What is the difference between cut and paste, and copy and paste?

9. List the steps involved in finding and replacing text in a document.

SESSION 2.2

In this session you will make the formatting changes Brandi suggested. You'll use a variety of formatting commands to change the margins, line spacing, text alignment, and paragraph indents. Also, you'll learn how to use the Format Painter, how to create bulleted and numbered lists, and how to change fonts, font sizes, and emphasis.

Changing the Margins

In general, it's best to begin formatting by making the changes that affect the document's overall appearance. Then you can make changes that affect only selected text. In this case, you need to adjust the margin settings of the annuity plan summary.

Word uses default margins of 1.25 inches for the left and right margins and 1 inch for the top and bottom margins. The numbers on the ruler (displayed below the Formatting toolbar) indicate the distance in inches from the left margin, not from the left edge of the paper. Unless you specify otherwise, changes you make to the margins will affect the entire document, not just the current paragraph or page.

<u>Changing Margins for the Entire Document</u>
- With the insertion point anywhere in your document and no text selected, click File on the menu bar, and then click Page Setup.
- If necessary, click the Margins tab to display the margin settings.
- Use the arrows to change the settings in the Top, Bottom, Left, or Right text boxes, or type a new margin value in each text box.
- Make sure the Apply to list box displays Whole document.
- Click the OK button.

You need to change the top margin to 1.5 inches and the left margin to 1.75 inches, as Brandi requested. The left margin needs to be wider than usual to allow space for making holes so that the document can be inserted in a three-ring binder. In the next set of steps, you'll change the margins with the Page Setup command. You also can change margins in print layout view; you'll practice that method in the Review Assignments.

To change the margins in the annuity plan document:

1. If you took a break after the last lesson, make sure Word is running, the RHS Annuity Plan document is open, and nonprinting characters are displayed.

2. Click once anywhere in the document to make sure no text is selected.

3. Click **File** on the menu bar, and then click **Page Setup** to open the Page Setup dialog box.

4. If necessary, click the **Margins** tab to display the margin settings. The Top margin setting is selected. See Figure 2-16.

| Figure 2-16 | PAGE SETUP DIALOG BOX |

margins tab selected

Top margin setting

new margin settings will apply to whole document

5. Type **1.5** to change the Top margin setting. (You do not have to type the inches symbol.)

6. Press the **Tab** key twice to move to the Left text box and select the current margin setting. Notice how the text area in the Preview box moves down to reflect the larger top margin.

7. Type **1.75** and then press the **Tab** key. Watch the Preview box to see how the margin increases.

8. Make sure the **Whole document** option is selected in the Apply to list box, and then click the **OK** button to return to your document. Notice that the right margin on the ruler has changed to reflect the larger margins and the reduced page area that results. See Figure 2-17.

Figure 2-17	RULER AFTER SETTING LEFT MARGIN TO 1.75 INCHES

ruler

text width now 5.5 inches

TROUBLE? If a double dotted line and the words "Section Break" appear in your document, text was selected in the document and Whole document wasn't specified in the Apply to list box. If this occurs, click the Undo button on the Standard toolbar and then repeat Steps 1 through 8, making sure you select the Whole document option in the Apply to list box.

Now that you've made numerous changes to your document, it's a good idea to save it with a new name. That way, if the file you are working on somehow becomes corrupted, you can at least return to the earlier draft, rather than having to start all over again.

To save the document with a new name:

1. Click **File** on the menu bar, then click **Save As**.

2. Verify that the Tutorial subfolder within the Tutorial.02 folder appears in the Save in list box, change the filename to **RHS Annuity Plan Copy 2**, and then click the **Save** button. The document is saved with the new margin settings and a new name.

Next you will change the amount of space between lines of text.

Changing **Line Spacing**

The line spacing in a document determines the amount of vertical space between lines of text. You have a choice of three basic types of line spacing: **single spacing** (which allows for the largest character in a particular line as well as a small amount of extra space); **1.5 line spacing** (which allows for one and one-half times the space of single spacing); and **double spacing** (which allows for twice the space of single spacing). The annuity plan document is currently single-spaced because Word uses single spacing by default. Before changing the line-spacing setting, you should select the text you want to change. You can change line spacing by using the Paragraph command on the Format menu, or by using your keyboard.

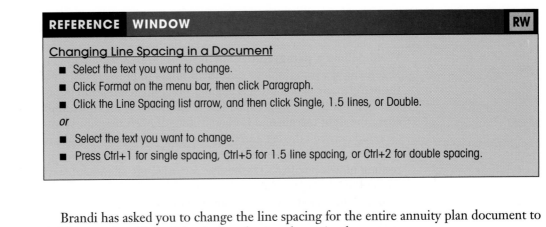

REFERENCE WINDOW | **RW**

Changing Line Spacing in a Document

- Select the text you want to change.
- Click Format on the menu bar, then click Paragraph.
- Click the Line Spacing list arrow, and then click Single, 1.5 lines, or Double.

or

- Select the text you want to change.
- Press Ctrl+1 for single spacing, Ctrl+5 for 1.5 line spacing, or Ctrl+2 for double spacing.

Brandi has asked you to change the line spacing for the entire annuity plan document to 1.5 line spacing. You will begin by selecting the entire document.

To change the document's line spacing:

1. Triple-click in the selection bar to select the entire document.

2. Click **Format** on the menu bar, and then click **Paragraph** to open the Paragraph dialog box.

3. If necessary, click the **Indents and Spacing** tab.

4. Click the **Line spacing** list arrow, and then click **1.5 lines**. The Preview box shows the results of the new line spacing. See Figure 2-18.

| Figure 2-18 | CHANGING THE DOCUMENT'S LINE SPACING |

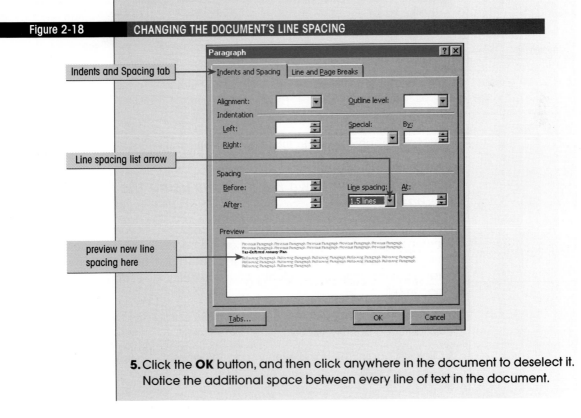

5. Click the **OK** button, and then click anywhere in the document to deselect it. Notice the additional space between every line of text in the document.

Now, you are ready to make formatting changes that affect individual paragraphs.

Aligning Text

Word defines a **paragraph** as any text that ends with a paragraph mark symbol (¶). The alignment of a paragraph or document refers to how the text lines up horizontally between the margins. By default, text is aligned along the left margin but is **ragged**, or uneven, along the right margin. This is called **left alignment**. With **right alignment**, the text is aligned along the right margin and is ragged along the left margin. With **center alignment**, text is centered between the left and right margins. With **justified alignment**, full lines of text are spaced between or aligned along both the left and the right margins. The paragraph you are reading now is justified. The easiest way to apply alignment settings is by clicking buttons on the Formatting toolbar.

Brandi indicated that the title of the annuity plan description should be centered and that the main paragraphs should be justified. First, you'll center the title.

To center-align the title:

1. Click anywhere in the title "Tax-Deferred Annuity Plan" at the beginning of the document.

2. Click the **Center** button on the Formatting toolbar. The text centers between the left and right margins. See Figure 2-19.

Figure 2-19   TITLE CENTERED

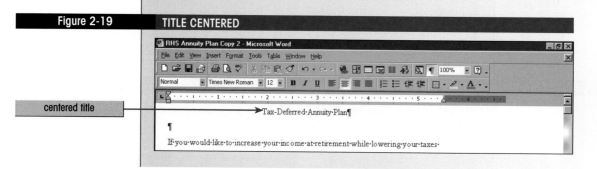

centered title

Now, you'll justify the text in the first two main paragraphs.

To justify the first two paragraphs using the Formatting toolbar:

1. Click anywhere in the first paragraph, which begins "If you would like to increase...," and click the **Justify** button on the Formatting toolbar. The justification would be easier to see if the paragraph had more lines of text. You'll see the effects more clearly after you justify the second paragraph in the document.

2. Move the insertion point to the second main paragraph, which begins "A tax-deferred annuity allows... ."

3. Click again. The text is evenly spaced between the left and right margins. See Figure 2-20.

| Figure 2-20 | TEXT JUSTIFIED USING THE FORMATTING TOOLBAR |

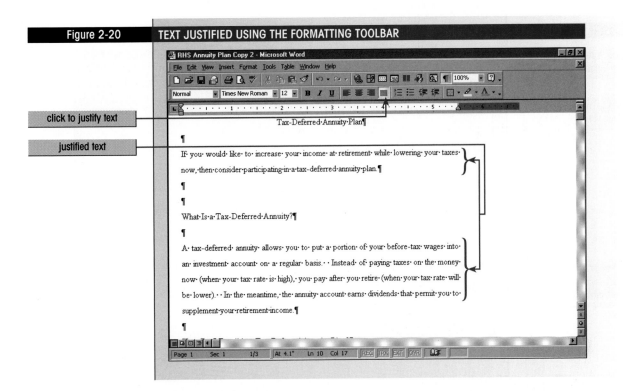

You'll justify the other paragraphs later. Now that you've learned how to change the paragraph alignment, you can turn your attention to indenting a paragraph.

Indenting a Paragraph

When you become a more experienced Word user, you might want to use some special forms of paragraph formatting, such as a **hanging indent** (where all lines except the first line of the paragraph are indented from the left margin) or a **right indent** (where all lines of the paragraph are indented from the right margin). You can select these types of indents on the Indents and Spacing tab of the Paragraph dialog box.

In this document, though, you'll need to indent only the main paragraphs 0.5 inches from the left margin. This left indent is a simple kind of paragraph indent, which requires only a quick click on the Formatting toolbar's Increase Indent button. According to Brandi's notes, you need to indent all of the main paragraphs, starting with the second paragraph.

To indent a paragraph using the Increase Indent button:

1. Make sure the insertion point is still located anywhere within the second paragraph, which begins "A tax-deferred annuity allows... ."

2. Click the **Increase Indent** button 📰 on the Formatting toolbar twice. (Don't click the Decrease Indent button by mistake.) The entire paragraph moves right 0.5 inches each time you click the Increase Indent button. The paragraph is indented 1 inch, 0.5 inches more than Brandi wants.

3. Click the **Decrease Indent** button 📰 on the Formatting toolbar to move the paragraph left 0.5 inches. The paragraph is now indented 0.5 inches from the left margin, as shown in Figure 2-21.

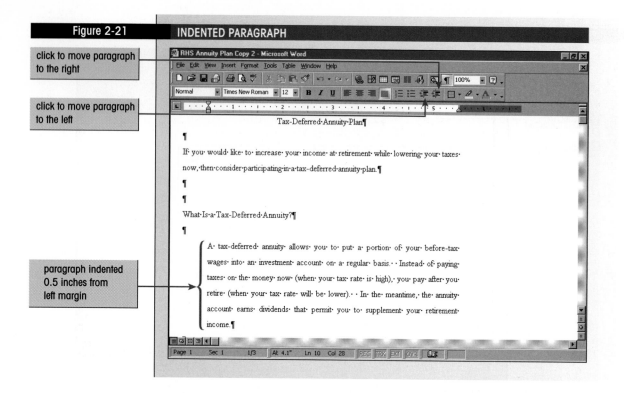

Figure 2-21   INDENTED PARAGRAPH

click to move paragraph to the right

click to move paragraph to the left

paragraph indented 0.5 inches from left margin

You could continue to indent, and then justify, each paragraph individually, but there's an easier way—the Format Painter command. The Format Painter allows you to copy both the indentation and alignment changes to all the other main paragraphs in the document.

Using Format Painter

The **Format Painter** makes it easy to copy all the formatting features of one paragraph to one or more other paragraphs. You'll use the Format Painter now to copy the formatting of the second paragraph to other main paragraphs. Begin by highlighting the paragraph whose format you want to copy. (Note that you can't simply move the insertion point to that paragraph.)

To copy paragraph formatting with the Format Painter:

1. Double-click in the selection bar to select the second paragraph, which is indented and justified and begins "A tax-deferred annuity... ."

2. Double-click the **Format Painter** button 🖌 on the Standard toolbar. The Format Painter button will stay pressed until you click the button again. When you move the pointer over text, the pointer changes to 🖌I to indicate that the format of the selected paragraph can be painted (or copied) onto another paragraph.

3. Scroll down, and then click anywhere in the third paragraph, which begins "As a full-time employee... ." The format of the third paragraph shifts to match the format of the selected paragraph. See Figure 2-22. As you can see, both paragraphs are now indented and justified. The pointer remains as the Format Painter pointer.

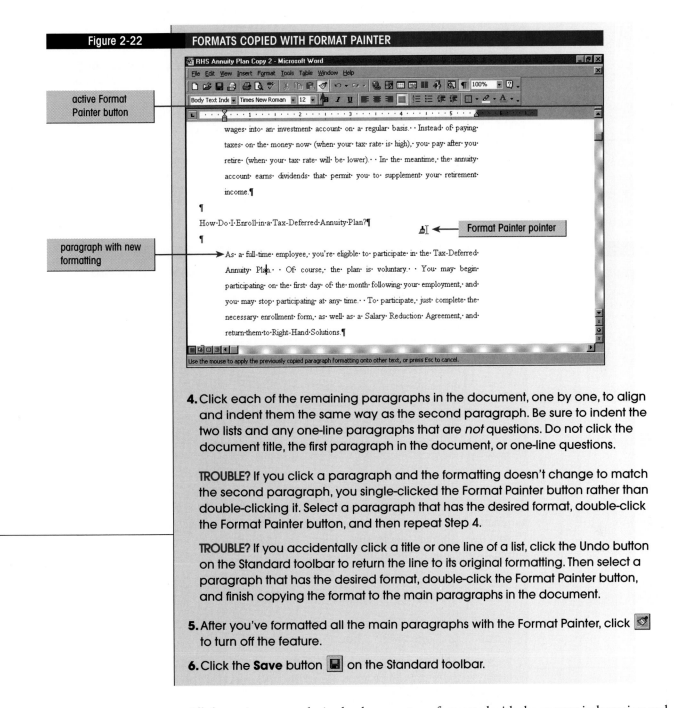

Figure 2-22 — **FORMATS COPIED WITH FORMAT PAINTER**

active Format Painter button

paragraph with new formatting

Format Painter pointer

4. Click each of the remaining paragraphs in the document, one by one, to align and indent them the same way as the second paragraph. Be sure to indent the two lists and any one-line paragraphs that are *not* questions. Do not click the document title, the first paragraph in the document, or one-line questions.

TROUBLE? If you click a paragraph and the formatting doesn't change to match the second paragraph, you single-clicked the Format Painter button rather than double-clicking it. Select a paragraph that has the desired format, double-click the Format Painter button, and then repeat Step 4.

TROUBLE? If you accidentally click a title or one line of a list, click the Undo button on the Standard toolbar to return the line to its original formatting. Then select a paragraph that has the desired format, double-click the Format Painter button, and finish copying the format to the main paragraphs in the document.

5. After you've formatted all the main paragraphs with the Format Painter, click to turn off the feature.

6. Click the **Save** button on the Standard toolbar.

All the main paragraphs in the document are formatted with the correct indentation and alignment. Your next job is to make the lists easier to read by adding bullets and numbers.

Adding **Bullets and Numbers**

You can emphasize a list of items by adding a heavy dot, known as a **bullet**, before each item in the list. For consecutive items, you can use numbers instead of bullets. Brandi requested that you add bullets to the list of financial needs on page 3 to make them stand out.

To apply bullets to a list of items:

1. Scroll the document until you see the list of financial needs below the sentence "The following are considered to be immediate and severe financial needs."

2. Select the four items that appear in the middle of page 3 (from "medical expenses" to "Internal Revenue Service").

3. Click the **Bullets** button on the Formatting toolbar to activate the Bullets feature. A rounded bullet, a special character, appears in front of each item, and each line indents to make room for the bullet.

4. Click anywhere within the document window to deselect the text. Figure 2-23 shows the indented bulleted list.

| Figure 2-23 | INDENTED BULLETED LIST |

bulleted list

Next you need to add numbers to the list that explains when benefits can be received, in the section below the bulleted list. For this, you'll use the Numbering button, which automatically numbers the selected paragraphs with consecutive numbers and aligns them. If you insert a new paragraph, delete a paragraph, or reorder the paragraphs, Word automatically adjusts the numbers to make sure they remain consecutive.

To apply numbers to the list of items:

1. Scroll down to the next section, and then select the list that begins "reach the age..." and ends with "...become disabled."

2. Click the **Numbering** button on the Formatting toolbar. Consecutive numbers appear in front of each item in the indented list. The list is indented, similar to the bulleted list above.

3. Click anywhere in the document to deselect the text. Figure 2-24 shows the indented and numbered list.

Figure 2-24	INDENTED NUMBERED LIST

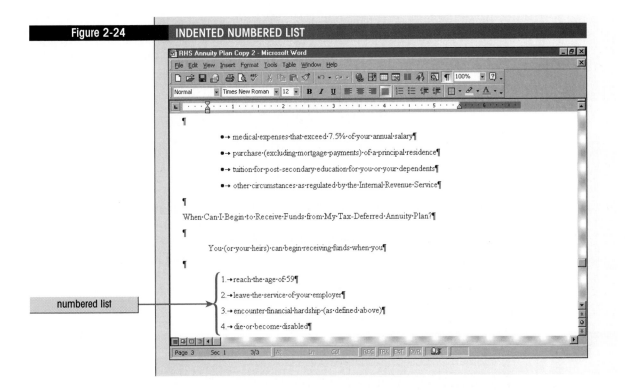

numbered list

The text of the document is now properly aligned and indented. The bullets and numbers make the lists easy to read and give readers visual clues about the type of information they contain. Next, you need to adjust the formatting of individual words.

Changing the Font and Font Size

All of Brandi's remaining changes concern changing fonts, adjusting font sizes, and emphasizing text with font styles. The first step is to change the font of the title from 12-point Times New Roman to 14-point Arial. This will make the title stand out from the rest of the text.

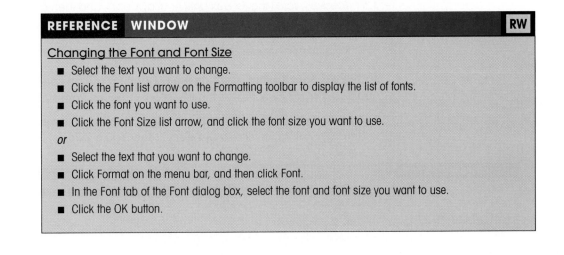

REFERENCE WINDOW   **RW**

Changing the Font and Font Size
- Select the text you want to change.
- Click the Font list arrow on the Formatting toolbar to display the list of fonts.
- Click the font you want to use.
- Click the Font Size list arrow, and click the font size you want to use.

or

- Select the text that you want to change.
- Click Format on the menu bar, and then click Font.
- In the Font tab of the Font dialog box, select the font and font size you want to use.
- Click the OK button.

Brandi wants you to change the font of the title as well as its size and style. To do this, you'll use the Formatting toolbar. Brandi wants you to use a **sans serif** font, which is a font that does not have the small horizontal lines (called serifs) at the tops and bottoms of the letters. Sans serif fonts are often used in titles so they contrast with the body text. Times New Roman is a serif font, and Arial is a sans serif font. The text you are reading now is a serif font, and the text in the steps below is a sans serif font.

To change the attributes of the title using the Font command:

1. Press **Ctrl+Home** to move to the beginning of the document, and then select the title.

2. Click the **Font** list arrow on the Formatting toolbar. A list of available fonts appears in alphabetical order, with the name of the current font highlighted in the font list and in the Font text box. See Figure 2-25. (Your list of fonts might be different from those shown.) Fonts that have been used recently might appear above a double line. Note that each name in the list is formatted with that font. For example, "Arial" appears in the Arial font, and "Times New Roman" appears in the Times New Roman font.

Figure 2-25   FONT LIST

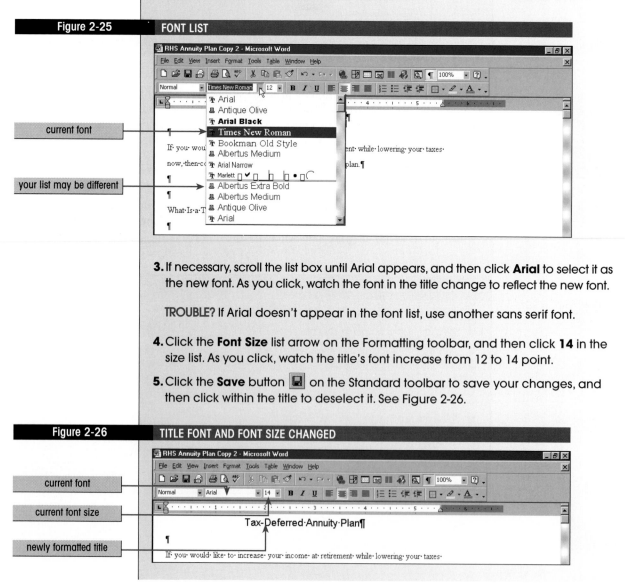

3. If necessary, scroll the list box until Arial appears, and then click **Arial** to select it as the new font. As you click, watch the font in the title change to reflect the new font.

TROUBLE? If Arial doesn't appear in the font list, use another sans serif font.

4. Click the **Font Size** list arrow on the Formatting toolbar, and then click **14** in the size list. As you click, watch the title's font increase from 12 to 14 point.

5. Click the **Save** button on the Standard toolbar to save your changes, and then click within the title to deselect it. See Figure 2-26.

Figure 2-26   TITLE FONT AND FONT SIZE CHANGED

TROUBLE? If your font and font size settings don't match those in Figure 2-26, you may not have selected the title. Select the title, view the font and font size settings displayed on the Formatting toolbar, and then make the necessary changes. Because of differences in fonts and monitors, the characters in your document might look different from the figure.

Emphasizing **Text with Boldface, Underlining, and Italics**

You can emphasize words in your document with boldface, underlining, or italics. These styles help you make specific thoughts, ideas, words, or phrases stand out. Brandi marked a few words on the document draft (shown in Figure 2-1) that need this kind of special emphasis. You add boldface, underlining, or italics by using the relevant buttons on the Formatting toolbar. Note that these buttons are toggle buttons, which means you can click them once to format the selected text, and then click again to remove the formatting from the selected text.

Bolding Text

Brandi wants to make sure that clients' employees see that the tax-deferred annuity plan can be terminated only under certain conditions. You will do this by bolding the word "only."

To change the font style to boldface:

1. Scroll down so you can view the first line of the paragraph beneath the question "Can My Tax-Deferred Annuity Plan Be Terminated?" on page 2.

2. Select the word "only" (immediately after the word "terminated").

3. Click the **Bold** button **B** on the Formatting toolbar, and then click anywhere in the document to deselect the text. The word appears in bold, as shown in Figure 2-27. After reviewing this change, you wonder if the word would look better without boldface. As you will see in the next step, you can easily remove the boldface by selecting the text and clicking the Bold button again to turn off boldfacing.

Figure 2-27	WORD IN BOLDFACE

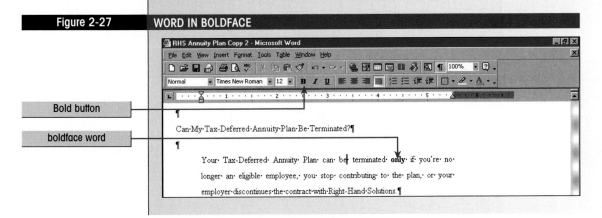

Bold button

boldface word

4. Double-click the word **only** to select it, then click **B**. The word now appears without boldface. You decide you prefer to emphasize the word with boldface after all.

5. Verify that the word "only" is still selected, and then click **B**. The word appears in boldface again.

Underlining Text

The Underline command works in the same way as the Bold command. Brandi's edits indicate that the word "Note" should be inserted and underlined at the beginning of the final paragraph. You'll make both of these changes at once using the Underline command.

To underline text:

1. Press **Ctrl+End** to move the insertion point to the end of the document. Then move the insertion point to the left of the word "Get" in the first line of the final paragraph.

2. Click the **Underline** button **U** on the Formatting toolbar to turn on underlining. Notice that the Underline button remains pressed. Now, whatever text you type will be underlined on your screen and in your printed document.

3. Type **Note:** and then click **U** to turn off underlining. Notice that the Underline button is no longer pressed, and "Note:" is underlined.

4. Press the **spacebar** twice. See Figure 2-28.

Figure 2-28	WORD TYPED WITH UNDERLINE

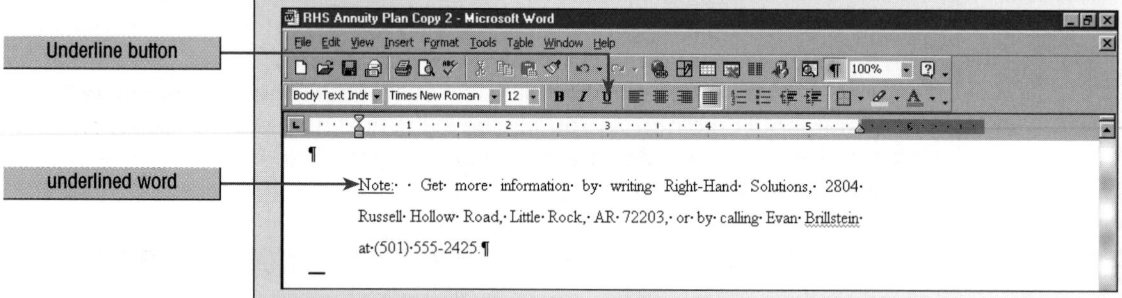

Underline button

underlined word

Note: · Get· more· information· by· writing· Right-Hand· Solutions,· 2804· Russell· Hollow· Road,· Little· Rock,· AR· 72203,· or· by· calling· Evan· Brillstein· at·(501)·555-2425.¶

Italicizing Text

Next, you'll make the annuity plan conform with the other documents that Right-Hand Solutions produces by changing each question (heading) in the document to italics. This makes the document easier to read by clearly separating the sections. You'll begin with the first heading.

To italicize the question headings:

1. Press **Ctrl+Home** to return to the beginning of the document, and then select the text of the first heading, "What Is a Tax-Deferred Annuity?," by triple-clicking the text.

2. Click the **Italic** button *I* on the Formatting toolbar. The heading changes from regular to italic text.

3. Repeat Steps 1 and 2 to italicize the next heading. Now try a shorter way to italicize the text by repeating the formatting you just applied.

4. Select the next heading, and then press the **F4** key. Repeat for each of the remaining four questions (headings) in the document. The italicized headings stand out from the rest of the text and help give the document a visual structure.

Saving and Printing

You have made all the editing and formatting changes that Brandi requested for the annuity plan description. When a document is complete, it's a good idea to save it with a name that indicates that it is final. After saving the document, you can preview and print it. It's especially useful to preview a document before printing when you made a number of formatting changes because the Print Preview window makes it easy to spot text that is not aligned correctly.

To save, preview, and print the document:

1. Click **File** on the menu bar, and then click **Save As**. Save the file as **RHS Annuity Plan Final Copy** in the Tutorial subfolder, within the Tutorial.02 folder.

2. Move the insertion point to the beginning of the document.

3. Click the **Print Preview** button on the Standard toolbar, and examine the first page of the document. Use the vertical scroll bar to display the second and third pages. (If you notice any headings as the last line of a page or other formatting errors, click the Close button on the Print Preview toolbar, correct the errors in normal view, and then return to the Print Preview window. To move a heading to the next page with its paragraph, click at the beginning of the heading and press **Ctrl+Enter** to insert a manual page break.)

4. Click the **Print** button on the Print Preview toolbar. After a pause, the document prints.

5. Click the **Close** button on the Print Preview toolbar, and then click the **Close** button X on the program window to close your document and exit Word.

You now have a hardcopy of the final annuity plan description, as shown in Figure 2-29.

Figure 2-29	FINAL VERSION OF RHS ANNUITY PLAN

Tax-Deferred Annuity Plan

If you would like to increase your income at retirement while lowering your taxes now, then consider participating in a tax-deferred annuity plan.

What Is a Tax-Deferred Annuity?

A tax-deferred annuity allows you to put a portion of your before-tax wages into an investment account on a regular basis. Instead of paying taxes on the money now (when your tax rate is high), you pay after you retire (when your tax rate will be lower). In the meantime, the annuity account earns dividends that permit you to supplement your retirement income.

How Do I Enroll in a Tax-Deferred Annuity Plan?

As a full-time employee, you're eligible to participate in the Tax-Deferred Annuity Plan. Of course, the plan is voluntary. You may begin participating on the first day of the month following your employment, and you may stop participating at any time. To participate, just complete the necessary enrollment form, as well as a Salary Reduction Agreement, and return them to Right-Hand Solutions.

How Will My Money Be Invested?

On your annuity application you can allocate your premiums among several options, such as stocks, money markets, bonds, and world equities. A

typical allocation might be similar to the following: stock (30%); money market (25%); bond market (25%); world equities (15%); other (5%).

You can change your allocation at any time by calling our Customer Service Center at (501) 555-2425. Right-Hand Solutions will make every effort to invest your money safely and effectively so you will realize the maximum possible earnings.

How Will I Know How Well My Investments Are Doing?

Right-Hand Solutions will send you a report annually, showing your total accumulation. Every quarter you'll receive a statement containing a complete history of all financial transactions and showing the interest credited you've earned. You'll also receive our regular newsletter.

For the purposes of this plan, accumulation is defined as all tax-deferred contributions, minus the Right-Hand Solutions service charges.

Can My Tax-Deferred Annuity Plan Be Terminated?

Your Tax-Deferred Annuity Plan can be terminated **only** if you're no longer an eligible employee, you stop contributing to the plan, or your employer discontinues the contract with Right-Hand Solutions.

Can I Withdraw Money from My Tax-Deferred Annuity Plan?

Normally, if you make an early withdrawal from your tax-deferred annuity plan, you will incur substantial financial penalties. However, you can

withdraw money without penalty if you have an immediate and severe financial need (as defined below) and the money from your plan is necessary to meet those needs. Under current law, these withdrawals are subject to ordinary income taxes.

The following are considered to be immediate and severe financial needs:

• medical expenses that exceed 7.5% of your annual salary
• purchase (excluding mortgage payments) of a principal residence
• tuition for post-secondary education for you or your dependents
• other circumstances as regulated by the Internal Revenue Service

When Can I Begin to Receive Funds from My Tax-Deferred Annuity Plan?

You (or your heirs) can begin receiving funds when you

1. reach the age of 59
2. leave the service of your employer
3. encounter financial hardship (as defined above)
4. die or become disabled

Note: Get more information by writing Right-Hand Solutions, 2804 Russell Hollow Road, Little Rock, AR 72203, or by calling Evan Brillstein at (501) 555-2425.

In this tutorial, you have helped Reginald plan, edit, and format the annuity plan that will appear in the employee handbooks of Right-Hand Solutions' clients. Now that you have fine-tuned the content, adjusted the text appearance and alignment, and added a bulleted list and a numbered list, the plan is visually appealing and easy to read.

You give the hardcopy to Reginald, who makes two photocopies—one for Brandi and one for the copy center, which copies and distributes the document to all clients of Right-Hand Solutions.

Session 2.2 QUICK CHECK

1. What are Word's default margins for the left and right margins? For the top and bottom margins?
2. Describe the four types of text alignment.
3. Explain how to indent a paragraph 1 inch or more from the left margin.
4. Describe a situation in which you would use the Format Painter.
5. Explain how to add underlining to a word as you type it.
6. Explain how to transform a series of short paragraphs into a numbered list.

7. Explain how to format a title in 14-point Arial.
8. Describe the steps involved in changing the line spacing in a document.

REVIEW ASSIGNMENTS

Now that you have completed the description of the annuity plan, Brandi explains that she also wants to include a sample quarterly statement and a sample contract change notice in the client's employee handbooks to show employees how easy the statements are to read. You'll open and format this document now.

1. If necessary, start Word, make sure your Data Disk is in the appropriate disk drive, and check your screen to make sure your settings match those in the tutorial.
2. Open the file **RHSQuart** from the Review folder for Tutorial 2 on your Data Disk, and save the document as **RHS Quarterly Report**.
3. Use the Spelling and Grammar checker to correct any spelling or grammatical errors. If the Suggestions list box does not include the correct replacement, click outside the Spelling and Grammar dialog box, type the correction yourself, click Resume in the Spelling and Grammar dialog box, and continue checking the document. After you finish using the Spelling and Grammar checker, proofread the document carefully to check for any additional errors, especially words that are spelled correctly but used improperly. Pay special attention to the second main paragraph of the letter.
4. Make all edits and formatting changes marked on Figure 2-30. To substitute "Right-Hand Solutions" for "We" in the first paragraph, copy the company name from the top of the letter (without the paragraph mark) and paste it into the first paragraph as marked. (Copy and paste this text *before* you format it in Arial 14 point.)

Figure 2-30

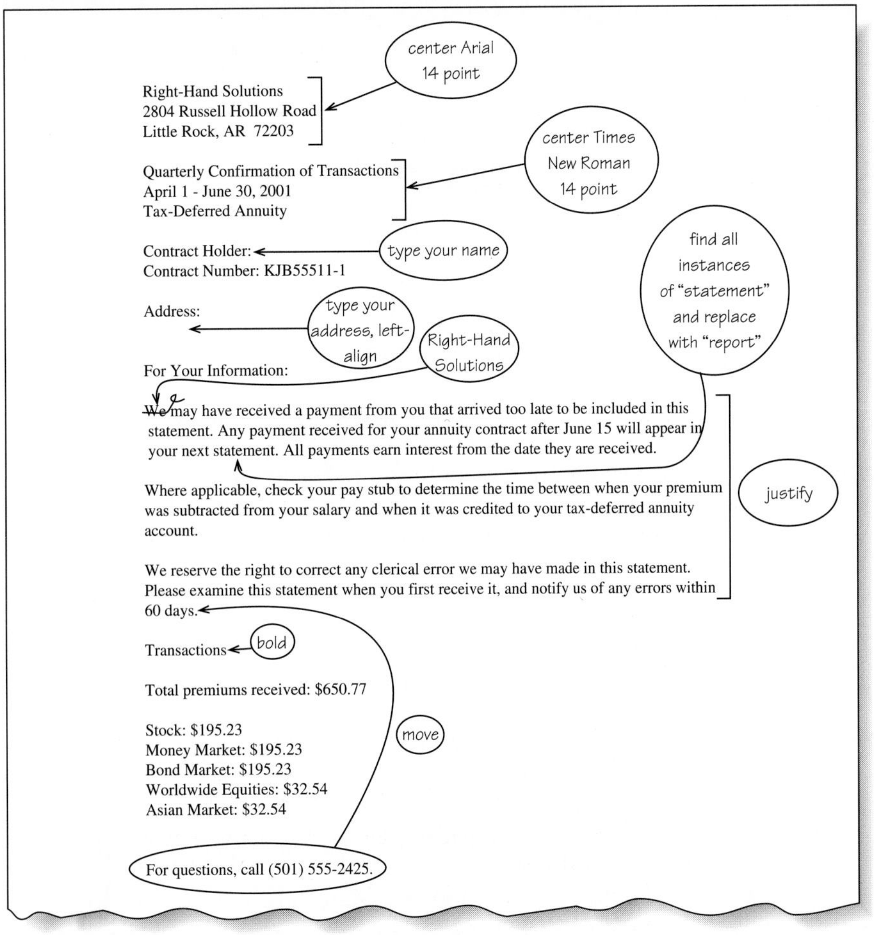
Right-Hand Solutions
2804 Russell Hollow Road
Little Rock, AR 72203

Quarterly Confirmation of Transactions
April 1 - June 30, 2001
Tax-Deferred Annuity

Contract Holder:
Contract Number: KJB55511-1

Address:

For Your Information:

We may have received a payment from you that arrived too late to be included in this statement. Any payment received for your annuity contract after June 15 will appear in your next statement. All payments earn interest from the date they are received.

Where applicable, check your pay stub to determine the time between when your premium was subtracted from your salary and when it was credited to your tax-deferred annuity account.

We reserve the right to correct any clerical error we may have made in this statement. Please examine this statement when you first receive it, and notify us of any errors within 60 days.

Transactions

Total premiums received: $650.77

Stock: $195.23
Money Market: $195.23
Bond Market: $195.23
Worldwide Equities: $32.54
Asian Market: $32.54

For questions, call (501) 555-2425.

5. Save the document, preview it, and then print it.

6. Close th document.

7. Open the file **RHSPort** from the Review folder for Tutorial 2 on your Data Disk, and save the file as **RHS Portfolio Changes**.

Explore 8. Make all the edits and formatting changes marked on Figure 2-31. However, instead of using the Formatting toolbar to change Current Allocation Accounts to underline 14 point, click Format on the menu bar, and then click Font to open the Font dialog box. Click the appropriate selections in the Underline style and Size list boxes. Notice that you should only replace "Right-Hand Solutions" with "RHS" in the list of Allocation Accounts. To skip an instance of "Right-Hand Solutions" without changing it, click the Find Next button in the Find and Replace dialog box.

Figure 2-31

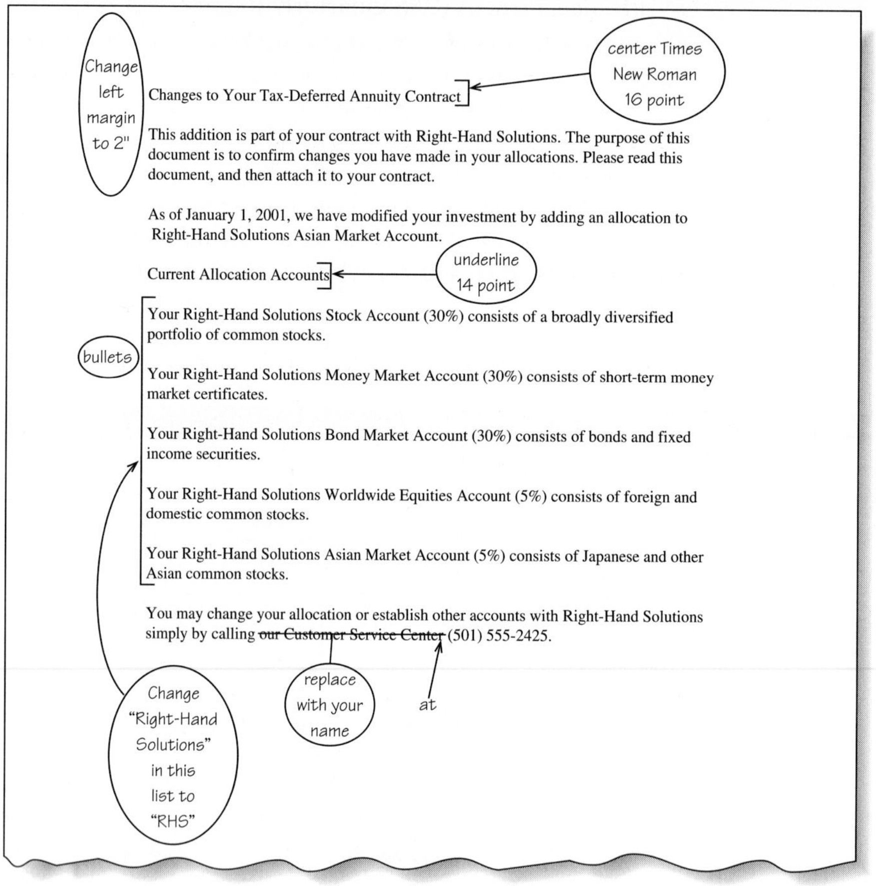

Explore 9. Change the right margin using the ruler in print layout view:

a. Click the Print Layout View button, and then select the entire document.

b. Position the pointer on the ruler at the right margin, above the Right Indent marker (a small, gray triangle).

c. Press and hold down the mouse button. A dotted line appears in the document window, indicating the current right margin. Drag the margin left to the 5-inch mark on the ruler, and then release the mouse button.

d. Click the Normal View button to return to normal view.

e. Save the document.

Explore 10. Change the line spacing of individual paragraphs within the document.

a. Select the first two paragraphs in the document, immediately under the heading "Changes to Your Tax-Deferred Annuity Contract."

b. Press Ctrl+5 to change the line spacing of the selected paragraphs to 1.5 line spacing.

c. Save the document.

11. Cut and paste text using the Clipboard:

    a. Select the second sentence in the document ("The purpose of this document is to confirm…"), and then click the Cut button on the Standard toolbar to remove the sentence from the document. If the Clipboard toolbar appears, leave it open while you continue with the next step.

    b. Select the last sentence in the document ("You may change your allocation…"), and then click the Cut button on the Standard toolbar to remove the sentence from the document. If the Clipboard toolbar did not open at the end of the previous step, it should be open now.

    c. Move the insertion point to the beginning of the first sentence, to the left of the "T" in "This addition is part of your contract… ." Move the pointer over the icons on the Clipboard toolbar, until you find one labeled "The purpose of this document is to confirm… ." Click that icon to insert the sentence (which was originally the second sentence in the document) at the insertion point. Insert an extra space, if necessary.

    d. Repeat the previous step to insert the sentence beginning, "You may change your allocation or establish other…" at the end of the second paragraph.

    e. Click the Clear Clipboard button on the Clipboard toolbar to erase the contents of the Clipboard, and then click the Close button to close the Clipboard toolbar.

12. Click the Print Preview button on the Standard toolbar to check your work.

Explore ▶ 13. Use the Print command on the File menu to open the Print dialog box. Print two copies of the document by changing the Number of copies setting in the Print dialog box.

Explore ▶ 14. You can find out the number of words in your documents by using the Word Count command on the Tools menu. Use this command to determine the number of words in the document, and then write that number in the upper-right corner of one of the printouts.

15. Save and close the document.

CASE PROBLEMS

Case 1. Store-It-All Katie Strainchamps manages Store-It-All, a storage facility in Huntsville, Alabama. She has written the draft of a tenant-information sheet outlining Store-It-All's policies for new customers. She asks you to edit and format the document for her.

1. If necessary, start Word, make sure your Data Disk is in the appropriate disk drive, and check your screen to make sure your settings match those in the tutorials.

2. Open the file **Store** from the Tutorial 2 Cases folder on your Data Disk, and save it as **Store-It-All Policies**.

3. Use the Spelling and Grammar checker to correct any errors in the document. Then proofread the document to check for errors the Spelling and Grammar checker missed. Pay particular attention to the paragraph under "Rental Payments" and the company name throughout the document.

4. Delete the word "basic" from the first sentence of the first full paragraph. (Remember to use the Undo and Redo buttons as you work to correct any editing mistakes.)

5. Delete the second sentence in the second paragraph, which begins "You renew your contract… ."

6. Insert the bolded sentence "A bill will not be sent to you." before the first sentence under the heading "Rental Payments."

7. Under the heading "Insurance," delete the sentence in parentheses and the extra paragraph mark.

8. Change all of the margins (top, bottom, left, and right) to 1.75 inches.

9. For each paragraph following a heading, set the alignment to justify. (*Hint:* Format the first paragraph and then use the Format Painter to format each successive paragraph.)

10. Find the phrase "not negotiable" using the Find command and italicize it.

11. Indent the four-item list under the heading "Delinquent Accounts" 0.5-inch and add bullets.

12. Change both lines of the title to 14-point Arial (or another sans serif font of your choice).

13. Center and bold both lines of the title.

14. Underline all of the headings.

15. Insert two blank lines at the end of the document, and then type the following, making sure to replace *"your name"* with your first and last name: Direct all questions to *your name* in the main office.

16. Save, preview, and print the rental information sheet, and close the document.

Case 2. UpTime   Matt Patterson is UpTime's marketing director for the Northeast region. The company provides productivity training for large companies across the country. Matt wants to provide interested clients with a one-page summary of UpTime's productivity training.

1. If necessary, start Word, make sure your Data Disk is in the appropriate disk drive, and check your screen to make sure your settings match those in the tutorials.

2. Open the file **UpTime** from the Tutorial 2 Cases folder on your Data Disk, and save it as **UpTime Training Summary**.

3. Change the title at the beginning of the document to a 16-point serif font other than Times New Roman. Be sure to pick a font that looks professional and is easy to read. (Remember to use the Undo and Redo buttons as you work to correct any editing mistakes.)

4. Center and bold the title.

5. Delete the word "general" from the second sentence of the first paragraph after the document title.

6. Convert the list of training components following the first paragraph to an indented, numbered list.

7. Under the heading "Personal Productivity Training Seminar," delete the third sentence from the first paragraph.

8. Under the heading "Personal Productivity Training Seminar," delete the phrase "at the seminar" from the first sentence in the second paragraph.

9. In the first paragraph under the heading "Management Productivity Training," move the first sentence (beginning with "UpTime provides management training…") to the end of the paragraph.

10. Switch the order of the first and second paragraphs under the "Field Services Technology and Training" heading.

11. Search for the text "your name," and replace it with your first and last name.

12. Change the top margin to 1.5 inches.

13. Change the left margin to 1.75 inches.

14. Bold each of the headings.

15. Italicize both occurrences of the word "free" in the second paragraph under the "Field Services Technology and Training" heading.

16. Save and preview the document.

17. Print the document, and then close the file.

Case 3. Ridge Top   Thomas McGee is vice president of sales and marketing at Ridge Top, an outdoor and sporting-gear store in Conshohocken, Pennsylvania. Each year, Thomas and his staff mail a description of new products to Ridge Top's regular customers. Ralph has asked you to edit and format the first few pages of this year's new products' description.

1. If necessary, start Word, make sure your Data Disk is in the appropriate disk drive, and check your screen to make sure your settings match those in the tutorials.

2. Open the file **Ridge** from the Tutorial 2 Cases folder on your Data Disk, and save it as **Ridge Top Guide**.

3. Use the Spelling and Grammar checker to correct any errors in the document. Because of the nature of this document, it contains some words that the Word dictionary on your computer may not recognize. It also contains headings that the Spelling and Grammar checker may consider sentence fragments. As you use the Spelling and Grammar checker, use the Ignore All button, if necessary, to skip over brand names. Use the Ignore Rule button to skip over sentence fragments.

4. Delete the phrase "a great deal" from the first sentence of the paragraph below the heading "Snuggle Up to These Prices." (Remember to use the Undo and Redo buttons to correct any editing mistakes as you work.)

5. Reverse the order of the first two paragraphs under the heading, "You'll Eat Up the Prices of This Camp Cooking Gear!"

6. Cut the last sentence of the first full paragraph ("Prices are good through...") from the document. Then move the insertion point to the end of the document, press the Enter key twice, and insert the cut sentence as a new paragraph. Format it in 12-point Arial, and italicize it.

7. Format the Ridge Top tip items as a numbered list.

Explore   8. Reorder the items under the "Ridge Top Tips!" heading by moving the fourth product idea and the following paragraph to the top of the list.

9. Search for the text "your name," and replace with your first and last name.

Explore   10. Experiment with two special paragraph alignment options: first line and hanging. First, select everything from the heading "Ridge Top Guarantees Warmth at Cool Prices" through the paragraph just before the heading "Ridge Top Tips." Next, click Format on the menu bar, click Paragraph, click Indents and Spacing tab, click the Help button in the upper-right corner of the dialog box, click the Special list arrow, and review the information on the special alignment options. Experiment with both the First line and the Hanging options. When you are finished, return the document to its original format by choosing the none option.

11. Justify all the paragraphs in the document. (*Hint:* To select all paragraphs in the document at one time, click Edit on the menu bar, and then click Select All.)

12. Replace all occurrences of "RidgeTop" with "Ridge Top."

13. Apply a 12-point, bold, sans serif font to each of the headings. Be sure to pick a font that looks professional and is easy to read. (*Hint:* Use the Format Painter.)

14. Change the title's font to the same font you used for the headings, except set the size to 16 point.

15. Bold both lines of the title.

16. Underline the names and prices for all of the brandname products in the Trekker's Guide. Make sure you don't underline spaces or periods. (*Hint:* Use the Words only underline style option in the Font dialog box.)

17. Save and preview the document. Print the document, and then close the file.

Case 4. Restaurant Review   Your student newspaper has asked you to review four restaurants in your area.

1. If necessary, start Word, make sure your Data Disk is in the appropriate disk drive, and check your screen to make sure your settings match those in the tutorials.

2. Write a brief summary (one to two paragraphs) for each restaurant and provide a rating for each one. Correct any spelling or grammatical errors.

3. Add a title and subtitle to your review. The subtitle should include your name.

4. Save the document as **Restaurant Review** in the Tutorial 2 Cases folder on your Data Disk, and print it.

5. Rearrange the order in which you discuss the restaurants to alphabetical order. (Remember to use the Undo and Redo buttons as you work to correct any editing mistakes.)

6. Change the top margin to 2 inches.

7. Change the left margin to 1.75 inches.

8. Center and bold the title and subtitle.

9. Change the paragraph alignment to justify.

10. Italicize the title of each restaurant.

11. Save the edited document as **Edited Restaurant Review**.

12. Print the document.

13. Save and close your document.

INTERNET ASSIGNMENTS

The purpose of the Internet Assignments is to challenge you to find information on the Internet that you can use to create effective documents. The actual assignments are updated and maintained on the Course Technology Web site. Log on to the Internet and use your Web browser to go to the Student Online Companion to accompany this text at **www.course.com/NewPerspectives/office2000**. Click the Word link, and then click the link for Tutorial 2.

QUICK | CHECK ANSWERS

Session 2.1

1. Click the Open button on the Standard toolbar, or click File, click Open, and double-click the file. Click File, click Save As, select the location, type the new filename, and then click OK.

2. (a) ↓; (b) Ctrl+End; (c) Page Down

3. The process of first selecting the text to be modified, and then performing the operations such as moving, formatting, or deleting.

4. (a) The blank space in the left margin area of the document window, which allows you to easily select entire lines or large blocks of text. (b) The button on the Standard toolbar that redoes an action you previously reversed using the Undo button. (c) The process of moving text by first selecting the text, then pressing and holding the mouse button while moving the text to its new location in the document, and finally releasing the mouse button.

5. To select a single word, double-click the word, or click at the beginning of the word, and drag the pointer to the end of the word. To select a complete paragraph, triple-click in the selection bar next to the paragraph, or click at the beginning of the paragraph and drag the pointer to the end of the paragraph.

6. You might use the Undo button to remove the bold formatting you had just applied to a word. You could then use the Redo button to restore the bold formatting to the word.

7. False

8. Cut and paste removes the selected material from its original location and inserts it in a new location. Copy and paste makes a copy of the selected material and inserts the copy in a new location; the original material remains in its original location.

9. Click the Select Browse Object button, click the Find button, click the Replace tab, type the search text in the Find what text box, type the replacement text in the Replace with text box, click Find Next or click Replace all.

Session 2.2

1. The default top and bottom margins are 1 inch. The default left and right margins are 1.25 inches.

2. Align-left: each line flush left, ragged right.
   Align-right: each line flush right, ragged left.
   Center: each line centered, ragged right and left.
   Justify: each line flush left and flush right.

3. Click in the paragraph you want to indent, and then click the Increase Indent button on the Formatting toolbar once for each half-inch you want to indent.

4. You might use the Format Painter to copy the formatting of a heading with bold italic to the other headings in the document.

5. Click the Underline button on the Formatting toolbar, type the word, and then click the Underline button again to turn off underlining.

6. Select the paragraphs, and then click the Numbering button on the Formatting toolbar.

7. Select the title, click the Font list arrow, and click Arial in the list of fonts. Then click the Font Size list arrow, and click 14.

8. Select the text you want to change, click Format on the menu bar, click Paragraph, click the Line Spacing list arrow, and then click Single, 1.5, or Double. Or, select the text, and then press Ctrl+1 for single spacing, Ctrl+5 for 1.5 line spacing, or Ctrl+2 for double spacing.

OBJECTIVES

In this tutorial you will:

- Set tab stops

- Divide a document into sections

- Change the vertical alignment of a section

- Center a page between the top and bottom margins

- Create a header with page numbers

- Create a table

- Sort the rows in a table

- Modify a table's structure

- Total a column of numbers with AutoSum

- Format a table

CREATING A MULTIPLE-PAGE REPORT

Writing a Recommendation Report for AgriTechnology

CASE

AgriTechnology

Brittany Jones works for AgriTechnology, a biotechnology company that develops genetically engineered food products. Recently, AgriTechnology began shipping the EverRipe tomato to supermarkets. The EverRipe tomato is genetically engineered to stay ripe and fresh nearly twice as long as other varieties. Because of its longer shelf life and vine-ripened taste, the new tomato is popular with supermarkets, and demand for it has been high. Unfortunately, the EverRipe tomato also is more susceptible to bruising than standard varieties. Nearly 20 percent of the first year's crop was unmarketable because of damage sustained during shipping and handling. AgriTechnology's vice president, Ramon Espinoza, appointed Brittany to head a task force to determine how to increase the profitability of the EverRipe. The task force is ready to present the results of their study in the form of a report with an accompanying table. Brittany asks you to help prepare the report.

In this tutorial, you will format the report's title page so that it has a different layout from the rest of the report. The title page will contain only the title and subtitle and will not have page numbers like the rest of the report. You also will add a table to the AgriTechnology report that summarizes the task force's recommendations.

SESSION 3.1

In this session you will review the task force's recommendation report. Then you will learn how to set tab stops, divide a document into sections, center a page between the top and bottom margins, create a header, and create a table.

Planning **the Document**

As head of the task force, Brittany divided the responsibility for the report among the members of the group. Each person gathered information about one aspect of the problem and wrote the appropriate section of the report. Now, Brittany must compile all the findings into a coherent and unified report. In addition, she also must follow the company's style guidelines for the content, organization, style, and format.

The report content includes the results of the study—obtained from interviews with other employees and visits to the packaging and distribution plant, trucking company, and so forth—and recommendations for action.

Because Brittany knows some executives will not have time to read the entire report, she organized the report so it begins with an executive summary. The body of the report provides an in-depth statement of the problem and recommendations for solving that problem. At the end of the report, she summarizes the cost of the improvements.

The report's style follows established standards of business writing, and emphasizes clarity, simplicity, and directness.

In accordance with AgriTechnology's style guide, Brittany's report will begin with a title page, with the text centered between the top and bottom margins. Every page except the title page will include a line of text at the top, giving a descriptive name for the report, as well as the page number. The text and headings will be formatted to match all AgriTechnology's reports, and will follow company guidelines for layout and text style.

At the end of the report, there will be a table that summarizes the costs of the proposed changes.

Opening **the Report**

Brittany already has combined the individual sections into one document. She also has begun formatting the report by changing the font size of headings, adding elements such as bold and italics, and by indenting paragraphs. You'll open the document and perform the remaining formatting tasks on page 1, as indicated in Figure 3-1.

Figure 3-1 INITIAL DRAFT OF TASK FORCE'S REPORT WITH EDITS (PAGE 1)

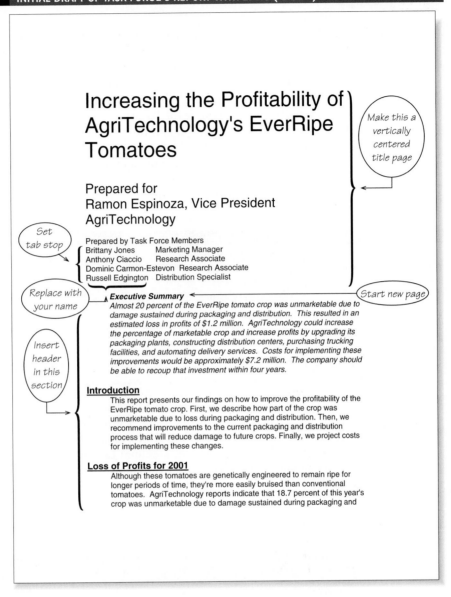

To open the document:

1. Start Word, and place your Data Disk in the appropriate drive. Make sure your screen matches the figures in this tutorial. In particular, be sure to display the nonprinting characters.

2. Open the file **EverRipe** from the **Tutorial** folder in the **Tutorial.03** folder on your Data Disk.

3. To avoid altering the original file, save the document as **EverRipe Report** in the same folder.

4. In the first page, replace the name "Russell Edgington" with your name.

Setting Tab Stops

Tabs are useful for indenting paragraphs and for vertically aligning text or numerical data in columns. A **tab** adds space between the margin and text in a column or between text in one column and text in another column. A **tab stop** is the location where text moves when you press the Tab key. When the Show/Hide ¶ button is pressed, the nonprinting tab character → appears wherever you press the Tab key. A tab character is just like any other character you type; you can delete it by pressing the Backspace key or the Delete key.

Word provides several **tab-stop alignment styles**. The five major styles are left, center, right, decimal, and bar, as shown in Figure 3-2. The first three tab-stop styles position text in a similar way to the Align Left, Center, and Align Right buttons on the Formatting toolbar. The difference is that with a tab, you determine line by line precisely where the left, center, or right alignment should occur.

| Figure 3-2 | TAB STOP ALIGNMENT STYLES |

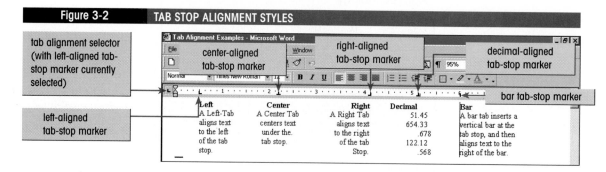

The default tab stops on the ruler are **Left tabs**, which position the left edge of text at the tab stop and extend the text to the right. **Center tabs** position text so that it's centered evenly on both sides of the tab stop. **Right tabs** position the right edge of text at the tab stop and extend the text to the left. **Decimal tabs** position numbers so that their decimal points are aligned at the tab stop. **Bar tabs** insert a vertical bar at the tab stop and then align text to the right of the bar. In addition, you also can use a **First Line Indent tab**, which indents the first line of a paragraph, and the **Hanging Indent tab**, which indents every line of a paragraph *except* the first line.

REFERENCE WINDOW **RW**

Setting Tab Stops

- Select the text for which you want to change the tab alignment.
- Click the tab alignment selector on the far left of the horizontal ruler until the appropriate tab-stop alignment style appears.
- Click the horizontal ruler where you want to set the tab stop.
- To remove a tab stop, click it and drag it off the horizontal ruler.

The Word default tab-stop settings are every one-half inch, as indicated by the small gray ticks at the bottom of the ruler shown in Figure 3-3. You set a new tab stop by selecting a tab-stop alignment style (from the tab alignment selector at the left end of the horizontal ruler) and then clicking on the horizontal ruler to insert the tab stop. You can remove a tab stop from the ruler by clicking it and dragging the tab stop off the ruler.

Figure 3-3 RULER WITH TAB STOPS

ruler

tab stops every one-half inch

You should never try to align columns of text by adding extra spaces with the spacebar. Although the text might seem precisely aligned in the document window, it might not be aligned when you print the document. Furthermore, if you edit the text, the extra spaces might disturb the alignment. However, if you edit text aligned with tabs, the alignment remains intact. If you want to align a lot of text in many columns, it is better to use a table, as described later in this tutorial.

To align columns using tabs, you can type some text, and press the Tab key. The insertion point will then move to the next tab stop to the right, where you can type more text. You can continue in this way until you have typed the first row of each column. Then you can press the Enter key, and begin typing the next row of each column.

However, sometimes you'll find that text in a column stretches beyond the next default tab stop, and as a result the columns will fail to line up evenly. In this situation, you need to set new tab stops on the horizontal ruler. For example, even though the list of task force members in the EverRipe report contains tab stops, the columns do not line up evenly. To fix this formatting problem, you need to move the tab stop farther to the right.

To add a new tab stop on the ruler:

1. Make sure the current tab-stop alignment style is left tab **L**, as shown in Figure 3-3. If **L** doesn't appear at that location, click the tab alignment selector one or more times until **L** appears.

2. Select the list of task force members and their titles on page 1. (Do not select the heading "Prepared by Task Force Members.")

3. Click the tick mark on the ruler that occurs at 3.0 inches. Word automatically inserts a left tab stop at that location and removes the tick marks to its left. The second column of text shifts to the new tab stop.

4. Deselect the highlighted text and then move the insertion point anywhere in the list of names and titles. See Figure 3-4.

To see the document in Print Preview:

1. Click the **Print Preview** button 🔍 on the Standard toolbar to open the Print Preview window.

2. Click the **Multiple Pages** button 🔲 on the Print Preview toolbar, and then click and drag across the top three pages in the list box to select "1 x 3 Pages." The three pages of the report are reduced in size and appear side-by-side. See Figure 3-7. Although you cannot read the text on the pages, you can see the general layout.

Figure 3-7	PRINT PREVIEW OF REPORT

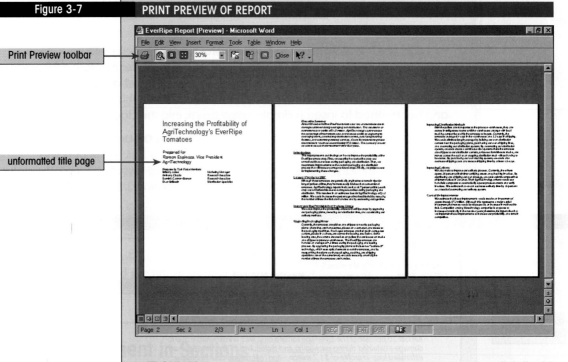

Print Preview toolbar

unformatted title page

TROUBLE? If you see the vertical and horizontal rulers, you can click the View Ruler button on the Print Preview toolbar to hide the rulers.

Now, you can change the vertical alignment to center the lines of text between the top and bottom margins. The **vertical alignment** specifies how a page of text is positioned on the page between the top and bottom margins—flush at the top, flush at the bottom, or centered between the top and bottom margins.

REFERENCE WINDOW   **RW**

Vertically Aligning a Section

- Insert a section break to create a separate section for the page you want to align.
- Move the insertion point within the section you want to align.
- Click File on the menu bar, click Page Setup, click the Layout tab, and then select the vertical alignment option you want.
- Make sure This section appears in the Apply to list box.
- Click the OK button.

You'll center the title page text from within the Print Preview window.

To change the vertical alignment of the title page:

1. If the **Magnifier** button 🔍 is selected, click it once to deselect it.

2. Click the leftmost page in the Print Preview window to make sure the current page is page 1 (the title page). The status bar in the Print Preview window indicates the current page.

3. Click **File** on the menu bar, and then click **Page Setup**. The Page Setup dialog box opens.

4. Click the **Layout** tab. In the Apply to list box, click **This section** (if it is not already selected) so that the layout change affects only the first section, not both sections, of your document.

5. Click the **Vertical alignment** list arrow, and then click **Center** to center the pages of the current section—in this case, just page 1—vertically between the top and bottom margins.

6. Click the **OK** button to return to the Print Preview window. The text of the title page is centered vertically, as shown in Figure 3-8.

| Figure 3-8 | TITLE PAGE VERTICALLY CENTERED |

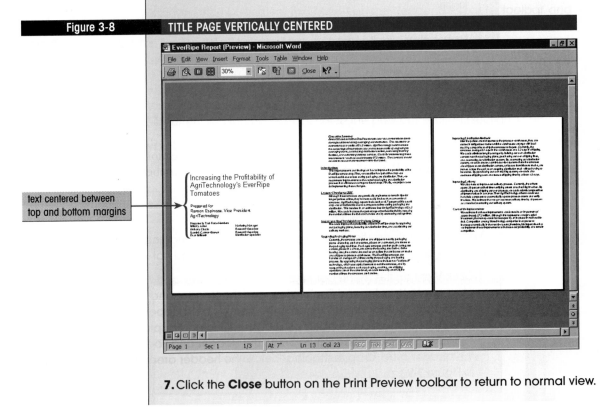

text centered between top and bottom margins

7. Click the **Close** button on the Print Preview toolbar to return to normal view.

You have successfully centered the title page text. Next you turn your attention to placing a descriptive name for the report and the page number at the top of every page.

2. Position the pointer in the upper-left cell of the grid, and then click and drag the pointer down and across the grid until you highlight five rows and four columns. As you drag the pointer across the grid, Word indicates the size of the table (rows by columns) at the bottom of the grid. See Figure 3-14.

Figure 3-14	SELECTING ROWS AND COLUMNS

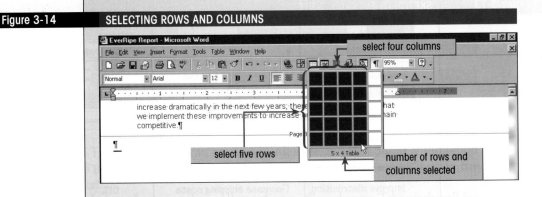

3. Release the mouse button. An empty table, five rows by four columns, appears in your document with the insertion point blinking in the upper-left corner (cell A1). See Figure 3-15.

Figure 3-15	EMPTY TABLE INSERTED INTO DOCUMENT

The table is outlined with borders, and the four columns are of equal width. The column widths are indicated by column markers on the ruler. Each cell contains an end-of-cell mark, and each row contains an end-of-row mark.

TROUBLE? If you don't see the end-of-cell and end-of-row marks, you need to show nonprinting characters. Click the Show/Hide ¶ button on the Standard toolbar to show nonprinting characters.

TROUBLE? If you see the Tables and Borders toolbar displayed along with the new blank table, simply continue with this tutorial. You will learn how to use the Tables and Borders toolbar in the next session.

Entering Text in a Table

You can enter text in a table by moving the insertion point to a cell and typing. If the text takes up more than one line in the cell, Word automatically wraps the text to the next line and increases the height of that cell and all the cells in that row. To move the insertion point to another cell in the table, you can either click in that cell or use the Tab key. Figure 3-16 summarizes the keystrokes for moving within a table.

Figure 3-16	KEYSTROKES FOR MOVING AROUND A TABLE

PRESS	TO MOVE THE INSERTION POINT
Tab or →	One cell to the right, or to the first cell in the next row.
Shift+Tab or ←	One cell to the left, or to the last cell in the previous row.
Alt+Home	To first cell of current row.
Alt+End	To last cell of current row.
Alt+PageUp	To top cell of current column.
Alt+PageDown	To bottom cell of current column.
↑	One cell up in current column.
↓	One cell down in current column.

Now, you are ready to insert information into the table.

To insert data into the table:

1. Verify that the insertion point is located in cell **A1** (in the upper-left corner).

2. Type **Projected Improvement**.

3. Press the **Tab** key to move to cell B1. See Figure 3-17.

Figure 3-17	ADDING TEXT TO THE TABLE

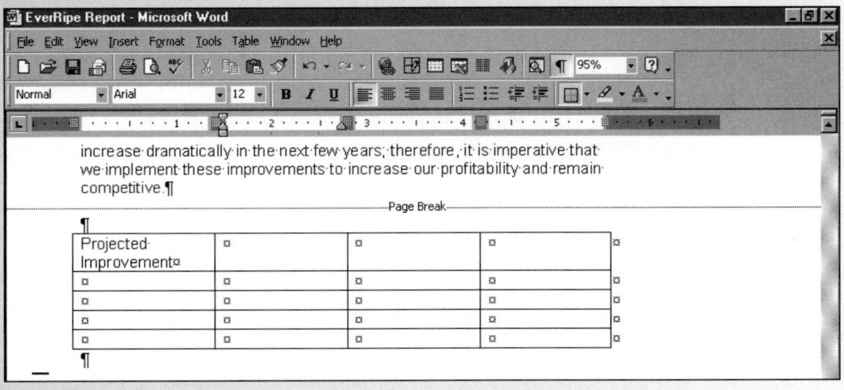

TROUBLE? If Word created a new paragraph in cell A1 rather than moving the insertion point to cell B1, you accidentally pressed the Enter key instead of the Tab key. Press the Backspace key to remove the paragraph mark, and then press the Tab key to move to cell B1.

4. Type **Benefit**, and then press the **Tab** key to move to cell C1.

5. Type **Percent of Total Cost**, and then press the **Tab** key to move to cell D1.

6. Type **Initial Cost**, and then press the **Tab** key to move the insertion point from cell D1 to cell A2. Notice that when you press the Tab key in the last column of the table, the insertion point moves to the first column in the next row.

You have entered the **heading row**, the row that identifies the information in each column.

7. Type the remaining information for the table, as shown in Figure 3-18, pressing the **Tab** key to move from cell to cell. Don't worry if the text in your table doesn't wrap the same way as shown here. You'll change the column widths in the next session.

Figure 3-18 **TABLE WITH COMPLETED INFORMATION**

Projected Improvement	Benefit	Percent of Total Cost	Initial Cost	
Upgrade packaging plants	Reduce by one-half the number of times tomatoes are handled	21%	$1,000,000	
Administrative improvements	Facilitate transition to new system	0.2%	$200,000	
Improve distribution methods	Decrease shipping costs and reduce shipping time by 1.5 days	51%	$3,700,000	
Automate delivery paperwork	Decrease delivery time by 15%	3.5%	$2,500,000	

TROUBLE? If a new row (row 6) appeared in your table, you pressed the Tab key when the insertion point was in cell D5, the last cell in the table. Click the Undo button on the Standard toolbar to remove row 6 from the table.

You've now completed a substantial amount of work on the report document, so you decide to save the document with a new name. That way, if for some reason the current document becomes corrupted, you still will have a previous version.

8. Save the document as **EverRipe Report Copy 2** in the **Tutorial** folder of the **Tutorial.03** folder.

Keep in mind that many document-editing features, such as the Backspace key, the copy-and-paste feature, the Undo button, and the AutoCorrect feature, work the same way in a table. Just like in a paragraph, you must select text within a table in order to edit it. You will edit and format this table in the next session.

Session 3.1 QUICK CHECK

1. Define the following in your own words:

   a. tab stop
   b. cell
   c. table
   d. decimal-aligned tab stop
   e. section (of a document)

2. Explain how to center the title page vertically between the top and bottom margins.

3. What is the difference between a header and a footer?

4. Describe how to insert a blank table consisting of four columns and six rows.

5. How do you move the insertion point from one row to the next in a table?

6. How do you insert the page number in a header?

7. Explain how to insert a new tab stop.

8. Describe a situation in which you would want to divide a document into sections.

9. Describe a situation in which it would be better to use a table rather than tab stops.

10. Explain how to select an entire table.

SESSION 3.2

In this session you will learn how to make changes to the table you just created. First you will rearrange the existing rows, and then you will learn how to add and delete rows. Next you will use the AutoSum feature to total a column of numbers, and then format the table to improve its appearance. You also will learn how to merge and split cells as well as how to rotate text within a cell.

Sorting Rows in a Table

The term **sort** refers to the process of rearranging information in alphabetical, numerical, or chronological order. When you sort a table, you arrange the rows based on the contents of one of the columns. For example, you could sort the table you just created based on the contents of the Projected Improvement column—either in ascending alphabetical order (from A to Z) or in descending alphabetical order (from Z to A). Alternatively, you could sort the table based on the contents of the Initial Cost column—either in descending numerical order (highest to lowest) or in ascending numerical order (lowest to highest). When you sort table data, Word usually does not sort the heading row along with the other information, but instead leaves the heading row at the top of the table.

The easiest way to sort a table is to use the Sort buttons on the **Tables and Borders toolbar**. You'll display the Tables and Borders toolbar in the following steps. As you will see, it contains a number of useful buttons that simplify the process of working with tables.

1. If you took a break after the last session, make sure Word is running and that the EverRipe Report Copy 2 document is open. Check that the nonprinting characters are displayed and that the document is displayed in normal view.

2. Right-click the **Standard toolbar**, and then click **Tables and Borders** in the shortcut menu. The Tables and Borders toolbar appears.

3. If necessary, drag the Tables and Borders toolbar down and to the right, so that it doesn't block your view of the EverRipe table. See Figure 3-19.

| Figure 3-19 | TABLE AND BORDERS TOOLBAR |

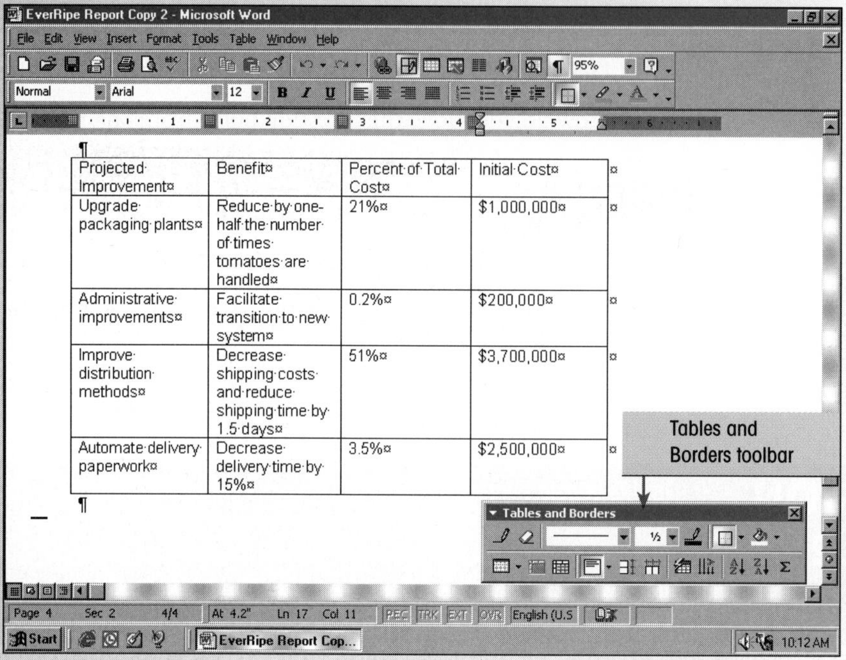

Tables and Borders toolbar

Brittany would like you to sort the table in ascending numerical order, based on the contents of the Initial Cost column. You start by positioning the insertion point in that column.

To sort the information in the table:

1. Click cell **D2** (which contains the value $1,000,000). The insertion point is now located in the Initial Cost column.

2. Click the **Sort Ascending** button on the Tables and Borders toolbar. Rows 2 through 5 now are arranged numerically from the lowest to the highest according to the numbers in the Initial Cost column. See Figure 3-20.

Figure 3-20   **TABLE AFTER BEING SORTED**

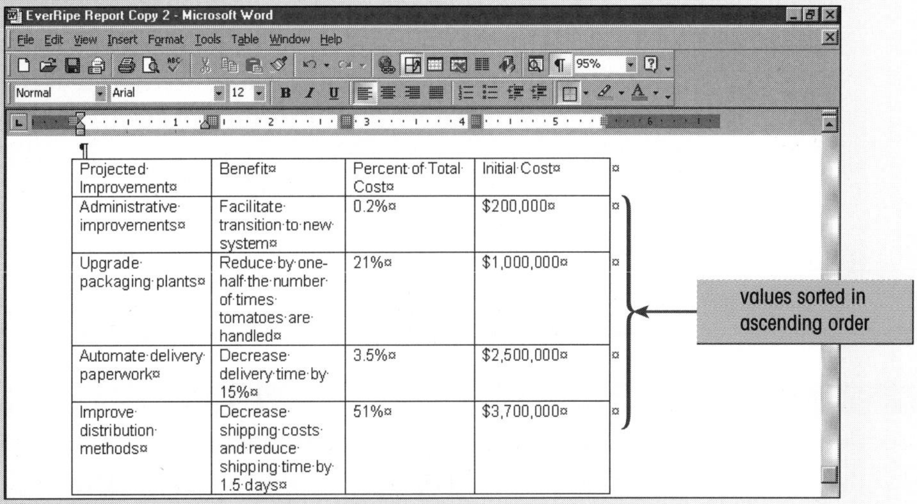

Projected Improvement¤	Benefit¤	Percent of Total Cost¤	Initial Cost¤	¤
Administrative improvements¤	Facilitate transition to new system¤	0.2%¤	$200,000¤	¤
Upgrade packaging plants¤	Reduce by one-half the number of times tomatoes are handled¤	21%¤	$1,000,000¤	¤
Automate delivery paperwork¤	Decrease delivery time by 15%¤	3.5%¤	$2,500,000¤	¤
Improve distribution methods¤	Decrease shipping costs and reduce shipping time by 1.5 days¤	51%¤	$3,700,000¤	¤

values sorted in ascending order

TROUBLE? If the sort was unsuccessful, immediately click the Undo button on the Standard toolbar, and then repeat Steps 1 and 2 to retry the sort.

Brittany stops by and asks you to delete the "Administrative improvements" row because it represents such a small percentage of the total cost. She also would like you to insert a new row to display the total of the Initial Cost column. You'll need to modify the structure of the table in order to complete these tasks.

Modifying an Existing Table Structure

Often, after you create a table, you'll need to delete extra rows and columns or insert additional ones. Figure 3-21 summarizes ways to insert or delete rows and columns in a table.

Figure 3-21   **WAYS TO INSERT OR DELETE TABLE ROWS AND COLUMNS**

TO	DO THIS
Insert a row within a table	Select the row below where you want the row added, click Table on the menu bar, point to Insert, and then click Rows Above.
	Select the row below where you want the row added, and then click the Insert Rows button on the Standard toolbar.
Insert a row at the end of a table	Position the insertion point in the rightmost cell of the bottom row, and then press the Tab key.
Insert a column within a table	Select the column to the right of where you want the column added, click Table on the menu bar, point to Insert, and then click Columns to the Right.
	Select the column to the right of where you want the column added, and then click the Insert Columns button on the Standard toolbar.
Insert a column at the end of a table	Select the end-of-row markers to the right of the table, click Table on the menu bar, point to Insert, and then click Columns to the Left.
	Select the end-of-row markers to the right of the table, and then click the Insert Columns button on the Standard toolbar.
Delete a row	Select the row or rows to be deleted, click Table on the menu bar, point to Delete, and then click Row
Delete a column	Select the column or columns to be deleted, click Table on the menu bar, point to Delete, and th Columns.

Deleting Rows and Columns in a Table

With Word, you can delete either the contents of the cells or the structure of the cells. To delete the contents of the cells in a selected row, you press the Delete key. However, to delete both the contents and structure of a selected row or column from the table entirely, you must use one of the methods described in Figure 3-21.

To delete a row using the Table menu:

1. Click the selection bar next to row 2 to select the Administrative improvements row.

2. Click **Table** on the menu bar, point to **Delete**, and then click **Rows**. The selected row is deleted from the table structure. See Figure 3-22.

Figure 3-22   TABLE AFTER DELETING ROW

row removed from table

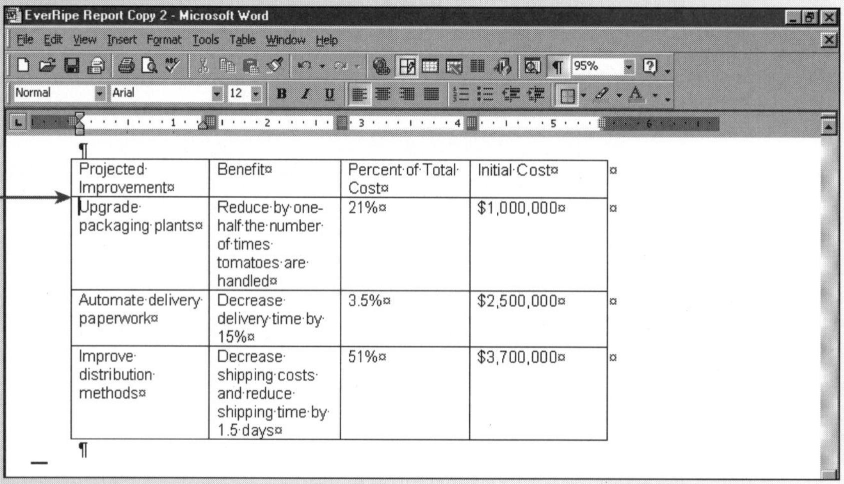

Inserting Additional Rows in a Table

You can insert additional rows within the table or at the end of a table. You now need to insert a row at the bottom of the table, so you can include the total of the Initial Cost column.

To insert a row at the bottom of the table:

1. Click cell **D4**, the last cell of the last row in the table, which contains the number "$3,700,000."

2. Press the **Tab** key. A blank row is added to the bottom of the table.

   TROUBLE? If a blank row is not added to the bottom of the table, click the Undo button on the Standard toolbar. Check to make sure the insertion point is in the last cell of the last row, and then press the Tab key.

3. Type **Total** in cell A5.

...re nearly ready to insert the total of the Initial Cost column in cell D5. First, you ...ake it clear that the "Total" heading only applies to the Initial Cost column. You ...t by combining cell A5 with cells at the bottom of the Benefit and Percent of Total ...ns.

Merging Cells

In addition to adding and deleting rows and columns, you also can change the structure of a table by changing the structure of individual cells. Specifically, you can combine, or **merge**, cells. You also can **split** one cell into multiple rows or columns.

REFERENCE WINDOW **RW**

Merging and Splitting Cells

- Select the cells you want to merge, and then click the Merge Cells button on the Tables and Borders toolbar. Or click the Draw Table button on the Tables and Borders toolbar, draw additional columns or row borders, and then press the Esc key to turn off the Draw Table pointer.
- Move the insertion point to the cell you want to split, click Table on the menu bar, and then click Split Cells; or click the Split Cells button on the Tables and Borders toolbar. In the Split Cells dialog box, specify the number of cells or rows into which you want to divide the cell, and then click OK.

You decide to merge cells A5, B5, and C5 to avoid the impression that you intend to insert totals at the bottom of the Benefit column or the Percent of Total Cost column.

To merge cells A5, B5, and C5:

1. Click cell **A5** (containing the word "Total") and drag the pointer to cells **B5** and **C5**. The three cells are now selected.

2. Click the **Merge Cells** button on the Tables and Borders toolbar, and then click anywhere within the table to deselect the cells. The borders between the three cells disappear. The three cells are now one, as shown in Figure 3-23.

Figure 3-23 **MERGED CELL**

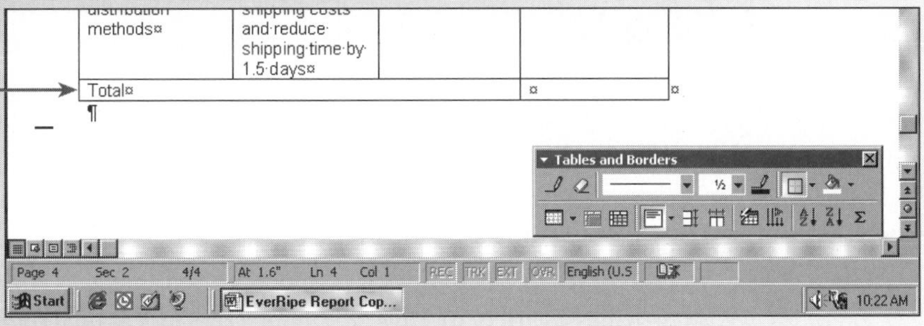

three cells merged into one

Eventually you need to format the text "Total" so that it is aligned next to the Initial Cost column. You will do that later in this tutorial, when you align the percentage values in column C. Now you are ready to calculate the total of the Initial Cost column.

Using AutoSum to Total a Table Column

Rather than calculating column totals by hand and entering them, you can have Word compute the totals of numeric columns in a table. The **AutoSum** feature automatically totals a column of numbers. Note that if you edit any number in the column, you need to click the cell containing the formula, and then press the F9 key to recalculate the total.

To total the values in the Initial Cost column:

1. Click the bottom cell in the Initial Cost column.

2. Click the **AutoSum** button ⎡Σ⎤ on the Tables and Borders toolbar. The total of the column appears in the cell formatted with a dollar sign and two decimal places. Although you see a number ($7,200,000.00), the cell contains a formula that calculates the total of all the numbers in the column. You can change the way the total looks by formatting the formula. In this case, you want to remove the decimal point and the two zeros.

3. Click the total to select it. The total becomes highlighted in gray.

4. Click **Table** on the menu bar, and then click **Formula**. The Formula dialog box opens.

5. Click the **Number format** list arrow, and select the only format with a dollar sign. You'll remove the part of the formula that specifies how to format negative numbers as well as the decimal codes.

6. In the Number format text box, click to the right of the format and press the **Backspace** key until only $#, ##0 remains, as shown in Figure 3-24.

Figure 3-24	FORMULA DIALOG BOX AFTER ADJUSTING NUMBER FORMAT

Formula
revised number format

Formula

Formula:
=SUM(ABOVE)

Number format:
$#,##0

Paste function:

Paste bookmark:

OK   Cancel

7. Click **OK**. The Initial Cost total is now formatted like the numbers above it.

You have finished creating the table, entering data, and modifying the table's structure. Now, you can concentrate on improving the table's appearance.

Formatting Tables

Word provides a variety of ways to enhance the appearance of the tables you create: You can alter the width of the columns and the height of the rows, or change the alignment of text within the cells or the alignment of the table between the left and right margins. You also can change the appearance of the table borders, add a shaded background, and rotate the text within cells.

Changing Column Width and Row Height

Sometimes, you'll want to adjust the column widths in a table to make the text easier to read. If you want to specify an exact width for a column, you should use the Table Properties command on the Table menu. However, it's usually easiest to drag the column's right border to a new position. Note that when adjusting columns and rows, you should switch to print layout view so that the vertical ruler is displayed.

The Percent of Total Cost column (column C) is too wide for the information it contains and should be narrowed. The values in the Initial Cost column look crowded and would be easier to read if the column were wider. You'll change these widths by dragging the column borders, using the ruler as a guide. Keep in mind that to change the width of a column, you need to drag the column's rightmost border.

To change the width of columns by dragging the borders:

1. Switch to print layout view.

2. Position the insertion point anywhere in the EverRipe table (without selecting any text or cells) and then move the pointer over the table without clicking. Notice that in print layout view, the Table move handle and the Table resize handle appear whenever you move the pointer over the table. You will learn more about these two handles in the Review Assignments at the end of this tutorial.

3. Move the pointer over the border between columns C and D (in other words, over the right border of column C, the Percent of Total Cost column). The pointer changes to ⊣┃⊢.

4. Press and hold down the **Alt** key and the mouse button. The column widths are displayed in the ruler, as shown in Figure 3-25.

Figure 3-25	COLUMN WIDTHS DISPLAYED IN RULER

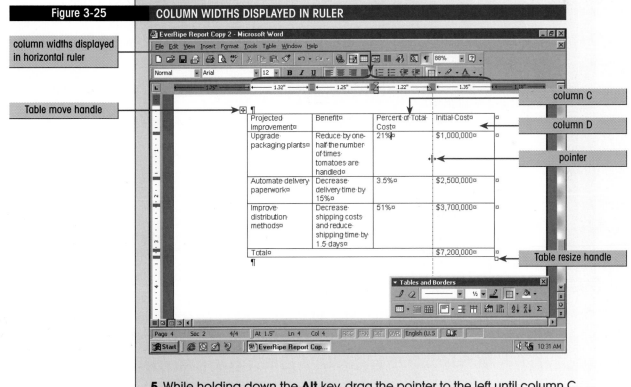

5. While holding down the **Alt** key, drag the pointer to the left until column C (the Percent of Total Cost column) is about **0.75** inches wide, and then release the mouse button. Notice that column C decreases in width and the width of column D (the Initial Cost column) increases. However, the overall width of the table does not change. See Figure 3-26.

Figure 3-26 | **TABLE AFTER DECREASING THE WIDTH OF COLUMN C**

column C reduced to 0.75 inches

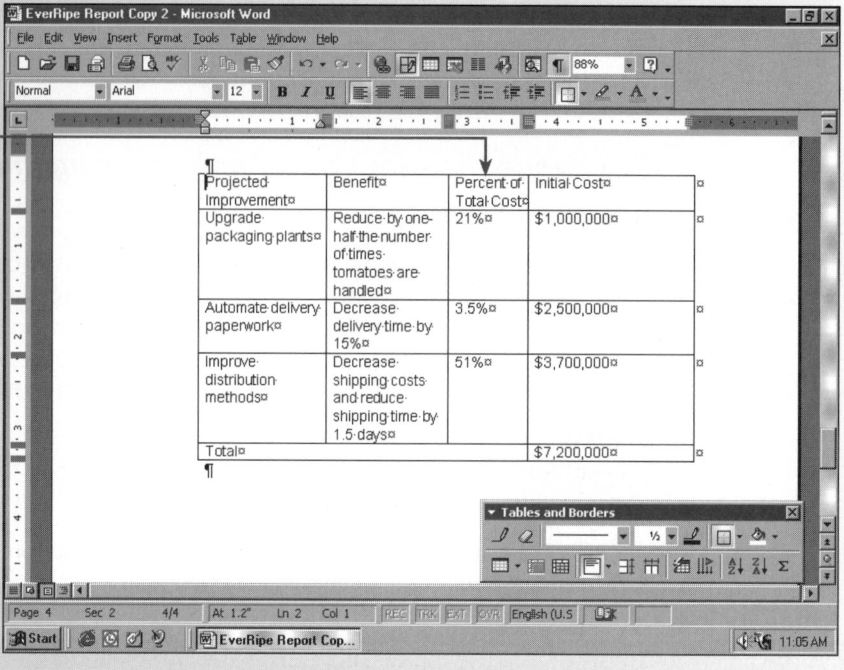

Projected Improvement¤	Benefit¤	Percent of Total Cost¤	Initial Cost¤	¤
Upgrade packaging plants¤	Reduce by one-half the number of times tomatoes are handled¤	21%¤	$1,000,000¤	¤
Automate delivery paperwork¤	Decrease delivery time by 15%¤	3.5%¤	$2,500,000¤	¤
Improve distribution methods¤	Decrease shipping costs and reduce shipping time by 1.5 days¤	51%¤	$3,700,000¤	¤
Total¤			$7,200,000¤	¤

TROUBLE? If you can't get the column width to exactly 0.75 inches, make it as close to that width as possible.

6. Use the same technique to decrease the Initial Cost column to approximately 1 inch.

You also can change the height of rows by dragging a border. You'll make row 1 (the header row) taller so it is more prominent.

To change the height of row 1:

1. Position the pointer over the bottom border of the header row. The pointer changes to $\div$.

2. Press and hold down the **Alt** key and the mouse button. The row heights are displayed in the vertical ruler.

3. While holding down the **Alt** key, drag the pointer down until row 1 is about **1** inch high, and then release the mouse button. Notice that the height of the other rows in the table is not affected by this change.

The EverRipe table now looks much better with its new column width and row height. Next you'll align the text to make the table even more attractive.

Aligning Text Within Cells

Aligning the text within the cells of a table makes the information easier to read. For example, aligning a column of numbers or percentages along the right margin helps the reader to quickly compare the values. At the same time, centering a row of headings makes a table more visually appealing. You can align text within the active cell the same way you do other text—with the alignment buttons on the Formatting toolbar. However, the alignment buttons on the Tables and Borders toolbar provide more options.

The percentage and dollar amounts in columns C and D would be much easier to read if you were to align the numbers on the right side of the cells. In the process of right-aligning the numbers, you can also right-align the word "Total" in the merged cell at the bottom of columns A, B, and C. The table also would look better with the headings centered. You'll begin by selecting and formatting all of columns C and D.

To right-align the numerical data and center the headings:

1. Move the pointer to the top of column C until the pointer changes to ↓, and then click the top of the column to select the entire column (including the merged cell at the bottom of the column.)

2. Drag the pointer to the right to select column D as well. Now that you've selected the columns, you can align the text within them.

3. Click the **Align Right** button ▤ on the Formatting toolbar. The numbers line up along the right edges of the cells. In addition, the word "Total" in the merged cell aligns next to the bottom cell in the Initial Cost column.

   TROUBLE? If more than just the numbers, column headings, and Total cell are right-aligned within the table, you may have selected the wrong block of cells. Click the Undo button on the Standard toolbar, and then repeat Steps 1 through 3.

   Notice that in the process of formatting Columns C and D, you right-aligned two of the headings ("Percent of Total Cost" and "Initial Cost"). You will reformat those headings in the next step, when you center the text in row 1 both horizontally and vertically in each cell.

4. Click the selection bar next to row 1. All of row 1 is selected.

5. Click the **Align** list arrow on the Tables and Borders toolbar to display a palette of nine alignment options.

6. Click the **Align Center** button ▣ in the middle of the palette. The text becomes centered both horizontally and vertically in the row.

7. Click anywhere in the table to deselect the row. See Figure 3-27.

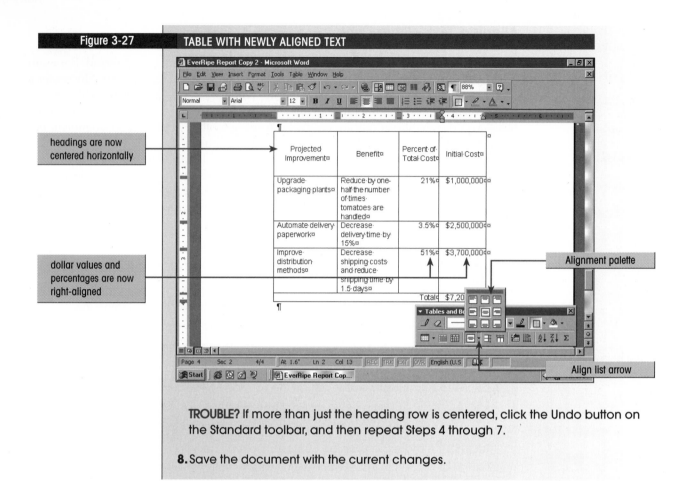

Figure 3-27   **TABLE WITH NEWLY ALIGNED TEXT**

headings are now centered horizontally

dollar values and percentages are now right-aligned

Alignment palette

Align list arrow

TROUBLE? If more than just the heading row is centered, click the Undo button on the Standard toolbar, and then repeat Steps 4 through 7.

8. Save the document with the current changes.

The tables look better with the headings centered and the numbers right-aligned. You now decide to make the table more attractive and easier to read by changing the table's borders and rules.

Changing Borders

It's important to keep in mind the distinction between gridlines and borders. Gridlines are light gray lines that indicate the structure of the table on the screen and that do not show up on the printed page. Borders are darker lines overlaying the gridlines, which do appear on the printed page. When you create a table using the Insert Table button, Word automatically applies a thin black border, so you can't actually see the underlying gridlines.

After you have created a table, you can add new borders, erase existing borders, or modify existing borders by changing their line weights and line styles. **Line weight** refers to the thickness of the border. You can use any combination of these formats you like.

> *To modify the table's existing borders:*
>
> **1.** Verify that the insertion point is located within the table.
>
> **2.** Click the **Line Weight** list arrow on the Tables and Borders toolbar, and then click **2¼ pt**.
>
> **TROUBLE?** If the Office Assistant opens, click the Cancel button to close it. Then continue with Step 3.

3. Move the Draw Table pointer ✏ to the upper-left corner of the table, and then click the top of each cell in row 1. The top border becomes a thicker line.

4. Repeat Step 3 to draw a thicker line below the header row, above the Totals row, and at the bottom of the table. If you make a mistake, click the Undo button ↶ on the Standard toolbar to reverse it.

Now you'll use a similar method to remove borders (without removing the underlying gridlines) between rows of the table.

5. Click the **Line Style** list arrow on the Tables and Borders toolbar, and then click **No Border**.

6. Click the bottom of each cell in row 2. Only the light gray gridline remains between the first two rows of data.

TROUBLE? If you don't see the light gray gridline, click Table on the menu bar and then click Show Gridlines.

7. Repeat Step 6 to remove the horizontal line below row 3.

8. Press the **Esc** key to turn off the Draw Table pointer. See Figure 3-28.

Figure 3-28	TABLE AFTER CHANGING LINE WEIGHTS AND STYLES

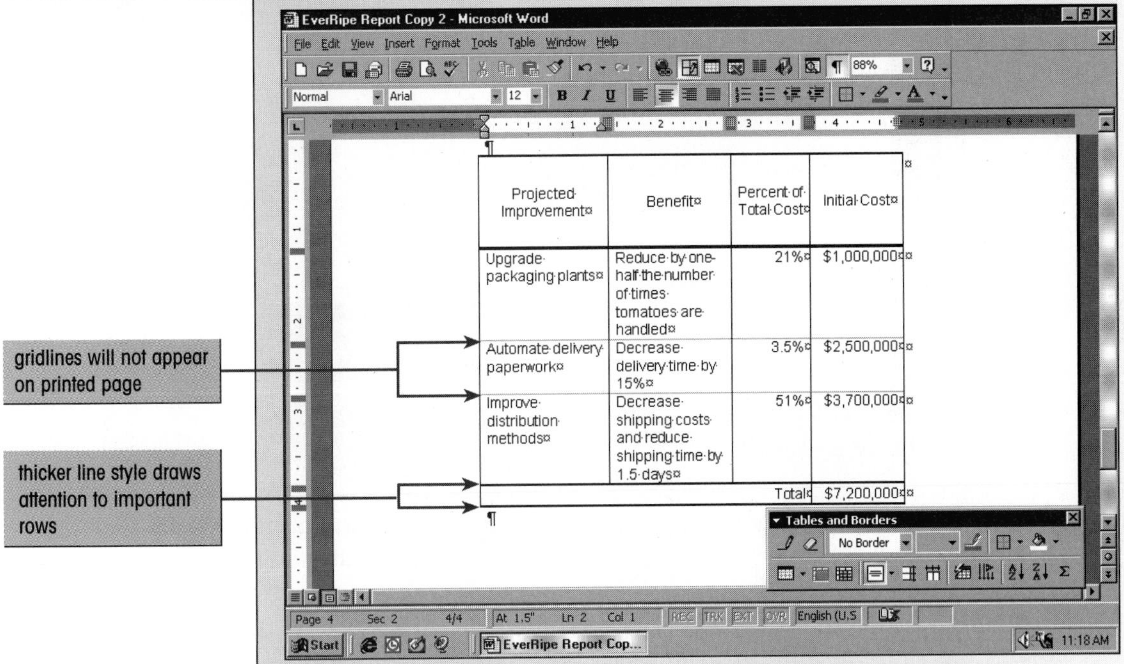

gridlines will not appear on printed page

thicker line style draws attention to important rows

9. Save your work.

Changing the borders has made the table more attractive. You finish formatting the table by adding shading to the cells containing the headings.

Adding Shading

With the Borders and Shading dialog box, adding **shading** (a gray or colored background) to text is a simple task. Shading is especially useful in tables when you want to emphasize headings, totals, or other important items. In most cases, when you add shading to a table, you also need to bold format the shaded text to make it easier to read.

You now will add a light gray shading to the heading row and format the headings in bold.

To add shading to the heading row and change the headings to bold:

1. Click the selection bar to the left of row 1 to select the heading row of the table.

2. Click the **Shading Color** list arrow on the Tables and Borders toolbar. A palette of shading options opens.

3. Point to the fifth gray square from the left, in the top row. The ScreenTip "Gray-15%" appears. See Figure 3-29.

| Figure 3-29 | SHADING OPTIONS |

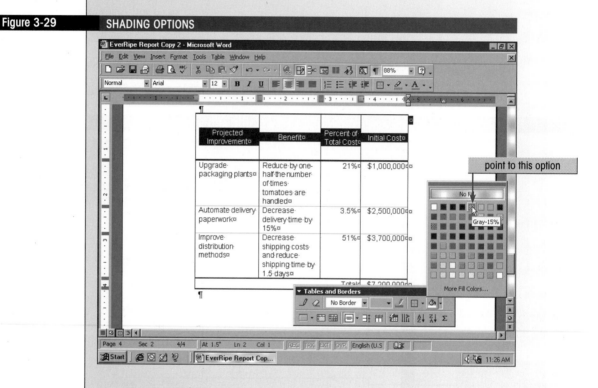

4. Click the **Gray-15%** square. A light gray background appears in the heading row. Now you need to format the text in bold to make the headings stand out from the shading.

5. Click the **Bold** button **B** on the Formatting toolbar to make the headings bold.

TROUBLE? If any of the headings break incorrectly (for example, if the "t" in "Cost" moves to the next line), you might need to widen columns to accommodate the bold letters. Drag the column borders as necessary to adjust the column widths so that all the column headings are displayed correctly.

6. Click in the selection bar next to the last row to select the Total row.

7. Click **B**. The Total row now appears in bold.

8. Click anywhere outside the Total row to deselect it. Your table should look like Figure 3-30.

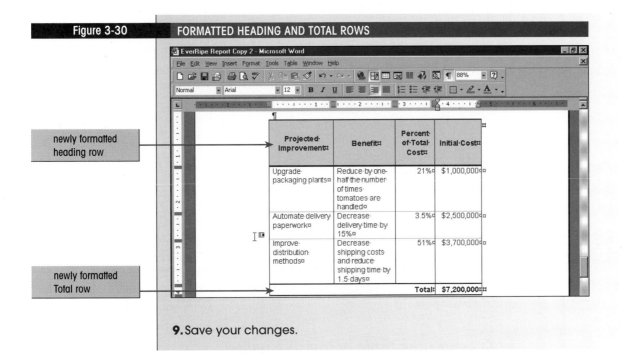

Figure 3-30   FORMATTED HEADING AND TOTAL ROWS

newly formatted heading row

newly formatted Total row

9. Save your changes.

Rotating Text in a Cell

Brittany stops by to take a look at the table so far. She mentions that it is possible to rotate text within the cells of a table. You decide to try rotating the headings to a vertical position to see how they look.

To rotate the headings vertically:

1. Select the heading row.

2. Click the **Change Text Direction** button in the Tables and Borders toolbar, and then click anywhere in the table to deselect the heading row. The table headings are now formatted vertically in their cells, as shown in Figure 3-31.

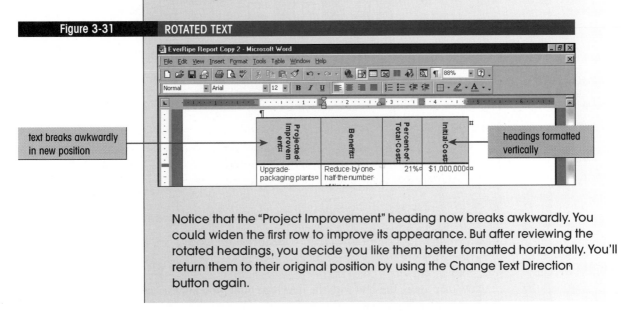

Figure 3-31   ROTATED TEXT

text breaks awkwardly in new position

headings formatted vertically

Notice that the "Project Improvement" heading now breaks awkwardly. You could widen the first row to improve its appearance. But after reviewing the rotated headings, you decide you like them better formatted horizontally. You'll return them to their original position by using the Change Text Direction button again.

3. Select the heading row, and then click 📊 again. The headings are still formatted vertically, but now the text flows from bottom to top.

4. Click 📄 again. The headings are now formatted horizontally. Because you are finished with the Tables and Borders toolbar, you will close it.

5. Click the **Close** button ✖ on the Tables and Borders toolbar to close the toolbar.

You will finish formatting your table by centering it on the page.

Centering a Table

If a table doesn't fill the entire page width, you can center it between the left and right margins. The Center button on the Formatting toolbar centers only text within each selected cell. It does not center the entire table across the page. To center a table across the page (between the left and right margins), you use the Table Properties command.

The EverRipe table will stand out more and look better if it is centered between the left and right margins.

To center the table across the page:

1. Click anywhere in the table, click **Table** on the menu bar, and then click **Table Properties**. The Table Properties dialog box opens.

2. Click the **Table** tab if necessary.

3. In the Alignment section click the **Center** option. See Figure 3-32.

Figure 3-32	TABLE TAB OF THE TABLE PROPERTIES DIALOG BOX

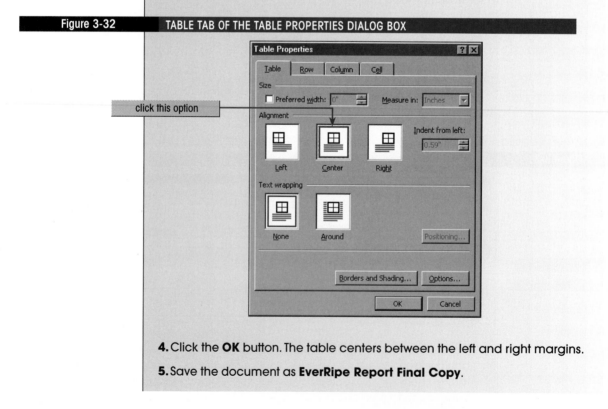

4. Click the **OK** button. The table centers between the left and right margins.

5. Save the document as **EverRipe Report Final Copy**.

Now that you're finished with the EverRipe table, you want to print a copy of the full report for Brittany. You'll preview the report first to make sure the table fits on the fourth page.

To preview the table:

1. Click the **Print Preview** button 🔍 on the Standard toolbar to open the Print Preview window.

2. Scroll to view all the pages of the report.

3. Click the **Print** button 🖨 on the Print Preview toolbar to print the report, then close the document and exit Word.

You now have a hardcopy of the EverRipe report including the table, which summarizes the report text. Your four-page finished report should look like Figure 3-33.

| Figure 3-33 | FINISHED EVERRIPE REPORT |

Page 1:

Increasing the Profitability of AgriTechnology's EverRipe Tomatoes

Prepared for
Ramon Espinoza, Vice President
AgriTechnology

Prepared by Task Force Members

Brittany Jones	Marketing Manager
Anthony Ciaccio	Research Associate
Dominic Carmon-Estevon	Research Associate
Evan Brillstein	Distribution Specialist

Page 2:

EverRipe Recommendation Report — Page 2

Executive Summary
Almost 20 percent of the EverRipe tomato crop was unmarketable due to damage sustained during packaging and distribution. This resulted in an estimated loss in profits of $1.2 million. AgriTechnology could increase the percentage of marketable crop and increase profits by upgrading its packaging plants, constructing distribution centers, purchasing trucking facilities, and automating delivery services. Costs for implementing these improvements would be approximately $7.2 million. The company should be able to recoup that investment within four years.

Introduction
This report presents our findings on how to improve the profitability of the EverRipe tomato crop. First, we describe how part of the crop was unmarketable due to losses during packaging and distribution. Then, we recommend improvements to the current packaging and distribution process that will reduce damage to future crops. Finally, we project costs for implementing these changes.

Loss of Profits for 2001
Although these tomatoes are genetically engineered to remain ripe for longer periods of time, they're more easily bruised than conventional tomatoes. AgriTechnology reports indicate that 18.7 percent of this year's crop was unmarketable due to damage sustained during packaging and distribution. This resulted in an estimated loss for AgriTechnology of $1.2 million. We could increase the percentage of marketable fruit by reducing the number of times the fruit are handled and by decreasing storage time.

Improving the Profitability of Future Crops
We could improve the profitability of future EverRipe crops by upgrading our packaging plants, reducing our distribution time, and accelerating our delivery methods.

Upgrading Packaging Plants
Currently, the tomatoes are picked and shipped to nearby packaging plants where they are hand-sorted, placed on a conveyor, and routed to the packaging machines. Packaged tomatoes are then put in corrugated cartons, placed in a chute, and sent to the loading area below. At the loading area, the cartons are stacked on pallets that are loaded on trucks and shipped to produce warehouses. The EverRipe tomatoes are handled an average of 4.3 times during the packaging and loading process. By upgrading the packaging plants to include new "soft touch" technology, which uses optical sensors to sort the tomatoes, and by reorganizing the plants so that packaging, stacking, and shipping operations are on the same level, we could reduce by one-half, the number of times the tomatoes are handled.

Page 3:

EverRipe Recommendation Report — Page 3

Improving Distribution Methods
After the pallets are transported to the produce warehouses, they are stored in refrigerated rooms until the warehouses arrange with local trucking companies to ship the tomatoes to buyers. Currently, the tomatoes average 8.4 days in the warehouses and 3.2 days in shipping. We could eliminate lengthy storage by building our own distribution centers near the packaging plants, purchasing our own shipping lines, and automating our distribution system. By automating our distribution system, we could create a continuous-flow system where the tomatoes are shipped to our distribution centers, unloaded from inbound trucks, and moved across the dock to an outgoing distribution truck without having to be stored. By purchasing our own trucking system, we would also decrease shipping costs and reduce shipping time by at least 1.5 days.

Improving Delivery
We also need to improve our delivery process. Currently, the drivers spend 20 percent of their time verifying orders and checking invoices. By distributing and shipping our own produce, we could submit computerized shipment notices in advance. Then AgriTechnology drivers would use handheld computers to automatically update produce orders and verify invoices. We estimate that we can decrease delivery time by 15 percent as a result of automating our delivery system.

Cost of the Improvements
We estimate that these improvements would require an investment of approximately $7.2 million. Although this represents a major capital investment, the money would be recouped by an increase in marketable fruit. Competition among biotechnology companies is expected to increase dramatically in the next few years; therefore, it is imperative that we implement these improvements to increase our profitability and remain competitive.

Page 4:

EverRipe Recommendation Report — Page 4

Projected Improvement	Benefit	Percent of Total Cost	Initial Cost
Upgrade packaging plants	Reduce by one-half the number of times tomatoes are handled.	21%	$1,000,000
Automate delivery paperwork	Decrease delivery time by 15%.	35%	$2,500,000
Improve distribution methods	Decrease shipping costs and reduce shipping time by 1.5 days.	51%	$3,700,000
		Total	$7,200,000

In this tutorial, you have planned and formatted Brittany's recommendation report and added a table to summarize the report recommendations. As a result, the report information is readily available to readers who want to skim for the most important points, as well as to those who want more detailed information.

Session 3.2 QUICK CHECK

1. How do you adjust the width of the columns in a table?

2. Why would you usually right-align numbers in a table?

3. Define the following terms in your own words:

    a. merge
    b. rotate
    c. border
    d. shading

4. Explain how to add a row to the bottom of a table.

5. Explain how to total a column of numbers in a table.

6. In what order would the following numbers appear in a table if you sorted them in ascending numerical order: 25, 10, 75, 45?

7. How do you center a table between the left and right margins?

REVIEW ASSIGNMENTS

AgriTechnology adopted the recommendations the task force made in the EverRipe report. It is now two years later and the task force is issuing a report on the progress of the new packaging, distribution, and delivery policies. You'll format this report now.

1. If necessary, start Word and make sure your Data Disk is in the appropriate disk drive, and check your screen to make sure your settings match those in the tutorial. Display nonprinting characters as necessary.

2. Open the file **StatRep** from the Review folder for Tutorial 3 on your Data Disk, and then save it as **AgTech Status Report**.

3. Select the list of task force members and their titles, and then insert a left tab stop 2.5 inches from the left margin.

4. Click after the "t" in "Distribution Specialist," press the Enter key, and then type your name. Press the Tab key to move the insertion point to the tab stop, and then type a title for yourself.

5. Divide the document into two sections. Insert a section break so that the executive summary begins on a new page.

Explore

6. Vertically align the first section of the document using the Justified alignment option in the Page Setup dialog box, and view the results in Print Preview.

Explore   7. Add a footer to section 2. Click View on the menu bar, and then click Header and Footer. Use the Word online Help system to learn the functions of the buttons on the Header and Footer toolbar. Then, on the Header and Footer toolbar, click the Switch Between Header and Footer button to move to the footer area of section 2. Click the Same as Previous button to deselect it. Using the same techniques you used to create a header in the tutorial, create a footer for section 2 that reads "EverRipe Status Report" at the left margin. Insert the current date at the right margin. (*Hint:* Use the Insert Date button on the Header and Footer toolbar to insert the date.) Use the Formatting toolbar to format the footer and date in 9-point bold Arial.

Explore   8. Create a header for section 2 that aligns your name at the left margin and centers the page number preceded by the word "Page." Don't forget to deselect the Same as Previous button. (*Hint:* To center the page number, use the second tab stop.) Click Close on the Header and Footer toolbar.

9. Save, preview, and print the document; then close it.

Open the file **ZonReq** from the Review folder for Tutorial 3 on your Data Disk, save the document as **Zoning Request**, and then complete the following:

10. On the first page, replace "Your Name" with your first and last name.

11. Under the heading "Benefits to the Community," select the three lines of text containing tabs. Insert a left tab stop 3 inches from the left margin.

12. Divide the document into two sections. Begin the second section with the introduction on a new page.

13. Use the Ctrl+Enter key combination to insert a page break before the line "The new jobs would be divided as follows:".

14. Vertically align the first section of the document using the Center alignment option in the Page Setup dialog box.

15. Create a header for section 2 that prints "Zoning Request" at the left margin and has a right-aligned page number preceded by the word "Page." (*Hint*: Deselect the Same as Previous button on the Header and Footer toolbar.)

16. On the Header and Footer toolbar, click the Switch Between Header and Footer button to move to the footer area of section 2. Using the same techniques you used to create a header in the tutorial, create a footer for section 2 that aligns your name at the left margin and the date on the right margin.

17. Click the Close button on the Header and Footer toolbar, then review the new headers and footers in print layout view.

Explore   18. Modify the page number in the header so that it indicates the total number of pages in the document. Click View on the menu bar, click Header and Footer, click to the right of the page number, press the spacebar, type "of" (without the quotation marks), press the spacebar, and then click the Insert Number of Pages button on the Header and Footer toolbar.

19. Save the document.

20. Insert a page break at the end of the document.

21. Insert a table consisting of four rows and three columns.

22. Type the headings "Project," "Cost," and "Jobs Added" in row 1.

23. In row 2, type "Expand Packaging Plant," "$1,200,000," and "175" in the appropriate cells.

24. In row 3, type "Miscellaneous Items," "$200,000," and "2" in the appropriate cells.

25. In row 4, type "Build Distribution Center," "$1,300,000," and "125" in the appropriate cells.

26. Sort the table in ascending numerical order, by the Jobs Added column.

27. Select the entire Project column, click Table on the menu bar, point to Insert, and then click Columns to the Right to insert a new column between the Project column and the Cost column. Type the heading "Priority" in the new cell B1, press the down arrow, type 3, press the down arrow, type 2, press the down arrow, and then type 1.

28. Add a new row to the bottom of the table. Type "Total" in the new cell A5, at the bottom of the Project column.

29. Merge the "Total" cell with the cell to its right. Align the word "Total" on the right of the newly merged cell.

30. Use the AutoSum button on the Tables and Borders toolbar to total the Cost and Jobs Added columns. Click the Cost total to select it, and then format it without decimal points using the Formula command on the Table menu. Notice that the Total of the Cost column is $2,700,000, and the total of the Jobs Added column is 302.

31. Delete the Miscellaneous Items row.

Explore ▶ 32. Update both AutoSum formulas to reflect the deleted row. To update a formula, select the cell containing the formula, and then press the F9 key. The totals are updated to include only the rows currently in the table. The total of the Cost column should now be $2,500,000. The total of the Jobs Added column should now be 300.

33. Center the table on the page.

34. Drag the right border of column C (the Cost column) to the left until the column is about 0.8 inches wide. Drag the right border of column D (the Jobs Added column) to the left until the column is about 0.9 inches wide.

Explore ▶ 35. Switch to print layout view, if necessary, and then use the Table move handle to select the entire table, and then format the text as 14-point Times New Roman.

Explore ▶ 36. Try adjusting the column widths to accommodate the newly formatted text by double-clicking the borders between columns. First click anywhere within the table to deselect any selected text or cells. Double-click the border between columns A and B. The width of column A adjusts automatically to accommodate the longest entry. Adjust the widths of the other columns by clicking on their right borders.

37. Right-align the numbers in the table. The "Total" label should also be right-aligned.

38. Format the heading row by adding a light gray shading. Format the headings in bold as well.

39. Use the Line Weight list arrow on the Tables and Borders toolbar to add a 2¼-point border around the outside of the table. Also, change the border above the Total row to 2¼ point. Instead of clicking the borders you want to change, try drawing with the pointer. If you don't drag the pointer far enough, the Office Assistant may appear to offer some advice. Read the information it provides and click OK. To turn off the Draw Tables pointer, press the Esc key.

40. Increase the height of the heading row to approximately 0.8 inches. Center the headings vertically and horizontally using the Align Center option on the Tables and Borders toolbar.

41. Save, preview, print, and close the document.

Word will convert text separated by commas, paragraph marks, or tabs into a table. To try this feature, open the file **Members** from the Review folder for Tutorial 3 on your Data Disk, and save it as **Zoning Board Members**. Then complete the following:

42. Select the list of zoning board members (including the heading), click Table on the menu bar, and point to Convert, and then click Text to Table. In the Convert Text to Table dialog box, make sure the settings indicate that the table should have two columns and that the text is separated by commas. Then click the OK button. Word converts the list of task force members into a table.

43. Click cell B5, in the lower-right corner of the table, and then press the Tab key. Type your own name in the new cell A6, press the Tab key, and then type "Ward 2" in cell B6.

44. Format the table appropriately using the techniques you learned in the tutorial. Be sure to adjust the column widths to close up any extra space.

Explore   45. Place the pointer over the Table resize handle, just outside the lower-right corner of the table. Drag the double-arrow pointer to increase the size of the height and width of each cell. Notice that all the parts of the table increase proportionally. Click the Undo button to return the table to its original format.

46. Save the document; then preview and print it.

CASE PROBLEMS

Case 1. Ocean Breeze Bookstore Annual Report   As manager of Ocean Breeze Bookstore in San Diego, California, you must submit an annual report to the Board of Directors.

1. If necessary, start Word, make sure your Data Disk is in the appropriate drive, and check your screen to make sure your settings match those in the tutorials.

2. Open the file **OceanRep** from the Cases folder for Tutorial 3 on your Data Disk, and save it as **Ocean Breeze Report**.

3. Divide the document into two sections. Begin section 2 with the introduction on a new page.

4. Format the title ("Annual Report") and the subtitle ("Ocean Breeze Bookstore") using the font and font size of your choice. Vertically align the first section using the alignment option of your choice.

Explore   5. Move the insertion point to section 2. Create a header for the entire document that aligns "Ocean Breeze Annual Report" on the left margin, your name in the center, and the current date on the right margin. Click the Show Previous button on the Header and Footer toolbar to view the header text for section 1.

6. Select the list of members under the heading "Board of Directors." Insert a left tab stop 4.5 inches from the left margin.

7. Preview and save the document.

8. Insert a page break at the end of the document.

9. Insert a table consisting of four rows and three columns.

10. Insert the headings "Name," "Title," and "Duties." Fill in the rows with the relevant information about the store personnel, which you will find listed in the report. Add new rows as needed.

11. Adjust the table column widths so the information is presented attractively.

12. Increase the height of the heading row, center the column headings horizontally and vertically, and then bold them.

Explore   13. Use Help to learn how to insert a row within a table. Insert a row in the middle of the table, and add your name to the list of store managers. Readjust the column widths as needed.

14. Format the heading row with a light gray shading of your choice.

15. Change the outside border of the table to 2¼-point line weight.

16. Save, preview, print, and close the document.

Case 2. Ultimate Travel's "Europe on a Budget" Report   As director of Ultimate Travel's "Europe on a Budget" tour, you need to write a report summarizing this year's tour.

1. If necessary, start Word, make sure your Data Disk is in the appropriate drive, and check your screen to make sure your settings match those in the tutorials.

2. Open the file **Europe** from the Cases folder for Tutorial 3 on your Data Disk, and save it as **Europe Tour Report**.

3. Replace "Your Name" in the first page with your first and last name.

4. Divide the document into two sections. Begin the second section on a new page, with the summary that starts "This report summarizes and evaluates...."

5. Vertically align the first section using the Center alignment option.

6. Create a header for section 2 that contains the centered text "Ultimate Travel." (*Hint:* To center text in the header, use the second tab stop. Deselect the Same as Previous button before you begin.)

7. On the Header and Footer toolbar, click the Switch Between Header and Footer button to move to the footer area of the document. Using the same techniques you used to create a header in the tutorial, create a footer for section 2 that aligns "Evaluation Report" on the left margin and the date on the right margin. (*Hint:* Deselect the Same as Previous button first.)

8. In the table, bold the text in column A (the left column), and then rotate it so that text is formatted vertically, from bottom to top.

9. Adjust the row and column widths as necessary.

10. Delete the blank row 2.

11. Format column A with a light gray shading.

12. Change the border around column A to 2¼-point line weight.

13. Save, preview, print, and close the document.

Case 3. Classical CD Sales at The Master's Touch   Austin Cornelius is the purchasing agent for The Master's Touch, a music store in Little Rock, Arkansas. Each month, Austin publishes a list of the classical CDs that are on sale at The Master's Touch. He has asked you to create a table showing this month's list of sale items.

1. Open the file **Classics** from the Cases folder for Tutorial 3 on your Data Disk, and save it as **Classical Music CDs**.

Explore

2. Highlight the list of CDs—Chopin Nocturnes through The Nine Symphonies—separated by commas, and convert it into a table. (*Hint:* Click Table on the menu bar, point to Convert, and then click Text to Table. In the dialog box, select Commas as the Separate text at option. Make sure the Number of columns is set to 5.)

Explore

3. Insert an additional row for headings by selecting the top row of the table, and then clicking the Insert Rows button in the Standard toolbar.

4. Type the following headings (in a sans serif boldface font) in this order: "Title," "Artist," "Label," "Number of CDs in Set," and "Price."

5. Insert a row below "The Best of Chopin," and then type the following in the cells: "Beethoven Piano Sonatas," "Alfred Brendel," "Vox," "2," "18.95."

6. Open the Tables and Borders toolbar if necessary, and then sort the rows in the table in ascending alphabetical order by title.

7. Center the numbers in the "Number of CDs in Set" column.

Explore

8. Split cells to allow for two columns of pricing information. Select the cells containing prices (cells E2 through E10), and then click the Split Cells button on the Tables and Borders toolbar. In the Split Cells dialog box, deselect the "Merge cells before split" check box. (If you keep this option selected, Word moves all the prices into one cell before splitting each of the cells into two.) Verify that the Number of columns setting is 2, so that Word will divide each cell into two cells (or columns). Click OK.

Explore

9. Click the Line Weight list arrow on the Tables and Borders toolbar, click 1½ pt, and then use the Draw Table pointer to draw a horizontal line in cell E1 directly below the word "Price." Next, use the Split Cells button again to divide the new, empty cell below the "Price" cell into two. In the new, empty cell on the left (directly above the column of prices), type "CD Club Members." In the new, blank cell on the right (directly above the blank column), type "Non-Members." For each title, enter a Non-Members' price that is $1.00 more than the CD Club Members price.

10. Adjust column widths as necessary.

11. Add 2¼-point horizontal borders to make the table easier to read.

12. Save your document; then preview, print, and close it.

*Case 4. **Computer Training at Pottery Row, Inc.*** Joseph Keats is the director of the Human Resources department at Pottery Row, Inc., a mail-order firm specializing in home furnishings. He has contracted with Bright Star Learning systems for a series of in-house training seminars on intermediate and advanced word processing skills. He asks you to create an informational flier for posting on bulletin boards around the office. Among other things, the flier should include Bright Star Learning Systems' corporate logo (an orange, five-pointed star). You begin by drawing a sketch, similar to the one shown in Figure 3-34. You decide to take advantage of the Word table features to structure the information in the flier.

Figure 3-34   **SKETCH FOR BRIGHT STAR FLIER**

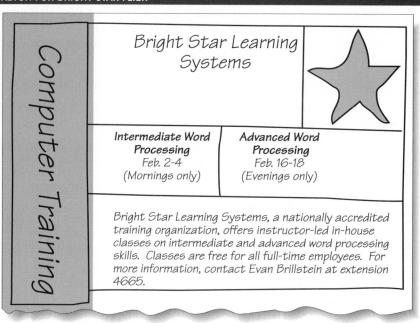

1. Open a new, blank document and save it as **Bright Star Training** in the Cases folder for Tutorial 3.

2. If necessary, switch to print layout view and display the Tables and Borders toolbar.

Explore

3. Click the Draw Table button on the Tables and Borders toolbar, if necessary, to select the button and change the pointer to a pencil shape. Click in the upper-left corner of the document (near the paragraph mark), and drag down and to the right to draw a rectangle about 6 inches wide and 3.5 inches high.

Explore

4. Continue to use the Draw Table pointer to draw the columns and rows shown in Figure 3-34. For example, to draw the column border for the "Computer Training" column, click at the top of the rectangle, where you want the column to begin, and drag down to the bottom of the rectangle. Use the same technique to draw rows. If you make a mistake, use the Undo button. To delete a border, click the Eraser button in the Tables and Borders toolbar, click the border you want to erase, and then click the Eraser button again to turn it off. Keep in mind that you can also merge cells, if necessary. Don't expect to draw the table perfectly the first time. You may have to practice a while until you become comfortable with the Draw Table pointer, but once you can use it well, you will find it a helpful tool for creating complex tables.

5. In the left column, type the text "Computer Training," rotate the text to position it vertically in the table, and format the text in 26-point Times New Roman, so that it fills the height of the column. If the text does not fit in one row, drag the table border down until it does. (*Hint:* You will probably have to adjust and readjust the row and column borders throughout this project, until all the elements of the table are positioned properly.)

6. Type the remaining text, as shown in Figure 3-34. Replace the name "Evan Brillstein" with your own name. Use bold and italic as necessary to draw attention to key elements. Use the font styles, font sizes, and alignment options you think appropriate.

Explore

7. Click the Drawing button on the Standard toolbar to display the Drawing toolbar. Now you can insert the Bright Star corporate logo in the upper-right cell, using one of the tools on the Drawing toolbar. Click the AutoShapes button on the Drawing toolbar, point to Stars and Banners, and then click the 5-Point Star. Move the cross-hair pointer over the upper-right cell, then click and drag to draw a star that fits roughly within the cell borders. After you draw the star, it remains selected, as indicated by the square boxes, called selection handles, that surround it. Click the lower-right selection handle, and drag up or down to adjust the size of the star so that it fits within the cell borders more precisely. With the star still selected, click the Fill Color list arrow on the Drawing toolbar, and then click a gold color in the color palette.

8. Use the Shading Color button on the Tables and Borders toolbar to add the same color background to the "Computer Training" column.

9. Adjust column widths and row heights so that the table is attractive and easy-to-read.

Explore

10. Now that you have organized the information using the Word table tools, you can remove the borders so that the printed flier doesn't look like a table. Click the Table move handle to select the entire table, click Table on the menu bar, click Table Properties, click the Table tab, click the Borders and Shading button, and then click the Borders tab, click the None option, click the OK button, and then click the OK button again. The borders are removed from the flier, leaving only the underlying gridlines, which will not appear on the printed page.

11. Save your work, preview the flier, make any necessary adjustments, print it, and then close the document.

INTERNET ASSIGNMENTS

The purpose of the Internet Assignments is to challenge you to find information on the Internet that you can use to create effective documents. The actual assignments are updated and maintained on the Course Technology Web site. Log on to the Internet and use your Web browser to go to the Student Online Companion to accompany this text at **www.course.com/NewPerspectives/office2000**. Click the Word link, and then click the link for Tutorial 3.

QUICK CHECK ANSWERS

Session 3.1

1. **a.** The location where text moves when you press the Tab key.

   b. The intersection of a row and a column in a table.

   c. Information arranged in horizontal rows and vertical columns.

   d. A tab stop that aligns numerical data on the decimal point.

   e. A unit or part of a document that can have its own page orientation, margins, headers, footers, and vertical alignment.

2. Insert a section break, move the insertion point within the section you want to align, click File, click Page Setup, click the Layout tab, select Center in the Vertical alignment list box, make sure This section is selected in the Apply to list box, and then click OK.

3. A header appears at the top of a page, whereas a footer appears at the bottom of a page.

4. Move the insertion point to the location where you want the table to appear. Click the Insert Table button on the Standard toolbar. In the grid, click and drag to select four columns and six rows, and then release the mouse button

5. If the insertion point is in the rightmost cell in a row, press the Tab key. Otherwise, press the ↓ key.

6. Click View on the menu bar, click Header and Footer, verify that the insertion point is located in the Header area, press Tab to move the insertion point to where you want the page number to appear, and then click the Insert Page Number button on the Header and Footer toolbar.

7. Select the text whose tab alignment you want to change, click the tab alignment selector on the far left of the horizontal ruler until the appropriate tab stop alignment style appears, and then click in the horizontal ruler where you want to set the new tab stop.

8. You might want to divide a document into sections if you wanted to center part of the document between the top and bottom margins.

9. It's better to use a table rather than tab stops when you need to organize a lot of complicated information.

10. Click the Table move handle.

Session 3.2

1. Drag the right border of each column to a new position.

2. Right-aligning numbers in a table makes the numbers easier to read.

3. a. Combine two or more cells into one.

   b. Move text in a cell so that it is formatted vertically rather than horizontally.

   c. The outline of a row, cell, column, or table.

   d. A gray or colored background used to highlight parts of a table.

4. Click the rightmost cell in the bottom row of the table, and then press the Tab key.

5. Click the cell where you want the total to appear, click the AutoSum button on the Tables and Borders toolbar, click the total to select it, click Table on the menu bar, click Formula, select the number format you want, and then click OK.

6. 10, 25, 45, 75

7. Click anywhere in the table, click Table on the menu bar, click Table Properties, click the Table tab, click Center, and then click OK.

In this tutorial you will:

- Identify desktop-publishing features

- Create a title with WordArt

- Create newspaper-style columns

- Insert clip art

- Wrap text around a graphic

- Incorporate drop caps

- Use symbols and special typographic characters

- Add a page border

DESKTOP PUBLISHING A NEWSLETTER

Creating a Newsletter for FastFad Manufacturing Company

CASE

FastFad Manufacturing Company

Gerrit Polansky works for FastFad Manufacturing Company, which designs and manufactures plastic figures (action figures, vehicles, and other toys) for promotional sales and giveaways in the fast-food and cereal industries. Gerrit keeps FastFad's sales staff informed about new products by producing and distributing a monthly newsletter that briefly describes these new items and gives ideas for marketing them. Recently, FastFad added MiniMovers—small plastic cars, trucks, and other vehicles—to its line of plastic toys. Gerrit needs to get the information about these products to the sales staff quickly so that the company can market the toys to FastFad's clients while the toys are still popular. He has asked you to help him create the newsletter.

The newsletter must be eye-catching because the quantity of printed product material sales reps get makes it difficult for them to focus on any one product. Gerrit also wants you to create a newsletter that is neat, organized, and professional-looking. He would like it to contain headings (so the sales reps can scan it quickly for the major points) as well as graphics that will give the newsletter a memorable "look." He wants you to include a picture that will reinforce the newsletter content and distinguish the product.

In this tutorial, you'll plan the layout of the newsletter, keeping in mind the audience (the sales representatives). Then you'll get acquainted with the desktop-publishing features and elements you'll need to use to create the newsletter. Also, you'll learn how desktop publishing differs from other word-processing tasks. You'll format the title using an eye-catching design and divide the document into newspaper-style columns to make it easier for the sales reps to read. To add interest and focus to the text, you'll include a piece of pre-designed art. You'll then fine-tune the newsletter layout, give it a more professional appearance with typographic characters, and put a border around the page to give the newsletter a finished look.

In this session you will see how Gerrit planned his newsletter and learn about desktop-publishing features and elements. Then you will create the newsletter title using WordArt, modify the title's appearance, and format the text of the newsletter into newspaper-style columns.

Planning the Document

The newsletter will provide a brief overview of the new FastFad products, followed by a short explanation of what the MiniMovers are and why children will like them. Like most newsletters, it will be written in an informal style that conveys information quickly. The newsletter title will be eye-catching and will help readers quickly identify the document. Newsletter text will be split into two columns to make it easier to read, and headings will help readers scan the information quickly. A picture will add interest and illustrate the newsletter content. Drop caps and other desktop-publishing elements will help draw readers' attention to certain information and make the newsletter design attractive and professional.

Elements of Desktop Publishing

Desktop publishing is the production of commercial-quality printed material using a desktop computer system from which you can enter and edit text, create graphics, compose or lay out pages, and print documents. The following elements are commonly associated with desktop publishing:

- **High-quality printing**. A laser printer or high-resolution inkjet printer produces final output.
- **Multiple fonts.** Two or three font types and sizes provide visual interest, guide the reader through the text, and convey the tone of the document.
- **Graphics.** Graphics, such as horizontal or vertical lines (called **rules**), boxes, electronic art, and digitized photographs help illustrate a concept or product, draw a reader's attention to the document, and make the text visually appealing.
- **Typographic characters**. Typographic characters such as typographic long dashes, called **em dashes** (—), in place of double hyphens (--), separate dependent clauses; typographic medium-width dashes, called en dashes (–), are used in place of hyphens (-) as minus signs and in ranges of numbers; and typographic bullets (•) signal items in a list.
- **Columns and other formatting features.** Columns of text, **pull quotes** (small portions of text pulled out of the main text and enlarged), page borders, and other special formatting features that you don't frequently see in letters and other documents distinguish desktop-published documents.

You'll incorporate many of these desktop-publishing elements into the FastFad newsletter for Gerrit.

Word's Desktop-Publishing Features

Successful desktop publishing requires that you first know what elements professionals use to desktop publish a document. Figure 4-1 defines some of the desktop-publishing features included in Word. Gerrit wants you to use these features to produce the final newsletter shown in Figure 4-2. The newsletter includes some of the typical desktop-publishing elements that you can add to a document using Word.

Figure 4-1	WORD DESKTOP PUBLISHING FEATURES
ELEMENT	**DESCRIPTION**
Columns	Two or more vertical blocks of text that fit on one page
WordArt	Text modified with special effects, such as rotated, curved, bent, shadowed, or shaded letters
Clip art	Prepared graphic images that are ready to be inserted into a document
Drop cap	Oversized first letter of word beginning a paragraph that extends vertically into two or more lines of the paragraph
Typographical symbols	Special characters that are not part of the standard keyboard, such as em dashes (—), copyright symbols (©), or curly quotation marks (")

Figure 4-2	FASTFAD NEWSLETTER

Announcing FastFad's New Line of Plastic Toys

Remember GI Joe and the Power Rangers? They've come and gone. And Transformers and Match Box cars? They're a thing of the past. But the next craze sure to sweep the country is MiniMovers®.

What Are MiniMovers?

MiniMovers are bright, colorful plastic models with parts that move. With just a push, these pint-size vehicles scoot across the floor; the wheels spin, the propellers turn, and the horns honk. MiniMovers are perfectly sized for pretend play, and they're stylish too.

Why Will Kids Love Them?

These child-size models encourage imaginativeness and play. Made of nearly indestructible plastic, MiniMovers help kids get serious about having fun! We used real experts, kids, as our official toy testers. And based on their play-packed screening, these toys will be the hot new items this year.

Mini Size, Mighty Fun!

MiniMovers let kids visit great places without ever leaving home.

Here's the rundown on our figures:

- Farm set—kids will love the horns on the truck, tractor, and old jalopy.
- Recreation set—ride in style with the beach patrol jeep, dune buggy, and three-wheeler.
- Transportation set—the propellers actually turn on our helicopter, plane, and boat.

After the kids have a full set, they can order our CargoCarrier™, a truck with a detachable trailer, which can carry two MiniMovers inside and one on top.

Just Right for Fun Packs

Our new line of MiniMovers are just right for putting in fun packs for kids ages 4 to 10 years.

MiniMovers are safe and tons of fun. They're perfect for the "Happy Meal" generation.

Your first step is to create the newsletter's title.

Using WordArt to Create the Newsletter Title

Gerrit wants the title of the newsletter, "FastFad Update," to be eye-catching and dramatic, as shown in Figure 4-2. **WordArt**, available in Word as well as other Microsoft Office programs, provides great flexibility in designing text with special effects that expresses the image or mood you want to convey in your printed documents. With WordArt, you can apply color and shading, as well as alter the shape and size of the text. You can easily "wrap" the document text around WordArt shapes.

You begin creating a WordArt image by choosing a text design. Then you type in the text you want to enhance and format it.

When you create a WordArt image, Word switches to print layout view because WordArt images are not visible in normal view. Print layout view is the most appropriate view to use when you are desktop publishing with Word because it shows you exactly how the text and graphics fit on the page. The vertical ruler that appears in print layout view helps you position graphical elements more precisely.

REFERENCE WINDOW   RW

Creating Special Text Effects Using WordArt
- Click the Drawing button on the Standard toolbar to display the Drawing toolbar.
- Click the Insert WordArt button on the Drawing toolbar.
- Click the style of text you want to insert, and then click the OK button.
- Type the text you want in the Edit WordArt Text dialog box.
- Click the Font and Size list arrows to select the font and font size you want.
- If you want, click the Bold or Italic button, or both.
- Click the OK button.
- With the WordArt selected, drag any handle to reshape and resize it. To keep the text in the same proportions as the original, press and hold down the Shift key while you drag a handle.

To begin, you'll open the file that contains the unformatted text of the newsletter, often called **copy**, and then you'll use WordArt to create the newsletter title.

To create the title of the newsletter using WordArt:

1. Start Word and insert your Data Disk in the appropriate drive. Make sure your screen matches the figures in this tutorial, and display the nonprinting characters so you can see more accurately where to insert text and graphics.

2. Open the file **MiniInfo** from the Tutorial folder for Tutorial 4 on your Data Disk, and then save it as **FastFad Newsletter** in the same folder.

3. With the insertion point at the beginning of the document, click the **Drawing** button 🔲 on the Standard toolbar to display the Drawing toolbar, which appears at the bottom of the screen, if it is not already displayed.

TROUBLE? If the Drawing toolbar is not positioned at the bottom of the document window, drag it there by its title bar. If you do not see the Drawing toolbar anywhere, right-click the Standard toolbar, and then click Drawing on the shortcut menu.

4. Click the **Insert WordArt** button 🔳 on the Drawing toolbar. The WordArt Gallery dialog box opens, displaying the 30 WordArt styles available.

5. Click the WordArt style in the bottom row, the fourth column from the left, as shown in Figure 4-3.

Figure 4-3	WORDART GALLERY STYLES

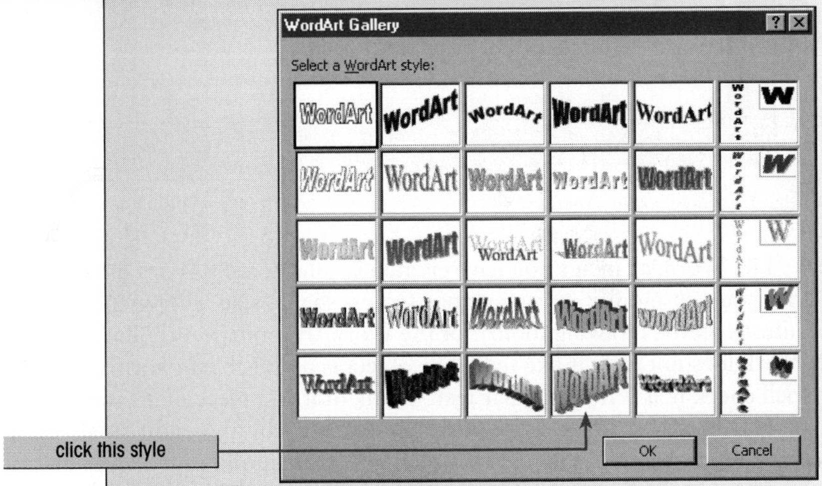

click this style

6. Click the **OK** button. The Edit WordArt Text dialog box opens, displaying the default text "Your Text Here," which you will replace with the newsletter title.

7. Type **FastFad Update**. Make sure you make "FastFad" one word with no space.

8. Click the **OK** button.

The WordArt image appears over the existing text at the top of the newsletter, the WordArt toolbar appears on the screen, and the document changes to print lay-out view. See Figure 4-4. Don't be concerned that the image partially covers the newsletter text or if it's below the first paragraph. You'll fix that later. Note that the position of the WordArt object relative to the text is indicated by a small anchor symbol in the left margin. If you want to add text before the WordArt object, you need to type the text before the anchor symbol. If you want to add a section break to the document after the WordArt, you need to insert a section break after the anchor symbol.

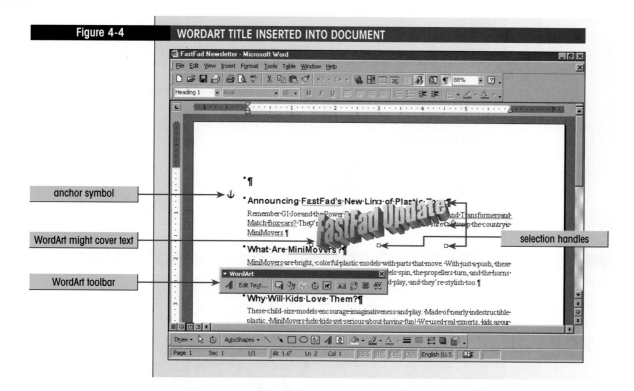

Figure 4-4 **WORDART TITLE INSERTED INTO DOCUMENT**

The WordArt image you have created is considered a Word drawing **object**. This means that you can modify its appearance (color, shape, size, alignment, and so forth) using the buttons on the Drawing toolbar or the WordArt toolbar. Although the object looks like text, Word does not treat it like text. The object is not visible in normal view, and Word will not spell check it as it does regular text. Think of it as a piece of art rather than as text.

The WordArt object is selected, as indicated by the eight small squares, called **resize handles,** surrounding it, and the small yellow diamond called an **adjustment handle**. The resize and adjustment handles let you change the size and shape of the selected object. Before you change the size of the object, you'll first alter its font size and formatting. The default font for this WordArt style is Impact (a sans serif font), but Gerrit wants you to change it to Times New Roman (a serif font) to provide contrast to the sans serif headings in the newsletter.

To change the font and formatting of the WordArt object:

1. Verify that the WordArt object is selected, as indicated by the selection handles.

2. Click the **Edit Text** button on the WordArt toolbar. The Edit WordArt Text dialog box opens.

3. Click the **Font** list arrow, scroll to and then click **Times New Roman**. The text in the preview box changes to Times New Roman.

   TROUBLE? If you do not have Times New Roman available, choose another serif font.

4. Click the **Size** list arrow, scroll to and then click **40**, click the **Bold** button B , and then click the **Italic** button I . The text in the preview box enlarges to 40-point bold, italic.

5. Click the **OK** button. The newsletter title changes to 40-point, bold, italic Times New Roman.

The default shape of the WordArt style you selected is an upward-slanting shape called Cascade Up. Gerrit wants something a little more symmetrical. In WordArt, you can change the object to any of the WordArt shapes.

To change the shape of the WordArt object:

1. Click the **WordArt Shape** button Abc on the WordArt toolbar. The palette of shapes appears, with the Cascade Up shape selected.

2. Click the **Deflate** shape (fourth row down, second column from the left), as shown in Figure 4-5.

| Figure 4-5 | WORDART SHAPES |

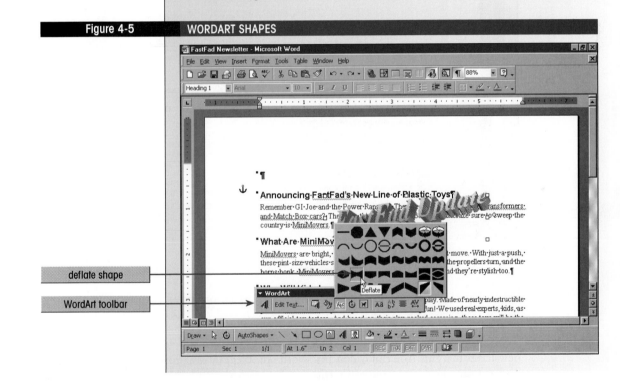

deflate shape

WordArt toolbar

The newsletter title changes to the new WordArt shape.

Editing a WordArt Object

Now that the newsletter title is the font and shape you want, you'll move the title to the top of the newsletter and wrap the newsletter text below the WordArt object. **Text wrapping** is often used in newsletters to prevent text and graphic objects from overlapping, to add interest, and to prevent excessive open areas, called **white space**, from appearing on the page. You can wrap text around objects many different ways in Word. For example, you can have the text wrap above and below the object, through it, or wrap the text to follow the shape of the object, even if the graphic has an irregular shape. The Text Wrapping button on the WordArt or Picture toolbar provides some basic choices, whereas the Layout tab of the Format Picture dialog box provides more advanced options. Because you want a simple wrap, you'll use the Text Wrapping button on the WordArt toolbar.

To insert space between the WordArt object and the newsletter text:

1. With the WordArt object selected, click the **Text Wrapping** button 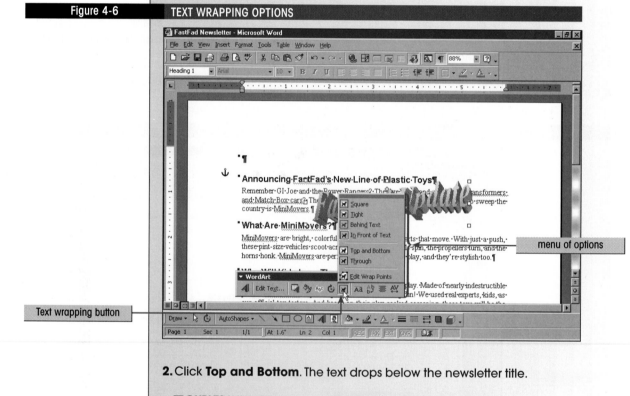 on the WordArt toolbar. A menu of text-wrapping options opens. See Figure 4-6.

Figure 4-6   **TEXT WRAPPING OPTIONS**

Text wrapping button

menu of options

2. Click **Top and Bottom**. The text drops below the newsletter title.

   TROUBLE? If the title is not above the text, drag it there now.

Next, you'll position the title and widen it proportionally so it fits neatly within the newsletter margins. You can widen any WordArt object by dragging one of its resize handles. To keep the object the same proportion as the original, you hold down the Shift key as you drag the resize handle. This prevents "stretching" the object more in one direction than the other. After you stretch the WordArt, you'll rotate it slightly so it looks more balanced. Then you'll check the position of its anchor to make sure it is located in a separate paragraph from the text of the newsletter.

To position, enlarge, and rotate the WordArt object:

1. Drag the WordArt object to the left until the lower-left corner of the first "F" in the word "FastFad" is aligned with the left margin and then release the mouse button. Because you can see only the text outline (not the text itself) as you drag the object, you might need to repeat the procedure. Use the left edge of the text or the left margin in the ruler as a guide.

2. With the WordArt object still selected, position the pointer over its lower-right resize handle. The pointer changes to ↖.

3. Press and hold the **Shift** key while you drag the resize handle to the right margin, using the horizontal ruler as a guide. See Figure 4-7. As you drag the handle, the pointer changes to ┼. If necessary, repeat the procedure to make the rightmost edge of the "e" in the word "Update" line up with the right margin. Note that in the process of resizing, the anchor symbol might have moved. You'll fix that later. Now, you'll lower the right side of the WordArt object.

Figure 4-7	RESIZING THE WORDART OBJECT

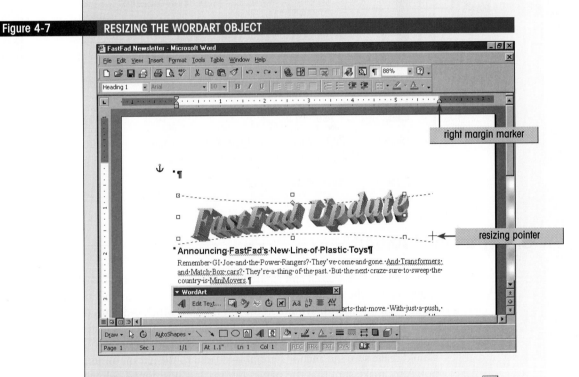

4. With the WordArt object still selected, click the **Free Rotate** button ⟳ on the WordArt toolbar. Round, green rotation handles surround the object.

5. Move the pointer anywhere on the document except over the WordArt text. The pointer changes to ⟳.

6. Position the pointer over the green circle on the lower-right corner of the object, and then drag the rotation handle clockwise about a half inch, or until the title text appears to be horizontal. See Figure 4-8.

Figure 4-8 | ROTATING THE WORDART OBJECT

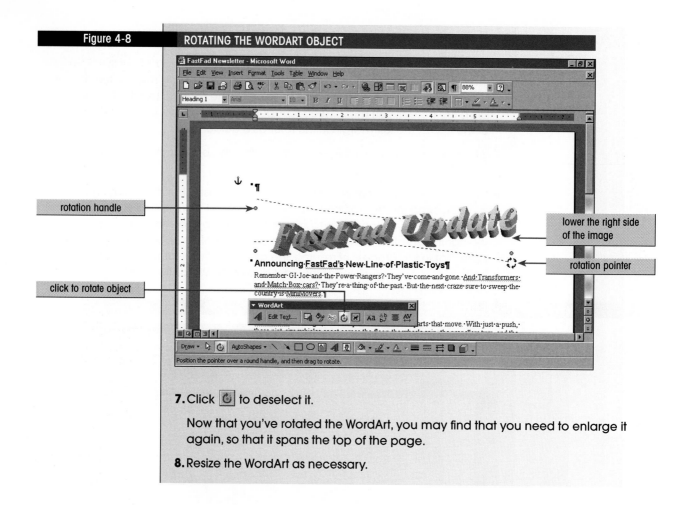

rotation handle

lower the right side
of the image

rotation pointer

click to rotate object

7. Click 🔄 to deselect it.

Now that you've rotated the WordArt, you may find that you need to enlarge it again, so that it spans the top of the page.

8. Resize the WordArt as necessary.

Anchoring the WordArt

Now that you have sized and rotated the WordArt, you need to make sure it is properly positioned within the document as a whole—a process known as anchoring. The process draws its name from the **anchor** symbol in the left margin, which indicates the position of the WordArt relative to the text. To ensure that changes to the text (such as section breaks) do not affect the WordArt, you need to anchor the WordArt to a blank paragraph before the text. That is, you should make sure the anchor symbol is located to the left of, or just above, the paragraph symbol. Also, make sure that the paragraph mark is positioned below the WordArt image on the screen. Depending on exactly how you sized and rotated your WordArt, the anchor and paragraph symbols may or may not be in the proper position now. For instance, in Figure 4-8, the anchor is located just above the paragraph symbol, just as it should be. However, the paragraph symbol itself is located above the WordArt rather than below. It's up to you to decide if your WordArt is anchored properly.

To anchor the FastFad WordArt:

1. Drag the WordArt image up or down as necessary, until the anchor symbol and the paragraph symbol are positioned similarly to Figure 4-9.

Figure 4-9   PROPERLY ANCHORED WORDART

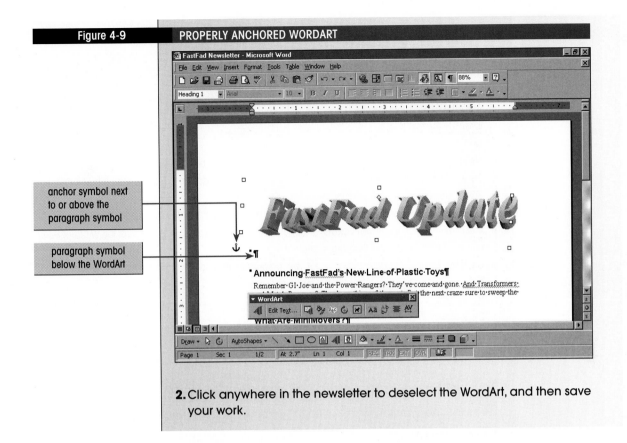

anchor symbol next to or above the paragraph symbol

paragraph symbol below the WordArt

2. Click anywhere in the newsletter to deselect the WordArt, and then save your work.

Your WordArt is now finished. The formatted WordArt title will draw the sales reps' attention to the newsletter as they review this document.

Formatting Text into Newspaper-Style Columns

Because newsletters are meant for quick reading, they usually are laid out in newspaper-style columns. In **newspaper-style columns**, a page is divided into two or more vertical blocks, or columns. Text flows down one column, continues at the top of the next column, flows down that column, and so forth. Newspaper-style columns are easier to read because the columns tend to be narrow and the type size is a bit smaller than the text in a letter. This enables the eye to see more text in one glance than when text is set in longer line lengths and in a larger font size.

If you want some of your text to be in columns and other text to be in full line lengths, you must insert section breaks into your document and apply the column format only to those sections you want in columns. You could select the text and use the Columns button on the Standard toolbar to automatically insert the needed section breaks and divide the text into columns. But because Gerrit wants you to divide the text below the title into two columns and add a vertical line between them, you'll use the Columns command on the Format menu. This lets you do both actions and insert a section break in the location you specify. Without the section break, the line between the columns would extend up through the title.

REFERENCE WINDOW **RW**

Formatting Text Into Newspaper-Style Columns

- Select the text you want to divide into columns, or don't select any text if you want the entire document divided into columns.
- Click the Columns button on the Standard toolbar, and highlight the number of columns you want to divide the text into.

  or

- Move the insertion point to the location where you want the columns to begin.
- Click Format on the menu bar, and then click Columns to open the Columns dialog box.
- Select the column style you want in the Presets section.
- Deselect the Line between check box if you do *not* want a vertical line between columns.
- If necessary, click the Equal column width check box to deselect it, and then set the width of each column in the Width and spacing section.
- Click the Apply to list arrow, and select This point forward if you want Word to insert a section break. Otherwise, select the Whole document option.
- If you want a vertical rule between the columns, click the Line between check box and click the OK button.

To apply newspaper-style columns to the body of the newsletter:

1. Position the insertion point to the left of the word "Announcing" just below the title.

2. Click **Format** on the menu bar, and then click **Columns**. The Columns dialog box opens.

3. In the Presets section, click the **Two** icon.

4. If necessary, click the **Line between** check box to select it. The text in the Preview box changes to a two-column format with a vertical rule between the columns.

   You want these changes to affect only the text after the title, so you'll need to insert a section break and apply the column formatting to the text after the insertion point.

5. Click the **Apply to** list arrow, and then click **This point forward** to have Word automatically insert a section break at the insertion point. See Figure 4-10.

| Figure 4-10 | COMPLETED COLUMNS DIALOG BOX |

creates two columns of the same width

places a line between columns

shows how columns will look with current settings

adds section break at insertion point

6. Click the **OK** button to return to the document window. A section break appears, and the insertion point is now positioned in section 2. The text in section 2 is formatted in two columns.

TROUBLE? If the WordArt moves below the section break, drag it above the section break, and then click anywhere in the newsletter text to deselect the WordArt object.

Viewing the Whole Page

As you create a desktop-published document, you should periodically look at the whole page to get a sense of the overall layout. You can view the page in Print Preview as you've done before, or you can use the Zoom list arrow on the Standard toolbar to enlarge or reduce the percentage of the page you see onscreen.

To zoom out and view the whole page:

1. Click the **Zoom** list arrow on the Standard toolbar, and then click **Whole Page**. Word displays the entire page of the newsletter so you can see how the two-column format looks on the page. See Figure 4-11.

| Figure 4-11 | WHOLE PAGE VIEW SHOWING THE TWO COLUMNS |

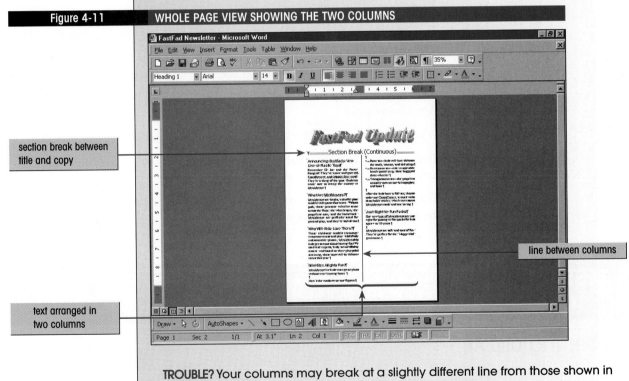

section break between title and copy

line between columns

text arranged in two columns

TROUBLE? Your columns may break at a slightly different line from those shown in the figure. This is not a problem; just continue with the tutorial.

The newsletter title is centered on the page, and the copy is in a two-column format. The text fills the left column but not the right column. You'll fix this later, after you add a graphic and format some of the text.

2. Click the **Zoom** list arrow again, and then click **Page Width**. Now you can read the text again. Finally, you should save the document with a new name.

3. Save the document as **FastFad Newsletter Copy 2** in the Tutorial folder for Tutorial 4.

You have set up an eye-catching title for the FastFad newsletter and formatted the text in newspaper-style columns to make it easier to read. Next, you will insert a graphic that illustrates the newsletter content. After you add clip art, you'll add more graphic interest by formatting some of the text. Then you'll finish the newsletter by making the columns equal in length and adding a border to the page.

Session 4.1 QUICK CHECK

1. Describe four elements commonly associated with desktop publishing.

2. In your own words, define the following terms:
   a. desktop publishing
   b. drawing object
   c. copy
   d. anchor

3. True or False: When using Word's desktop-publishing features, you should display your document in normal view.

4. True or False: Word treats WordArt the same way as any other document text.

5. How do you change the size of a WordArt object after you have inserted it into a Word document?

6. What is the purpose of the WordArt Shape button on the WordArt toolbar?

7. True or False: To format part of a document in newspaper-style columns, you need to insert a section break.

8. True or False: When you first format a document into newspaper-style columns, the columns will not necessarily be of equal length.

SESSION 4.2

In this session you will insert, resize, and crop clip art, and change the way the text wraps around the clip art. Then you'll create drop caps, insert typographic symbols, balance columns, place a border around the newsletter, and print the newsletter.

Inserting Clip Art

Graphics, which can include artwork, photographs, charts, tables, designs, or even designed text such as WordArt, add variety to documents and are especially appropriate for newsletters. Word allows you to draw pictures in your document, using the buttons on the Drawing toolbar. To produce professional-looking graphics, though, it's best to use one of two methods. In the first method, you begin by drawing a picture in a special graphics program or by scanning an existing image, such as a photograph. You can then save the graphic (often in a picture format known as a bitmapped graphic) and insert it into your document using the Picture command on the Insert menu. (You will have a chance to practice adding a bitmapped graphic to a document in Case Projects at the end of this tutorial.)

In the second method, you simply choose from a collection of pre-made, copyright-free images included along with Word. To add visual appeal to the FastFad newsletter, you will insert a piece of clip art now. Gerrit wants you to use a graphic that reflects the newsletter content.

REFERENCE WINDOW **RW**

Working With Clip Art
- Move the insertion point to the location in your document where you want the graphic image to appear.
- Click the Insert Clip Art button on the Drawing toolbar, or click Insert on the menu bar, point to Picture, and then click Clip Art to open the Insert ClipArt window.
- If necessary, click the Pictures tab.
- Click the category that best represents the type of art you need.
- Click the image you want to use.
- Click the Insert Clip icon.
- If you plan to use a particular clip art regularly, click the Add to Favorites or other category icon, verify that Favorites is selected in the list box, and then click OK. Click the Add to Favorites or other category icon again to hide the list box.
- To search for a particular image, type a description of the image you want in the Search for clips text box, and then press the Enter key.
- To re-display all the categories of clip art, click the All Categories button in the toolbar at the top of the Insert ClipArt window.
- To delete a graphic from a document, select it, and then press the Delete key.

To insert the clip-art image of an airplane into the newsletter:

1. If you took a break after the last session, make sure Word is running, the FastFad Newsletter is open, the document is in print layout view, and the nonprinting characters are displayed. Verify that the Drawing toolbar is displayed also.

2. Position the insertion point to the left of the word "MiniMovers" in the second paragraph of the newsletter just below the heading "What are MiniMovers?"

3. Click the **Insert Clip Art** button 🖾 on the Drawing toolbar. The Insert ClipArt window opens.

4. If necessary, click the **Pictures** tab.

5. Click the **All Categories** 🔲 button to make sure all the clip art categories are displayed.

6. Scroll down and click the Transportation category. The Pictures tab now displays a variety of transportation-related images.

TROUBLE? If you click the wrong category by mistake, click the All Categories button at the top of the Insert ClipArt window to redisplay all categories, and then click the Transportation category.

7. Scroll down, and click the airplane image. A menu of options opens, as shown in Figure 4-12.

Figure 4-12   **PICTURES TAB OF THE INSERT CLIPART WINDOW**

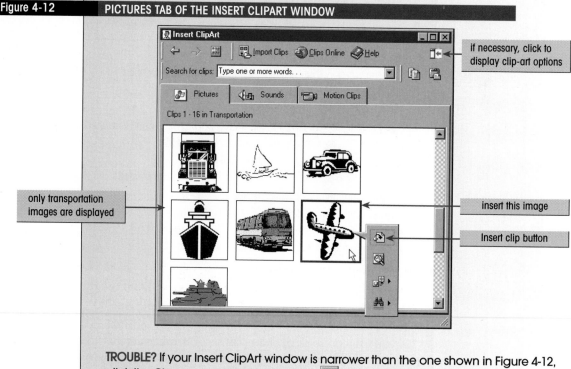

if necessary, click to display clip-art options

only transportation images are displayed

insert this image

Insert clip button

TROUBLE? If your Insert ClipArt window is narrower than the one shown in Figure 4-12, click the Change to Full Window button 🔲 at the top of the Insert ClipArt window, and then repeat Step 7.

8. Click the **Insert clip** button 🖻 to insert the airplane in the newsletter at the insertion point.

9. Click the **Close** button ❌ to close the Insert ClipArt window.

10. Save the document. The airplane clip art fills the left column. The text below the heading moves down to make room for the image.

11. Click the airplane image to select it. Like the WordArt object you worked with earlier, the clip-art image is a graphic object with resize handles that you can use to change its size. The Picture toolbar appears whenever the clip-art object is selected. See Figure 4-13.

Figure 4-13 **THE NEWSLETTER WITH THE CLIP ART OBJECT INSERTED**

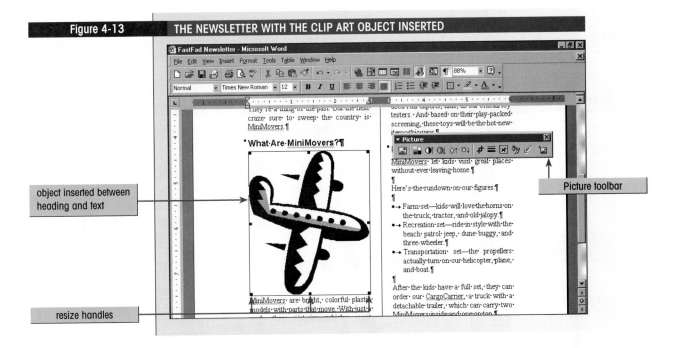

object inserted between heading and text

resize handles

Picture toolbar

Gerrit would like the image to be smaller so it doesn't distract attention from the text.

Resizing a Graphic

Often, you need to change the size of a graphic so that it fits into your document better. This is called **scaling** the image. You can resize a graphic by either dragging its resize handles or, for more precise control, by using the Format Picture dialog box.

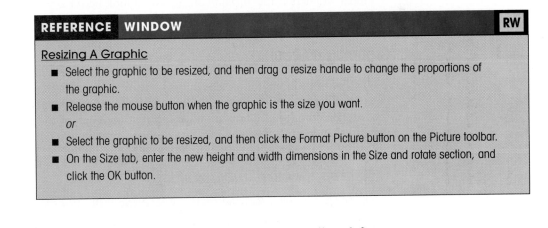

REFERENCE   WINDOW   **RW**

Resizing A Graphic
- Select the graphic to be resized, and then drag a resize handle to change the proportions of the graphic.
- Release the mouse button when the graphic is the size you want.
  or
- Select the graphic to be resized, and then click the Format Picture button on the Picture toolbar.
- On the Size tab, enter the new height and width dimensions in the Size and rotate section, and click the OK button.

For Gerrit's newsletter, the dragging technique will work fine.

To resize the clip-art graphic:

1. Make sure the clip-art graphic is selected, and scroll down so you can see the lower-right resize handle of the object.

2. Drag the lower-right resize handle up and to the left until the dotted outline forms a rectangle about 1.5 inches wide by 1.75 inches high. (Note that you don't have to hold down the Shift key, as you do with WordArt, to resize the picture proportionally.) See Figure 4-14.

| Figure 4-14 | RESIZING THE AIRPLANE GRAPHIC |

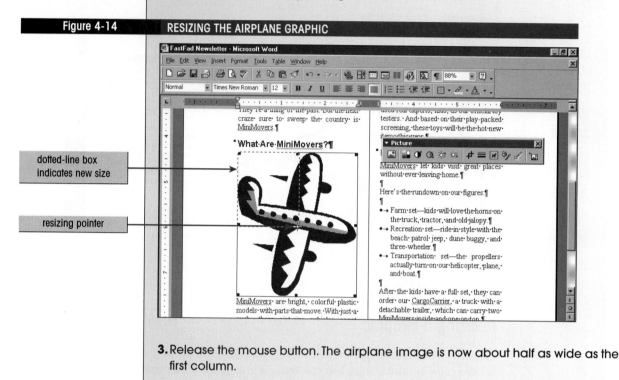

dotted-line box indicates new size

resizing pointer

3. Release the mouse button. The airplane image is now about half as wide as the first column.

Gerrit wonders if the airplane image would look better if you cut off the back end and showed only the front half.

Cropping a Graphic

You can **crop** the graphic—that is, cut off one or more of its edges—using either the Crop button on the Picture toolbar or the Format Picture dialog box. Once you crop a graphic, the part you cropped is hidden from view. It remains a part of the graphic image, though, so you can change your mind and restore a cropped graphic to its original form.

To crop the airplane graphic:

1. If necessary, click the clip art to select it. The resize handles appear.

2. Click the **Crop** button ⊞ on the Picture toolbar.

3. Position the pointer directly over the middle resize handle on the left side of the picture. The pointer changes to ⤢.

4. Press and hold down the mouse button, and drag the handle to the right so that only the wings and the nose of the plane are visible. See Figure 4-15.

| Figure 4-15 | CROPPING THE AIRPLANE GRAPHIC |

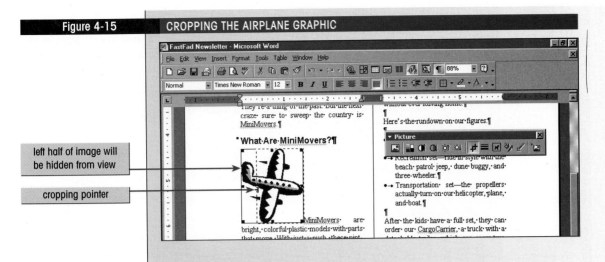

left half of image will be hidden from view

cropping pointer

5. Release the mouse button.

Gerrit decides he prefers to display the whole airplane, so he asks you to return to the original image.

6. Click the **Undo** button on the Standard toolbar. The cropping action is reversed, and the full image of the airplane reappears.

Now Gerrit wants you to make the text to wrap to the right of the graphic, making the airplane look as if it's flying into the text.

Wrapping Text Around a Graphic

For the airplane to look as though it flies into the newsletter text, you need to make the text wrap around the image. Earlier, you used text wrapping to position the WordArt title above the columns of text. Now you'll try a more advanced text-wrapping option to make the text follow the shape of the plane. You'll use the Format Picture dialog box to do this because it gives you more control over how the text flows around the picture.

To wrap text around the airplane graphic:

1. Verify that the airplane graphic is selected.

2. Click the **Format Picture** button on the Picture toolbar. The Format Picture dialog box opens.

3. Click the **Layout** tab. This tab contains a number of text-wrapping options, but to fine-tune the way text flows around the graphic, you need a more advanced set of options. You want the text to flow around the graphic, but only on the right side of the plane.

4. Click the **Advanced** button. The Advanced Layout dialog box opens.

5. Click the **Text Wrapping** tab, if necessary.

6. In the Wrapping style section, click the **Tight** icon, the second icon from the left.

7. In the Wrap text section, click the **Right only** option button. This option ensures that all text will flow to the right of the graphic. If you had used the options in the Layout tab (which you saw in Step 4), some of the text would have flowed into the white space to the left of the airplane, making the text difficult to read.

8. In the Distance from text section, click the **Right** up arrow once to display 0.2". Don't worry about the Left setting because the text will wrap only around the right side.

9. Click the **OK** button. You return to the Format Picture dialog box.

10. Click the **OK** button. The Format Picture dialog box closes.

11. Scroll down, if necessary, to view the picture. The text wraps to the right of the airplane, following its shape.

12. Click anywhere in the text to deselect the graphic, and then save the newsletter. Your screen should look similar to Figure 4-16.

Figure 4-16   TEXT WRAPPED AROUND GRAPHIC

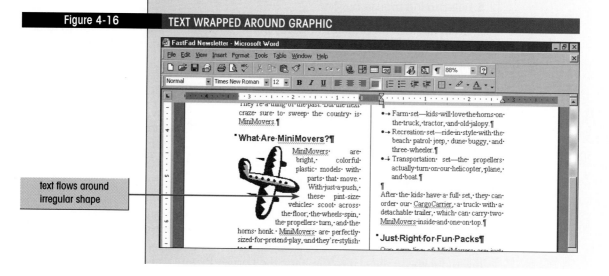

text flows around irregular shape

The image of the airplane draws the reader's attention to the beginning of the newsletter, but the rest of the text looks plain. Gerrit suggests adding a drop cap at the beginning of each section.

Inserting Drop Caps

A **drop cap** is a large, uppercase (capital) letter that highlights the beginning of the text of a newsletter, chapter, or some other document section. The drop cap usually extends from the top of the first line of the paragraph down two or three succeeding lines of the paragraph. The text of the paragraph wraps around the drop cap. Word allows you to create a drop cap for the first letter of the first word of a paragraph.

You will create a drop cap for the first paragraph following each heading in the newsletter (except for the first heading, where the clip-art image is located). The drop cap will extend two lines into the paragraph.

Inserting Drop Caps

- Click in the paragraph for which you want to create a drop cap.
- Click Format on the menu bar, and then click Drop Cap to open the Drop Cap dialog box.
- In the Position section, click the icon for the type of drop cap you want: Dropped or In Margin.
- Click the Font list arrow, and select the font you want for the drop cap.
- Set the appropriate number in the Lines to drop text box. This setting indicates the number of lines the drop cap will extend vertically into the text.
- If necessary, enter a new value for the Distance from text option, and click the OK button.

To insert drop caps in the newsletter:

1. Click in the paragraph following the first heading that starts with the word "Remember."

2. Click **Format** on the menu bar, and then click **Drop Cap**. The Drop Cap dialog box opens.

3. In the Position section, click the **Dropped** icon.

4. Click the **Lines to** drop down arrow once to display 2. You don't need to change the default distance from the text. See Figure 4-17.

Figure 4-17	DROP CAP DIALOG BOX

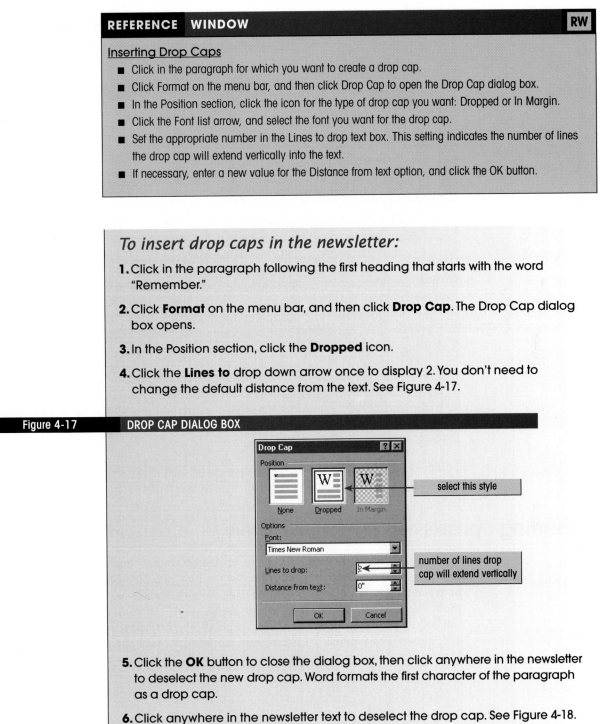

5. Click the **OK** button to close the dialog box, then click anywhere in the newsletter to deselect the new drop cap. Word formats the first character of the paragraph as a drop cap.

6. Click anywhere in the newsletter text to deselect the drop cap. See Figure 4-18.

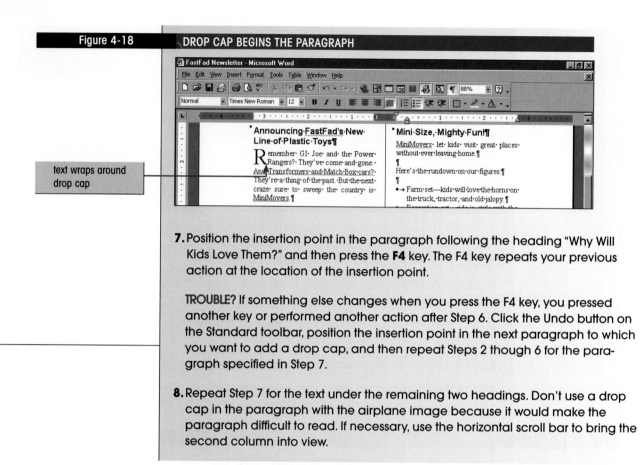

Figure 4-18   DROP CAP BEGINS THE PARAGRAPH

text wraps around drop cap

7. Position the insertion point in the paragraph following the heading "Why Will Kids Love Them?" and then press the **F4** key. The F4 key repeats your previous action at the location of the insertion point.

TROUBLE? If something else changes when you press the F4 key, you pressed another key or performed another action after Step 6. Click the Undo button on the Standard toolbar, position the insertion point in the next paragraph to which you want to add a drop cap, and then repeat Steps 2 though 6 for the paragraph specified in Step 7.

8. Repeat Step 7 for the text under the remaining two headings. Don't use a drop cap in the paragraph with the airplane image because it would make the paragraph difficult to read. If necessary, use the horizontal scroll bar to bring the second column into view.

The newsletter looks more lively with the drop caps. Next, you turn your attention to the issue of inserting a registered trademark symbol beside the trademark names.

Inserting Symbols and Special Characters

Gerrit used standard word-processing characters rather than **typographic characters** (special symbols and punctuation marks) when he typed the newsletter copy. For example, he typed two dashes in place of an em dash. Word's AutoCorrect feature converts some of these standard characters (such as the dashes) into more polished-looking typographic symbols as you type. Figure 4-19 lists some of the characters that AutoCorrect automatically converts to symbols. In some cases, you need to press the spacebar before Word will convert the characters to the appropriate symbol.

Figure 4-19   COMMON TYPOGRAPHICAL SYMBOLS

TO INSERT THIS SYMBOL OR CHARACTER	TYPE	WORD CONVERTS IT TO
em dash	word--word	word—word
smiley	:)	☺
copyright symbol	(c)	©
registered trademark symbol	(r)	®
trademark symbol	(tm)	™
ordinal numbers	1st, 2nd, 3rd, etc.	1ST, 2ND, 3RD, etc.
fractions	1/2, 1/4	½, ¼
arrows	--> or <--	→ or ←

To insert typographic characters into a document after you've finished typing it, you also can use the Symbol command on the Insert menu.

REFERENCE WINDOW   **RW**

Inserting Symbols And Special Characters
- Move the insertion point to the location where you want to insert a particular symbol or special character.
- Click Insert on the menu bar, and then click Symbol to open the Symbol dialog box.
- Click the appropriate symbol from those shown in the symbol character set on the Symbols tab, or click the name from the list on the Special Characters tab.
- Click the Insert button.
- Click the Close button.

To make the newsletter look professionally formatted, you'll insert two special characters now—a registered trademark symbol and a trademark symbol—at the appropriate places.

FastFad protects the names of its products by registering the names as trademarks. You'll indicate that in the newsletter by inserting the registered trademark symbol (®) at the first occurrence of the trademark name "MiniMovers" and a trademark symbol (™) for the first occurrence of "CargoCarrier."

To insert the registered trademark symbol:

1. Position the insertion point at the end of the word "MiniMovers" in the first paragraph, just before the period.

2. Click **Insert** on the menu bar, and then click **Symbol** to open the Symbol dialog box.

3. If necessary, click the **Special Characters** tab. See Figure 4-20.

Figure 4-20   SPECIAL CHARACTERS TAB IN SYMBOL DIALOG BOX

click to display this tab

insert this symbol

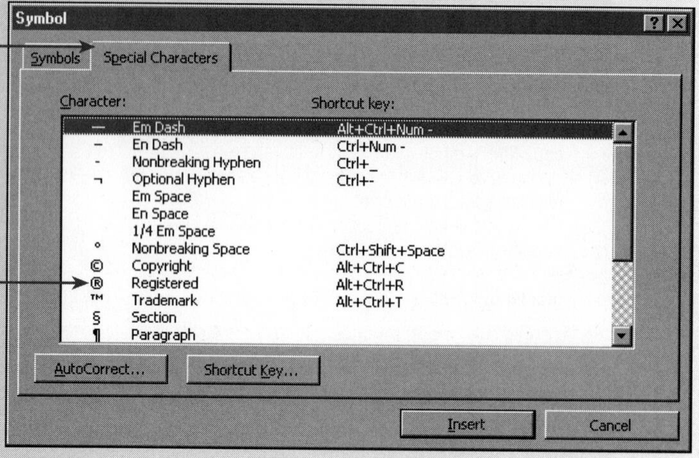

4. Click **Registered** to select it, and then click the **Insert** button. The dialog box stays open so you can insert additional symbols and characters in this location.

5. Click the **Close** button to close the Symbol dialog box. Word has inserted ® immediately after the word "MiniMovers."

If you have to insert symbols repeatedly, or if you want to insert them quickly as you type, it's often easier to use the Word AutoCorrect feature to insert them. You'll use AutoCorrect now to insert the trademark symbol (™) after the first occurrence of CargoCarrier. First, you'll look in the AutoCorrect settings to make sure the correct entry is there.

To enter a symbol using AutoCorrect:

1. Click **Tools** on the menu bar, and then click **AutoCorrect**. The AutoCorrect tab of the AutoCorrect dialog box opens. In the Replace column on the left side of the dialog box, you see (tm), which means that any occurrence of (tm) in the document will change to the trademark symbol. Now that you know the symbol is there, you'll try entering it in the document.

2. Click the **Cancel** button.

3. Position the insertion point just after the word "CargoCarrier" in the second column, in the paragraph above the heading "Just Right for Fun Packs."

4. Type **(tm)**. Word converts your typed characters into the trademark symbol.

The trademark symbols ensure that everyone who reads the newsletter is aware that these names are protected. Next, you decide to adjust the columns of text so they are approximately the same lengths.

Balancing the Columns

You could shift text from one column to another by adding blank paragraphs to move the text into the next column or by deleting blank paragraphs to shorten the text so it will fit into one column. The problem with this approach is that any edits you make could throw off the balance. Instead, Word can automatically balance the columns, or make them of equal length.

To balance the columns:

1. Position the insertion point at the end of the text in the right column, just after the period following the word "generation." Next, you need to change the zoom to Whole Page so you can see the full effect of the change.

2. Click the **Zoom** list arrow on the Standard toolbar, and then click **Whole Page**.

3. Click **Insert** on the menu bar, and then click **Break**. The Break dialog box opens.

4. Below "section break types," click the **Continuous** option button.

5. Click the **OK** button. Word inserts a continuous section break at the end of the text, which, along with the first section break you inserted earlier, defines the area in which it should balance the columns. As shown in Figure 4-21, Word balances the text between the two section breaks.

Figure 4-21	NEWSLETTER WITH BALANCED COLUMNS

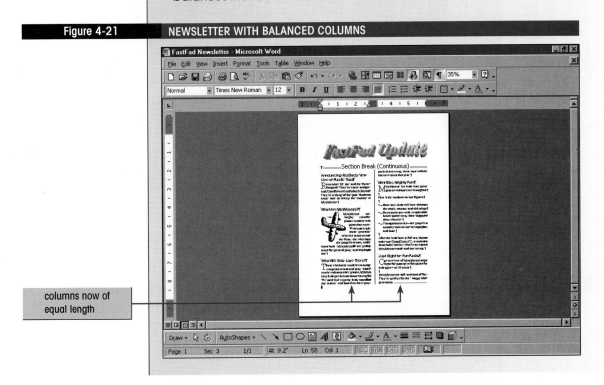

columns now of equal length

Drawing a Border Around the Page

Gerrit wants to give the newsletter a little more pizzazz. He suggests adding a border around the newsletter.

To draw a border around the newsletter:

1. Make sure the document is in print layout view and that the zoom setting is set to Whole Page so that you can see the entire newsletter.

2. Click **Format** on the menu bar, and then click **Borders and Shading**. The Borders and Shading dialog box opens.

3. Click the **Page Border** tab. You can use the Setting options, on the left side, to specify the type of border you want. In this case, you want a simple box.

4. In the Setting section, click the **Box** option. Now that you have selected the type of border you want, you can choose the style of line that will be used to create the border.

5. In the Style list box, scroll down and select the ninth style down from the top (the thick line with the thin line underneath), and then verify that the Apply to list option is set to Whole document. See Figure 4-22.

Figure 4-22   BORDERS AND SHADING DIALOG BOX

box type border

line style

apply to whole document

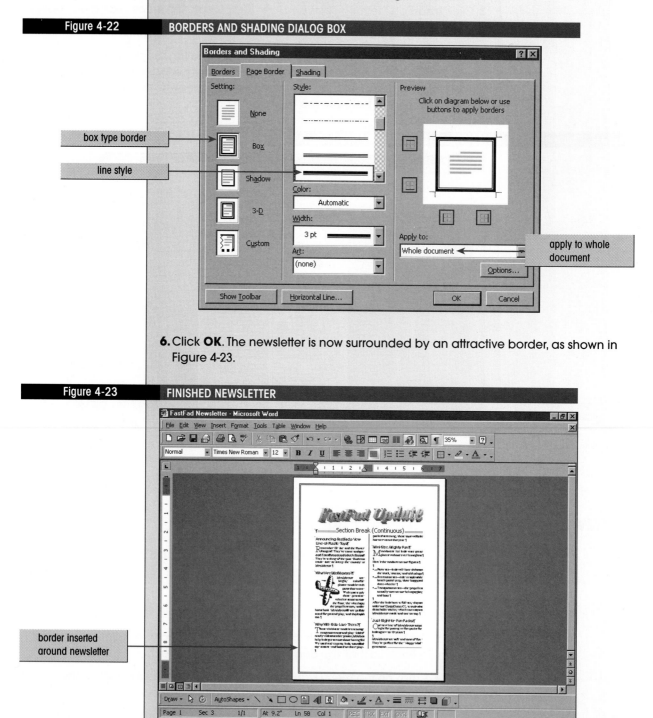

6. Click **OK**. The newsletter is now surrounded by an attractive border, as shown in Figure 4-23.

Figure 4-23   FINISHED NEWSLETTER

border inserted around newsletter

7. Save the completed newsletter as **FastFind Newsletter Final Copy** in the Tutorial folder for Tutorial 4.

8. Create a footer that centers "Prepared by *your name*" at the bottom of the document. Be sure to replace *your name* with your first and last name. Format the footer in a small font to make it as unobtrusive as possible.

9. Preview the newsletter and then print it. Unless you have a color printer, the orange and yellow letters of the title and the airplane will print in black and white.

10. If necessary, click the **Close** button on the Print Preview toolbar to return to print layout view, then close the newsletter and exit Word.

You give the printed newsletter to Gerrit, along with a copy on disk. He thinks it looks great and thanks you for your help. He'll print it later on a high-quality color printer (to get the best resolution for printing multiple copies) and distribute the newsletter to FastFad's sales staff.

Session 4.2 QUICK CHECK

1. Define the following in your own words:
   a. drop cap
   b. scaling
   c. clip art
   d. balance

2. Explain how to insert a clip-art graphic in Word.

3. Describe a situation in which you would want to scale a graphic. Describe a situation in which you would want to crop a graphic.

4. True or False: When inserting a drop cap, you can specify the number of lines you want the drop cap to extend into the document vertically.

5. Describe two different methods for inserting the registered trademark symbol in a document.

6. Besides the Symbol command on the Insert menu, what is another way of entering typographic symbols?

7. Describe the process for drawing a border around the page.

REVIEW ASSIGNMENTS

Gerrit's FastFad newsletter was a success; the sales representatives all seemed to have good product knowledge, and the sales for MiniMovers were brisk. Now the sales reps want a product information sheet (similar to the newsletter) about another product, FastFad Action Pros, that they can print and send directly to their clients. You'll create that newsletter now.

1. If necessary, start Word and make sure your Data Disk is in the appropriate disk drive. Check your screen to make sure your settings match those in the tutorial and that the nonprinting characters and Drawing toolbar are displayed.

2. Open the file **FigSpecs** from the Review folder for Tutorial 4 on your Data Disk, and then save it as **Action Pros**.

3. In the second-to-last line of the document, replace "our toll free-number" with your name.

4. Click the Insert WordArt button on the Drawing toolbar.

5. Choose the WordArt style in the fourth row down, second column from the left.

6. Type "FastFad Pros" in the Edit WordArt Text dialog box, and then click OK.

7. Drag the WordArt above the first heading so that the anchor symbol is positioned to the left of the first paragraph symbol and so that the paragraph symbol is positioned below the WordArt on the screen.

8. Use the WordArt Shape button on the WordArt toolbar to apply the Inflate shape (fourth row down, leftmost column).

9. Click the Edit Text button on the WordArt toolbar and change the font to 32-point Times New Roman bold.

10. Use the Text Wrapping button on the WordArt toolbar to apply the Top and Bottom wrapping style.

11. Drag the lower-right and then the lower-left resize handles to enlarge the image to span the entire width between the left and right margins. Be sure to hold down the Shift key while you drag. Size the WordArt to make it approximately two-inches tall.

12. Save the document.

13. Position the insertion point to the left of the first word in the first heading, and then format the text into two columns using the Columns dialog box. Insert a section break so that the columns appear from this point forward. Do not insert a line between columns.

14. View the whole newsletter in print layout view, using the Whole Page zoom setting.

15. Return to Page Width zoom, and then position the insertion point at the beginning of the first paragraph, right before the phrase "FastFad Action Pros are the latest…".

16. Use the Insert Clip Art button on the Drawing toolbar to insert the baseball player clip-art image from the Sports & Leisure category.

17. Select and resize the sports image so it fits in the left half of the first column.

18. Click the Crop button on the Picture toolbar, and then try cropping the image horizontally and vertically by dragging the appropriate selection handles.

19. Use the Undo button to uncrop the image.

20. Select the picture, click the Format Picture button on the Picture toolbar, click the Layout tab, and then click the Advanced button. Set the Wrapping style to Tight, and wrap the text around the right side of the image.

21. Format a drop cap for the first paragraph following the "Five Sets of Figures" heading, using the default settings for the Dropped position.

22. Insert the trademark symbol after the first occurrence of "FastFad Action Pros."

Explore   23. As you might have noticed, Word automatically justifies text in newspaper columns, but you can easily change that alignment. Select both columns of text by clicking before the first word of text ("Product"), pressing and holding down the Shift key, and then clicking after the last word of text in the second column ("business"). Use the Align Left button on the Formatting toolbar to change the columns' text alignment to left alignment.

24. Make the columns of equal length by balancing the columns. Position the insertion point at the end of the document, click Insert on the menu bar, and then click Break. Below Section break types, click the Continuous option button, and then click the OK button.

Explore 25. A pull quote is a phrase or quotation taken from the text that summarizes a key point. To insert a pull quote, click the Text Box button on the Drawing toolbar, and then drag the pointer below the two columns to draw a text box that spans the page width and fills the space between the columns and the bottom margin. Use the Enter key to center the insertion point vertically in the text box. Type "FastFad: Playing is our business." Now format the text in the text box as 18-point Times New Roman italic, bold, and then use the Center button to center the text horizontally in the box.

Explore 26. You can use the Replace command to replace standard word-processing characters with typographic characters. To replace every occurrence of -- (two dashes) with — (an em dash), position the insertion point at the beginning of the first paragraph of text. Click Edit on the menu bar, and then click Replace. In the Find what text box, type "--" (two hyphens), and then press the Tab key to move the insertion point to the Replace with text box. Click the More button to display additional options and then click the Special button at the bottom of the dialog box. Click Em Dash in the list to display the special code Word has for em dashes in the Replace with text box. Click the Replace All button. When the operation is complete, click the OK button, and then click the Close button.

27. Add a border to the page using the Page Border command and the line style of your choice.

28. Look at the newsletter in print layout view, using the Whole Page zoom setting.

29. Preview, save, and print the document.

CASE PROBLEMS

Case 1. City of Madison, Wisconsin Claudia Mora is the manager of information systems for the city of Madison. She and her staff, along with the city manager, have just decided to convert all city computers from the Windows 3.1 operating system to Windows 98 and to standardize applications software on Microsoft Office 2000. Claudia writes a monthly newsletter on computer operations and training, so this month she decides to devote the newsletter to the conversion to Windows 98 and Microsoft Office 2000.

1. If necessary, start Word, make sure your Data Disk is in the appropriate drive, and check your screen to make sure your settings match those in the tutorial.

2. Open the file **CityComp** from the Cases folder for Tutorial 4 on your Data Disk, and then save the file as **Computer**.

Explore 3. If the text you want to format as WordArt has already been typed, you can cut it from the document and paste it into the WordArt dialog box. You can try this technique now. Cut the text of the newsletter title, "Computer News." Click the Insert WordArt button on the Drawing toolbar, and then choose the WordArt style in the third row down, second column from the left. Paste the text (using the Ctrl+V shortcut keys) into the Edit WordArt Text dialog box, and then click OK.

4. Drag the WordArt to the top of the newsletter, so that the anchor symbol is positioned to the left of the first paragraph symbol, and set the wrapping style to Top and Bottom.

5. In the Edit WordArt Text dialog box, set the font to 32-point Arial bold, then use the WordArt Shape button on the Drawing toolbar to apply the Arch Up (Curve) shape.

Explore 6. Experiment with changing the shape of the WordArt object by dragging the yellow adjustment handle.

7. Resize the WordArt object so that it spans the width of the page from left margin to right margin and so that its maximum height is about 1 inch. (*Hint:* Use the resize handles while watching the horizontal and vertical rulers in print layout view to adjust the object to the appropriate size.)

8. Center and italicize the subtitle of the newsletter, "Newsletter from the Madison Information Management Office."

9. Replace "INSERT YOUR NAME HERE" with your name, then center and italicize it.

10. Insert a continuous section break before the subtitle. (*Hint:* The section break may appear above the WordArt title, depending on where the anchor is positioned, but this is not a problem.)

Explore 11. To emphasize the subtitle paragraph with the city name, insert a border around all four sides and shade the paragraph using the Borders and Shading command. (*Hint:* In the Borders and Shading dialog box, click the Shading tab, select a light, see-through color from the Fill grid, such as Gray-15%, and then click OK.)

12. Move the insertion point to the beginning of the heading "The Big Switch." Then format the body of the newsletter into two newspaper-style columns; set the format of the columns so that no vertical rule appears between the columns. Use the This point forward option in the Apply to list box to make the columns a separate section.

13. Position the insertion point at the beginning of the first paragraph under the heading "Training on MS Office 2000," and insert the clip-art image from the Business category that shows a person using a laptop computer in front of a group.

Explore 14. Resize the picture so that it is 35 percent of its original size. Instead of dragging the resize handles as you did in the tutorial, use the Size tab in the Format Picture dialog box to scale the image. Adjust the Height and Width settings to 35 percent in the Scale section, and make sure the Lock aspect ratio check box is selected.

Explore 15. Click the Text Wrapping button on the Picture toolbar and select the Tight option.

16. Replace any double hyphens with typographic em dashes.

17. Make sure the newsletter fits on one page; if necessary, decrease the height of the WordArt title until the newsletter fits on one page.

18. Insert a border around the newsletter.

19. If necessary, balance the columns.

20. Save and print the newsletter, and then close it.

Case 2. *Morning Star Movers* Martin Lott is the executive secretary to Whitney Kremer, director of personnel for Morning Star Movers (MSM), a national moving company with headquarters in Minneapolis, Minnesota. Whitney assigned you the task of preparing the monthly newsletter News and Views, which provides news about MSM employees. You decide to update the layout and to use the desktop-publishing capabilities of Word to design the newsletter. You will use text assembled by other MSM employees for the body of the newsletter.

1. If necessary, start Word, make sure your Data Disk is in the appropriate drive, and check your screen to make sure your settings match those in the tutorial.

2. Open the file **MSM_NEWS** from the Cases folder for Tutorial 4 on your Data Disk, and then save it as **MSM Newsletter**.

3. Use the Find and Replace command to replace all instances of the name "Katrina" with your first name. Then replace all instances of "Pollei" with your last name.

4. Create a "News and Views" WordArt title for the newsletter, and set the font to 24-point Arial bold. Use the WordArt style in the third row, fourth column from the left, and set the shape of the text to Wave 2 (third row, sixth column from the left).

5. Drag the WordArt title to the top of the newsletter so that the anchor symbol is positioned to the left of the first paragraph symbol, and set the wrapping style to Top and Bottom.

6. Resize the WordArt proportionally so that the title spans the width of the page from left margin to right margin and so that the height of the title is about 1 inch. (*Hint:* Use the resize handles while watching the horizontal and vertical rulers in print layout view to adjust the object to the appropriate size.)

7. Format the body of the newsletter into two newspaper-style columns, and place a vertical rule between the columns.

Explore ▶ 8. You can change the structure of a newsletter by reformatting it with additional columns. Change the number of columns from two to three using the same technique you used in the previous step (that is, the Columns command on the Format menu). Make sure that the Equal column width check box is selected.

Explore ▶ 9. You can insert your own bitmapped graphics, stored on a disk, just as easily as you can insert clip art. Position the insertion point at the beginning of the paragraph below the heading "MSM Chess Team Takes Third." Click Insert on the menu bar, point to Picture, and then click From File. Look in the Cases folder for Tutorial 4 on your Data Disk, select the file named **Knight**, and then click the Insert button.

Explore ▶ 10. You can easily delete a graphic by selecting it, and then pressing the Delete key. To practice this technique, click the Knight graphic to select it, and then press the Delete key. To reinsert the graphic, click the Undo button.

Explore ▶ 11. Scale the height and the width of the picture to 60 percent of its original size. (*Hint:* To scale the size, use the Format Picture button on the Picture toolbar, and then set the Scale values on the Size tab, making sure the Lock aspect ratio check box is selected.)

Explore ▶ 12. Use the Picture tab in the Format Picture dialog box, and change the values in the Crop from text boxes. Crop 0.3, 0.4, 0.2, and 0.4 inches from the left, right, top, and bottom of the picture, respectively.

13. Wrap the text around the clip art.

14. Format drop caps in the first paragraph after each heading except the "MSM Chess Team Takes Third" heading. Use the default settings for number of lines, but change the font of the drop cap to Arial.

15. View the entire page. If necessary, decrease the height of the WordArt title or change the page margins until the entire newsletter fits onto one page and until each column starts with a heading.

16. Add a border around the entire page of the newsletter using the Page Border command.

17. Save the newsletter, and then preview and print it. Close the document.

Case 3. Lake Mendota Wellness Clinic   The Lake Mendota Wellness Clinic, located in Vicksburg, Mississippi, is a private company that contracts with small and large businesses to promote health and fitness among their employees. Mary Anne Logan, an exercise physiologist, is director of health and fitness at the clinic. As part of her job, she writes a newsletter for the employees of the companies with which the clinic contracts. She's asked you to transform her document into a polished, desktop-published newsletter.

1. If necessary, start Word, make sure your Data Disk is in the appropriate drive, and check your screen to make sure your settings match those in the tutorials.

2. Open the file **Wellness** from the Cases folder for Tutorial 4 on your Data Disk, and then save it as **Wellness Newsletter**.

3. In the third line, replace "YOUR NAME HERE" with your first and last names.

4. At the beginning of the newsletter, create a WordArt title "Feeling Good." Choose any WordArt style that you feel would be appropriate to the newsletter content, and set the font to 24-point, italic Times New Roman.

5. Set the shape of the text to any option that looks appropriate to the subject matter.

6. Move the title to the top of the document, so the anchor symbol is positioned to the left of the first paragraph symbol.

Explore   7. Add a shadow to the WordArt title (or adjust the existing one) by clicking the Shadow button on the Drawing toolbar and selecting a Shadow option. Then use the Shadow Settings option on the Shadow button to open the Shadow Settings toolbar. Click the Shadow Color button on the Shadow Settings toolbar, select a good color for the shadow, then close the Shadow Settings toolbar. For the purpose of this exercise, choose a shadow style that is behind the text, not in front of it.

Explore   8. Rotate the WordArt 90 degrees. (*Hint:* In the Format WordArt dialog box, click the Size tab and set the Rotation option to 90 degrees.)

Explore   9. Resize the WordArt graphic box so that the WordArt object spans the height of the page from the top margin to the bottom margin and the width of the object is about 1 inch. (*Hint:* Use the resize handles while watching the horizontal and vertical rulers in print layout view to adjust the object to the appropriate size.)

10. Drag the WordArt object to the right edge of the page.

11. Use the Advanced wrapping options to change the Wrapping style to Square and Left only.

12. At the top of the page, italicize the subtitles, the line that contains the issue volume and number of the newsletter, and the line that contains your name.

13. Format the body of the newsletter as a separate section, in two newspaper-style columns with a vertical rule between the columns. (*Hint:* The columns' widths will be uneven because the WordArt title takes up part of the second column space.)

14. To the right of each of the words "NordicTrack" and "HealthRider," insert a registered trademark symbol (®), and then change the font size of the symbol to 8 points. (*Hint:* Highlight the symbol and change the font size.)

15. Balance the columns.

16. Save the newsletter, and then preview and print it. Close the document.

Case 4. New Home Newsletter You've just moved to a new part of the country and decide to send out a newsletter to friends and family describing your new home. In the one-page newsletter, you'll include articles about you and your family or friends, your new job, your new abode, and future plans. You'll desktop publish the copy into a professional-looking newsletter.

1. If necessary, start Word, make sure your Data Disk is in the appropriate drive, and check your screen to make sure your settings match those in the tutorials.

2. Write two articles to include in the newsletter; save each article in a separate file.

3. Plan the general layout of your newsletter.

4. Create a title ("New Home News") for your newsletter with WordArt.

5. Save the document as **New Home** in the Cases folder for Tutorial 4.

6. Insert the current date and your name as editor below the title.

Explore
7. Insert the articles you wrote into your newsletter. Position the insertion point where you want the first article to appear, click Insert on the menu bar, click File, select the article you want to insert, and then click the Insert button. Repeat to insert the second article.

8. Format your newsletter with multiple columns.

9. Insert at least one clip-art picture into your newsletter, and wrap text around it.

10. Format at least two drop caps in the newsletter.

Explore
11. Create a border around the page and then add shading to the entire document using the Shading and Borders command on the Format menu. (*Hint:* Click CTRL+A to select the entire document, open the Borders and Shading dialog box, select a page border, click the Shading tab, select a light, see-through color from the Fill grid, such as Gray-15%, and then click OK.)

12. Save and print the newsletter, and then close the document.

INTERNET ASSIGNMENTS

The purpose of the Internet Assignments is to challenge you to find information on the Internet that you can use to create effective documents. The actual assignments are updated and maintained on the Course Technology Web site. Log on to the Internet and use your Web browser to go to the Student Online Companion to accompany this text at **www.course.com/NewPerspectives/office2000**. Click the Word link, and then click the link for Tutorial 4.

Quick Check answers

Session 4.1

1. (list 4) The printing is high-quality; the document uses multiple fonts; the document incorporates graphics; the document uses typographic characters; the document uses columns and other special formatting features.

2. (a) Using a desktop computer system to producing commercial-quality printed material. With desktop publishing you can enter and edit text, create graphics, lay out pages, and print documents. (b) An image whose appearance you can change using the Drawing toolbar or WordArt toolbar (c) The unformatted text of a newsletter (d) A symbol that appears in the left margin, which shows a WordArt object's position in relation to the text

3. False

4. False

5. To resize a WordArt object, select the object and drag its resize handles. To resize the WordArt object proportionally, press and hold the Shift key as you drag a resize handle.

6. The WordArt Shape button allows you to change the basic shape of a WordArt object.

7. True

8. True

Session 4.2

1. (a) a large, uppercase letter that highlights the beginning of the text of a newsletter, chapter, or some other document section; (b) resizing an image to better fit a document; (c) existing, copyright-free artwork that you can insert into your document; (d) to make columns of equal length

2. Position the insertion point at the location where you want to insert the image, click the Insert Clip Art button on the Drawing toolbar, click the Pictures tab in the Insert ClipArt window, click the category that best represents the type of art you need, click the image you want to use, click the Insert clip button.

3. You might scale a graphic to better fit the width of a column of text. You might crop a graphic to emphasize or draw attention to a particular part of the image or to eliminate unnecessary borders.

4. True

5. Click where you want to insert the symbol in the document, click Insert on the menu bar, click Symbol, click the Special Characters tab in the Symbol dialog box, click Registered Trademark in the list, click the Insert button, and then click the Close button. Type (tm).

6. Using the AutoCorrect feature, which lets you type certain characters and then changes those characters into the corresponding symbol

7. Click Format on the menu bar, click Borders and Shading, click the Page Border tab in the Borders and Shading dialog box, select the border type you want in the Setting section, choose a line style from the Style list box, make sure Whole document appears in the Apply to list box, and then click OK.

New Perspectives on

MICROSOFT®
WORD 2000

Read This Before You Begin

To the Student

Data Disks

To complete the Level II tutorials, Review Assignments, and Case Problems in this book, you need three Data Disks. Your instructor will either provide you with Data Disks or ask you to make your own.

If you are making your own Data Disks, you will need three blank, formatted high-density disks. You will need to copy a set of folders from a file server or standalone computer or the Web onto your disks. Your instructor will tell you which computer, drive letter, and folders contain the files you need. You could also download the files by going to www.course.com, clicking Data Disk Files, and following the instructions on the screen.

The following list shows you which folders go on each of your disks, so that you will have enough disk space to complete all the tutorials, Review Assignments, and Case Problems:

Data Disk 1

Write this on the disk label:
Data Disk 1: Level II Tutorial 5

Put these folders on the disk:
Tutorial.05

Data Disk 2

Write this on the disk label:
Data Disk 2: Level II Tutorial 6

Put these folders on the disk:
Tutorial.06

Data Disk 3

Write this on the disk label:
Data Disk 3: Level II Tutorial 7

These folders need to be put on the hard drive:
Tutorial.07

When you begin each tutorial, be sure you are using the correct Data Disk. See the inside front or inside back cover of this book for more information on Data Disk files, or ask your instructor or technical support person for assistance.

Course Lab

The Level II tutorials in this book feature one interactive Course Lab to help you understand Internet World Wide Web concepts. There are Lab Assignments at the end of Tutorial 7 that relate to this Lab.

To start a Lab, click the **Start** button on the Windows taskbar, point to **Programs**, point to **Course Labs**, point to **New Perspectives Applications**, and click The Internet World Wide Web.

Using Your Own Computer

If you are going to work through this book using your own computer, you need:

- **Computer System** Microsoft Word 2000 and Windows 95 or higher must be installed on your computer. This book assumes a complete installation of Word 2000.

- **Data Disks** You will not be able to complete the tutorials or exercises in this book using your own computer until you have Data Disks.

- **Course Lab** See your instructor or technical support person to obtain the Course Lab software for use on your own computer.

Visit Our World Wide Web Site

Additional materials designed especially for you are available on the World Wide Web. Go to http://www.course.com.

To the Instructor

The Data Files and Course Lab are available on the Instructor's Resource Kit for this title. Follow the instructions in the Help file on the CD-ROM to install the programs to your network or standalone computer. For information on creating Data Disks or the Course Lab, see the "To the Student" section above. Please note, students need to install the data files for Tutorial 7 onto their hard drives due to the complexity of the tutorial.

You are granted a license to copy the Data Files and Course Lab to any computer or computer network used by students who have purchased this book.

OBJECTIVES

In this tutorial you will:

- Use the Thesaurus

- Create a new folder

- Use fonts appropriately to add interest to a document

- Create and modify styles

- Attach a template to a document and create a new one

- Create and modify an outline

- Hyphenate the document

- Add footnotes and endnotes

- Insert text with Click and Type

- Apply text highlighting

- Adjust Character and Paragraph spacing

- Create a table of contents and browse by headings

CREATING
STYLES, OUTLINES, TABLES, AND TABLES OF CONTENTS

Writing a Business Plan for EstimaTech

CASE

EstimaTech

Chiu Lee Hwang and Robert Camberlango, recent college graduates majoring in computer science, earned their college tuition by working summers and vacations for a company that specializes in historically accurate renovations of older homes. Their employer asked them to use their computer skills to help him estimate the cost of restoring or renovating buildings and homes. They developed a computer program for the task that lets them easily create well-formatted documents they can present to potential customers. It has worked so well that Chiu Lee and Robert have decided to develop it commercially and call it EstimaQuote. They hope to sell the product to contractors, subcontractors, and individuals, as well as to agencies and foundations.

To bring the product to market, Chiu Lee and Robert must secure a $475,000 loan from Commercial Financial Bank of New England for the start-up of EstimaTech, the company that will let them fine-tune the product for commercial use and let them market the software. To obtain the necessary financing, Chiu Lee and Robert are writing a business plan—a report that details all aspects of starting a new business, including market, operations, financial information, and personnel. They have written a draft of the plan and asked you to help them complete it.

SESSION 5.1

In this session, you'll see how Chiu Lee and Robert planned their report. Then you'll open the report and use the Microsoft Word Thesaurus to edit the report. You'll learn about using fonts and then modify, create, and apply styles to format the report.

Planning the Document

A thorough business plan informs prospective investors about the purpose, organization, goals, and projected profits of the proposed business. It also analyzes the target industry, including available market research. A business plan should convince readers that the venture is viable, well-thought-out, and worthy of funding. Chapter 2 of the EstimaTech business plan analyzes the industry and discusses the market research on potential customers for the new cost-estimating software.

Chiu Lee and Robert want to follow a standard business plan organization. The industry analysis begins by explaining how they performed the market research, followed by a summary of the results. They also want to include a table of contents for the chapter. Chiu Lee and Robert use facts and statistics in their business plan to convince potential investors that the company would be profitable and that the cost-estimating software would fill an existing need in the marketplace. They write in a formal business style.

Chiu Lee and Robert have begun to format the document but want you to check the fonts, headers, and styles and make sure the formatting is consistent. They also need you to create a table of contents. You'll start by creating a new folder in which to store your version of the document.

Creating a New Folder

Chiu Lee and Robert have written a draft of Chapter 2 of their business plan. You'll begin by opening a draft of Chapter 2. Robert wants you to create a new folder for this chapter. You'll create the folder and then save the document in the new folder, using a different filename.

To open the document and save it in a new folder:

1. Start Word, if necessary, make sure your Data Disk is in the appropriate drive, and check the screen. For this tutorial, make sure that the ruler appears below the Formatting toolbar and that the nonprinting characters are displayed.

2. Open the file **Industry** from the Tutorial subfolder in the Tutorial.05 folder on your Data Disk.

3. Click **File** on the menu bar, and then click **Save As** to display the Save As dialog box. You'll now create a new folder called Chapter 2 within the Tutorial folder.

4. Click the **Create New Folder** button 📁 located near the top of the Save As dialog box. The New Folder dialog box opens, as shown in Figure 5-1.

Figure 5-1	NEW FOLDER DIALOG BOX

location of your
Tutorial.05 folder
may differ

New Folder   ? X

Current Folder:

A:\Tutorial.05\Tutorial

Name:

OK

Cancel

5. Type **Chapter 2**, the name of the new folder, and then click the **OK** button. The new folder now appears in the Save in list box, at the top of the Save As dialog box.

6. Save the document in the new Chapter 2 folder using the filename **Industry Analysis**.

Now, the **Industry Analysis** document is in the Chapter 2 folder. Before you begin formatting this document, read through it carefully to check for word usage.

Using the Thesaurus

Under the heading "Size of the Market" on page 2, the word "restore" occurs twice, and Robert has asked you to find another word that has the same meaning for the second occurrence. You can do this easily using the Thesaurus. The **Thesaurus** is a Word feature that contains a list of words and their synonyms. Similar to a thesaurus reference book, the Word Thesaurus lets you look up a specific word and then find its synonyms and related words. After you have found an appropriate replacement word, you can immediately substitute the word you looked up with its synonym. The Thesaurus is a good editing tool to help make your word choices varied and exact.

REFERENCE WINDOW	**RW**

Using the Thesaurus
- Move the insertion point anywhere within the word that you want to replace with a synonym.
- Click Tools on the menu bar, point to Language, and then click Thesaurus.
- In the Meanings list box, click the word that most closely defines the selected word.
- In the Replace with Synonym list box, scroll to find a good replacement word.
- Click the replacement word, and then click the Replace button.

You'll use the Thesaurus to find a synonym for the word "restore" in the "Size of Market" paragraph.

To find a synonym for "restore" using the Thesaurus:

1. Below the heading "Size of Market," click the second occurrence of the word "restore". If necessary, you can use the Find command on the Edit menu to find the first occurrence and then click the Find Next button to go to the second occurrence.

2. Click **Tools** on the menu bar, point to **Language**, and then click **Thesaurus**. The Thesaurus: English (U.S.) dialog box opens. The word "restore" appears in the Looked Up list box. Two words, each representing a related definition, appear in the Meanings list box, and several synonyms of the selected meaning "reinstate" appear in the Replace with Synonym list box.

The meaning of "restore" closest to your meaning is "refurbish."

3. Click **refurbish (v.)** in the Meanings list box. The synonyms for "refurbish" appear in the Replace with Synonyms list box on the right. Your Thesaurus dialog box should look similar to Figure 5-2, although your list of synonyms may differ. Robert feels that "renovate" is the best synonym.

Figure 5-2	THESAURUS DIALOG BOX WITH SYNONYMS FOR "RESTORE"

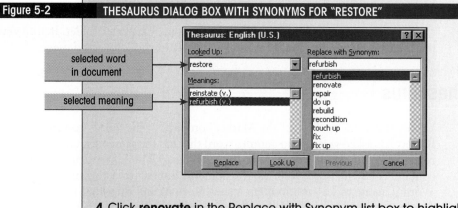

4. Click **renovate** in the Replace with Synonym list box to highlight it, and then click the **Replace** button. The Thesaurus dialog box closes and the word "renovate" replaces the word "restore" in the document.

As you can see, the Thesaurus helps you increase your word power as you write. Now that you know that the text of the chapter is finished, you work on its appearance. To create a professional-looking document, you need to understand how to use fonts effectively, as the following section explains.

Choosing Fonts

Although the Word default font is Times New Roman, this is not the best font for many documents. In fact, Times New Roman was specifically designed for narrow-column newspaper text. For books, manuals, and other documents that have wider columns, a wider font is easier to read. Here are some general principles that might help you decide which fonts to use in your documents:

■ Use a serif font as the main text of your documents. A **serif** is a small embellishment at the tips of the lines of a character, as shown in Figure 5-3.

Figure 5-3	SERIF AND SANS SERIF FONTS

Serif font: ABCabc

serifs

Sans serif font: ABCabc

■ Common serif fonts include Baskerville Old Face, Book Antiqua, Century Schoolbook (also called New Century Schoolbook), Courier, Garamond, Goudy Old Style, Rockwell, and Times New Roman, some of which are shown in Figure 5-4. Because serif fonts are easy to read, they are appropriate not only for the main text but also for titles and headings.

Figure 5-4	SAMPLE SERIF FONTS

Century Schoolbook
Courier
Garamond
Times New Roman

■ "Sans" is French for "without"; thus, a **sans serif font** is a font without the embellishments. Generally, you should avoid sans serif fonts except in titles, headings, headers and footers, captions, and other special parts of the document. Examples of common sans serif fonts include Arial, Arial Narrow, Century Gothic, Eras Light, Eurostile, Franklin Gothic Book, and Lucida Sans, some of which are shown in Figure 5-5. Studies have shown that large blocks of text in sans serif font are harder to read than serif fonts. However, sans serif fonts in titles and headings are attractive and legible.

Figure 5-5	SAMPLE SANS SERIF FONTS

Arial
Arial Narrow
Century Gothic
Franklin Gothic Book

■ Avoid all-uppercase sans serif text, which is difficult to read. All-uppercase serif font is easier to read, but mixed uppercase and lowercase text in any font is better still.

■ Avoid unusual or fancy fonts except for use in certificates, invitations, advertisements, and other specialty documents. Examples of fonts that might be appropriate in these specialty documents include Brush Script, Braggadocio, French Script, Lucida Blackletter, Monotype Corsiva, and Stencil, as shown in Figure 5-6.

Using a Word Template

A **template** is a set of predefined styles designed for a specific type of document. For example, Word provides templates for formatting reports, brochures, memos, letters, or resumes. The Word default template, the Normal template, contains the Normal paragraph style described earlier. You can change the available styles by attaching a different template to a document. Also, you can use a Word template as the basis for a completely new document.

Another Word feature, related to templates, is known as a theme. A **theme** is a unified design for a document that can include background colors, horizontal and vertical lines, and graphics. Themes are designed for documents you plan to present online. Because elements of a theme can be distracting, you should use templates rather than themes for professional documents, especially those you'll print on a black and white printer.

Attaching a template requires two steps. First, you attach the template to the document. Then you apply the template's styles to the various parts of the document. You'll begin by attaching a new template to Robert's document. Notice that the process of attaching a predefined Word template is different from attaching a template you create yourself. In this section, you'll learn how to attach a Word template. Later in this chapter, you'll learn how to attach a newly created template. You'll have a chance to use a template as the basis for a brand-new document in the review assignments at the end of this chapter.

REFERENCE WINDOW **RW**

Attaching a Word Template to a Document

- Click Format on the menu bar, click Theme, and then click the Style Gallery button to open the Style Gallery dialog box.
- In the Template list box, click the template you want to preview.
- In the Preview box, click the Document option button to see how the template's Normal styles look when applied to your document, or click the Example option button to see a sample file that uses all the template styles.
- Click the OK button to attach the template to your document.

Robert would like to use the Elegant Report template for his document. He asks you to preview the template to see what it looks like and then attach it to the draft of Chapter 2.

To preview and attach the Elegant Report template to your document:

1. Click **Format** on the menu bar, and then click **Theme**. The Theme dialog box opens.

2. Click the **Style Gallery** button. The Style Gallery dialog box opens, with the first page of the document displayed in the Preview window.

3. Scroll to and then click **Elegant Report** in the Template list box to select the template. In the Preview window, the text of your document changes to reflect the new Normal style for the Elegant Report template. See Figure 5-9.

Figure 5-9	STYLE GALLERY WITH PREVIEW OF ELEGANT REPORT TEMPLATE

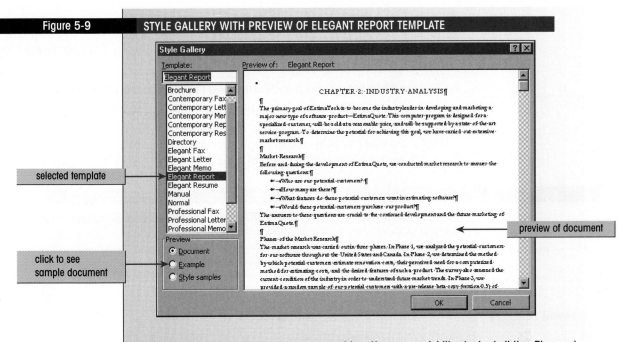

selected template

click to see
sample document

preview of document

TROUBLE? If you see a message asking if you would like to install the Elegant Report template, insert the Office 2000 CD into your CD-ROM drive, and then click Yes. If the Office 2000 CD is not available to you, choose another template.

4. In the Preview box, click the **Example** option button to see a sample document that uses all the Elegant Report template styles. Scroll through the sample document to preview all the styles that are available in this template.

5. Click the **OK** button to attach the template to the report and return to the document window. The template's Normal style (11-point Garamond) is applied to the entire document except for the title, which is formatted in 12 point Garamond. You'll see the various styles of the Elegant Report template when you apply them in the next section.

6. Click the **Style list arrow** on the Formatting toolbar. Scroll through the style list to verify that the styles of the Elegant Report template are now available in this document, and then click the **Style list arrow** again to close the style list.

Now that the Elegant Report template is attached to the report, you can begin applying its styles to the document.

Applying Styles

The best way to apply a template's styles to a document is to move the insertion point to (or highlight) individual parts of the document and then select the appropriate style from the Style list on the Formatting toolbar. For example, to format the chapter title, you could highlight "Chapter 2: Industry Analysis" at the top of the first page and then select the Heading 1 style from the Style list.

You'll apply the Elegant Report template styles now, beginning with the chapter title.

To apply styles to the chapter:

1. Click anywhere within the chapter title ("Chapter 2: Industry Analysis") near the top of the first page.

2. Click the **Style list** arrow on the Formatting toolbar to open the Style list.

3. Scroll down the list, and then click **Heading 1**. Word applies the style to the selected text. Notice that the font of the Heading 1 style is 9-point Garamond bold. Note that this style also changes the title to all capital letters and centers the title on the page, with horizontal lines above and below. See Figure 5-10.

| Figure 5-10 | TITLE FORMATTED WITH CHAPTER TITLE STYLE |

Heading 1 text

normal text

4. Use the Heading 2 style to format all the other headings in the document: "Market Research," "Phases of the Market Research," "Market Definition," "Demographic Description of Target Users," "Size of the Market," "Current Competition," "Customer Needs," and "Market Trends." Rather than using the Style list arrow to apply the heading every time, remember that you use the F4 key to repeat your previous action. Notice that the Heading 2 style formats text as 9-point Garamond bold, centered, in all capital letters.

The newly formatted headings are attractive and make the chapter easier to read by breaking it up into distinct sections. Robert suggests that the headings within the chapter would look better in a larger point size.

Modifying a Predefined Style

Now that you have applied the heading styles, you're ready to modify them. Robert asks that you change the font size of the headings from 9-point to 10-point. To do this, you need to change the style definition, which specifies the particular font, size, and format for that style. Once you change the style definition, all the headings with that style applied to them will automatically be reformatted with the new, modified style. (You don't have to go back and reapply any of the styles with new definitions.) This automatic updating capability makes styles one of the most flexible and helpful Word tools.

To change the Heading 2 style to 10-point:

1. Make sure the insertion point is located within one of the headings formatted with the Heading 2 style. Click **Format** on the menu bar, and then click **Style**. The Style dialog box opens.

2. Verify that **Heading 2** is selected in the Style list box. (It should be selected because the insertion point was located in text formatted with that style when you opened the Style dialog box.)

3. Click the **Modify** button. The Modify Style dialog box opens.

4. Click the **Format** button, and then click **Font**. The Font dialog box opens, as shown in Figure 5-11. The name of the current font, Garamond, is highlighted in the Font text box, and the font size, 9, appears in the Size text box. The Font style is set to bold.

Figure 5-11	FONT DIALOG BOX

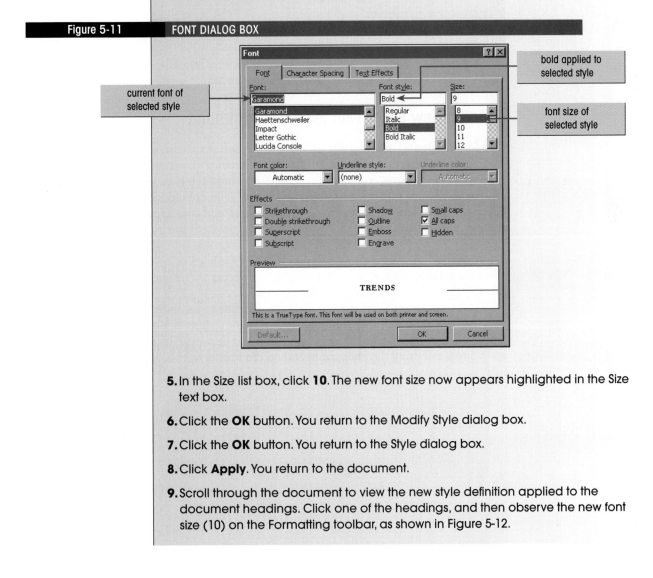

current font of selected style

bold applied to selected style

font size of selected style

5. In the Size list box, click **10**. The new font size now appears highlighted in the Size text box.

6. Click the **OK** button. You return to the Modify Style dialog box.

7. Click the **OK** button. You return to the Style dialog box.

8. Click **Apply**. You return to the document.

9. Scroll through the document to view the new style definition applied to the document headings. Click one of the headings, and then observe the new font size (10) on the Formatting toolbar, as shown in Figure 5-12.

Figure 5-12	NEW FONT DEFINITION APPLIED TO DOCUMENT

new font size

Industry Analysis - Microsoft Word

File   Edit   View   Insert   Format   Tools   Table   Window   Help

Heading 2   Garamond   10   B I U

EstimaTech·will·operate·in·the·national·and·international·market.·After·completing·version·2·of·EstimaQuote·in·English,·we·plan·to·expand·to·Spanish,·French,·German,·and·Japanese·versions·over·the·next·four·years.·We·will·continue·to·improve·our·software·in·all·languages.¶

¶

DEMOGRAPHIC·DESCRIPTION·OF·TARGET·USERS¶

Our·target·users·have·the·following·characteristics:·Prepare·frequent·estimates;·use·printed·forms;·use·computer·spreadsheet,·database,·or·calculator;·prepare·multiple·calculations;·provide·high-·and·low-end·options.¶

text formatted in Heading 2 style is now 10-point

10. Click anywhere in the document *except* within the chapter title, and then use the same technique to change the Heading 1 style to **12-point Garamond bold**. Note that this time you need to select the Heading 1 style in the Style dialog box before you can modify it. Also, to close the Style dialog box, click **Close** rather than Apply. (If you clicked Apply, Word would apply the modified Heading 1 style to the text containing the insertion point.)

11. Save the document.

The Heading 2 style in the document now appears in a 10-point font size, whereas the Heading 1 style is in 12-point. This emphasizes the headings and makes them easier to read.

Defining New Styles with the Style Command

To add interest and improve the appearance of each chapter in their business plan, Robert asks you to define a new style for the introductory (first) paragraph of each chapter. **Defining**, or creating, a new style is similar to modifying an existing style. To define a new style, you assign it a name and give it a new style definition. You can define a style by example by formatting document text, selecting it, and then typing the new style name in the style list box, or by using the Style command on the Format menu. If you use the latter method, you must specify whether the style is a paragraph style or a character style. As mentioned earlier, a paragraph style is one that you apply to complete paragraphs, including short paragraphs such as titles and headings, whereas a character style is one you apply to a single character or to a range of characters.

Word automatically adds any new styles you define to the style list (in the Style list box) of your current document, but it doesn't attach a new style to the template unless you specify that it should. Word provides two ways to define a new style: using an existing paragraph as an example and using the Style command on the Format menu.

<u>Defining a Style</u>
- Format a paragraph with the font, margins, alignment, spacing, and so forth, that you want for the style, and then select the paragraph.
- Click the Style text box on the Formatting toolbar.
- Type the name of the new style (replacing the current style name), and then press the Enter key.
  or
- Select the text for which you want to define a style.
- Click Format on the menu bar, click Style, click the New button, and type the name of the new style in the Name text box.
- Click the OK button, and then click the Apply button.

Now, Robert wants you to define a new style to apply to the first paragraph of each chapter in their business plan. He wants the first paragraph to present the major topic and set the direction for the entire chapter. Therefore, he would like the first paragraph to be indented and justified and to appear in Arial font. You'll now define a style, called First Paragraph, that contains these formatting features.

To define the new style:

1. Move the insertion point anywhere within the first paragraph of the document, below the chapter title. You'll now define the style.

2. Click **Format** on the menu bar, and then click **Style**. The Style dialog box opens. See Figure 5-13.

Figure 5-13   **STYLE DIALOG BOX**

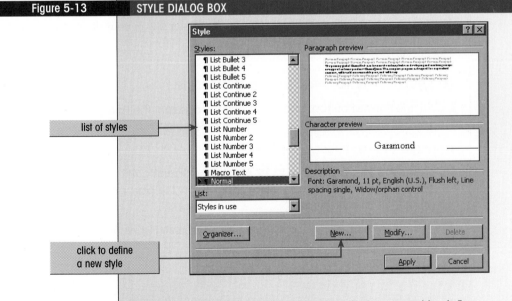

list of styles

click to define
a new style

---

3. Click the **New** button. This tells Word that you want to define a new style. The New Style dialog box opens. The default name Style1 is highlighted and ready to be replaced with your style name.

4. Type **First Paragraph**, the name of your new style. Now, you need to make sure that your new style is a paragraph style, based on the settings of the Normal style.

5. Verify that "Paragraph" appears in the Style type list box and that "Normal" appears in the Based on text box. Now you need to specify the style you want to follow your new style by default.

6. Click the **Style for following paragraph** list arrow, scroll down, and then click **Normal**. This setting specifies that if you apply the First Paragraph style to a paragraph and then press the Enter key at the end of the paragraph, the new paragraph will have the Normal style. See Figure 5-14.

Figure 5-14 | **NEW STYLE DIALOG BOX**

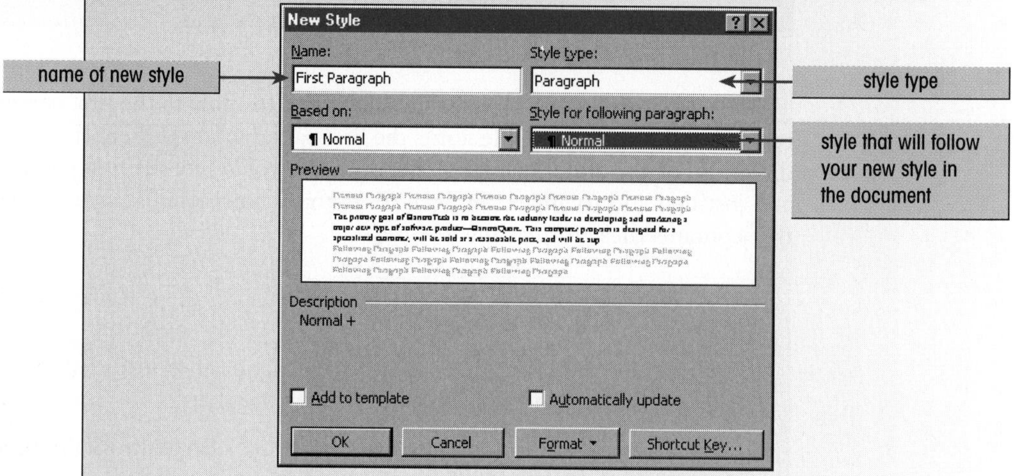

name of new style → **Name:** First Paragraph

Based on: ¶ Normal

Style type: Paragraph ← style type

Style for following paragraph: ¶ Normal → style that will follow your new style in the document

Preview

Description
Normal +

☐ Add to template   ☐ Automatically update

OK   Cancel   Format ▾   Shortcut Key...

You have specified the name and type of the new style as well as the style that should apply to any paragraph after it when you press the Enter key in your document. Now you're ready to specify the format of the new style.

To specify the format of the new style:

1. Click the **Format** button, and then click **Paragraph**. The Paragraph dialog box opens. If necessary, click the **Indents and Spacing** tab.

2. Change the Alignment to **Justified**.

3. Change the Spacing Before to **12 pt** and the Spacing After to **6 pt**. These settings will add white space above and below the paragraph so it stands out from the text surrounding it.

4. In the Indentation section, change Left to **0.5"**. See Figure 5-15.

Figure 5-15	PARAGRAPH DIALOG BOX

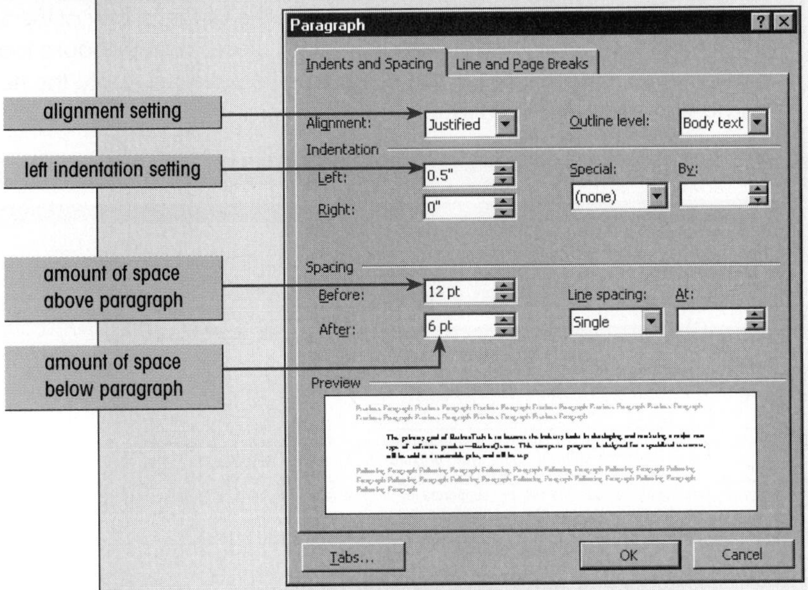

This completes the paragraph formatting. Next, you'll change the font of the style from Garamond to Arial.

5. Click the **OK** button. The Paragraph dialog box closes, and you return to the New Style dialog box.

6. Click the **Format** button, and then click **Font**. The Font dialog box opens.

7. Change the font to Arial. Leave the font style as Regular and the font size as 11-point.

8. Click the **OK** button. The Font dialog box closes. Now, you'll add a border around the paragraph.

9. Click the **Format** button, and then click **Border**. The Borders and Shading dialog box opens. If necessary, click the **Borders** tab.

10. In the Setting section of the dialog box, click the **Box** icon to place a box border around the paragraph, and then click the **OK** button.

11. Look over the New Style dialog box, especially the Description, to make sure you have defined the style as you would like it. At this point, you could click the **Add to template** check box to add this new style to the Elegant Report template. However, because you may want to use the Elegant Report template later for some other purpose besides Robert's business plan, you won't add the new style to the template now. Instead, you'll simply apply the new style; in the process, Word will add it to the style list for the current document. In the next section, you'll learn how to save the current document as a completely new template, which you can use to create new chapters of the business plan.

12. Click the **OK** button to close the New Style dialog box.

13. With the First Paragraph style highlighted in the Styles list box of the Style dialog box, click the **Apply** button. The dialog box closes and, because the insertion point was in the first paragraph at the time you clicked Apply, the new paragraph style is applied to it. See Figure 5-16.

| Figure 5-16 | NEWLY DEFINED STYLE |

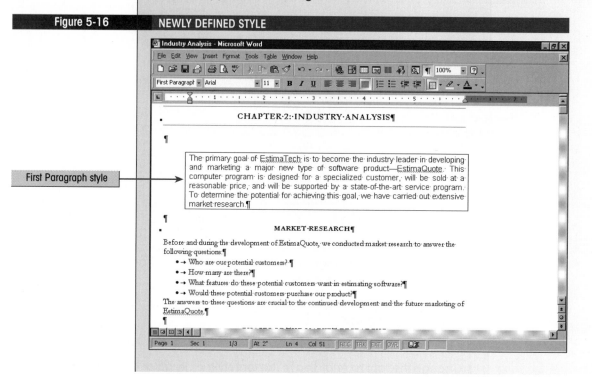

You have defined and applied the new paragraph style called First Paragraph. In the next section, you'll learn how to use this document's styles to create other documents.

Creating a New Template

Now that the document contains all the styles needed for future chapters, you'll save it as a new template. By default, Word will offer to save your new template in the Template folder. Any templates saved to this folder can be accessed later by the New command on the File menu. For this tutorial, however, you'll choose to save your template in the same folder as the rest of your data files.

<u>Creating and Using a New Template</u>

- Create a new document containing all the styles you want to include in your template, save it as a Word document, and then delete all text from the document.
- Click File on the menu bar, click Save As, click the Save As type list arrow, and then click Document Template.
- Verify that the Templates folder is displayed in the Save in list box. If you save your template to this folder, it will appear as one of the options in the New dialog box. If you prefer, you can save the template in a different location, such as your Data Disk.
- Type a descriptive name for the template in the filename text box, click Save, and then close the template.
- To begin creating a document based on a template stored in the Template folder, click File on the menu bar, click New, click the icon for your template in the General tab, and then click OK. Begin typing the text of your new document, applying styles as necessary. Save the new document as a Word document.
- To begin creating a document based on a template saved in any location, open a blank document, click Tools on the menu bar, click Templates and Add-ins, and then click the Attach button to open the Attach Template dialog box. Use the Look in list box to locate and select your template, and then click the Open button to return to the Templates and Add-ins dialog box. Click the Automatically update document styles check box to select it, and then click the OK button to return to the current document. Verify that the template styles are available in the Styles list box.

You're ready to save the styles in the **Industry Analysis** document as a new template. You'll save the template to the Chapter 2 folder that you created earlier, so that you can easily give it to Robert.

To save the styles of the current document as a new template:

1. Save the Industry Analysis document to preserve all the work you've done so far. *Be absolutely certain you have saved the document before proceeding to the next step.*

2. Press **Ctrl+A**, and then press **Delete.** The text of the document is selected and then deleted, but the styles are still available from the Style list box.

3. Click **File** on the menu bar, click **Save As,** click the **Save As type** list arrow and then click **Document Template**.

4. Verify that the Templates folder is displayed in the Save in list box. Because you want your new template handy, so you can pass it on to Robert easily, you'll save it to a different location.

5. Use the **Save in list** arrow to switch to the Chapter 2 file on your Data Disk, where you originally saved the Industry Analysis document.

6. Change the filename to **Business Plan Template,** click Save, and then close the template.

The new template is now saved and ready for whenever Robert wants to begin creating a new chapter of the business plan. He asks you to show him exactly how to begin using the new template. You explain that the process of attaching the template, which you just created, is different from attaching a predefined Word template. Earlier in this tutorial, you attached a predefined Word template with the Theme command on the Format menu. To attach a newly created template to an existing document, you use the Templates and Add-ins command on the Tools menu. You'll try attaching the template you just created to a new document now.

To attach the new template to a new document:

1. Open a new, blank document.

2. Click **Tools** on the menu bar, click **Templates and Add-ins**, and then click the **Attach** button. The Attach Template dialog box opens.

3. Use the Look in list box to locate and select your template, and then click the **Open** button to return to the Templates and Add-ins dialog box.

4. Click the **Automatically update document styles** check box to select it. Note that if you did not select this option, the template styles would not be available in the Styles list box. See Figure 5-17.

| Figure 5-17 | TEMPLATES AND ADD-INS DIALOG BOX |

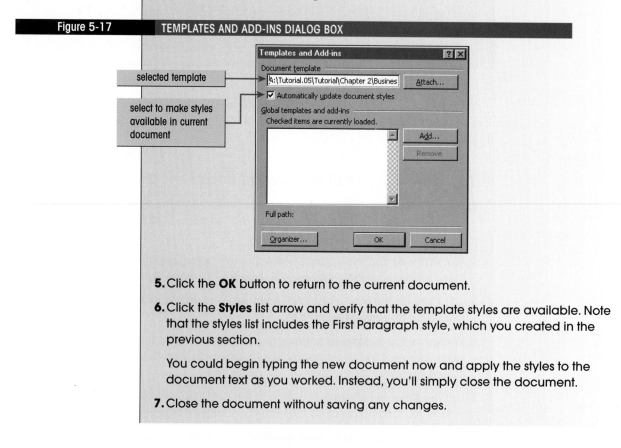

selected template

select to make styles available in current document

5. Click the **OK** button to return to the current document.

6. Click the **Styles** list arrow and verify that the template styles are available. Note that the styles list includes the First Paragraph style, which you created in the previous section.

You could begin typing the new document now and apply the styles to the document text as you worked. Instead, you'll simply close the document.

7. Close the document without saving any changes.

The template you have just created will make it easy for Robert and Chiu Lee to create new chapters. You'll give them a copy on a disk after you have completed the rest of the Chapter 2 document.

Session 5.1 QUICK CHECK

1. Explain how to create a new folder.

2. What is the Thesaurus?

3. List at least two synonyms that the Thesaurus provides for the word "restore."

4. Define serif and sans serif fonts. When would you use each of these types of fonts? Give two examples of each.

5. Explain how to attach a Word template to a document.

6. Explain how to create a new template and attach it to a document.

7. How do you modify a predefined style?

8. Describe one method for defining a new style.

You have improved the EstimaTech business plan chapter by modifying the word choice and writing style, by selecting proper fonts, and by using styles to give the plan a consistent look. Next, you'll change the business plan's organization using Outline view.

SESSION 5.2

In this session, you'll learn how to rearrange the document using outline view. You'll also learn how to improve the appearance of the right margin by hyphenating the document. Finally, you'll add a footnote to the document that will help readers locate additional information.

Creating and Editing an Outline

Chiu Lee and Robert created an outline of their business plan with the Word Outline feature. An **outline** is a list of the basic points of a document and the order in which they are presented. You can create an outline before typing any other text of a document, or you can view and edit the outline of an existing document. To construct an outline when you first create a document, you open a blank document and change to Outline view. Word then automatically applies heading styles (Heading 1, Heading 2, and so forth) to the outline paragraphs that you type. To create an outline as you type the text of a document in Normal view or Print layout view, you must apply heading styles (Heading 1, Heading 2, and so forth) to all the headings in your document. Chiu Lee and Robert used this latter method as they wrote their business plan. You'll change to Outline view to modify and reorganize the outline.

In Outline view, you can see and edit as many as nine levels of headings in a document. As with any outline, the broadest or most general topic is the first-level heading (in Heading 1 style), and the remaining topics become increasingly narrow or more specific with second-level headings (in Heading 2 style) and in subsequent headings (in Heading 3 style, and so on).

After reviewing the organization of the business plan, you realize that the topic "Current Competition" should appear after the topic "Market Trends." Also, the topic "Size of the Market" should appear before "Demographic Description of Target Users." Because you have applied the predefined heading styles to the headings, you can easily reorder the text in Outline view. As you reorder the headings, the text below the headings will move as well. Notice that in Outline view, the Outline toolbar replaces the ruler.

REFERENCE WINDOW **RW**

Creating and Editing Outlines
- Click the Outline View button.
- Click the appropriate Show Heading button to show only the desired number of headings in your document.
- Enter new heading text or edit existing headings.
- Click the Move Up button or the Move Down button to reorder text.
- Click the Promote button or the Demote button to increase or decrease the levels of headings.
- Click the All button to display the entire document again.
- Click the Normal View button.

Now you're ready to reorganize the order of topics in outline view.

To use Outline view:

1. If you took a break after the last session, make sure Word is running.

2. Open the **Industry Analysis** document in the Tutorial sub-folder in the Tutorial.05 folder. Display nonprinting characters, and switch to Print Layout view.

3. Make sure the insertion point is at the beginning of the document, and then click the **Outline View** button ▣. The Outline toolbar replaces the horizontal ruler.

   TROUBLE? Depending on how your machine is set up, your Outline toolbar may be in a different location.

4. Click the **Show Heading 3** button ③ on the Outline toolbar to display three levels of headings. In outline terminology, text formatted in the Heading 1 style is considered a level-1 head, text formatted in the Heading 2 style is considered a level-2 heading, and so on. Although the document has only two levels of headings now, you'll add a third level soon. Notice that the headings are displayed in the outline without the rest of the document text. The plus sign next to each line of text indicates that the text is a heading, rather than part of the main text of the document. See Figure 5-18.

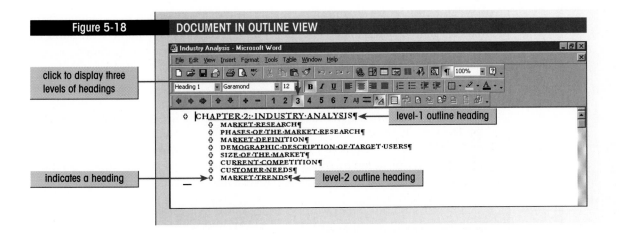

Figure 5-18   **DOCUMENT IN OUTLINE VIEW**

click to display three levels of headings

indicates a heading

level-1 outline heading

level-2 outline heading

Now that you see only the headings of the business plan, you can change the organization by reordering some headings and by changing the level of others.

Moving Headings Up and Down in an Outline

You can rearrange the order of topics in an outline by moving the headings up and down. When you move a heading in outline view, any text below that heading (indicated by the underline) moves with it. First, you'll move the section "Current Competition" (and its accompanying text) to follow the section "Market Trends." As you work in outline view, keep in mind that the Undo button will reverse any mistakes, just as in Normal view.

To move headings in outline view:

1. Place the insertion point anywhere in the heading "Current Competition," and then click the **Move Down** button ⬇ on the Outline toolbar. The heading and the text below it move down one line to follow the heading "Customer Needs," which does not move.

2. Click ⬇ again to move the "Current Competition" heading to the end of the chapter, after "Market Trends."

   Next, you can move the heading "Size of the Market" up, to position it before "Demographic Description of Target Users."

3. Place the insertion point anywhere in the heading "Size of the Market," and then click the **Move Up** button ⬆ on the Outline toolbar. The heading (and the text below it) move up one line to just below "Market Definition."

Now that the topics of the outline are in a better order, you realize that some level-2 headings (text in Heading 2 style) should be level-3 headings (in Heading 3 style).

Promoting and Demoting Headings in an Outline

You can easily change the levels of headings in outline view. To **promote** a heading means to increase the level of a heading—for example, to change an item from a level-3 heading to a level-2 heading. To **demote** a heading means to decrease the level—for example, to change a level-1 heading to a level-2 heading.

While reviewing Chapter 2 of the business plan, you realize that the headings "Size of the Market" and "Demographic Description of Target Users" should be subheadings that follow the heading "Market Definition." You'll now demote these two headings.

To demote headings:

1. While still in Outline view, make sure the insertion point is in the heading "Size of the Market" and then click the **Demote** button ⬚ on the Outline toolbar. (Take care not to click the Demote to Body Text button by mistake, which would make the heading part of the main text of the document, rather than a heading.) The heading moves right and becomes a level-3 heading with the Heading 3 style.

    TROUBLE? If the heading now has a square next to it, rather than a plus sign, you clicked the Demote to Body Text button by mistake. Click the Undo button ⬚, and then repeat Step 1.

2. Place the insertion point anywhere in the heading "Demographic Description of Target Users," and then click ⬚. Again, the heading moves right and becomes a level-3 heading. See Figure 5-19.

| Figure 5-19 | PROMOTING AND DEMOTING HEADINGS |

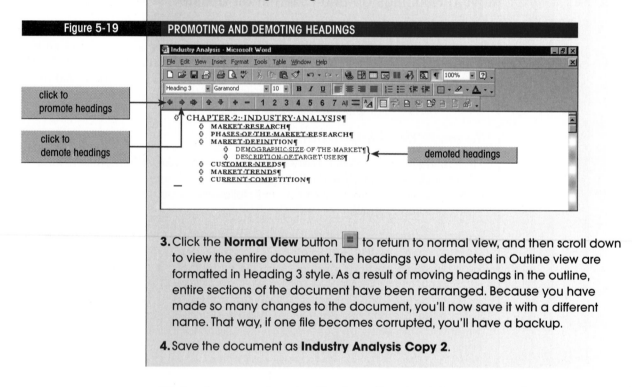

3. Click the **Normal View** button ⬚ to return to normal view, and then scroll down to view the entire document. The headings you demoted in Outline view are formatted in Heading 3 style. As a result of moving headings in the outline, entire sections of the document have been rearranged. Because you have made so many changes to the document, you'll now save it with a different name. That way, if one file becomes corrupted, you'll have a backup.

4. Save the document as **Industry Analysis Copy 2**.

Notice that promoting a heading in outline view is just as easy as demoting. You simply place the insertion point in the desired heading and click the Promote button.

Printing the Outline

Word makes it easy to print whatever you see on the screen in outline view. Robert asks you to print the outline of Chapter 2, so he can refer to it in his conversation with the bank personnel. Before you do so, you'll turn off the formatting of the headings, to make them easier to read.

To print the outline:

1. Click the **Outline View** button 🔲.

2. Click the **Show Formatting** button 🔳 on the Outline toolbar to deselect it. Word converts the outline to the Normal style. In the closely spaced lines of the outline, a simpler style like this is much easier to read.

3. Click the **Print** button 🔳 on the Standard toolbar to print the outline. See Figure 5-20.

| Figure 5-20 | THE PRINTED OUTLINE |

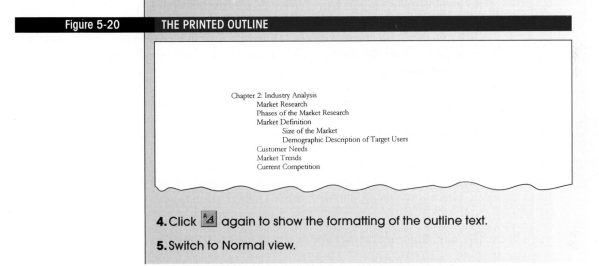

4. Click 🔳 again to show the formatting of the outline text.

5. Switch to Normal view.

You have reorganized Chapter 2 of the business plan and printed the outline. Now you're ready to address some other concerns. First, Robert has noticed that the right edges of most of the paragraphs in the document are rather uneven. You'll correct this problem in the next section.

Hyphenating a Document

One potential problem with left-aligned text is excessive raggedness along the right margin. You can solve the problem of raggedness by justifying the text, but that introduces another problem: Word inserts extra white space between words to stretch the lines of text to align along the right margin. Sometimes, this causes unsightly **rivers**, that is, blank areas running through the text of a page, as shown in Figure 5-21.

Figure 5-21 | **RIVERS WITHIN A JUSTIFIED COLUMN OF TEXT**

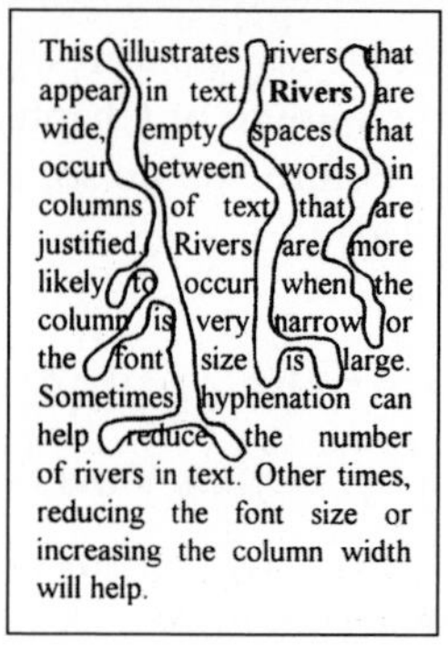

> This illustrates rivers that appear in text. **Rivers** are wide, empty spaces that occur between words in columns of text that are justified. Rivers are more likely to occur when the column is very narrow or the font size is large. Sometimes hyphenation can help reduce the number of rivers in text. Other times, reducing the font size or increasing the column width will help.

Hyphenating the text can sometimes reduce the raggedness in left-aligned text or reduce the rivers in justified text. The Hyphenation feature allows you to hyphenate a document either automatically—in which case, Word decides the exact point at which to divide a word—or manually, in which case you can accept, reject, or change the suggested hyphenation.

To hyphenate a document, you need to specify a width for the **hyphenation zone**, which is the distance from the right margin within which words will be hyphenated. A smaller hyphenation zone results in more words being hyphenated but creates a less-ragged right margin. A larger hyphenation zone results in fewer hyphenated words but a more ragged right margin. In justified text, increasing the number of hyphenated words reduces the amount of white space inserted between words. Notice that to decrease the total number of hyphenated words, you can increase the size of the hyphenation zone. You also can specify the number of successive lines that can end with hyphenated words. Too many lines in a row ending in a hyphen can be distracting and difficult to read.

Robert asks you to hyphenate the business plan to eliminate as much raggedness as possible. This means you need to decrease the hyphenation zone.

To set the hyphenation zone and to hyphenate the newsletter:

1. With the insertion point anywhere in the document, click **Tools** on the menu bar, point to **Language**, and then click **Hyphenation**. The Hyphenation dialog box opens.

2. Decrease the Hyphenation zone to **0.1"**.

3. Change the Limit consecutive hyphens setting to **3**. This prevents Word from hyphenating words at the end of more than three lines in a row.

4. Click the **Automatically hyphenate document** check box. See Figure 5-22.

Figure 5-22 | **HYPHENATION DIALOG BOX**

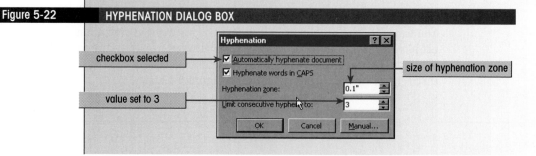

5. Click the **OK** button. Word hyphenates words in the document as needed. For example, scroll the document so that the heading "Phases of Market Research" is at the top of the document window. You can now see several hyphenated words as shown in Figure 5-23.

TROUBLE? If you see a message asking if you would like to install the hyphenation feature, insert the Office 2000 CD into the CD-ROM drive, and then click Yes.

Figure 5-23	DOCUMENT WITH AUTOMATIC HYPHENATION

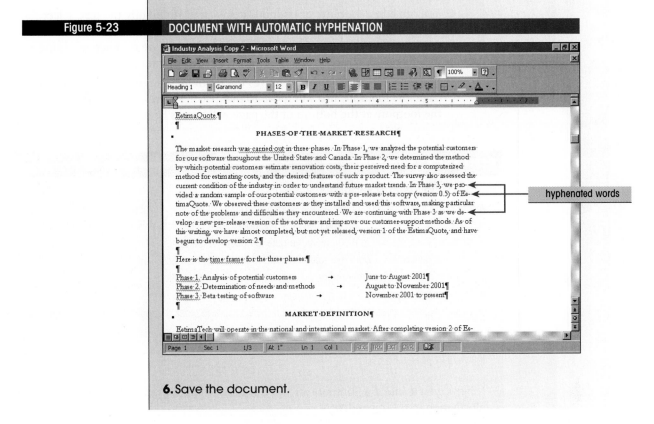

6. Save the document.

You should look through your document to make sure you like how Word has hyphenated it. If you don't like its hyphenations, you can click the Undo button, repeat the preceding steps, and then click the Manual button instead. Then Word will stop at each word before it is hyphenated to let you accept or reject the suggested hyphenation. In this case, Robert is satisfied with the automatic hyphenation.

Adding **Footnotes and Endnotes**

As you read through the chapter, you realize that under the heading "Customer Needs," the text refers to the results of a survey. Robert wants to include the survey results in an appendix at the end of the business plan and wants a cross-reference to this fact in a footnote.

A **footnote** is a line of text that appears at the bottom of the printed page and often includes an explanation, the name of a source, or a cross-reference to another place in the document. When all notes for a document are gathered together and printed at the end of the document, instead of at the bottom of each page, they are called **endnotes**. Usually, a document will contain footnotes or endnotes, but not both. You can insert footnotes and endnotes into a Word document quickly and easily with the Footnote command on the Insert menu.

The Footnote feature provides several benefits over simply typing notes at the bottom of a page or at the end of a document:

■ Word numbers footnotes or endnotes automatically. If you add a note anywhere in the document, delete a note, or move a note, Word automatically renumbers all the remaining footnotes or endnotes consecutively.

■ Word automatically formats the footnote text at the bottom of the page or the endnote text at the end of the document.

■ You can edit a footnote or endnote at any time. To modify the text, select Footnotes from the View menu and then use the same editing commands you use in the document window. (You'll have a chance to practice editing a footnote in the case problems at the end of this chapter.)

■ If you add or delete text that moves the footnote reference onto a different page, the footnote also will move to that page. The reference in the text and the footnote at the bottom of the page will always be on the same page.

REFERENCE WINDOW   **RW**

Inserting Footnotes or Endnotes

■ Position the insertion point where you want the footnote or endnote number to appear.

■ Click Insert on the menu bar, and then click Footnote to open the Footnote and Endnote dialog box.

■ Click the Footnote button if you want the note to appear at the bottom of the page, or click the Endnote button if you want the note to appear at the end of the document.

■ Select a method for numbering the note, and then click the OK button.

■ Type the text in the footnote or endnote window.

■ Click the Close button on the Footnote or Endnote toolbar to close the footnote or endnote window and return to the document window.

Now, you'll insert a footnote in the business plan that refersthe reader to the survey information in the appendix.

To insert a footnote:

1. Switch to normal view if necessary, scroll down until you can see the heading "Customer Needs," and then position the insertion point after the period at the end of the first sentence, which ends "such as EstimaQuote." This is where you will add the first footnote number.

2. Click **Insert** on the menu bar, and then click **Footnote**. The Footnote and Endnote dialog box opens.

3. Make sure the Footnote option button is selected, make sure the AutoNumber option button is selected, and then click the **OK** button. The footnote number appears in the text and the insertion point moves to a blank footnote window at the bottom of the page. See Figure 5-24.

Figure 5-24 CREATING A FOOTNOTE

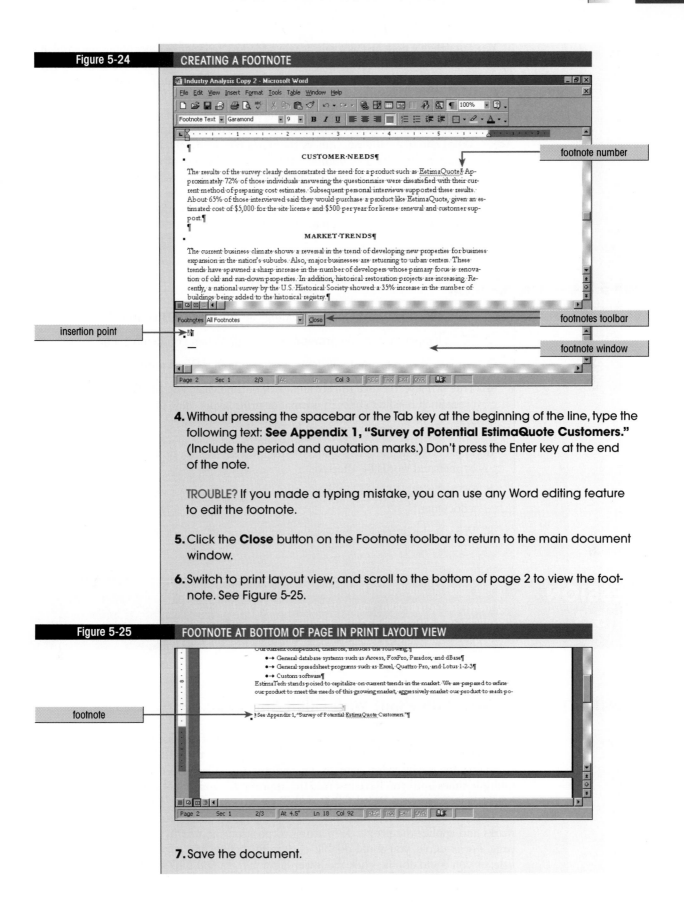

4. Without pressing the spacebar or the Tab key at the beginning of the line, type the following text: **See Appendix 1, "Survey of Potential EstimaQuote Customers."** (Include the period and quotation marks.) Don't press the Enter key at the end of the note.

TROUBLE? If you made a typing mistake, you can use any Word editing feature to edit the footnote.

5. Click the **Close** button on the Footnote toolbar to return to the main document window.

6. Switch to print layout view, and scroll to the bottom of page 2 to view the footnote. See Figure 5-25.

Figure 5-25 FOOTNOTE AT BOTTOM OF PAGE IN PRINT LAYOUT VIEW

7. Save the document.

You can delete a note just as easily as you added it. To delete a footnote or endnote, highlight the footnote or endnote number in the document and press the Delete key. When you delete the number, Word automatically deletes the text of the footnote or endnote and renumbers the remaining notes consecutively.

You can move a footnote or endnote using the cut-and-paste method. Simply highlight and cut the note number from the document, and then paste it anywhere in your document. Again, Word automatically renumbers the notes consecutively and places the footnote on the same page as its reference number. You can edit the text of an endnote or footnote by clicking in the footnote or endnote while in print layout view. Finally, note that you can display the text of the footnote in a ScreenTip, by placing the pointer over the footnote number in the document. This feature is especially useful when you are sharing documents in electronic form only, rather than distributing printouts.

Session 5.2 QUICK CHECK

1. Why would you want to move headings up and down in an outline?

2. What happens when you promote a heading? When you demote a heading?

3. Explain how to promote or demote a heading in a Word outline.

4. True or False: To take full advantage of outline view, you should apply the Word predefined heading styles in normal or print layout view first.

5. What does the term *river* mean in relation to justified text.

6. What is the hyphenation zone? If you increase its size, how will the number of hyphenated words be affected?

7. What are the advantages of using the Footnote feature to insert footnotes into a document?

8. What is the difference between a footnote and an endnote?

SESSION 5.3

In this session, you'll learn how to position the insertion point with Click and Type and how to insert the current date. You'll also learn how to highlight text with colors and adjust character and paragraph spacing. Finally, you'll create a table of contents and browse through the document by quickly jumping from one heading to another.

Positioning the Insertion Point with Click and Type

Your next task is to create a cover page at the beginning of the document. To draw attention to the text of the new cover page, you want it to appear in the middle of a separate page. You could position the insertion point at the beginning of a blank page by pressing the Enter key multiple times until you have inserted the appropriate number of paragraph marks. But it is much easier to use the Word **Click and Type** feature, which allows you to double-click a blank area of a page and immediately begin typing. Word inserts the necessary paragraph marks and applies the proper formatting to position the text in that particular area of the page. For example, you could double-click in the center of a page and then type a centered title; or you could double-click the lower-right margin and type a right-aligned date.

Keep in mind that Click and Type only works in print layout view. As you move the pointer over a blank area of a page, the pointer changes shape to reflect the alignment that will be applied to text inserted in that particular area of the page. For example, when you move the pointer over the center of the page, the pointer indicates that text inserted there will be formatted with center alignment. Table 5-1 describes some useful Click and Type pointers.

Table 5-1	CLICK AND TYPE POINTERS
POINTER	**DESCRIPTION**
I≣	Aligns text on the left side of the page.
≣I	Aligns text on the right side of the page.
I≣	Centers text on the page.
▪≣ I	Formats text to flow around the right side of a graphic.

To create the new cover page for the document, you'll first verify that the Click and Type feature is turned on. Then, you'll insert a new page, double-click the center of the blank page, and begin typing the centered text.

To create a title page using Click and Type:

1. Verify that the **Industry Analysis Copy 2** document is open, that nonprinting characters are displayed, and that the document is displayed in print layout view.

2. Click **Tools** on the menu bar, click **Options**. The Options dialog box opens.

3. Click the Edit tab, verify that the **Enable click and type** check box is selected, and then click the **OK** button.

4. Press **Ctrl+Home** to move the insertion point to the blank paragraph at the beginning of the document.

5. Format the blank paragraph using the Normal style. Note that if you plan to insert a page *before* a heading in a document, it's a good idea to keep a blank paragraph (formatted with the Normal style) between the heading and the new page. Otherwise, you may have difficulties using styles you want on the new page.

6. Press **Ctrl+Enter**. Word inserts a page break at the beginning of the chapter.

7. Press the ↑ key to move the insertion point to the top of the new page.

8. Move the pointer over the center of the page, about 4 inches down from the top margin. (Use the vertical ruler on the left side of the screen as a guide.) The pointer changes to I≣.

9. Double-click the mouse. Word inserts the appropriate number of paragraph mark breaks and applies formatting to position the insertion point where you double-clicked. See Figure 5-26.

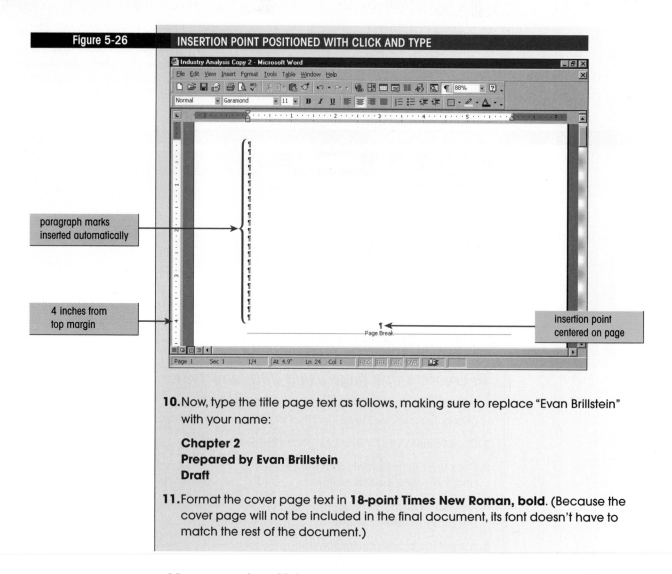

Figure 5-26   INSERTION POINT POSITIONED WITH CLICK AND TYPE

paragraph marks
inserted automatically

4 inches from
top margin

insertion point
centered on page

10. Now, type the title page text as follows, making sure to replace "Evan Brillstein"
    with your name:

    Chapter 2
    Prepared by Evan Brillstein
    Draft

11. Format the cover page text in **18-point Times New Roman, bold**. (Because the
    cover page will not be included in the final document, its font doesn't have to
    match the rest of the document.)

Next, you need to add the current date to the cover page.

Inserting the Current Date

You could begin typing the date and have Word finish it for you using AutoComplete. But
you decide to use the Insert Date and Time command on the Insert menu instead, to take
advantage of its many options. You can use this command to insert both the current date
and time into a document.

To insert the date into the title page:

1. Click at the end of your name, and then press **Enter** to move the insertion point
   to a new line.

2. Click **Insert** on the menu bar, and then click **Date and Time**. The Date and
   Time dialog box opens, as shown in Figure 5-27. The Available formats list box
   contains the current date and time in a variety of formats. Notice the Update
   automatically checkbox, which you could click if you wanted Word to update

the date and time each time you open the document. In this case, however, you simply want to insert today's date without having it updated automatically when you reopen the document.

| Figure 5-27 | DATE AND TIME DIALOG BOX |

leave unchecked so Word won't update date and time in document

current date

current time

3. In the Available formats list box, click the format that provides both the day of the week, and the date—for example, Monday, April 9, 2001.

4. Click **OK**. Word inserts the date into the title page.

5. Verify that the date is formatted in 18-point Times New Roman, bold, to match the rest of the title page text.

Robert is happy to have the day of the week included in the date because it will remind him that the final draft of the chapter is due exactly a week later. He plans to remove the cover page text in the final document. To make sure he remembers to do so, you offer to highlight it with a special color.

Highlighting **Text with Color**

The **Highlight** button on the Formatting toolbar serves the same function as a highlighting pen; you use it to add a shading of bright color over portions of a document. You'll find it useful when you need to draw attention to specific text. If you want, you can click the Highlight list arrow to select a highlighting color from the palette of options. But most people prefer yellow (which is selected by default) because its light shade makes it easy to read the text.

You'll use the yellow highlighting now to draw attention to the cover page text.

To highlight the title page text:

1. Select all the text on the cover page.

2. Place the pointer over the **Highlight** button 🖉 in the Formatting toolbar and observe the screentip, which indicates the selected highlighting color (for example, "Highlight (Yellow)"). Notice that the selected highlighting color also is displayed in the Highlight button itself.

3. If yellow is the selected color, click 🖉 to highlight the text. If yellow is *not* the

selected color, click the **Highlight list** arrow 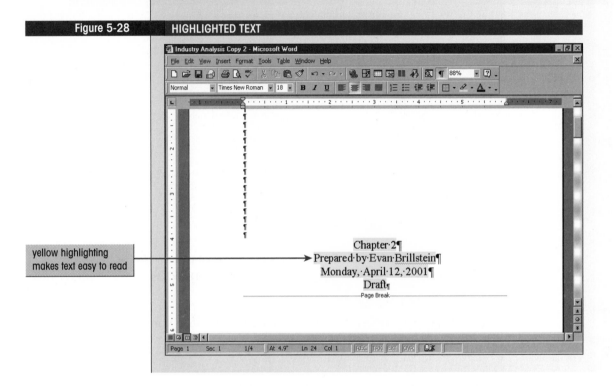 and then click the yellow square (top row, left-most square) in the color palette. The title page text is now highlighted in yellow. The highlighting will remind Robert to remove the cover page when the document is final. See Figure 5-28.

Figure 5-28   **HIGHLIGHTED TEXT**

yellow highlighting makes text easy to read

> Chapter 2¶
> Prepared by Evan Brillstein¶
> Monday, April 12, 2001¶
> Draft¶
> Page Break

Finally, you decide the cover page text would be easier to read if you adjusted the spacing between the characters. Specifically, you want to add space between the characters. While you're at it, you'll also adjust some paragraph spacing within the chapter.

Changing **Character and Paragraph Spacing**

As you know, you can quickly change the spacing between lines of a document to make it single-spaced, 1.5-spaced, or double-spaced. (If you prefer, you can choose even more precise line-spacing options by using the Paragraph command on the Format menu.)

To add polish to a document, you can also adjust the spacing between characters or between individual paragraphs. Adjusting **Character spacing** is useful when you want to emphasize titles, whereas adjusting **paragraph spacing** allows you to fine-tune the appearance of specially formatted elements, such as a bulleted list.

Adjusting Spacing between Characters

Word offers a number of ways to adjust the spacing between characters. In some situations, you might want to use **kerning**, the process of adjusting the spacing between specific combinations of characters to improve their appearance. In most documents, however, it's easiest to select a group of characters and then uniformly expand or condense the spacing between them. Notice that space between characters is measured in points, with one point equal to ½ of an inch.

Expanding or Condensing Spacing between Characters

- Select the text where you want to adjust character spacing.
- Click Format on the menu bar, click Font, and then click the Character Spacing tab.
- Click the Spacing list arrow, and then click Expanded or Condensed. If you like, you can increase or decrease the exact amount of spacing that will be applied to each character by adjusting the settings in the By text box.
- To switch from expanded or condensed spacing back to regular spacing, click the Spacing list arrow and then click Normal.
- Observe the newly formatted characters in the Preview box.
- Click OK to apply the new character spacing.

In this case, you want to expand the spacing between the characters in the cover page. You'll do that now.

To adjust character spacing in the cover page:

1. Select the four lines of the cover page.

2. Click **Format** on the menu bar, and then click **Font**. The Font dialog box opens.

3. If necessary, click the **Character Spacing** tab. This tab, shown in Figure 5-29, offers a number of ways to adjust the spacing between characters.

Figure 5-29   CHARACTER SPACING TAB IN THE FONT DIALOG BOX

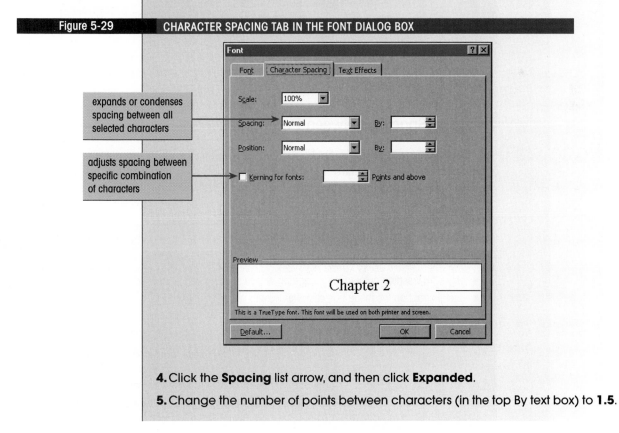

expands or condenses spacing between all selected characters

adjusts spacing between specific combination of characters

4. Click the **Spacing** list arrow, and then click **Expanded**.

5. Change the number of points between characters (in the top By text box) to **1.5**.

6. Observe the expanded spacing (applied to the first line of the selected text) in the Preview box.

7. Click **OK,** and then click anywhere in the cover page to deselect the text. The new character spacing is applied to the text of the cover page. See Figure 5-30.

Figure 5-30	EXPANDED CHARACTER SPACING IN TITLE PAGE

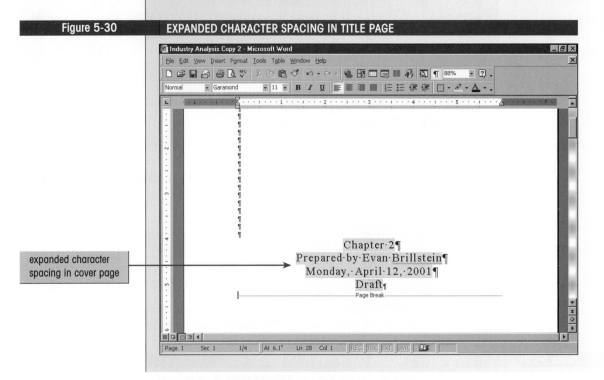

expanded character spacing in cover page

Now that the cover page is finished, you turn your attention to adjusting the spacing before and after the bulleted list on page 2 of the document.

Adjusting Spacing between Paragraphs

In a single-spaced document, such as the draft of Chapter 2, it's often a good idea to insert extra spacing before specially formatted items, such as a bulleted list. As with character spacing, paragraph spacing is measured in points.

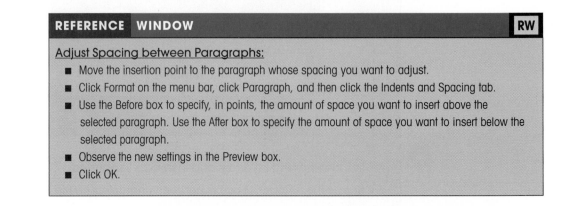

REFERENCE WINDOW **RW**

Adjust Spacing between Paragraphs:
- Move the insertion point to the paragraph whose spacing you want to adjust.
- Click Format on the menu bar, click Paragraph, and then click the Indents and Spacing tab.
- Use the Before box to specify, in points, the amount of space you want to insert above the selected paragraph. Use the After box to specify the amount of space you want to insert below the selected paragraph.
- Observe the new settings in the Preview box.
- Click OK.

Robert has asked you to insert extra space before and after the bulleted list on Page 2, under the heading "Market Research."

To change the paragraph spacing before and after the bulleted list:

1. Scroll to the second page of the document, and then click at the beginning of the first bullet ("Who are our potential customers?") under the heading "Market Research." Now you can insert extra space between this bullet and the introductory sentence before it.

2. Click **Format** on the menu bar, and then click **Paragraph**. The Paragraph dialog box opens.

3. If necessary, click the **Indents and Spacing** tab. See Figure 5-31. As mentioned earlier, you can use the Line spacing settings to choose precise line-spacing options. You'll use the Before box now to specify, in points, the amount of space you want to insert above the selected paragraph.

Figure 5-31   INDENTS AND SPACING TAB IN THE PARAGRAPH DIALOG BOX

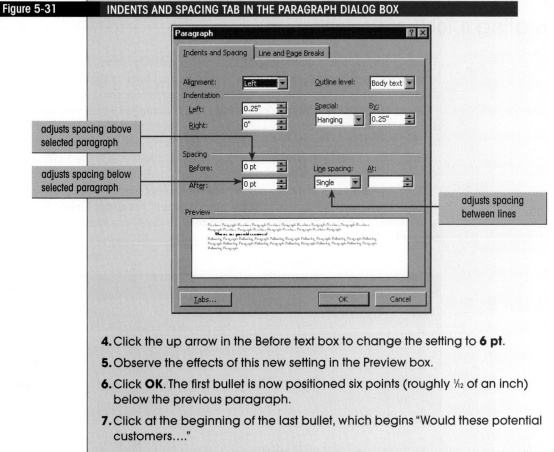

adjusts spacing above selected paragraph

adjusts spacing below selected paragraph

adjusts spacing between lines

4. Click the up arrow in the Before text box to change the setting to **6 pt**.

5. Observe the effects of this new setting in the Preview box.

6. Click **OK**. The first bullet is now positioned six points (roughly ½ of an inch) below the previous paragraph.

7. Click at the beginning of the last bullet, which begins "Would these potential customers...."

8. Insert 6 points of space after the last bullet. The newly formatted bulleted list, with space inserted above and below, is shown in Figure 5-32.

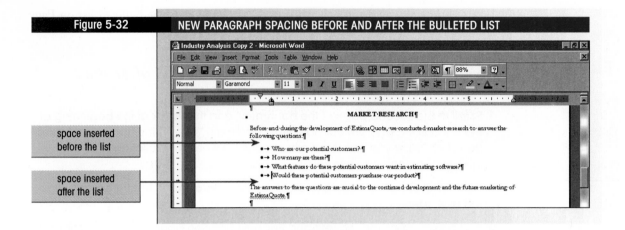

Figure 5-32   NEW PARAGRAPH SPACING BEFORE AND AFTER THE BULLETED LIST

space inserted before the list

space inserted after the list

The additional space draws attention to the bulleted list and makes it easier to read.

Now, Robert wants you create a table of contents, which should usually be one of the last tasks you perform in creating a document.

Creating a Table of Contents

Although this chapter of the business plan is relatively short, the entire business plan is lengthy, so Chiu Lee and Robert want to include a table of contents at the beginning of each chapter. Eventually, they will create a table of contents for the entire business plan.

Word can create a table of contents for any document to which you have applied heading styles in the form of Heading 1, Heading 2, Heading 3, and so forth. Word quickly creates a table of contents in the style you choose and inserts the relevant page numbers for each heading. Note that if you add or delete text later, so that one or more headings move to a new page, the table of contents will not be updated automatically. However, you can easily update the table of contents by clicking anywhere in the table of contents and pressing the F9 key.

To delete a table of contents, simply select it and press the Delete key. To modify the appearance of a table of contents, you need modify the document styles and then re-create a new table of contents.

REFERENCE WINDOW   **RW**

Creating a Table of Contents
- Make sure you have applied heading styles Heading 1, Heading 2, Heading 3, etc.
- Click Insert on the menu bar, and then click Index and Tables.
- Click the Table of Contents tab in the Index and Tables dialog box.
- Select a predefined style in the Formats list box, set the show levels number to the number of heading levels you want to show, and then click the OK button.

Now, you're ready to create a table of contents for Chapter 2 of the EstimaTech business plan, inserting it just below the title of the chapter.

To insert the table of contents for Chapter 2:

1. Move the insertion point to the blank line immediately below the chapter title on page 2.

2. Switch to normal view. First you need to type the heading for the table of contents.

3. Click the **Bold** button [B] on the Formatting toolbar, type **Contents**, click [B] again to turn off bold formatting, and then press **Enter** three times. The insertion point is now located where you want to insert the table of contents.

4. Click **Insert** on the menu bar, and then click **Index and Tables**. The Index and Tables dialog box opens.

5. If necessary, click the **Table of Contents** tab. Word provides a variety of formats for the Table of Contents page. In this case, you'll accept the From template setting in the Formats list box, which indicates that you want to format the table of contents using the Normal style from the current template.

6. Make sure **From template** is selected in the Formats list box. The Print Preview box shows a sample of the format. See Figure 5-33.

Figure 5-33	INDEX AND TABLES DIALOG BOX

sample of contents

use this setting

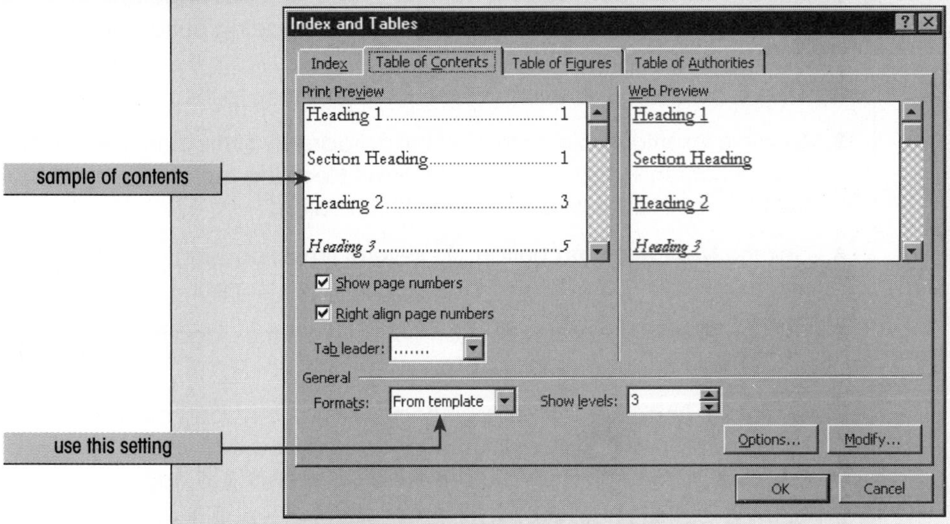

7. Click the **OK** button. Word searches for any text formatted with styles Heading 1, Heading 2, Heading 3, and so on, and then assembles that text and its corresponding page number in a table of contents. The table of contents appears below the "Contents" heading. When selected, the text is grayed to indicate that Word created the list and considers the text a single object.

8. Save the completed document.

With the table of contents at the beginning of the chapter, you're almost ready to print the document. Before you print, however, it's a good idea to review the document on-screen first. In the next section, you'll browse through the document by heading.

Browsing by Heading

Now that you have finished working on Chapter 2 of the business plan, you can print it for Robert and Chiu Lee. Before you print the business plan, however, you should browse through it to double-check its appearance and organization. Word provides various ways for you to move through a document quickly, a process known as **browsing.** For example, you could browse by headings (that is, move from one heading to another) or browse by page (that is, move from one page to another). The particular element by which you choose to browse (for example, headings or pages) is known as the **browse object.** Right now, you'll browse through the chapter by heading.

To browse by heading:

1. Click the **Select Browse Object** button located near the bottom of the vertical scroll bar. A palette of browse objects opens. To review these options, place the pointer over each object, and read its description in the gray box at the bottom of the palette. Note that if you don't see the browse object you need here, you can click the Go To button in the lower-left corner of the palette to display a dialog box with additional options.

2. Click the **Browse by Heading** button. The Previous Page button and Next Page button are now called the Previous Heading button and the Next Heading button, respectively. Note that they are also blue. When you click one of these buttons, Word will move the insertion point to the next heading.

3. Move the insertion point to the first full paragraph of the document, below the table of contents, and then click the **Next Heading** button. Word moves the insertion point to the heading, "Market Research."

4. Click the **Next Heading** button several times, pausing after each click to read the heading and view the format of the document.

5. Click the **Previous Heading** button several times, again pausing each time to read the heading.

   As you can imagine, browsing by heading in a very long document can allow you to move through a lot of material quickly. Now that you're finished browsing by heading, you'll change the browsing object back to pages.

6. Click, and then click the **Browse by Page** button. The Previous and Next buttons are black again, indicating that your browse object is now set back to Page.

7. Save the document as **Industry Analysis Final Copy**.

8. Preview, and then print the chapter. If Word displays a message about updating the table of contents, then click the **OK** button in the message dialog box. Your completed document should look like Figure 5-34. Notice that the yellow highlighting on the cover page appears as a gray background on a black and white print-out.

Figure 5-34	THE COMPLETED DOCUMENT (PAGES 1 AND 2)

Chapter 2
Prepared by Evan Brillstein
Monday, April 12, 2001
Draft

ESTIMATECH BUSINESS PLAN   INDUSTRY ANALYSIS PAGE 2

CHAPTER 2: INDUSTRY ANALYSIS

Contents

The primary goal of EstimaTech is to become the industry leader in developing and marketing a major new type of software product—EstimaQuote. This computer program is designed for a specialized customer, will be sold at a reasonable price, and will be supported by a state-of-the-art service program. To determine the potential for achieving this goal, we have carried out extensive market research.

MARKET RESEARCH

Before and during the development of EstimaQuote, we conducted market research to answer the following questions:

- Who are our potential customers?
- How many are there?
- What features do these potential customers want in estimating software?
- Would these potential customers purchase our product?

The answers to these questions are crucial to the continued development and the future marketing of EstimaQuote.

PHASES OF THE MARKET RESEARCH

The market research was carried out in three phases. In Phase 1, we analyzed the potential customers for our software throughout the United States and Canada. In Phase 2, we determined the method by which potential customers estimate renovation costs, their perceived need for a computerized

Figure 5-34   THE COMPLETED DOCUMENT (PAGES 3 AND 4)

ESTIMATECH BUSINESS PLAN   INDUSTRY ANALYSIS PAGE 3

method for estimating costs, and the desired features of such a product. The survey also assessed the current condition of the industry in order to understand future market trends. In Phase 3, we provided a random sample of our potential customers with a pre-release beta copy (version 0.5) of EstimaQuote. We observed these customers as they installed and used this software, making particular note of the problems and difficulties they encountered. We are continuing with Phase 3 as we develop a new pre-release version of the software and improve our customer-support methods. As of this writing, we have almost completed, but not yet released, version 1 of the EstimaQuote, and have begun to develop version 2.

Here is the time frame for the three phases:

Phase 1. Analysis of potential customers	June to August 2001
Phase 2. Determination of needs and methods	August to November 2001
Phase 3. Beta testing of software	November 2001 to present

MARKET DEFINITION

EstimaTech will operate in the national and international market. After completing version 2 of EstimaQuote in English, we plan to expand to Spanish, French, German, and Japanese versions over the next four years. We will continue to improve our software in all languages.

SIZE OF THE MARKET

Our primary customers include large- and medium-sized contracting companies that restore existing buildings. Our secondary customers are government and private agencies, and wealthy individuals who renovate historical homes and buildings. Our estimated market size (for the United States only) is approximately 35,000. This number includes only those organizations and individuals directly involved in restoration cost estimates.

DEMOGRAPHIC DESCRIPTION OF TARGET USERS

Our target users have the following characteristics: Prepare frequent estimates; use printed forms; use computer spreadsheet, database, or calculator; prepare multiple calculations; provide high- and low-end options

Our target users desire a software program that can: Provide a tabular view of data; calculate costs based on overall building requirements; perform a one-step calculation of high and low prices; update costs of materials and labor; interface with project management software

CUSTOMER NEEDS

The results of the survey clearly demonstrated the need for a product such as EstimaQuote.[1] Approximately 72% of those individuals answering the questionnaire were dissatisfied with their current method of preparing cost estimates. Subsequent personal interviews supported these results. About 65% of those interviewed said they would purchase a product like EstimaQuote, given an estimated cost of $5,000 for the site license and $500 per year for license renewal and customer support.

---
[1] See Appendix 1, "Survey of Potential EstimaQuote Customers."

ESTIMATECH BUSINESS PLAN   INDUSTRY ANALYSIS PAGE 4

MARKET TRENDS

The current business climate shows a reversal in the trend of developing new properties for business expansion in the nation's suburbs. Also, major businesses are returning to urban centers. These trends have spawned a sharp increase in the number of developers whose primary focus is renovation of old and run-down properties. In addition, historical restoration projects are increasing. Recently, a national survey by the U.S. Historical Society showed a 35% increase in the number of buildings being added to the historical registry.

CURRENT COMPETITION

No company currently has a specialized product like EstimaQuote. Many companies, however, use computerized database management systems and spreadsheets to develop estimates. Some companies have custom software designed for this purpose.

Our current competition, therefore, includes the following:
- General database systems such as Access, FoxPro, Paradox, and dBase
- General spreadsheet programs such as Excel, Quattro Pro, and Lotus 1-2-3
- Custom software

EstimaTech stands poised to capitalize on current trends in the market. We are prepared to refine our product to meet the needs of this growing market, aggressively market our product to reach potential customers, create new products as time goes on, and to withstand challenges from future competitors.

Potential customers indicate their need for the software we are developing. In addition, current market trends indicate that increased need for our software will continue.

Page breaks in your document might be at different locations, depending on the fonts you use. Don't be concerned about this. Simply scroll through your document and add return characters as necessary so that the lines of text are well-grouped.

9. Close the Preview window, close the document, and then exit Word.

You now have a hardcopy of the final Chapter 2 of the business plan, which you take to Robert and Chiu Lee.

Session 5.3 QUICK CHECK

1. Explain how to position the insertion point in the middle of a blank page without pressing Enter to insert paragraph marks.

2. True or False: If you use the Date and Time dialog box to insert the current date in your document, Word will automatically revise the date each time you open the document.

3. Describe a situation in which you might want to highlight text in a document, and then explain how to do so.

4. What is the difference between character spacing and paragraph spacing?

5. True or False: It is only possible to adjust the spacing before the selected paragraph.

6. Explain the steps required to create a table of contents in Word.

7. How do you browse by heading through a document?

In this tutorial, you have edited the business plan content with the Thesaurus and improved its appearance using fonts and styles. You reorganized the document in Outline view, hyphenated the document, and added a footnote. Also, you created a highlighted cover page, adjusted character and paragraph spacing, and added a table of contents. Chiu Lee and Robert plan to revise the chapter in the coming week. You also gave them a copy of the new document template, which they will use as they write additional chapters.

REVIEW ASSIGNMENTS

Chiu Lee and Robert have received the startup funding they wanted and are almost ready to begin marketing their software. They have written a summary of their customer training and support policies and have asked you to help edit and format the document.

1. Start Word, if necessary, and make sure that nonprinting characters and the ruler are displayed.

2. Open the file Training from the Review folder for Tutorial 5 on your Data Disk.

3. Open the Save As dialog box, and create a new folder called Policies (within the Review folder).

4. Save the file Training in the new folder as Training Courses.

5. Use the Thesaurus to replace "periodic" (in the first line of the first paragraph under the heading "Training") with a simpler word.

6. Attach the Word Contemporary Report template to the document. If this template is not available, choose another, and then use appropriate headings in the following step.

7. Apply the Chapter Label style to the first line of the document, "Training and Technical Support." Apply the Heading 1 style to all of the headings in the body of the document: "Training," "Introduction," "Technical Support," "Using Technical Support," "Average Wait Times," and "Frequently Asked Questions." Do not apply a style to the company address and phone number at the top of the document.

Explore 8. Create a new style by example for the company address and phone number at the top of the document. First, format the text as 12-point Arial bold, and then center it on the page. Change the character spacing to expanded, with 1.5 points between each character. Once the text is formatted properly, click Format on the menu bar, click Style, click the New button, name the new style "Company Information," review the style description, click OK, and then click Apply. (Do not save the new style to the template.) Click anywhere in the document outside the first six lines, and verify that the new style is available in the Style list box on the Formatting toolbar.

9. Modify the Chapter Label heading so that it formats text with center alignment, using the small caps font effect, in 20-point Times New Roman. (Look for the alignment setting on the Indents and Spacing tab of the Paragraph dialog box. Look for the font settings on the Font tab of the Font dialog box.)

10. Under the heading "Using Technical Support," select the list of technical support options (beginning "Call our telephone support….and ending with "…and then press Enter"), and then apply the List Bullet style. Under the heading "Average Wait Times," apply the List Bullet style to the list of waiting times for the four technical support plans (Bronze through Platinum). Modify the List Bullet Style by changing its paragraph spacing to 6 points before and 0 points after. (Do not save the modified style to the template.)

11. Using Outline view, reorganize the document so the Introduction section is the first section of the document.

12. Demote the headings "Using Technical Support," "Average Wait Times," and "Frequently Asked Questions" to make them level-2 headings, and then switch to Normal view to review your changes.

13. Below the heading, "Technical Support," after the period at the end of the second sentence, insert the following footnote: "As the needs and resources of your company change, you can change your technical support plan. Changes can be made only at the expiration of the current contract period."

Explore 14. Hyphenate the document with a hyphenation zone of 0.1", using manual hyphenation. Don't hyphenate words so that only two letters appear alone on a line.

15. Create a cover page for the document. Use Click and Type to insert your name, and the word "Draft" in the center of the page. Insert the current date and time, using the format of your choice.

16. Highlight the word "Draft" to call attention to it.

17. Save and preview your document.

18. Insert a table of contents immediately following the company address and phone numbers. In the Formats list box, specify the Distinctive format for your table of contents. (If the Distinctive format is not available, choose another.) Be sure to include the necessary number of heading levels.

Explore 19. A table of contents provides a quick way to move the insertion point to a document heading. Try clicking a heading in the table of contents, and watch the insertion point jump to that heading in the document.

Explore 20. Click at the top of the document, click the Select Browse Object button, click the Go To button, and then use the Go To dialog box to move the insertion point to the footnote.

21. Save the document, and then print it. If you are asked if you want to update the table of contents, click cancel.

22. Use the Training Courses document to create a new template called "Policy Template." Save the new template in the Policies folder.

23. Open a blank document, and attach the Policy Template to it. Verify that the template headings are available in the document, save the new document as "New Policy," and then close the document.

Explore 24. To experiment with using a Word template as the basis for a brand-new document, click File on the menu bar, and then click New. Click the tabs in the New dialog box to review the various templates provided with Word. Some tabs include icons for wizards, which guide you through the steps involved in creating complicated documents such as Web pages. Click the General tab. Note that if you create a new template, and save it in the Templates folder, it will appear as an option on this tab. Click the Reports tab, click the Contemporary Report icon, and then click OK. A document opens with placeholder text for all the elements of a report. For example, in the upper-right corner you see "Type Address Here." A place-holder company name, "blue sky associates," appears at the top of the first page formatted in the Company Name style. Review the remaining styles in the templates. To use this template, you could delete the placeholder text with text you type, and then save the document with a new name. When you're finished, close the document without saving changes. Open and examine two other templates.

25. Close any open documents.

CASE PROBLEMS

Case 1. Mountainland Nursery Raynal Stubbs is the sales manager of Mountainland Nursery in Steamboat Springs, Colorado. Twice each year, he provides sales representatives with guidelines for helping customers with their planting needs. Raynal has asked you to help him prepare this year's list of spring-blooming perennials.

1. Start Word, if necessary, open the file Flowers from the Cases folder for Tutorial 5 on your Data Disk, and save it as Mountainland Flowers.

2. Using outline view, promote the section "Guidelines for Helping Customers" to a first-level heading. (*Hint:* Show all text by clicking the Show All Headings button, so you can see the sentence to promote.)

3. Reorder the document so the introduction section is the first section of the document.

4. Make "Guidelines for Helping Customers" the last section in the document.

5. Print the outline, without showing the formatting of the headings.

6. Change the font of the Title style and the Heading 1 style to a sans serif font.

7. Change the font of the Normal style to a serif font other than Times New Roman.

8. Click at the end of the telephone number, at the top of the document press Enter twice, type "Draft Prepared by," and then type your name. Highlight the new line, using the color of your choice.

9. Format the four lines containing the nursery's name, address, and phone number using one of the font effects (such as small caps) available in the Font dialog box. Adjust the character spacing as necessary to make the text easy to read.

10. In the last item of the bulleted list, change "patrons" to one of its synonyms in the Thesaurus.

11. In the first sentence under the heading "Suggested Spring Blooming Perennials," after the word "perennials," insert a footnote reference. Type the following text for the footnote: "Information taken from Andrea Macula's *Gardening in the West*, published by Gladstone Press, Flagstaff, Arizona." Be sure to italicize the book title.

12. Hyphenate the document using automatic hyphenation.

13. Move the insertion point to the paragraph above the table, and change the paragraph spacing after the paragraph to 12-point.

Explore ▷ 14. Insert a table of contents for the document above the introduction, using the Formal style. Because the document is so short, there's no need for page numbers, so you can deselect the Show page numbers checkbox.

Explore ▷ 15. Change the heading "Guidelines for Helping Customers" to "Guidelines for Assisting Customers." Now that you've changed the heading, you need to update the table of contents, as follows: right-click the table of contents, and then click Update Field in the shortcut menu.

16. Save your changes. Preview the document for problems, fix any formatting problems, and print the document.

Explore ▷ 17. Word's Autocorrect feature allows you to preserve formatted text and then insert it into documents later simply by typing a few characters. To see how this works, select the nursery's name, address, and phone number at the top of the document, as well as the blank paragraph below the phone number. Click Tools on the menu bar, click AutoCorrect, click the AutoCorrect tab, type "mf address" (without the quotes) in the Replace text box, verify that the Formatted text option button is selected, click the Add button, and then click OK. To try out the new Autocorrect entry, close the Mountainland Flowers document, open a blank document, type mf address, and press the spacebar. Verify that the formatted text is inserted into the document, and then delete your AutoCorrect entry as follows: Click Tools, click AutoCorrect, scroll down and select the mn address entry in the list box, click Delete, and click OK.

Case 2. Menus for Classic Catering   Clarissa Ruffolo and Tom Jenkins own Classic Catering, an upscale catering service that specializes in home entertaining for people who like to socialize but don't have time to cook. Tom has prepared a brochure with the company's latest menu choices, which he formatted using the Word default heading styles. However, he is not happy with the brochure's appearance and has asked for your help.

1. Start Word, if necessary, and check your screen, making sure that nonprinting characters are displayed.

2. Open the file Catering from the Cases folder for Tutorial 5 on your Data Disk, and save it as Classic Catering.

Explore 3. Notice that the headings in the document are formatted using the Word default Heading 1 and Heading 2 styles. Now, use the Templates and Add-Ins command on the Tools menu to attach the template named Menu Template, which is stored in the Cases folder for Tutorial 5, to the current document. Remember to select the Automatically update document styles checkbox. Verify that the document's styles are updated to reflect the template's styles.

4. Apply the Bulleted List style to all the bulleted lists in the document.

5. In outline view, promote the headings "Lunch," "Dinner," and "Our Famous Desserts," to level-1 headings.

6. Move the "Our Famous Desserts" heading up, to make it the first heading in the document, above "Bagel Brunch."

7. Print the outline, with only the headings displayed.

8. In the first sentence under the heading "Our Famous Desserts," use the Thesaurus to find a synonym for "delectable."

Explore 9. Switch to print layout view, insert a new first page, move the insertion point up to the new page, select the Company Name style, then use Click and Type to insert "Classic Catering" (without the quotes) about 3 inches down, in the center of the document. Notice how the Click and Type Feature automatically applies the selected style.

10. Press [Enter], select the Company Address style, and then type the following:

    2567 Eton Ridge
    Madison, Wisconsin 53708
    Prepared by Your Name

    Be sure to replace "Your Name" with your first and last name. Then, insert the current date below your name, in the format of your choice.

11. Highlight your name in yellow.

12. Save, preview, and print the document.

Case 3. The Business of Basketball   As part of the requirements for your advanced writing class, your writing group has written a term paper on "The Business of Basketball." Your assignment is to edit the preliminary outline.

1. Start Word, if necessary, and check your screen, making sure that nonprinting characters are displayed. Open the file Business from the Cases folder for Tutorial 5 on your Data Disk.

2. Within the Cases folder for Tutorial 5, create a new folder called "Writing Project," and then save the document in the new folder as "Business of Basketball."

3. Using outline view, reorder the headings so that "Team Philosophy" follows "Management Style."

4. Demote the section "Marketing" to make it a second-level heading.

5. Print the completed outline of the document, with the Show Formatting feature turned off.

6. Use the Thesaurus to find a synonym to replace "lucrative" in the first sentence under the heading "Introduction."

7. Scroll to the table in the document, and then at the end of the table title, add the footnote with the text, "Data taken from *Financial World*, May 25, 2001, page 29." Scroll up and place the pointer over the footnote number, in the main document. Observe the text of the footnote displayed in a screen tip.

8. Change the Heading 1 style to a sans serif font.

9. Create a new paragraph style called Abstract. For this style, specify 12-point Arial, with single-line spacing. Add a box border around the paragraph. Apply the style to the paragraph under the heading "Abstract."

10. Add your name to the list of authors on the first page.

11. Below the class name, insert the current date, and on another line, the word "Draft". Highlight the date and the word "Draft" in yellow.

12. Insert a section break following the word "Draft" on the title page, so that the Table of Contents begins a new page.

13. Create a table of contents for the report to appear on its own page following the title page. Use the Formal style.

14. If the heading "Abstract" is on a separate page from the boxed paragraph below it, insert a hard page break above the heading "Abstract." Do the same for the table title, if necessary. (*Hint:* To insert a hard page break, move the insertion point to the desired location, and press Ctrl + Enter.)

15. Save the changes to your report; then preview and print it. Close the file.

Case 4. *Report on Median Family Income* Arlene Littlefield is an economic analyst for a consulting firm that helps minority businesses market their products. She is preparing a short report on the median family income of American families, from 1980 to 1991, based upon the ethnicity of the head of household. She has obtained a government report that contains two tables of data, which she gives to you as unformatted Word tables and asks you to help her analyze the information and write her report.

1. Start Word, if necessary, making sure that nonprinting characters are displayed. Open the file Income from the Cases folder for Tutorial 5 on your Data Disk, and print the document. Analyze the two tables. On scratch paper (or in a Word document window), jot down your observations, ideas, and conclusions about the data in the two tables. As you analyze the data, you might be interested in noting that the average family income for all families in the United States in 1950, 1960, and 1970 was $3,319, $5,630, and $9,867 in current dollars and $18,757, $25,850, and $34,636 in constant dollars. (Data for minorities during those time periods is scarce or unavailable.)

2. Plan a logical order of topics for your talk, with headings and subheadings. Your headings might be the following: "Introduction" (which explains the purpose of your report), "Income Increases During the 1980s" (with subheadings "Income Increase for Whites," "Income Increases for Blacks," and "Income Increases for Hispanics"), "Comparison of Incomes Based on Ethnicity," "Are Minorities Catching Up with Whites in Income?," and "Economic Progress during the 1980s: Did We Get Richer?," "Four Decades of Economic Progress in the U.S." You might want to use some of these sample headings or none of them. Organize your outline in a logical manner. Make sure your final heading is "Summary" or "Conclusion."

Explore ▶ 3. Open a new Word document, and type a title for your talk.

Explore ▶ 4. In addition to creating an outline using document headings, you can create a numbered list in outline format, using the Numbering button on the Formatting toolbar. To experiment with this feature now, move the insertion point to a new line, click the Numbering button on the Formatting toolbar, and type your first heading. Press Enter, and type the next heading. To demote a level-1 heading to a level-2 heading, click the Increase Indent button on the Formatting toolbar. To demote a level-2 heading to a level-3 heading, click the Increase Indent button again. Use the Decrease Indent to promote headings. You can promote and demote headings as you type or after you've typed all the headings. After you type the last item in the outline, press Enter twice.

Explore ▶ 5. Now that you have created your outline, you can format it using the Word default heading styles. Select your outline numbered list, click Format on the menu bar, click Bullets and Numbering, and then click the Outline Numbered tab, which offers two rows of formatting styles. Click the second style from the right, in the bottom row (which uses the form I. Heading 1, A. Heading 2), and then click OK.

6. Switch to outline view, and print two versions of your outline, using two different organizations.

7. Switch to print layout view, and write your report. One or two paragraphs under each heading is sufficient.

8. At the appropriate places in your document, copy the tables from the document Income into your document.

9. Format your tables to be attractive and readable. Make sure they are single-spaced and each table appears in its entirety on one page rather than spanning two pages.

10. At the end of each table title, insert a footnote with the citation for the table: U.S. Department of Commerce, Bureau of the Census, Current Population Reports, Series P-60, *Money Income of Families and Persons*, nos. 105 and 107. Use this same citation for both tables.

11. Change the fonts of the Normal and heading styles as desired.

12. Hyphenate your document as desired.

Explore   13. Edit the footnotes by adding "*in the United States*" after the word "Persons." The final footnote should read: "U.S. Department of Commerce, Bureau of the Census, Current Population Reports, Series P-60, *Money Income of Families and Persons in the United States*, nos. 105 and 107."

14. Create a table of contents at the appropriate location in your document.

15. Save your report as Median Family Income in the Cases folder for Tutorial 5 and then preview and print it. Close the documents.

QUICK | CHECK ANSWERS

Session 5.1

1. In the Save As dialog box, click the New Folder button, type the name of the folder, and then click OK.

2. The Thesaurus is a feature you can use to find synonyms for words in a document.

3. The following are synonyms for "restore" included in Word's Thesaurus: refurbish, renovate, repair, do up, rebuild, recondition, touch up, fix, fix up, reinstate, reestablish, bring back, and return.

4. A serif font is a font in which each character has a small embellishment (called a serif) at its tips. A sans serif font is a font in which the characters do not have serifs. Serif fonts are useful for the main text of a document because they are easy to read. Sans serif fonts are best for headings and titles. Two examples of serif fonts are Times New Roman and Garamond. Two examples of sans serif fonts include Arial and Century Gothic.

5. Click Format on the menu bar, click Theme, and then click the Style Gallery button. In the Template list box, click the template you want to preview. In the Preview box, click the Document option button to see how the template's Normal styles look when applied to your document, or click the Example option button to see a sample file that uses all the template styles. Click the OK button to attach the template to your document.

6. First, create a new document containing all the styles you want to include in your template, save it as a Word document, and delete all text from the document. Then save the file as a Document Template. Verify that the Templates folder is displayed in the Save in list box. If you save your template to this folder, it will appear as one of the options in the New dialog box. If you prefer, you can save the template in a different location, such as your data disk. To use a template saved in the Template folder, use the New command on the File menu. To attach a template saved in a different location, click Tools on the menu bar, click Templates and Add-ins, and then click the Attach button to open the Attach

Template dialog box. Use the Look in list box to locate and select your template, and then click the Open button to return to the Templates and Add-ins dialog box. Click the Automatically update document styles check box to select it, and then click the OK button to return to the current document.

7. Click Format on the menu bar, and then click Style. Select the style you want to modify in the Style list box, and then click the Modify button. Use the options available from the Format button to specify new settings for the style.

8. Format a paragraph with the font, margins, alignment, spacing, and so forth that you want for the style, and then select the paragraph. Click the Style text box on the Formatting toolbar. Type the name of the new style (replacing the current style name), and then press the Enter key. Or, select the text for which you want to define a style. Click Format on the menu bar, click Style, click the New button, and type the name of the new style in the Name text box. Finally, click the OK button, and then click the Apply button.

Session 5.2

1. By moving the headings in an outline, you can reorganize the document text.

2. When you promote a heading, it becomes a higher-level heading in the outline. For example, you could promote a level-2 heading to a level-1 heading. When you demote a heading, it becomes a lower-level heading. For example, you could demote a level-1 heading to a level-2 or level-3 heading.

3. To promote a heading, click that heading in outline view, and then click the Promote button on the Outline toolbar. To demote a heading, click that heading and then click the Demote button.

4. True

5. A river is a blank area running through the text of a page.

6. The hyphenation zone is the distance from the right margin within which words will be hyphenated. Increasing its size reduces the number of hyphenated words.

7. The advantages of using the Footnote feature are:

   - Word numbers footnotes or endnotes automatically. If you add a note anywhere in the document, delete a note, or move a note, Word automatically renumbers all the remaining footnotes or endnotes consecutively.

   - Word automatically formats the footnote text at the bottom of the page or the endnote text at the end of the document.

   - You can edit a footnote or endnote at any time. To modify the text, select Footnotes from the View menu and then use the same editing commands you use in the document window.

   - If you add or delete text that moves the footnote reference onto a different page, the footnote will also move to that page. The reference in the text and the footnote at the bottom of the page will always be on the same page.

8. A footnote appears at the bottom of a page, whereas an endnote appears at the end of a document.

Session 5.3

1. Double-click a blank area of a page using the Click and Type pointer.

2. False

3. It is sometimes helpful to highlight text that you'll want to delete from a document

later. To highlight text, first select it and then click the Highlight button on the Formatting toolbar.

4. Character spacing affects the positioning of individual characters, whereas paragraph spacing affects the spacing between paragraphs.

5. False

6. Make sure you have applied heading styles Heading 1, Heading 2, Heading 3, and so forth. Click Insert on the menu bar, and then click Index and Tables. Click the Table of Contents tab in the Index and Tables dialog box. Select a predefined style in the Formats list box, set the show-levels number to the number of heading levels you want to show, and then click the OK button.

7. Click the Select Browse Object button, click the Heading button, and then click the Previous Heading or Next Heading buttons.

OBJECTIVES

In this tutorial you will:

- Create, edit, and format a mail merge main document

- Create, edit, and format a mail merge data source

- Sort records in a data source

- Merge files to create personalized form letters

- Create, format, and print mailing labels

- Create a telephone list from a data source

CREATING FORM LETTERS AND MAILING LABELS

Writing a Sales Letter for The Pet Shoppe

CASE

The Pet Shoppe

Alicia Robles is vice-president of sales for The Pet Shoppe, a chain of 15 superstores based in Colorado Springs, Colorado. The Pet Shoppe, which has customers throughout the state, sells a wide variety of pets, pet food, supplies, and services. As part of her job, Alicia sends information about The Pet Shoppe's products and services to customers who request to be on the company's mailing list. Alicia needs to send the same information to many customers, but because of the large number of Pet Shoppe customers, she and her staff don't have the time to write personalized letters. Instead, she can create a **form letter** that contains the content she wants to send all customers and then add personal information for each customer, such as the name, address, type of pet, and so on, in specific places. To do this manually would be very time-consuming. Fortunately, Microsoft Word provides a time-saving method that simplifies Alicia's job. By using Word's Mail Merge feature, Alicia can produce multiple copies of the same letter yet personalize each copy with customer-specific information in about the same amount of time it takes to personalize just one letter. She also could use this feature to create such documents as catalogs, directories, and contracts.

The Pet Shoppe is celebrating its 10th anniversary. As a promotional tool, Alicia wants to send out a form letter to all customers on the mailing list telling them about the chain's 10th Anniversary Celebration and offering them a discount if they purchase a product or service anytime during the store's anniversary month. Alicia has already written the letter she wants to send, but she needs to add the personal information for each customer. She asks you to create the form letters and the mailing labels for the envelopes.

In this tutorial, you'll help Alicia create a form letter and mailing labels using Word's Mail Merge feature. First, you'll open the letter that will serve as the main document. Next, you'll create a data source document that contains the name and address of each customer who will receive the customized letter.

Then, you'll have Word merge the main document with the data source, which creates the customized letters, and sorts them in ZIP code order. You'll also send a special version of the letter offering special savings on surplus inventory to customers in a particular ZIP code. Finally, you'll use the data source document to create mailing labels Alicia can put on the envelopes and to create a telephone list so Alicia can have the sales representatives follow up the mailing with a phone call to each customer.

SESSION 6.1

In this session, you'll see how Alicia planned her letter. Then you'll open the form letter and create a document containing the specific customer information that will be inserted into the form letter using Word's Mail Merge feature.

Planning the Form Letter

Alicia hopes to generate increased sales for The Pet Shoppe chain by announcing a 10-percent discount on the purchase of any product or service as part of the company's 10th Anniversary Celebration. Alicia's sales letter will inform current customers about The Pet Shoppe's 10th Anniversary Celebration and offer them a special discount on products and services during November. Her letter is organized to capture the reader's attention. First, she cites a few examples of the need The Pet Shoppe fills, and then she briefly describes The Pet Shoppe's services and products. Finally, she offers a discount to encourage readers to visit their local stores.

Alicia writes in a persuasive, informal style. She illustrates the need and quality of The Pet Shoppe's services by including personal experiences of current customers. Alicia wants to send a professional-looking, personalized letter to each customer on The Pet Shoppe's mailing list. She uses a standard business-letter format and plans to print the letters on stationery preprinted with the company letterhead.

The Merge Process

Alicia asks you to use Word's Mail Merge feature to create the form letters. In general, a **merge** combines information from two separate documents to create many final documents, each of which contains customized information. In Word, the two separate documents are called a main document and a data source.

A **main document** is a document (such as a letter or a contract) that, in addition to text, contains areas of placeholder text (called **merge fields**) to mark where variable information (such as a name or an address) will be inserted. Alicia's main document is a letter that looks like Figure 6–1, except that merge fields will replace the red text to mark the locations of the customer's name, address, and other information.

Figure 6-1 ALICIA'S FORM LETTER

A **data source** is a document that contains information, such as customers' names and addresses that will be merged into the main document. Alicia's data source is a name and address list of The Pet Shoppe customers.

Inserting information from a data source into a main document produces a final document, called a **merged document**. Figure 6–2 illustrates how the data source and main document combine to form a merged document.

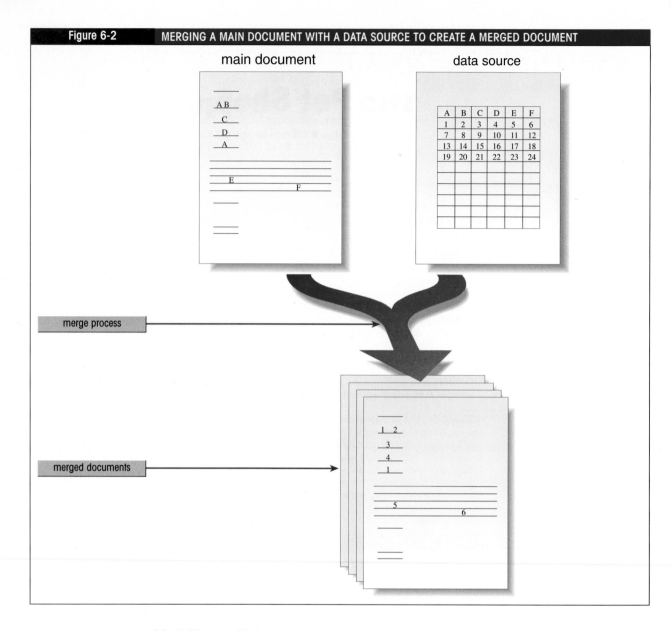

Figure 6-2 MERGING A MAIN DOCUMENT WITH A DATA SOURCE TO CREATE A MERGED DOCUMENT

Mail Merge Fields

During a mail merge, the **merge fields** (the placeholders for text that changes in the main document) instruct Word to retrieve specific information from the data source. For example, one merge field in the main document might retrieve a name from the data source, whereas another merge field might retrieve an address. For each complete set of data (in this instance, a name and address) in the data source, Word will create a new, separate page in the merged document. Thus, if Alicia has five sets of customer names and addresses in her data source, the merge will produce five versions of the main document, each one containing a different customer name and address in the appropriate places.

In addition to merge fields, a main document also can contain **Word fields**, which retrieve information from sources other than the data source. For example, a Word field might insert the current date into a main document, prompt you to input text from the keyboard, or print information only if certain, specified conditions are met. Figure 6–3 lists some of the most common Word and merge fields.

Figure 6-3	COMMON FIELDS USED IN MAIL MERGE
WORD FIELDS	**ACTION**
DATE	Inserts current date
FILLIN	Displays a prompt during merge; response is inserted into the merged document
IF	Prints information only if a specified condition is met
MERGEFIELD	Extracts information from the data source document and inserts it into the merged document

You can distinguish merge fields from the other text of the main document because each merge field name is enclosed by pairs of angled brackets like this: << >>. You don't type the merge field into your main document; instead, you use the Insert Merge Field command to place the merge fields into your main document, and Word automatically inserts the brackets.

Data Fields and Records

Data for a mail merge can come from many sources, including a Microsoft Word document, a Microsoft Excel workbook, or a Microsoft Access database. In the Review Assignments, you will learn how to use a Microsoft Excel workbook as a data source. For Alicia's mail merge, you will use a Word table in which information is organized into data fields and records, as shown in Figure 6–4. The **header row**, the first row of the table, contains the name of each merge field used in a main document in a separate cell. Every other cell of the table contains a **data field**, or the specific information that replaces the merge field in the main document. As shown in Figure 6–4, one data field might be the first name of a customer, another data field the customer's address, another data field the customer's city, and so forth. Each row of data fields in the table makes up a complete record, or all the information about one individual or object. For proper functioning of a mail merge, every record in the data source must have the same set of merge fields.

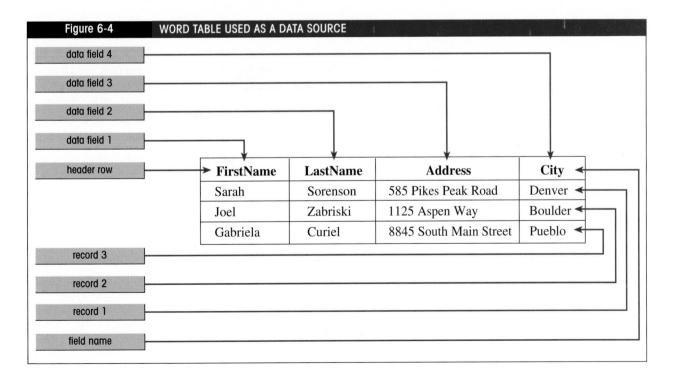

Figure 6-4   WORD TABLE USED AS A DATA SOURCE

Data sources are not limited to records about customers. You could create data sources with inventory records, records of suppliers, or records of equipment. After you understand how to manage and manipulate the records in a data source, you'll be able to use them for many applications.

Creating a Main Document

The main document contains the text that will appear in all the letters, as well as the merge fields that tell Word where to insert the information from the data source. In the first step of the merge process, you must indicate which document you intend to use as the main document. You can either create a new document or use an existing document as the main document.

Alicia has already written the letter she wants to send out to all Pet Shoppe customers, so you don't need to create a new document. Instead, you'll modify an existing document to create the main document.

REFERENCE WINDOW   **RW**

Creating a Main Document

- Click Tools on the menu bar, and then click Mail Merge to display the Mail Merge Helper dialog box.
- Click the Create button in the Main document section of the dialog box, and then click the type of main document that you want to create (such as Form Letters).
- Click the Active Window button to use the active, open document as the main document. Click the New Main Document button if you want to open a new, blank document as the main document.
- Click the Edit button on the Mail Merge Helper dialog box. If necessary, click the appropriate filename.
- Edit (or create) the text of the main document; add merge fields into the main document by clicking the Insert Merge Field button on the Mail Merge toolbar.

To start Word and create the main document:

1. Start Word as usual and insert your Data Disk in the appropriate drive, open the **PetShopp** file from the Tutorial folder for Tutorial 6 on your Data Disk, and then save the document on the disk as **Pet Shoppe Form Letter**. This is the text of the letter that Alicia wrote to send to Pet Shoppe customers and will become the main document of your form letter. You don't have to display nonprinting characters for this tutorial.

2. Click **Tools** on the menu bar, and then click **Mail Merge**. The Mail Merge Helper dialog box opens. See Figure 6-5. The Mail Merge Helper dialog box contains a checklist to help you create merged documents.

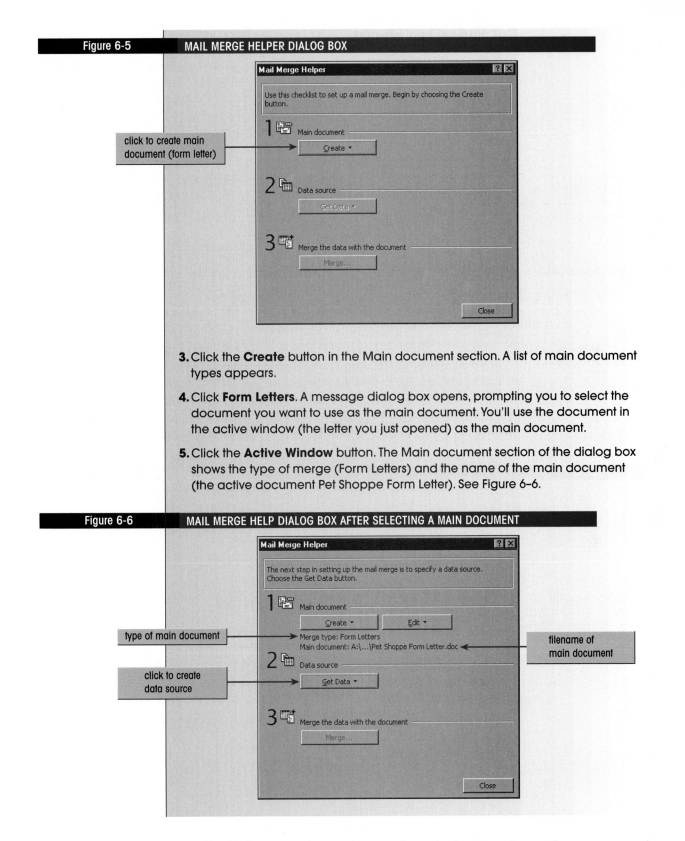

| Figure 6-5 | MAIL MERGE HELPER DIALOG BOX |

click to create main
document (form letter)

| Figure 6-6 | MAIL MERGE HELP DIALOG BOX AFTER SELECTING A MAIN DOCUMENT |

type of main document

click to create
data source

filename of
main document

3. Click the **Create** button in the Main document section. A list of main document types appears.

4. Click **Form Letters**. A message dialog box opens, prompting you to select the document you want to use as the main document. You'll use the document in the active window (the letter you just opened) as the main document.

5. Click the **Active Window** button. The Main document section of the dialog box shows the type of merge (Form Letters) and the name of the main document (the active document Pet Shoppe Form Letter). See Figure 6–6.

You'll add the merge instructions to the main document later, after you create the data source.

Creating a Data Source

As mentioned earlier, the data source for a mail merge can come from several different kinds of files, such as a Word file, an Excel file, or an Access file. You can use a file that already contains names and addresses, or you can create a new data source, enter names and addresses into it, and then merge it with the main document. In the Review Assignments at the end of this tutorial, you will use an Excel worksheet as a data source.

In this case, you will create a Word table to use as your data source. The table's header row will contain the merge field names. Just as a column label in a table indicates what kind of information is stored in the column below, each merge field name indicates the type of information contained in the data fields below it. For example, you'll use the field name FirstName to label the data field that contains the first name of Pet Shoppe customers. You must follow several conventions when choosing field names:

- Each field name in the header row must be unique; that is, you can't have two fields with the same name.
- Names of data fields can contain underscores, but not spaces.
- Names of data fields must begin with a letter.
- Names of data fields can be as long as 40 characters (including numbers and letters).

In a mail merge, you link the data source document to the main document so that Word will know in which file to find the information you want inserted into the main document.

You need to create a data source that contains all the information about The Pet Shoppe's customers. Alicia has given you a list of the type of information you'll merge into the letter and the field names you should use, as Figure 6–7 shows.

Figure 6-7	FIELD NAMES FOR THE RECORDS IN THE DATA SOURCE

Data Field Name	Description
FirstName	Customer's first name
LastName	Customer's last name
Address1	Customer's street address
City	Customer's city (in Colorado)
PostalCode	Customer's zip code
HomePhone	Customer's phone number
Branch	Location of The Pet Shoppe branch
PetKind	The kind of pet owned by the customer
PetName	The name of the customer's pet

Creating a Data Source

- Click Tools on the menu bar, click Mail Merge to open the Mail Merge Helper dialog box, and then select the main document.
- In the Data source section of the Mail Merge Helper dialog box, click the Get Data button, and then click Create Data Source. The Create Data Source dialog box opens.
- Add or delete field names in the Field names in header row list, and then click the OK button. The Save As dialog box opens.
- In the Save As dialog box, save the new data source file to your disk. A message dialog box opens, asking you what document you want to edit: the data source or the main document.
- Click the Edit Data Source button. The Data Form dialog box opens.
- Enter the information into the data fields for each record of the data source, and then click the OK button.

Attaching the Data Source and Creating the Header Row

The first step in creating a data source document is to specify the field names in the data source and then attach the data source to the main document. In this context, **attach** means to associate or link the data source to the main document so that Word knows where to find the specific information (data fields) that replace the merge fields in the main document. Although the order of field names in the data source doesn't affect their placement in the main document, you'll want to arrange them logically. This way, you can enter information quickly and efficiently. For example, you probably want first and last name fields adjacent, or city, state, and ZIP code fields adjacent.

Just as you did with the main document, you can either open an existing data source document and attach it to the main document, or you can create a new data source document and attach it to the main document. Alicia doesn't have an existing data source document, so you'll create a new one, and attach it to the file listed in the Main document section of the dialog box.

To attach the data source to the main document:

1. Click the **Get Data** button in the Data source section of the Mail Merge Helper dialog box. The Get Data list box opens. See Figure 6-8.

Figure 6-8   MAIL MERGE HELPER DIALOG BOX WITH GET DATA LIST BOX

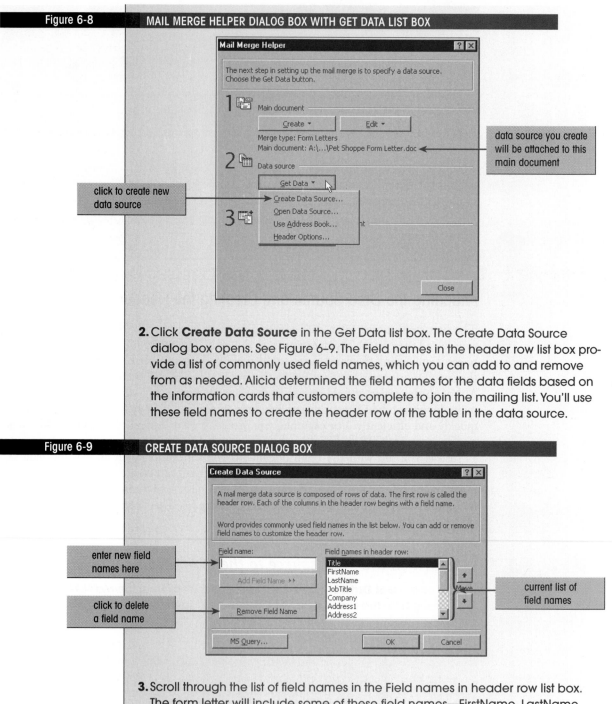

2. Click **Create Data Source** in the Get Data list box. The Create Data Source dialog box opens. See Figure 6–9. The Field names in the header row list box provide a list of commonly used field names, which you can add to and remove from as needed. Alicia determined the field names for the data fields based on the information cards that customers complete to join the mailing list. You'll use these field names to create the header row of the table in the data source.

Figure 6-9   CREATE DATA SOURCE DIALOG BOX

3. Scroll through the list of field names in the Field names in header row list box. The form letter will include some of these field names—FirstName, LastName, Address1, City, PostalCode, and HomePhone. However, you will need to create field names for the store branch, the type of pet, and the name of the pet.

4. In the Field name text box, type **Branch**, and then click the **Add Field Name** button to add "Branch" to the list of field names in the Field names in header row list box. This tells Word that one data field in each record will contain the name of The Pet Shoppe store nearest the customer.

5. Repeat Step 4 to add the field names **PetKind** and **PetName** to the Field names in the header row list box. Now, each customer record will contain fields with the kind of pet the customer owns and the name of that pet.

TROUBLE? If the Add Field Name button is dimmed, you might have entered "PetKind" or "PetName" as two separate words. Word won't accept field names that contain spaces. Delete the space between the words, and then click the Add Field Name button.

Some of the field names in the Field names in header row list box aren't applicable to The Pet Shoppe, so you'll remove those field names.

6. Scroll to the top of the Field names in header row list, click **Title** and click the **Remove Field Name** button. The field name "Title" disappears from the list.

7. Repeat Step 6 to remove the following field names: JobTitle, Company, Address2, State, Country, and WorkPhone. See Figure 6-10. Check the Field names in the header row list carefully to make sure it contains the following: FirstName, LastName, Address1, City, PostalCode, HomePhone, Branch, PetKind, and PetName.

| Figure 6-10 | COMPLETED CREATE DATA SOURCE DIALOG BOX |

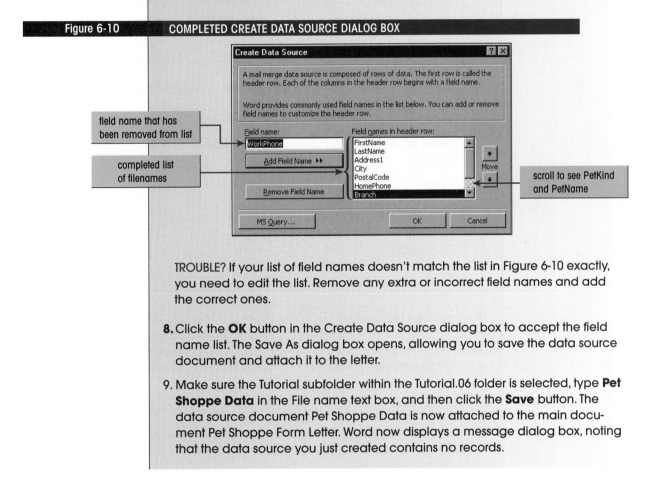

field name that has
been removed from list

completed list
of filenames

scroll to see PetKind
and PetName

TROUBLE? If your list of field names doesn't match the list in Figure 6-10 exactly, you need to edit the list. Remove any extra or incorrect field names and add the correct ones.

8. Click the **OK** button in the Create Data Source dialog box to accept the field name list. The Save As dialog box opens, allowing you to save the data source document and attach it to the letter.

9. Make sure the Tutorial subfolder within the Tutorial.06 folder is selected, type **Pet Shoppe Data** in the File name text box, and then click the **Save** button. The data source document Pet Shoppe Data is now attached to the main document Pet Shoppe Form Letter. Word now displays a message dialog box, noting that the data source you just created contains no records.

At this point you could edit either the data source or the main document. First, you'll edit the data source by entering the data for each customer record; in the next session, you'll edit the main document by adding the merge fields to it.

Entering Data into a Data Source

The Pet Shoppe staff uses customer information cards to collect data from their customers, as shown in Figure 6–11. The data source will contain a field for each piece of information on the card. You'll add the information for three customers (the first three records) into the data source document.

| Figure 6-11 | CUSTOMER INFORMATION TO BE USED AS A DATA RECORD |

The Pet Shoppe

First Name _Sarah_   Last Name _Sorenson_

Address _585 Pikes Peak Road_

City _Denver_ , Colorado

ZIP _80207_   Home Phone _303-555-8976_

Store Branch _High Prairie Mall_

Kind of Pet:

☒ dog   ☐ armadillo
☐ cat   ☐ Gila monster
☐ parrot   ☐ fish
☐ parakeet ☐ lizard
☐ turtle   ☐ Other _____
☐ pigeon

Name of Pet:

Rascal

Word provides two methods for adding records to the data source: entering data directly into a data source table, just as you would enter information into any other Word table, or using the Data Form dialog box, in which you can enter, edit, or delete records. You'll use the data form to enter information about three of The Pet Shoppe's customers into the data source.

To enter data into a record using the data form:

1. In the message dialog box, click the **Edit Data Source** button. The Data Form dialog box opens with blank text boxes beside each field name of the data source. See Figure 6-12.

Figure 6-12	DATA FORM DIALOG BOX

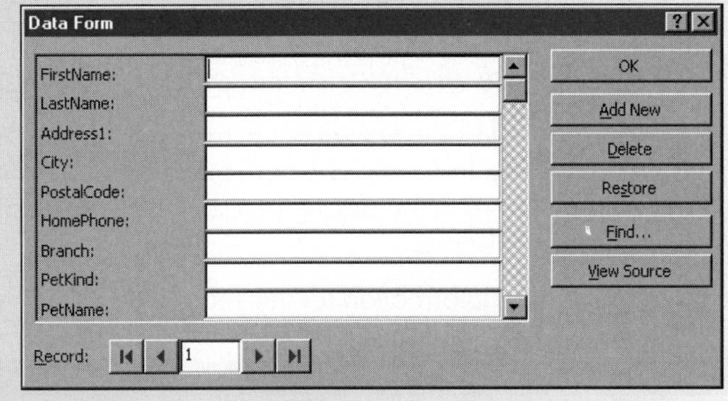

2. With the insertion point in the FirstName text box, type **Sarah** to enter the first name of the first customer. Make sure you do not press the spacebar after you finish typing any entry in the Data Form dialog box. If you do so, you'll add the necessary spaces in the text of the main document, not in the data source.

3. Press the **Enter** key to move the insertion point to the LastName field. You could also click in that text box, or you could press the Tab key to move the insertion point to the next field text box. You would press Shift + Tab to move to the previous text box.

4. Type **Sorenson**, and then press the **Enter** key to move the insertion point to the next field.

5. Type **585 Pikes Peak Road**, and then press the **Enter** key to move the insertion point to the next field.

6. Type **Denver**, and then press the Enter key to move the insertion point to the next field.

7. Type **80207**, and then press the Enter key to move to the next field.

8. Type **303-555-8076** and press **Enter**, type **High Prairie Mall** and press **Enter**, and then type **dog** and press **Enter**. You have inserted the customer's home phone number, the branch location of The Pet Shoppe, and the kind of pet the customer owns. The insertion point is now in the text box of the last field, PetName.

9. Type **Rascal**, but do not press the Enter key yet. Your Data Form dialog box should match Figure 6–13.

Figure 6-13	DATA FORM DIALOG BOX WITH COMPLETED RECORD 1

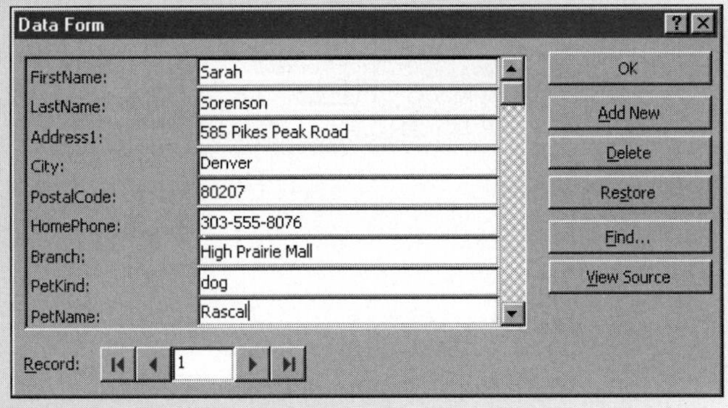

You have completed the information for the first record of the data source document. Now, you're ready to enter the information for the remaining two records.

To create additional records in the data source:

1. With the insertion point still at the end of the last field of the first record, press the **Enter** key. This creates a new, blank record. Notice that the Record text box at the bottom of the data form displays "2," indicating that you're editing the second record.

2. Enter the information for the second record, as shown in Figure 6–14.

Figure 6-14   **COMPLETED RECORD 2**

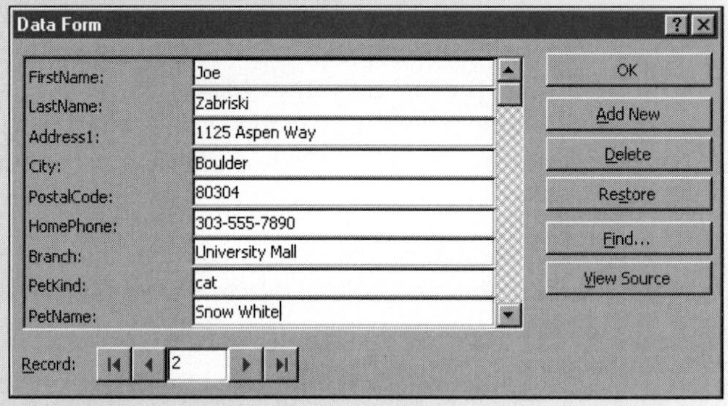

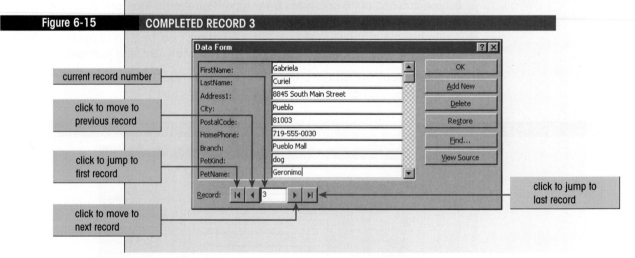

3. After entering data into the last field, click the **Add New** button to open another blank record. Notice that you can press the Enter key or click the Add New button to create a blank record.

4. Enter the information for the third record, as shown in Figure 6–15, but do not press the Enter key after the last field. If you were to press Enter or click the Add New button, you would add a blank record as the fourth record.

Figure 6-15   **COMPLETED RECORD 3**

> TROUBLE? If a new, blank record opens, you pressed the Enter key at the end of the third record or you clicked the Add New button in the Data Form dialog box. Click the Delete button in the Data Form dialog box to remove the unneeded fourth record.

You have entered the records for three customers. Next, you need to proofread each record to make sure you typed the information correctly. Any misspelled names or other typos will print in the final letters and reflect poorly on The Pet Shoppe. You can move among individual records within the data source by using the Record arrow buttons. You'll begin by proofreading the first data record.

To move to the first record within the data source:

1. Click the **First Record** button 14 at the bottom of the Data Form dialog box to move to the first record. The record number changes to 1, and the first record appears in the data form with the data you entered.

2. Proofread the data by comparing your information with Figure 6–13. Make any necessary corrections by selecting the text and retyping it.

3. Click the **Next Record** button ▶ at the bottom of the Data Form dialog box to move to the next record. The record number changes to 2, and the information for the second data record appears. Compare your record with Figure 6–14.

4. Click ▶ to review the third record. Compare your record with Figure 6–15. Make corrections where necessary.

You have entered and edited the three records using the data form. Also, you can add and edit records in the data source while viewing the records as a Word table.

Krishan, a Pet Shoppe employee, created a Word table with the other records you need to add to the data source. You'll view the data source as a table and add those records.

To view the data source as a table and add new records to the data form:

1. Click the **View Source** button in the **Data Form** dialog box. The data source table appears in the document window, and the Database toolbar appears above the document window. See Figure 6–16. Depending on your monitor, you may find the contents of the cells difficult to read because they wrap onto one or more lines or break between words. Don't worry about this. You won't be printing the table, but instead will only be merging the information it contains with the main document. Once the data is merged, it will be formatted properly in the main document. However, note that you could edit, format, or print the data source table just as you would any other Word table.

Figure 6-16   DATA SOURCE TABLE

database toolbar

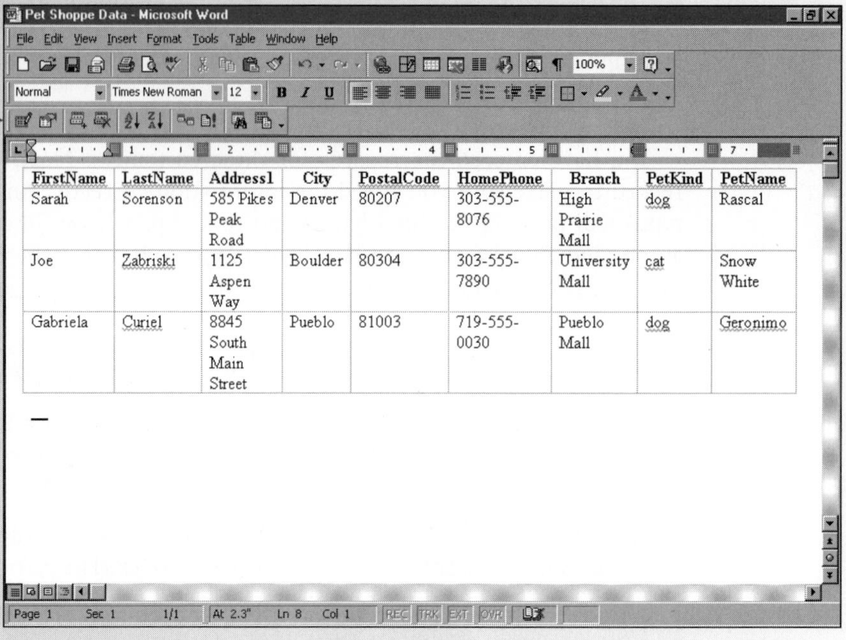

FirstName	LastName	Address1	City	PostalCode	HomePhone	Branch	PetKind	PetName
Sarah	Sorenson	585 Pikes Peak Road	Denver	80207	303-555-8076	High Prairie Mall	dog	Rascal
Joe	Zabriski	1125 Aspen Way	Boulder	80304	303-555-7890	University Mall	cat	Snow White
Gabriela	Curiel	8845 South Main Street	Pueblo	81003	719-555-0030	Pueblo Mall	dog	Geronimo

TROUBLE? If your data source table does not show the gridlines shown in Figure 6-16, display them by clicking Table on the menu bar and then clicking Show Gridlines.

2. Move the insertion point to the end of the document, to the blank line below the table. Now, you can insert the file containing additional customer information.

3. Click **Insert** on the menu bar, and then click **File**. The Insert File dialog box opens.

4. Make sure the Tutorial folder for Tutorial 6 on your Data Disk is selected, click the filename **ShopDat**, and then click the **Insert** button. Word automatically adds the 11 records in the ShopDat data source table to the three records of the Pet Shoppe Data source table.

5. Scroll up to view all 14 records in the data source table. On most computers, the column borders are not aligned properly. You'll fix that in the next step. (Even if your column borders are properly aligned, you should complete Step 6.)

6. Click **Table** on the menu bar, point to **Select**, click **Table** to select the entire table. Then click **Table** on the menu bar, click **Table AutoFormat**, select **(none)** in the list of formats, click the **OK** button, and then click anywhere in the table to deselect it. The header row is no longer formatted in boldface. All the columns in the table should now be aligned.

   Now that you've entered and edited records using the data form and inserted additional customer records, you should save the data source document.

7. Save the document. Word saves the file using the current filename, Pet Shoppe Data.

Alicia's data source eventually will contain hundreds of records for all The Pet Shoppe customers. The current data source, however, contains only the records Alicia wants to work with now.

You have opened the main document for the form letter and created the data source that will supply the customer-specific information for Alicia's mailings. In the next session, you'll insert merge fields into the main document and merge the main document with the data source. Then, you'll sort the data source by ZIP code and repeat the merge using the sorted data with the main document.

Session 6.1 QUICK CHECK

1. Define the following in your own words:

   a. form letter
   b. main document
   c. data source
   d. merge field
   e. record
   f. data field

2. Which of the following are valid field names?

   a. Number of Years on the Job
   b. PayGrade
   c. 3rdQuarterProfits
   d. StudentIdentificationNumber
   e. ThePetShoppeCompanyEmployeeSocialSecurityNumber
   f. Birth Date

3. All the information about one individual or object in a data source is called a
   _____.

4. True or False: For a mail merge to work properly, every record in the data source must have the same set of fields.

5. Suppose you want to insert information for a field named "Gender" into the data source. How would you do it?

6. What is the purpose of the data form?

7. How do you move to individual records within the data source?

SESSION 6.2

In this session, you'll return to the form letter main document and insert merge fields into it. Then you'll create the merged document. You'll also sort the data source and merge it with the main document. Finally, you'll filter the data source, edit the main document, and merge the two.

Editing a Main Document

You opened Alicia's sales letter earlier but didn't enter any of the merge instructions. Now that the data source contains all the records you need to use, you're ready to edit the sales letter.

Alicia wants the date to print below the company letterhead. Instead of just typing today's date, you'll insert a date field. By entering the date field, you won't have to modify the main document each time you send it; the date field will automatically insert the current date when you print the document.

To insert the date field:

1. If you took a break after the last session, make sure Word is running and the Pet Shoppe Form Letter and Pet Shoppe Data are open. The Pet Shoppe Data document should be displayed on the screen.

2. Click the **Mail Merge Main Document** button 🖼 on the Database toolbar to switch from the data source document to the main document, Pet Shoppe Form Letter. You should now be viewing Alicia's form letter. Notice that the Mail Merge toolbar appears below the Formatting toolbar. See Figure 6–17.

| Figure 6-17 | MAIN DOCUMENT BEFORE INSERTING MERGE FIELDS |

Mail merge toolbar

click to insert a merge field

Ten years ago, Stephen Mueller was unable to find suitable grooming facilities for his dog, Rusty. Maria Fuentes drove 100 miles to buy food for her cat, Sneakers. And Carole Cochran only dreamed of owning an armadillo lizard. Today, Stephen, Maria, and Carole are among The Pet Shoppe's loyal customers.

Established in 1988, The Pet Shoppe chain provides a complete line of high quality yet affordable pet supplies and services for customers throughout Colorado. We're committed to helping you meet the needs of your [kind of pet] in a caring manner.

We invite you and your pet to join us in our 10th Anniversary Celebration. Just bring this letter to The Pet Shoppe in the [branch] anytime during the month of November and you'll receive a 10% discount on the purchase of any product or service. And remember to register [pet's name] for our month-long "Purrfect Pet" drawing. We'll be giving away over $1,000 worth of prizes and services each week.

We look forward to seeing you at The Pet Shoppe.

Sincerely yours,

TROUBLE? If the main document, Pet Shoppe Form Letter, is already in the document window, your document window should match Figure 6–17. Continue with Step 3.

3. Make sure the insertion point is at the beginning of the form letter, on the first blank line, and then press the **Enter** key five times to position the insertion point approximately two inches from the top margin, leaving enough space for the company letterhead that is preprinted on the company stationery. Here, you'll insert the date.

Now, rather than typing today's date, you'll insert a Word date field, so that no matter when you print the document, the current date will appear.

4. Click **Insert** on the menu bar, and then click **Date and Time**. The Date and Time dialog box opens. You have used this dialog box before to insert the current date. Now, you will use the Update automatically check box to tell Word to revise the date every time you use the document.

5. Click the month-day-year format from the list of available formats, and then click the **Update automatically** check box to select it. See Figure 6–18.

Figure 6-18   DATE AND TIME DIALOG BOX

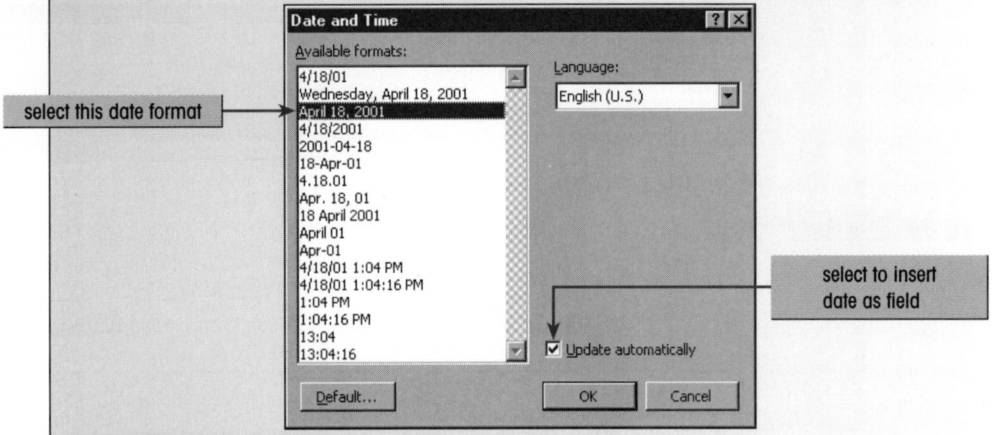

select this date format

select to insert
date as field

TROUBLE? The date that shows in your dialog box will differ from the one shown in Figure 6–18. Just click the format that lists the month, the day, and then the year.

6. Click the **OK** button. The current date appears in the document. Now, whenever you or Alicia print the merged document letter for Pet Shoppe's customers, the current date will print.

TROUBLE? If you see TIME \@ "MMMM d, yyyy"} instead of the date, then your system is set to view field codes. To view the date, click Tools on the menu bar, click Options, click the View tab, click the Field codes check box in the Show section of the View tab to deselect that option, and then click the OK button.

You're now ready to insert the merge fields for the inside address of the form letter.

Inserting Merge Fields

The sales letter is a standard business letter, so you'll place the customer's name and address below the date. You'll use merge fields for the customer's first name, last name, address, city, and ZIP code to create the inside address of the form letter. As you insert these merge fields into the main document, you must enter proper spacing and punctuation around the fields so that the information in the merged document will be formatted correctly.

To insert a merge field:

1. Press the **Enter** key six times to leave the standard number of blank lines between the date and the first line of the inside address.

2. Click the **Insert Merge Field** button on the Mail Merge toolbar. A list appears with all the field names that you created earlier in the data source. See Figure 6–19.

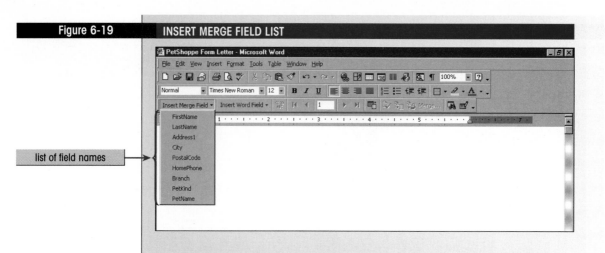

Figure 6-19   INSERT MERGE FIELD LIST

list of field names

3. Click **FirstName** in the list of field names. Word inserts the merge code for the field name, FirstName, in the form letter at the location of the insertion point.

Word places angled brackets << >>, also called chevrons, around the merge field to distinguish it from normal text.

TROUBLE? If you make a mistake and insert the wrong merge field, select the entire merge field, including the chevrons, press the Delete key, and then insert the correct merge field.

Later, when you merge the main document with the data source, Word will retrieve the first name from the data source and insert it into the letter at that location. Now, you're ready to insert the merge fields for the rest of the inside address. You'll add the spacing and punctuation to the main document as well.

To insert the remaining merge fields for the inside address:

1. Press the **spacebar** to insert a space after the FirstName field, click the **Insert Merge Field** button on the Mail Merge toolbar, and then click **LastName** in the Insert Merge Field list. Word inserts the LastName merge field into the form letter.

2. Press the **Enter** key to move the insertion point to the next line, click the **Insert Merge Field** button, and then click **Address1** in the Insert Merge Field list. Word inserts the Address1 merge field into the form letter.

3. Press the **Enter** key to move the insertion point to the next line, click the **Insert Merge Field** button, and then click **City** in the Insert Merge Field list. Word inserts the City merge field into the form letter.

4. Type **,** (a comma), press the **spacebar** to insert a space after the comma, and then type **CO** to insert the abbreviation for the state of Colorado. If The Pet Shoppe had customers outside Colorado, you would need to use the State field name in the data source and, here, in the main document form letter. Because all of the customers live in Colorado, you can make the state name part of the main document, where it will be the same for every letter.

5. Press the **spacebar** to insert a space after the state abbreviation, click the **Insert Merge Field** button, and then click **PostalCode** in the list of fields. Word inserts the PostalCode merge field into the form letter. See Figure 6-20.

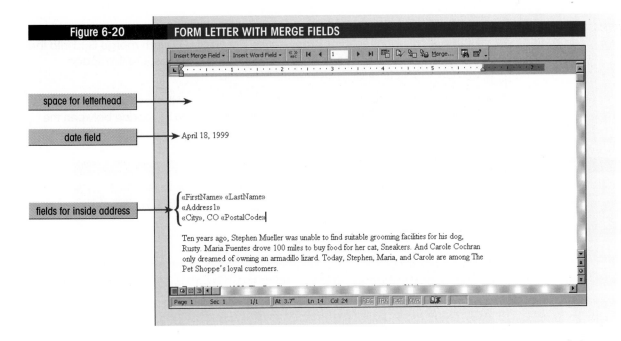

Figure 6-20   **FORM LETTER WITH MERGE FIELDS**

space for letterhead

date field

fields for inside address

The inside address is set up to match the form for a standard business letter. You can now add the salutation of the letter, which will contain each customer's first name.

To insert the merge field for the salutation:

1. Press the **Enter** key twice to leave a line between the inside address and the salutation, and then type **Dear** and press the **spacebar**.

2. Click the **Insert Merge Field** button on the Mail Merge toolbar, and then click **FirstName**. Word inserts the FirstName merge field into the form letter.

3. Type **:** (a colon). This completes the salutation.

   TROUBLE? If the Office Assistant asks if you want help writing the letter, click Simply type the letter without help.

Alicia wants each customer to know that The Pet Shoppe values its customers and remembers them and their pets. You'll personalize the letter even further by including the kind of pet each customer owns and the pet's name.

To finish personalizing the letter:

1. Select the placeholder **(kind of pet)** (including the brackets) in the second paragraph of the form letter. You'll replace this phrase with a merge field.

2. Click the **Insert Merge Field** button on the Mail Merge toolbar, and then click **PetKind**. Word replaces your placeholder with the PetKind merge field into the form letter. If necessary, press the **spacebar** to make sure there is a space between the field and the next word, "in."

3. Select **(branch)** in the third paragraph of the form letter, click the **Insert Merge Field** button, and then click **Branch**. Word inserts the Branch merge field into the form letter. Press the **spacebar** if necessary to make sure there is a space between the field and the next word, "anytime."

4. Similarly, replace **(pet's name)** in the third sentence of the third paragraph of the form letter with the **PetName** field, and make sure there is a space between the merge field and the next word, "for." Your document should look like Figure 6–21.

| Figure 6-21 | FORM LETTER AFTER INSERTING MERGE FIELDS |

click to view data merged into main document

Insert Merge Field ▾ | Insert Word Field ▾ | 《》ABC | I◀ ◀ | 1 | ▶ ▶I | ▦ ▯ ℞ ℞ Merge... | ▨ ▥ ▾

«FirstName» «LastName»
«Address1»
«City», CO «PostalCode»

Dear «FirstName»:

Ten years ago, Stephen Mueller was unable to find suitable grooming facilities for his dog, Rusty. Maria Fuentes drove 100 miles to buy food for her cat, Sneakers. And Carole Cochran only dreamed of owning an armadillo lizard. Today, Stephen, Maria, and Carole are among The Pet Shoppe's loyal customers.

Established in 1988, The Pet Shoppe chain provides a complete line of high quality yet affordable pet supplies and services for customers throughout Colorado. We're committed to helping you meet the needs of your «PetKind» in a caring manner.

fields inserted into text

We invite you and your pet to join us in our 10th Anniversary Celebration. Just bring this letter to The Pet Shoppe in the «Branch» anytime during the month of November and you'll receive a 10% discount on the purchase of any product or service. And remember to register «PetName» for our month-long "Purrfect Pet" drawing. We'll be giving away over $1,000 worth of prizes

Page 1 | Sec 1 | 1/1 | At 6.8" | Ln 29 Col 91 | REC TRK EXT OVR | 🗒

5. Carefully check your document to make sure all the field names and spacing are correct.

TROUBLE? If you see errors, use the Word editing commands to delete the error, and then insert the correct merge field or spacing.

You can use the View Merged Data button on the Mail Merge toolbar to see how the letter will look when the merge fields are replaced by actual data.

6. Click the **View Merged Data** button 《》ABC on the Mail Merge toolbar. The data for the first record replaces the merge fields in the form letter. See Figure 6–22. Scroll to the top of the document so you can see the inside address and salutation. Carefully check the letter to make sure the text and format are correct. In particular, check to make sure that the spaces before and after the merged data are correct because it is easy to omit spaces or add extraneous spaces around merge fields.

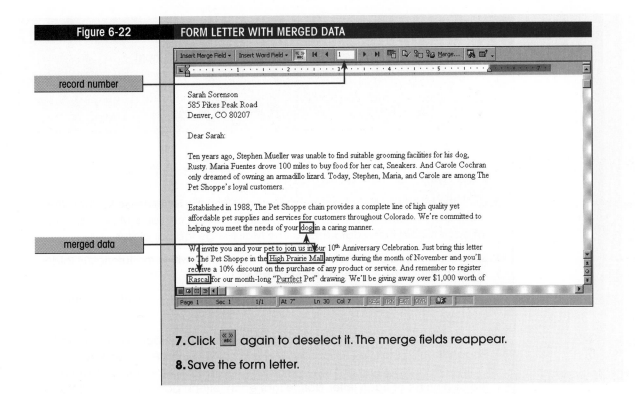

Figure 6-22 | FORM LETTER WITH MERGED DATA

7. Click again to deselect it. The merge fields reappear.

8. Save the form letter.

The form letter (main document) of the mail merge is complete. As you saw while creating the main document, merge fields are easy to use and flexible:

- You can use merge fields anywhere in the main document. For example, in Alicia's form letter, you inserted fields for the inside address and you placed fields within the body of the letter.

- You can use the same merge field more than once. For example, Alicia's form letter uses the FirstName field in the inside address and in the salutation.

- You don't have to use all the fields from the data source in your main document. For example, Alicia's form letter doesn't use the HomePhone field.

Merging the Main Document and Data Source

Now that you've created the form letter (main document) and the list of customer information (data source), you're ready to merge the two files and create personalized letters to send to The Pet Shoppe's customers. Because the data source consists of 14 records, you'll create a merged document with 14 pages, one letter per page.

You could merge the data source and main document directly to the printer using the Merge to Printer button on the Mail Merge toolbar, which is often quicker and doesn't require disk space. However, Alicia wants to keep a copy of the merged document on disk for her records. So you'll merge the data source and main document to a new document on disk.

REFERENCE **WINDOW** **RW**

Merging a Main Document and Data Source to a New Document
- Make sure the mail merge main document is in the document window with the Mail Merge toolbar above it.
- Click the Merge to New Document button on the Mail Merge toolbar.

To merge to a new document:

1. Click the **Merge to New Document** button on the Mail Merge toolbar. Word creates a new document called Form Letters1, which contains 14 pages, one for each record in the data source. The Mail Merge toolbar closes.

2. Save the merged document in the Tutorial subfolder within the Tutorial.06 folder, using the filename **Pet Shoppe Form Letters1**.

3. Click the **Print Preview** button on the Standard toolbar to switch to Print Preview.

4. Click the **Zoom Control** list arrow on the Print Preview toolbar, and then click **Page Width** so the text is large enough to read. Click the **Previous Page** button or **Next Page** button below the vertical scroll bar to move to the beginning of each letter. Notice that each letter is addressed to a different customer and the branch location, kind of pet, and pet name are different in each letter.

   TROUBLE? If the Next and Previous Page buttons are blue and don't display the beginning of each letter, click the Select Browse Object button and click the Browse by Page button.

5. Click the **Close** button on the Print Preview toolbar to return to the Normal view.

6. Press **Ctrl + End** to move the insertion point to the end of the document. Notice on the status bar that you're viewing page 14, the final letter in the merged document.

7. Click **File** on the menu bar, and then click **Print** to open the Print dialog box.

8. Click the **Current page** option button in the **Page** range section of the dialog box so Word will print only the current page (the last letter) of the merged document, and then click the **OK** button to print the document. Figure 6-23 shows what the letter will look like when Alicia prints it on company letterhead.

Figure 6-23	**LAST PAGE OF MERGED DOCUMENT**

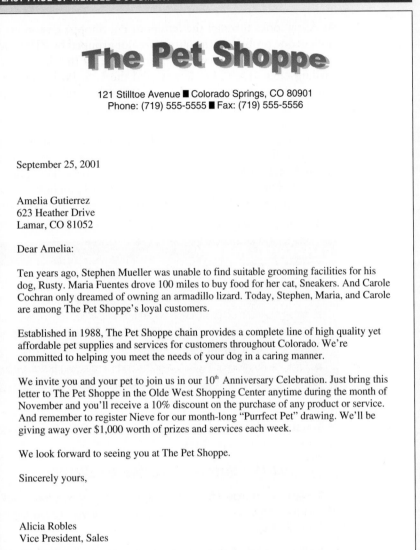

You have completed the mail merge and generated a merged document. Alicia stops by to see how the letters are coming.

Sorting Records

As Alicia looks through the letters to Pet Shoppe customers in the merged document, she notices one problem—the letters are not grouped by ZIP codes. Currently, the letters are in the order in which customers were added to the data source file. She plans to use bulk mailing rates to send her letters, and the U.S. Postal Service requires bulk mailings to be separated into groups according to ZIP code. She asks you to sort the data file by ZIP code (the PostalCode field) and perform another merge, this time merging the main document with the sorted data source.

You can sort information in a data source table just as you sort information in any other table. Recall that to sort means to rearrange a list or a document in alphabetical, numerical, or chronological order. You can sort information in ascending order (A to Z, lowest to highest, or earliest to latest) or in descending order (Z to A, highest to lowest, or latest to earliest) using the Sort Ascending button or the Sort Descending button on the Database toolbar.

REFERENCE WINDOW **RW**

Sorting a Data Source

- Make sure the data source is in the document window and the Database toolbar is visible.
- Move the insertion point to the field name in the header row whose data you want to sort. For example, if you want to sort by LastName, move the insertion point to the header cell containing the field name "LastName."
- Click the Sort Ascending button or the Sort Descending button on the Database toolbar.

You'll sort the records in ascending order of the PostalCode field in Pet Shoppe Data.

To sort the data source file by ZIP code:

1. With the merged file still in the document window, click **File** on the menu bar, and then click **Close** to close the file. If you're prompted to save your changes, click **Yes**.

2. Click the **Edit Data Source** button 🖼 on the Mail Merge toolbar to open the Data Form dialog box, and then click the **View Source** button. The data source table appears in the document window.

3. Position the insertion point in the PostalCode cell in the header row of the data table. The exact location of the insertion point in the cell doesn't matter.

4. Click the **Sort Ascending** button 🔼 on the Database toolbar. Word sorts the rows of the data table from lowest ZIP code number to highest. See Figure 6-24.

Figure 6-24   **DATA SOURCE TABLE AFTER SORTING BY POSTALCODE**

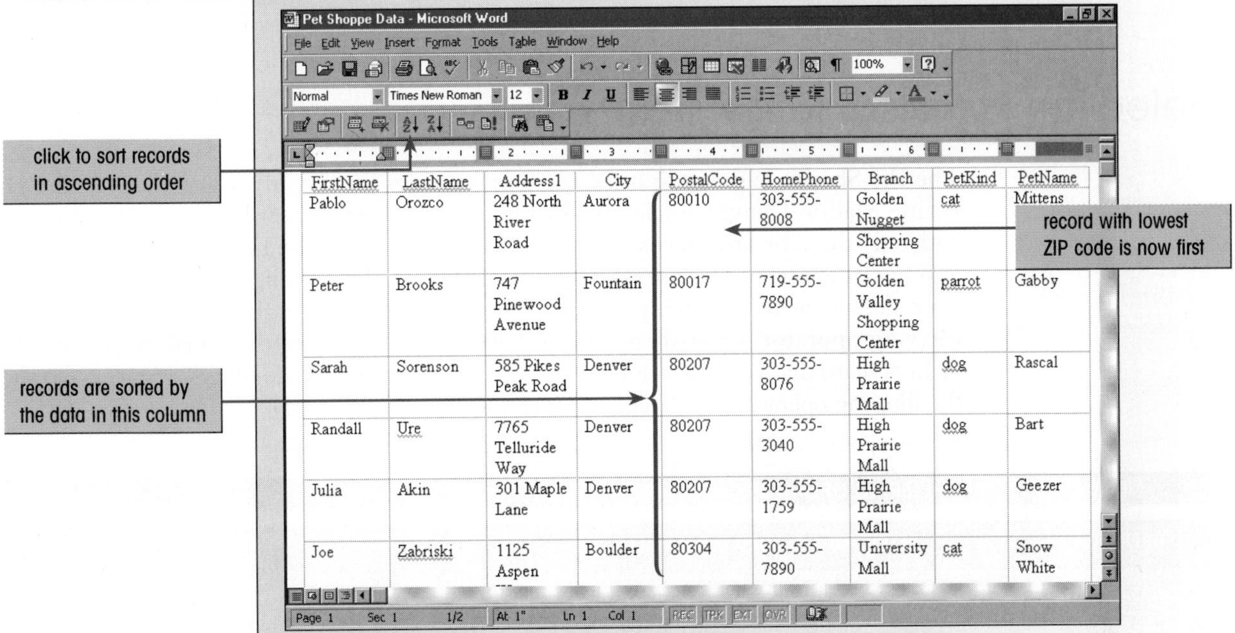

click to sort records in ascending order

record with lowest ZIP code is now first

records are sorted by the data in this column

FirstName	LastName	Address1	City	PostalCode	HomePhone	Branch	PetKind	PetName
Pablo	Orozco	248 North River Road	Aurora	80010	303-555-8008	Golden Nugget Shopping Center	cat	Mittens
Peter	Brooks	747 Pinewood Avenue	Fountain	80017	719-555-7890	Golden Valley Shopping Center	parrot	Gabby
Sarah	Sorenson	585 Pikes Peak Road	Denver	80207	303-555-8076	High Prairie Mall	dog	Rascal
Randall	Ure	7765 Telluride Way	Denver	80207	303-555-3040	High Prairie Mall	dog	Bart
Julia	Akin	301 Maple Lane	Denver	80207	303-555-1759	High Prairie Mall	dog	Geezer
Joe	Zabriski	1125 Aspen	Boulder	80304	303-555-7890	University Mall	cat	Snow White

Page 1   Sec 1   1/2   At 1"   Ln 1   Col 1

Now, when you merge the data source with the form letter, the letters will appear in the merged document in order of the ZIP codes.

5. Click the **Mail Merge Main Document** button 📇 on the Database toolbar to switch to the Pet Shoppe Form Letter.

6. Click the **Merge to New Document** button 📇 on the Mail Merge toolbar. Word generates the new merged document with 14 letters, one letter per page, as before, but this time the first letter is to Pablo Orozco, who has the lowest ZIP code (80010). See Figure 6–25.

Figure 6-25   **LETTER OF CUSTOMER WITH LOWEST ZIP CODE**

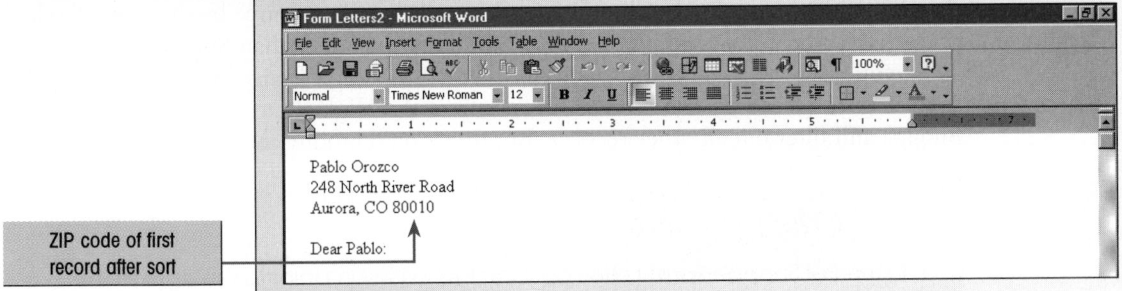

Pablo Orozco
248 North River Road
Aurora, CO 80010

Dear Pablo:

ZIP code of first record after sort

7. Scroll through the letters in the new merged document to see that they are in order of ZIP code.

8. Save the new merged document in the Tutorial subfolder within the Tutorial.06 folder, using the filename **Pet Shoppe Form Letters2**.

9. Close the document.

As Alicia requested, you've created a merged document with the letters to Pet Shoppe customers sorted by ZIP code. She stops back to tell you that the letters to customers who frequent one branch of The Pet Shoppe need additional information.

Selecting Records to Merge

The Pet Shoppe is going to offer additional savings on certain surplus items at the High Prairie Mall in Denver. Alicia wants to modify the form letter slightly and then merge it with only those records of customers of The Pet Shoppe in the High Prairie Mall.

You can select specific records from the data source, or **filter** records, to merge with the main document by specifying values for one or more fields with a filtering operation. A **filtering operator** is a mathematical or logical expression (such as Equal to, Not Equal to, or Less than) that you use to include certain records and exclude others. Figure 6–26 shows the filtering operators available for a mail merge.

Figure 6-26	FILTERING OPERATORS AVAILABLE IN WORD
OPERATOR	**RETRIEVES A RECORD IF DATA FIELD**
Equal to	Matches value of Compare to text box
Not Equal to	Does not match value of Compare to text box
Less than	Is less than the value of Compare to text box
Greater than	Is greater than the value of Compare to text box
Less than or Equal	Is less than or equal to the value of the Compare to text box
Greater than or Equal	Is greater than or equal to the value of the Compare to text box
Is Blank	Is blank or empty
Is Not Blank	Contains any value

A complete expression is called a **query**. An example of a query is "PostalCode Greater than 80010," which tells Word to filter the records in a data source by the PostalCode field and select any records that include a ZIP code that is higher than 80010. In the following steps, you'll set the Branch field so that it is equal to "High Prairie Mall." That way, Word will select only records of customers who shop at the High Prairie Mall branch of The Pet Shoppe and filter out all other records. But first, you'll modify the form letter.

To edit the form letter:

1. In the Pet Shoppe Form Letter, position the insertion point to the right of the phrase "10% discount on the purchase of any product or service" in the third paragraph of the form letter, just before the period.

2. Press the **spacebar**, and type **and a 25% discount on the purchase of selected items**. See Figure 6–27.

Figure 6-27	FORM LETTER WITH INSERTED TEXT

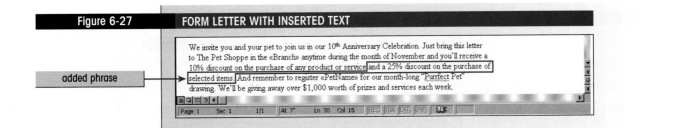

added phrase

> We invite you and your pet to join us in our 10ᵗʰ Anniversary Celebration. Just bring this letter to The Pet Shoppe in the «Branch» anytime during the month of November and you'll receive a 10% discount on the purchase of any product or service and a 25% discount on the purchase of selected items. And remember to register «PetName» for our month-long "Purrfect Pet" drawing. We'll be giving away over $1,000 worth of prizes and services each week.

Alicia wants to send this version of the letter only to customers of the High Prairie Mall store. You'll use the Equal to filtering operator to select only those records for High Prairie Mall, and then you'll merge the revised form letter with the records in the data source that match the query.

To filter records for a merge:

1. Make sure the main document appears in the document window, and then click the **Mail Merge Helper** button 🖹 on the Mail Merge toolbar. The Mail Merge Helper dialog box opens.

2. Click the **Query Options** button on the dialog box. The Query Options dialog box opens. If necessary, click the **Filter Records** tab. See Figure 6–28. This is where you'll specify the query using a filtering operator.

Figure 6-28	QUERY OPTIONS DIALOG BOX

select this tab

click to select field name

Query Options ? ✕

Filter Records | Sort Records

Field: | Comparison: | Compare to:

OK   Cancel   Clear All

3. Click the **Field** list arrow, and then scroll through the list of field names and click **Branch**. Word fills in the Field text box with Branch.

4. If necessary, click the **Comparison** list arrow, and then click **Equal to**. This selects the filtering (comparison) operator, which tells Word that you want the value of the Branch field to be equal to something.

Next, you'll specify what you want the Branch field to equal.

5. Position the insertion point in the Compare to text box, and type **High Prairie Mall**. Be careful to spell it exactly as shown. If any character or space differs, Word will fail to find any records that match. The completed Query Options dialog box should look like Figure 6–29. This is the only condition that Alicia needs to select customers who shop at High Prairie Mall.

Figure 6-29 **COMPLETED QUERY IN QUERY OPTIONS DIALOG BOX**

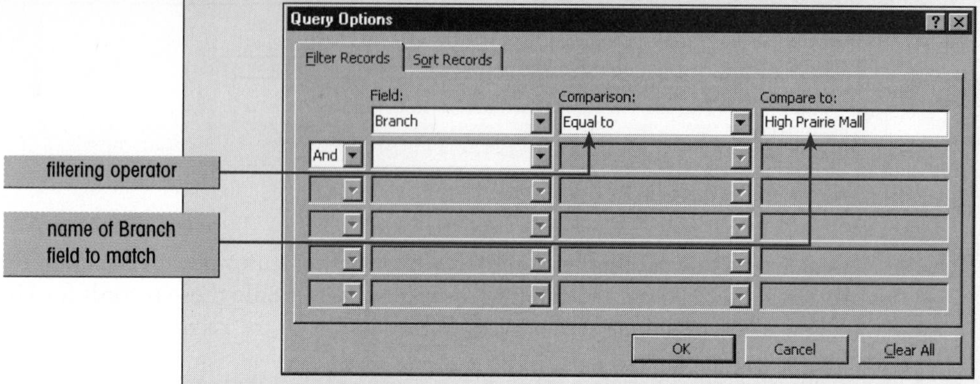

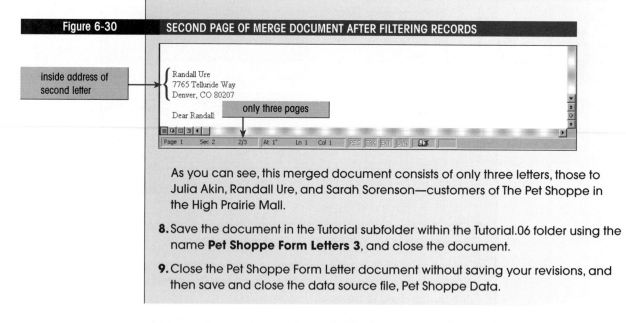

filtering operator

name of Branch field to match

6. Click the **OK** button to accept the query options and return to the Merge dialog box. Notice that, among other things, the phrase "Query Options have been set" appears at the bottom of the dialog box.

7. Click the **Merge** button in the Mail Merge Helper dialog box to display the Merge dialog box. Make sure the Merge to text box displays **New Document**, and then click the **Merge** button. Word performs the merge and creates a new document that merges the modified form letter with all the records that match the query. Notice that the document is only three pages because only three records list High Prairie Mall in the Branch field. Scroll through the merged document to see the three letters. See Figure 6–30.

Figure 6-30 **SECOND PAGE OF MERGE DOCUMENT AFTER FILTERING RECORDS**

inside address of second letter

Randall Ure
7765 Telluride Way
Denver, CO 80207

Dear Randall: *only three pages*

Page 1   Sec 2   2/3   At 1"   Ln 1   Col 1   REC   TRK   EXT   OVR

As you can see, this merged document consists of only three letters, those to Julia Akin, Randall Ure, and Sarah Sorenson—customers of The Pet Shoppe in the High Prairie Mall.

8. Save the document in the Tutorial subfolder within the Tutorial.06 folder using the name **Pet Shoppe Form Letters 3**, and close the document.

9. Close the Pet Shoppe Form Letter document without saving your revisions, and then save and close the data source file, Pet Shoppe Data.

You give the completed file to Alicia, who will print the letters on letterhead.

You now have created merged documents for a sorted data source file, filtered records in a data source, and an edited main document. In the next session, you'll create mailing labels and a phone list for Alicia to use when she has the sales reps make follow-up phone calls.

Session 6.2 QUICK CHECK

1. What is the purpose of a date merge in a main document?

2. How do you insert a merge field into a main document?

3. How can you distinguish the merge field from the rest of the text in a main document?

4. Define the following in your own words:

   a. merged document

   b. sort

   c. query

   d. filtering operator

5. Suppose one of the data fields contains the ZIP code of your customers. How would you select only those customers with a certain ZIP code?

6. How can you preview how the main document will look when the merge fields are replaced by actual data?

7. If your main document is a form letter and you have 23 records in your data source, how many letters will the merged document create?

8. Do you have to print every letter in a merged form-letter document?

SESSION 6.3

In this session, you'll create and print mailing labels for the form-letter envelopes and create a telephone list, both using the mail merge feature.

Creating Mailing Labels

Now that you've created and printed the personalized sales letters, Alicia is ready to prepare envelopes in which to mail the letters. She could print the names and addresses directly onto envelopes, or she could create mailing labels to attach to the envelopes. The latter method is easier because 14 labels come on each sheet, and the envelopes don't have to go through the printer one by one. Alicia asks you to create the mailing labels.

She has purchased Avery® Laser Printer labels, product number 5162™ Address. These labels, which are available in most office-supply stores, come in $8^{1}/_{2} \times 11$-inch sheets designed to feed through a laser printer. Each label measures 4×1.33 inches, and each sheet has seven rows of labels with two labels in each row, for a total of 14 labels per sheet, as shown in Figure 6–31. Word supports most of the Avery label formats.

Figure 6-31   **LAYOUT OF A SHEET OF AVERY 5162 LABELS**

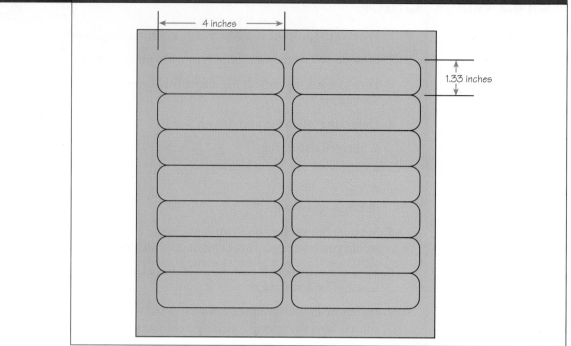

You can use the same data source file (Pet Shoppe Data) as you did earlier, but you'll have to create a new main document. The main document will be of type Mailing Labels instead of type Form Letters.

REFERENCE WINDOW   **RW**

Creating Mailing Labels

- Create a main document of type Mailing Labels. (Refer to the Reference Window "Creating a Main Document," except select Mailing Labels when you set up the main document.) The Labels Options dialog box opens.
- In the Labels Options dialog box, select the options for your printer type and tray location.
- In the Label products text box, select Avery Standard to print to letter-sized label sheets.
- In the Product number list, select the specific product number for the type of Avery labels that you have, and then click the OK button.

You'll begin creating the mailing labels by specifying the main document and data source.

To specify the main document and data source for creating mailing labels:

1. If you took a break after the last session, make sure Word is running and that your Data Disk is in the appropriate drive.

2. If a blank document doesn't already appear on your screen, click the **New Blank Document** button ▢ on the Standard toolbar to open a new, blank document.

3. Click **Tools** on the menu bar, and then click **Mail Merge** to open the Mail Merge Helper dialog box.

4. Click the **Create** button in the Main document section of the dialog box, and then click **Mailing Labels**. Word displays a message asking if you want to use the current document or a new one.

5. Click the **Active Window** button so that the current blank document window is the mailing label main document.

6. Click the **Get Data** button on the Mail Merge Helper dialog box, and then click **Open Data Source**. You'll use an existing data source—the table you created earlier that contains Pet Shoppe customer information. The Open Data Source dialog box opens.

7. Make sure the Tutorial subfolder within the Tutorial.06 folder is selected, click the filename **Pet Shoppe Data** (if necessary), and then click the **Open** button. Word displays a message advising that you need to set up your main document.

8. Click the **Set Up Main Document** button on the message dialog box. The Label Options dialog box opens.

You've specified the main document, which is the blank document in the document window, and the data source, which is the file Pet Shoppe Data. Now, you're ready to select the type of labels and create the merged document of labels.

To create the mailing labels:

1. In the Printer information section of the dialog box, select the type of printer you'll use—dot matrix or laser and ink-jet. If you use a laser or ink-jet printer, you might also have the option of specifying the printer tray that will contain the mailing-label sheets. For example, if you have an HP LaserJet 4000 printer, the printer type is a laser printer and the tray is tray 1. For other printers, the tray might be the upper tray. You should select the options that are appropriate for your printer.

    TROUBLE? If you're not sure which options to choose for your printer, consult your instructor or technical support person.

2. Make sure **Avery standard** displays in the Label products text box. Even if you don't have Avery labels, you can print the merged document in the format of an Avery label sheet on an $8\frac{1}{2} \times 11$-inch letter-sized sheet of paper.

3. Scroll down the Product number list box and click **5162 - Address**. Your dialog box should look like Figure 6–32, except your printer specifications might be different.

Figure 6-32   **LABEL OPTIONS DIALOG BOX**

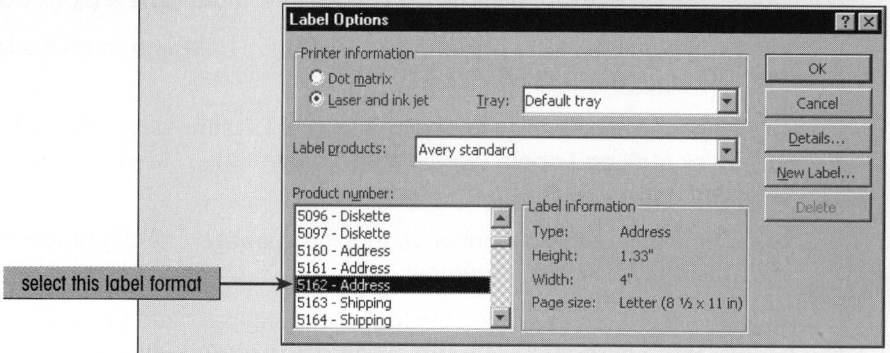

select this label format

4. Click the **OK** button. Word opens the Create Labels dialog box, which contains an area in which you can insert the merge fields in a sample label.

5. Click the **Insert Merge Field** button on the dialog box and click **FirstName** to insert the field, press the **spacebar** to insert a space between the first and last names, click the **Insert Merge Field** button, and then click **LastName** to insert the field.

6. Press the **Enter** key to move to the next line; use the same method as in Step 5 to insert the **Address1** field, press the **Enter** key, insert the **City** field, type **,** (a comma), press the **spacebar**, type **CO** (the abbreviation for Colorado), press the **spacebar**, and insert the **PostalCode** field. The completed Create Labels dialog box should look like Figure 6–33.

Figure 6-33   **CREATE LABELS DIALOG BOX**

inserted merge fields

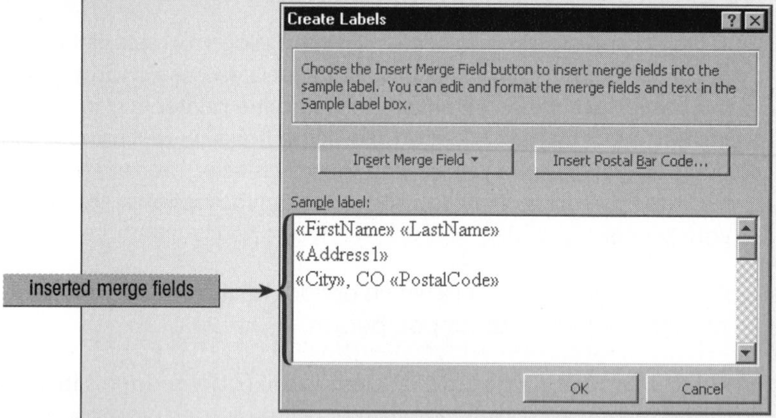

7. Click the **OK** button. The Mail Merge Helper dialog box is still open, and you're ready to merge the data source into the mailing-labels document.

8. Click the **Merge** button in the Merge the data with the document section. The Merge dialog box opens.

9. Make sure that the Merge to option is set to **New Document** and that the Records to be merged option is set to **All**, and then click the **Merge** button. Word creates a new merged document formatted for the Avery 5162 - Address mailing-label sheets. See Figure 6–34.

Figure 6-34	MERGED DOCUMENT WITH MAILING LABELS

The labels are all set up. All you need to do is save the document and print the labels. For now, you'll just print the labels on an 8½ × 11-inch sheet of paper so you can see what they look like. Later, Alicia will print them again on the sheet of labels.

To save and print the labels:

1. Save the merged document to the Tutorial subfolder within the Tutorial.06 folder using the filename **Pet Shoppe Labels**.

2. Scroll through the document to preview the labels.

3. Print the merged document of labels just as you would print any other document.

   TROUBLE? If you want to print on a sheet of labels, consult your instructor or technical support person about how to feed the sheet into the printer. If you're using a shared printer, you may need to make special arrangements so other users' documents aren't accidentally printed on your label sheets.

4. Close the merged document.

5. Save the main document to the Tutorial subfolder within the Tutorial.06 folder using the filename **Pet Shoppe Labels Form**, and then close the document.

6. If necessary, close the data source file, but do not exit Word.

If Alicia wanted you to print envelopes instead of mailing labels, you would have created a new main document similar to the one for creating mailing labels, except you would choose Envelopes as the type of main document rather than Mailing Labels.

Creating a Telephone List

As your final task, Alicia wants you to create a telephone list for all the customers in the data source table. She asked some of the sales personnel to call customers and remind them of The Pet Shoppe's anniversary sale; the sales reps will call all the customers on the phone list you create.

You'll begin by setting up a mail merge as before, except this time you'll use a Catalog type of main document rather than a Form Letter. Even though you aren't actually creating a catalog, you'll use the Catalog type because in Form Letter, Word automatically inserts a section break, which forces a page break, after each merged record. In a Catalog type of main document, all the entries (records) in the telephone list will print on one page rather than each record printing on its own page.

To prepare for creating the telephone list:

1. Click the **New Blank Document** button [ ] on the Standard toolbar to open a new, blank document window.

2. Click **Tools** on the menu bar, and then click **Mail Merge**. The Mail Merge Helper dialog box opens.

3. Click the **Create** button in the Main document section of the dialog box. A list of main document types appears.

4. Click **Catalog**.

5. Click the **Active Window** button.

6. Click the **Get Data** button, and then click **Open Data Source** and open **Pet Shoppe Data** from the Tutorial folder for Tutorial 6 on your Data Disk.

7. Click the **Edit Main Document** button in the message dialog box.

You're ready to create the main document for the telephone list and merge the main document with the data source. The format of the telephone list is the customer's name (last name first) at the left margin of the page and the phone number at the right margin. You'll set up the main document so that the phone number is preceded by a dot leader. A **dot leader** is a dotted line that extends from the last letter of text on the left margin to the beginning of text aligned at a tab stop.

To create the main document:

1. With the insertion point in a blank document window, insert the **LastName** merge field, type **,** (a comma), press the **spacebar**, and insert the **FirstName** merge field.

   Now, you'll set a tab stop at the right margin (position 6 inches) with a dot leader.

2. Click **Format** on the menu bar, and then click **Tabs** to open the Tabs dialog box.

3. Type **6** in the Tab stop position text box, click the **Right** option button in the Alignment section, and then click **2 ....** in the Leader section to create a dot leader. See Figure 6-35.

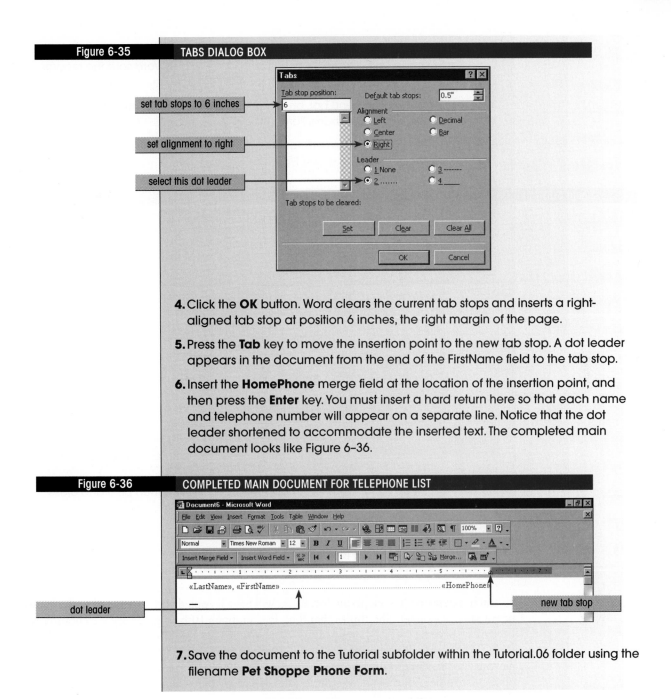

| Figure 6-35 | TABS DIALOG BOX |

set tab stops to 6 inches

set alignment to right

select this dot leader

4. Click the **OK** button. Word clears the current tab stops and inserts a right-aligned tab stop at position 6 inches, the right margin of the page.

5. Press the **Tab** key to move the insertion point to the new tab stop. A dot leader appears in the document from the end of the FirstName field to the tab stop.

6. Insert the **HomePhone** merge field at the location of the insertion point, and then press the **Enter** key. You must insert a hard return here so that each name and telephone number will appear on a separate line. Notice that the dot leader shortened to accommodate the inserted text. The completed main document looks like Figure 6–36.

| Figure 6-36 | COMPLETED MAIN DOCUMENT FOR TELEPHONE LIST |

dot leader

new tab stop

7. Save the document to the Tutorial subfolder within the Tutorial.06 folder using the filename **Pet Shoppe Phone Form**.

You're almost ready to merge this file with the data source, except that you want the name and phone numbers list to be alphabetized by the customers' last names. First, you'll sort the data source, and then you'll merge the files.

To sort the data source by last name and merge the files:

1. Click the **Edit Data Source** button 🖼 on the Mail Merge toolbar, and then click the **View Source** button to display the data table.

2. Move the insertion point to the LastName cell in the header row, and then click the **Sort Ascending** button 🔼 on the Database toolbar. Word sorts the records by customer last name. You're ready to perform the merge.

3. Click **Window** on the menu bar, and then click **Pet Shoppe Phone Form** to switch to the Pet Shoppe Phone Form.

4. Click the **Merge to New Document** button 🔳 on the Mail Merge toolbar. Word generates the telephone list. See Figure 6–37.

| Figure 6-37 | MERGED DOCUMENT OF TELEPHONE LIST |

```
Aimes, Barry ............................................................303-555-8898
Akin, Julia ...............................................................303-555-1759
Brooks, Peter ...........................................................719-555-7890
Curiel, Gabriela ........................................................719-555-0030
Freestone, Chad ........................................................719-555-5432
Gutierrez, Amelia ......................................................719-555-4464
Lazarov, Mirella ........................................................303-555-2940
Orozco, Pablo ...........................................................303-555-8008
Sorenson, Sarah ........................................................303-555-8076
Thomas, Sally ...........................................................303-555-2841
Ure, Randall .............................................................303-555-3040
Wolfgramm, Violette ..................................................719-555-6802
Yorgasen, Ruth .........................................................303-555-4563
Zabriski, Joe ............................................................303-555-7890
—
```

Page 1   Sec 1   1/1   At 1"   Ln 1   Col 1   REC TRK EXT OVR

5. Save the new merged file as **Pet Shoppe Phone List**, and then print and close the file.

6. Save, and close the Pet Shoppe Phone form.

7. Exit Word without saving the sorted data source file.

You have created the telephone list. Alicia will have it copied and distributed to the appropriate sales personnel. She thinks that The Pet Shoppe's 10th Anniversary Celebration will be a great success.

In this tutorial, you've created a form letter and merged it with a data source to create a personalized mailing to Pet Shoppe customers. You've also created mailing labels and a telephone list to help in their marketing efforts. Alicia thanks you for your help and prepares the letters for mailing to Pet Shoppe's customers.

Session 6.3 QUICK CHECK

1. Which of the following are not types of main documents:

   a. mailing labels

   b. merge fields

   c. envelopes

   d. telephone list

   e. form letters

2. True or False: To create mailing labels, you can use the same data source file you used for a form letter.

3. Describe the general process for creating and printing an address list that will print directly to envelopes.

4. True or False: Word automatically inserts an end of section break, which forces a page break, after each merged record in a Catalog type of main document.

5. What is a dot leader? (The telephone list you created in this tutorial used a dot leader.)

6. How do you display a data table?

7. How do you sort a data source using the LastName field so that all the customers are arranged in reverse alphabetical order (Z to A)?

REVIEW ASSIGNMENTS

The Pet Shoppe's 10th Anniversary Celebration was a great success, and Alicia was pleased with how convenient it was to send out form letters with the Word Mail Merge feature. She decides to use it to remind customers about the pet vaccines that the shop offers, using the services of a visiting veterinarian. She asks you to help her with a mailing.

1. If necessary, start Word and make sure your Data Disk is in the appropriate drive. Open the file **Vaccines** from the Review folder in the Tutorial.06 folder on your Data Disk, and then save it on your Data Disk as **Pet Shoppe Vaccines**.

2. In mail merge, create a form letter main document using the Pet Shoppe Vaccines file.

3. Create a data source document, using the filename Pet Vaccine Data, with the following eight field names: FirstName, LastName, Address1, City, PostalCode, Branch, PetKind, and PetName.

4. Create records using the following information:
   ■ Delbert Greenwood, 2483 Teluride Drive, Boulder, 80307, University Mall, dog, Barkley
   ■ Ariel Cornell, 471 S. Mountain View, Cortez, 81321, Cortez, dog, Charity
   ■ Edna Peacemaker, 372 Wildwood Ave., Greeley, 80631, Rocky Mountain Mall, cat, Tawny
   ■ Silvester Polansky, 988 Heather Circle #32, Denver, 80204, High Prairie Mall, cat, Simon.

5. Sort the data source by postal code from the lowest to the highest postal code.

6. Save your changes to the data source document Pet Vaccine Data.

7. Switch to the main document, and replace the text of the field names in brackets with actual merge fields. Remember to use a Word date field to replace "[Date]".

8. Save the changes to the main document, and then view the document as it will appear when it is merged. Check for any mistakes in the records you've added.

Explore ▶ 9. Print only those records for customers who own a dog.

10. Close all documents, saving changes as needed.

As you learned in the tutorial, you can use many types of files as your data source. For example, right now Alicia needs to send out a memo to her own employees regarding their payroll deductions. The data you'll need for this mail merge is stored in a Microsoft Excel worksheet named "Payroll Data," which contains the following field names: FirstName, LastName, Address1, WorkPhone, and Exemptions. To learn how to merge this alternate data source with a Word document, first open the file **Payroll** from the Review folder in the Tutorial.06 folder on your Data Disk, and then save it as **Pet Shoppe Payroll Memo**. Complete the following:

11. Create a form letter main document using Pet Shoppe Payroll Memo file.

Explore ▶ 12. Now, you can select an Excel worksheet as your data source. To select this data source, click Get Data in the Mail Merge Helper, and then click Open Data Source. Use the Look in arrow to select the Review folder for Tutorial 6. Click the Files of type list arrow, select MS Excel Worksheets, click the Payroll Data file, and then click Open. The Microsoft Excel dialog box opens. Verify that "Entire Spreadsheet" is selected in the Named or cell range text box, and then click OK. You see a message box indicating that the main document does not contain any merge fields. Click Edit Main Document. In the next step, you will edit the main document to insert the necessary merge fields. The Insert Merge Field button automatically displays the field names contained in the Excel file.

Edit the main document by doing the following:

13. Move the cursor to the right of "TO:," press the Tab key and insert the FirstName field (for the employee's first name), press the spacebar, and then insert the LastName field (for the employee's last name). Select the name fields, and turn off bold formatting.

14. To the right of "DATE:" in the memo, press the Tab key and insert the Word date field. Select the Word date field and toggle off the Bold button.

15. In the body of the memo, immediately before the word "exemption(s)," insert the Exemptions field followed by a space.

16. Save the main document with the changes, and then view the memo as it will appear when merged and check each record for any mistakes.

17. Merge to a new document. Scroll through the new document to verify that names and exemptions have been inserted into the memos correctly, and then save the new document as Pet Shoppe Payroll Memo 2.

Explore ▶ 18. Print only the memo for Minh Lien.

19. Close all documents, saving any changes. If Word asks if you want to save changes to a template, click No.

20. Create a new main document of the Envelopes type.

Explore ▶ 21. Select the Microsoft Excel worksheet "Payroll Data" as the data source, following the directions in Step 12, except that you will need to click Set Up Main Document, rather than Edit Main Document.

Explore ▶ 22. In the Envelope Options dialog box, select the Size 10 envelope in the Envelope size list box, and then click OK. (The steps that follow assume you will be printing the envelope text on a piece of paper rather than on an actual envelope. If you plan to print to an envelope, use the Envelope size list box to select the appropriate envelope size.)

Explore

23. In the Envelope Address dialog box, use the Insert Merge Field button to insert the FirstName, LastName, and Address1 fields into the Envelope Address dialog box, and then click OK. Click Close to close the Mail Merge Helper dialog box.

24. Save the envelopes main document as **Payroll Envelope Form**.

25. Merge the envelopes main document and data source Payroll Data, and then save the merged document as **Payroll Envelopes**. If Word asks you which return address to use, use the default return address, or substitute your own.

26. Print the last employee address on an 8½ × 11-inch sheet of paper, and then close all documents.

27. Open a new, blank document window and create a main document for generating a one-page telephone list. Use Payroll Data as the data source.

28. Create an employee telephone list by inserting the LastName and FirstName fields, separated by a comma and space, at the left margin. Insert the WorkPhone field at the right margin with a dot leader.

29. Format the main document so that each telephone number appears on a separate line, save the main document as **Employee Phone List Form**, and then sort the data source alphabetically by last name in ascending order.

30. Generate the telephone list, and save the new merged document as **Employee Phone List**.

31. Print the telephone list, and then close all documents, saving changes as needed.

CASE PROBLEMS

Case 1. Amber Christensen for Mayor Amber Christensen is preparing to run for the office of mayor of Joplin, Missouri. Amber's campaign staff is creating a data file of prospective supporters of her campaign, and asks you to help.

1. If necessary, start Word and make sure your Data Disk is in the appropriate drive. Open the file **Campaign** from the Cases folder in the Tutorial.06 folder on your Data Disk, and then save it as **Campaign Form Letter**.

2. Create a form letter main document using the Campaign Form Letter file.

Explore

3. Create a data source document with the following field names: LastName, FirstName, NickName, WorkField, Title, Company, Address1, and Phone. After you have added and removed the necessary fields, use the Move arrows in the Create Data Source dialog box to arrange the field names in the order given in this step. (To move a field name, select it in the Field names in header row list box, and then click the up or down arrow as necessary to move it up or down in the list.)

4. Save the data source document as **Supporters Data**.

5. Enter the following four records into the data source. (Don't include the commas in the records.)

   ■ Montoya, Andrea, Andrea, community, Chief Medical Officer, Joplin Medical Center, 1577 Lancelot Drive, 552-7740

   ■ Zabriski, David, Dave, business, President, Zabriski Appraisal Services, 633 Wentworth, 552-1095

■ Kinikini, Leilani, Lani, business, Business Manager, Astor and Bradford Architects, 4424 Bedford, 552-9850

■ Norman, Theodore, Tad, education, Principal, Joplin High School, 844 Tiger Way, 552-0180

Edit the Campaign Form Letter as follows:

6. At the beginning of the document, insert the Word date field, and then leave five blank lines between the date and the inside address.

7. Insert merge fields for the inside address. Include fields for each person's first and last name, title, company, and address. All the inside addresses should include the city (Joplin), the abbreviation for the state (MO), and the ZIP code (64801).

8. Insert a blank line below the fields for the inside address, and create the salutation of the letter. Use the field name NickName in the salutation. Make sure there is a blank line between the salutation and the body of the letter.

9. In the third paragraph, replace "[Nickname]" with the actual field name.

10. Save the edited main document.

11. Merge the files to create a set of letters to prospective contributors.

12. Save the merged letters document as **Campaign Letters**.

13. Print the first two letters.

Explore ▶ 14. Create a main document to print envelopes for the letters, and save the document as **Campaign Envelope Form**.

15. Merge the envelopes main document with the Supporters Data data source, and save the merged document as **Campaign Envelopes**.

16. Print the first page of the envelope file on an 8½ ×11-inch sheet of paper.

17. Sort the data source in descending order by phone numbers.

Explore ▶ 18. Create a telephone list of prospective contributors. Use a dot leader to separate the name on the left from the phone number on the right.

19. Save the main document for the telephone list as **Campaign Phone Form**.

20. Save the merged document of the telephone list as **Campaign Phone List**.

21. Print the telephone list on a sheet of paper.

22. Close the documents.

Case 2. Jeri's Gems Jeri Moak owns a small jewelry store in Dubuque, Iowa. Frequently, she notifies her regular customers (who live in nearby communities in Iowa, Wisconsin, and Illinois) of upcoming sales. She decides to prepare personalized form letters to mail to all her regular customers one month before their birthdays. She'll mail the letters in manila envelopes along with a two-page color catalog and a gift certificate. She asks you to help her perform a mail merge using Word.

1. If necessary, start Word and make sure your Data Disk is in the appropriate drive. Open the file **Gems** from the Cases folder in the Tutorial.06 folder of your Data Disk, and then save it as **Gems Form Letter**.

2. Create a form letter main document using the Gems Form Letter document.

3. Create a data source document with the following field names: FirstName, LastName, Address1, City, State, PostalCode, BirthDay, BirthMonth, BirthStone.

4. Save the data source document as **Gems Data**.

5. Enter the following five records into the data source. (Don't include the commas in the records.) Enter months by numbers (1, 2, 3), not names (January, February, March), so you can sort in chronological order.

   Kayleen, Mitchell, 882 River Way, Dubuque, IA, 52001, 23, 1, garnet
   Tammy, Minervini, 8244 Westbrook Way, Platteville, WI, 52143, 31, 8, sapphire
   Susan, Gardner, 804 Derby Road, Dubuque, IA, 52001, 14, 6, pearl
   Garth, Poduska, 77 Catskill Circle, Rockford, IL, 51345, 7, 1, garnet
   Oscar, Pike, 402 Waverly Avenue, Waterloo, IA, 53400, 22, 8, sapphire

6. At the beginning of the main document, Gems Form Letter, insert the date field and data fields for the inside address and salutation, in a proper business-letter format. Remember to include the state field in the inside address. Use the customer's first name in the salutation.

7. In the body of the letter, insert the fields BirthMonth, BirthDay, and BirthStone at the locations indicated by the bracketed words. Put a slash (/) between the BirthDay and BirthMonth.

8. Sort the data source alphabetically by the customer's last name.

9. Save the main document using its current filename.

Explore ▷ 10. Using Query Options, select those records for customers whose birthdays are in January, and then merge the main document with the data source.

11. Save the merged document as **Gems Letters**.

12. Print the letters that result from the merge.

13. Create a main document for generating mailing labels on sheets of Avery 5162 – Address Labels, using the Gems Data file as your data source.

14. Save the main document as **Gems Labels Form**.

15. Merge the main document and the data source to a new file.

16. Print the labels on an 8½ × 11-inch sheet of paper, and save the labels as **Gems Labels**.

17. Create a catalog main document for generating a list of customers, using the Gems Data file as your data source. Use the following example to format your merge fields, putting a blank line after the last line, and using bold formatting for the first line:

    Name: Garth Poduska
    Address: 77 Catskill Circle, Rockford, IL 51345
    Birth date: 1/7
    Birthstone: garnet

18. Save the main document as **Gems Customer List Form**.

Explore ▷ 19. Sort the data source in ascending order by birth month, then by birth day. (*Hint:* Click the Query Options button on the Mail Merge Helper dialog box, use the Sort Records tab, set the Sort by text box to BirthMonth and the Then by text box to BirthDay.)

20. Merge the customer list form with the data source.

21. Save the merged document as **Gems Customer List**.

22. Print the list.

23. Close the files.

Case 3. Liberty Auto Sales Tom Reynolds is the customer relations manager for Liberty Auto Sales in Cadillac, Michigan. After a customer purchases a new car, Tom sends out a Sales Satisfaction Survey accompanied by a personalized letter. He would like you to help him use the Word Mail Merge feature to perform this task.

1. If necessary, start Word and make sure your Data Disk is in the appropriate drive. Open the file **AutoSale** from the Cases folder in the Tutorial.06 folder on your Data Disk, and then save it as **Auto Sale Form Letter**.

2. Create a main document using the Auto Sale Form Letter file.

3. Create a data source with the following field names: FirstName, LastName, Address1, City, PostalCode, CarMake, CarModel, SalesRep.

4. Save the data source document as **Auto Sale Data**.

5. Enter the following five records into the data source. (Don't include the commas in the records.)

   ■ Donald, Meyers, 344 Spartan Avenue, Detroit, 48235, Honda, Civic, Bruce
   ■ Arlene, Snow, 46 North Alberta Road, Ecorse, 48229, Toyota, Camry, Lillie
   ■ Lance, Nakagawa, 4211 Livonia Drive, Kentwood, 49508, Honda, Accord, Martin
   ■ Peter, Siskel, 92 Waterford Place, Walker, 49504, Toyota, Corolla, Bruce
   ■ Marilee, Peterson, 8211 University Drive, Detroit, 48238, Honda, Civic, Lillie

6. Edit the main document to include the following in the letter, using a proper letter format: date, inside address, and salutation. (*Hint:* You'll need to add the state as text.)

7. Edit the body of the form letter to replace words in brackets with their corresponding merge field names.

8. Save the form letter. If Word asks if you want to save changes to a template, click No.

9. Sort the data source alphabetically by the last name.

Explore 10. Use the Query Option dialog box to select only those records whose sales representative was Lillie.

11. Merge the form letter with the data source.

12. Save the merged document as **Auto Letters**.

13. Print letters in the merged document.

Explore 14. Create a main document for printing envelopes for the letters that you printed.

15. Save the new main document as **Auto Envelopes Form**.

16. Merge the main document with the data to generate a file for printing envelopes.

17. Save the merged document as **Auto Envelopes**.

18. Print the envelopes in the file on 8½×11-inch sheets of paper.

19. Close all the files, saving any changes as needed.

Case 4. Graduation Announcements Mailing List Suppose that, upon your graduation from college, you want to send announcements to your friends and family telling them about this special event in your life. You can do this easily with Word's Mail Merge feature. Do the following:

1. If necessary, start Word and make sure your Data Disk is in the appropriate drive.

2. Open a new, blank document and use it to create a main document form letter.

3. Create a data source containing the names and addresses of at least five people. You can use real or fictitious names and addresses. Be sure to include addresses in at least two different states.

4. Save the data source document as **Graduation Guest Data** in the Cases folder in the Tutorial.06 folder on your Data Disk.

5. Write a brief form letter telling your friends and relatives about your graduation. Include the following in the letter:

   a. Word field for the current date
   b. merge fields for the inside address and salutation of the letter
   c. at least one merge field within the body of the letter
   d. information to your friends and family about the time, date, and location of the graduation exercises

6. Save the main document as **Graduation Form Letter**.

7. Sort the data source in ascending order by last name.

8. Merge the main document and data source.

9. Save the merged document as **Graduation Merge**.

10. Print the first two letters of the merged document.

11. Create a labels main document. You can use any printer label type you like, as long as each name and address fits on one label and all the labels fit on one page.

12. Save the labels main document as **Graduation Labels Form**.

13. Merge the files, and save the merged document of labels as **Graduation Labels**.

14. Print the labels on a plain sheet of paper.

Quick | Check answers

Session 6.1

1. a. A form letter is a document containing general information to be sent to many recipients, to which you can add personalized data for each recipient, such as name, address, and so on.

   b. A **main document** is a document (such as a letter or a contract) that, in addition to text, contains placeholder text to mark where variable information from the data source (such as a name or an address) will be inserted.

   c. A **data source** is a document (often in the form of a table) that contains information, such as customers' names and addresses, that can be merged with the main document.

   d. A merge field is placeholder text in a main document. When the main document and the data source are merged, merge fields are replaced by specific information from each record in the data source.

   e. A record is a collection of information about one individual or object in a data source. For example, a record might include the first name, last name, address and phone numbers for a customer.

   f. A **data field** is one specific piece of information a record. For example, a record might include a first name data field, a last name data field, and a phone number address field. Each row of data fields in a data source make up a complete record.

2. PayGrade and StudentIdentificationNumber are valid field names. Options a and f are invalid because they contain spaces. Option e is invalid because it is longer than 40 characters.

3. record

4. True

5. Type "Gender" in the Field name text box of the Create Data Source dialog box, and then click the Add Field Name button.

6. The data form simplifies the process of entering, editing, and deleting data records.

7. To move among records in the data source, open the data form, and then use the Record arrow buttons in the lower-left corner of the data form to move forward or backward to the record you want.

Session 6.2

1. Using a data field in a main document ensures that the current date will be inserted every time the document is printed.

2. To insert a merge field into a main document, click the Insert Merge Field button on the Mail Merge toolbar, and then click a field name.

3. Within the main document, a merge field is indicated by chevrons.

4. a. A merged document is a document containing the text of the main document, combined with the data from the data source.

   b. When you sort a list or a document, you rearrange its contents in alphabetical, numerical, or chronological order.

   c. A query is the process by which you can select specific records from a data source.

   d. A filtering operator is a mathematical or logical expression used to include or exclude certain records.

5. Open the Mail Merge Helper, click the Query Options button, click the Field list arrow and select the ZIP code field, verify that "Equal to" appears in the Comparison text box, type the desired ZIP code in the Compare to text box, and then click OK.

6. To preview the merged document, create a main document and a data source, verify that the main document is displayed in the document window, and then click the View Merged Data button on the Mail Merge toolbar.

7. 23

8. No, you do not have to print every letter in a merged form letter document.

Session 6.3

1. Merge fields (b) and telephone list (d) are not types of main documents.

2. True

3. Create main document of type Envelopes, specify the main document and the data source, select the type of printer, create a sample envelope with merge fields in the Create Envelopes dialog box, and then create a new merge document and print.

4. True

5. A dot leader is a dotted line extending from text on the left margin to text at the tab stop.

6. To display a data table, click the Edit Data Source button on the Mail Merge toolbar, and then click View Source.

7. Display the data table, move the insertion point to the LastName field, and then click the Sort Descending button on the Database toolbar.

OBJECTIVES

In this tutorial you will:

- Embed and modify an Excel worksheet

- Link an Excel chart

- Modify and update the linked chart

- Modify a document for online viewing

- Explore Web Layout view and the Document Map

- Save a Word document as a Web page

- Format a Web document

- View a Web document in a Web browser

LAB

The Internet: World Wide Web

INTEGRATING
WORD WITH OTHER PROGRAMS AND WITH THE WORLD WIDE WEB

Writing a Proposal to Open a New Branch of Family Style, Inc.

CASE

Family Style, Inc.

Nalani Tui is one of the founders and owners of Family Style, Inc., a retail company with six outlets in the central and southern regions of Indiana. When she and her partners founded Family Style in 1988, their concept was simple. They would buy high-quality used home merchandise—clothing, sports equipment, appliances, furniture, televisions, personal computers, and so forth—and resell it at a profit, but still for far less than consumers would pay for similar, new merchandise.

The concept was immediately popular. Customers who have items for sale can receive immediate cash, and customers who want to buy items can purchase them at very low prices. Family Style is successful because the outlets readily attract sellers and buyers and because the management has kept administrative, marketing, and overhead expenses low.

Nalani thinks that Family Style is ready to expand to cities in northern Indiana. She is preparing a written proposal for the other owners and investors of Family Style on the advantages and disadvantages of opening new outlet stores. The proposal will include an overview of the company's current financial picture, the rationale for expanding, possible sites for new outlets, and Nalani's recommendations for the first new branch site and manager. She wants you to help organize this information in the proposal document.

Nalani needs to make her proposal available to three different groups of people:

- Current owners and stockholders of the company, who live in different parts of the country

- The Family Style management team, who work in the Bloomington office

- Potential investors in the company, who could reside anywhere

Nalani can simply mail a printed copy of her proposal to the current owners and stockholders. For the company's management team, she can make the proposal available through the company's network. To reach a worldwide audience of potential investors, she can post her proposal on the company's World Wide Web site.

In this tutorial, you'll combine the text that Nalani has already written in Word with a worksheet file and a chart that other Family Style employees prepared using different software. Then, you'll prepare the document for online viewing on the company's network. Your modifications will enable online viewers to easily navigate the document and view additional, more detailed information. Finally, you'll save the document in a special format that is readable by Web browsers such as Internet Explorer or Netscape Navigator, and you'll enhance the Web document's appearance.

SESSION 7.1

In this session, you'll see how Nalani planned the proposal. Then you'll embed a worksheet file that was created in Microsoft Excel and modify it from within Word. Next, you'll insert a link to an Excel chart. You'll modify the chart from Excel and learn how to update it in Word to see the effects of your modifications.

Planning the Document

Nalani has written the text of the proposal in Word. She has asked you to add two other components to her proposal: a worksheet and a chart, both from Excel. Together, the text, data, and chart will show the company's current financial state and the possible sites for new retail outlets. The proposal also presents Nalani's recommendations for a new site and branch manager. Nalani gives you two files to combine with the Word document: a Microsoft Excel spreadsheet of financial data created by one of the store managers and an Excel chart created by the Accounting department. Figure 7-1 shows how Nalani wants to combine these elements into a complete proposal.

The proposal begins with an executive summary; then it reviews the company objectives, explains the current situation and future expansion ideas, suggests some location options, and gives a final recommendation.

Your immediate task is to place the Excel worksheet and chart into the Word proposal document.

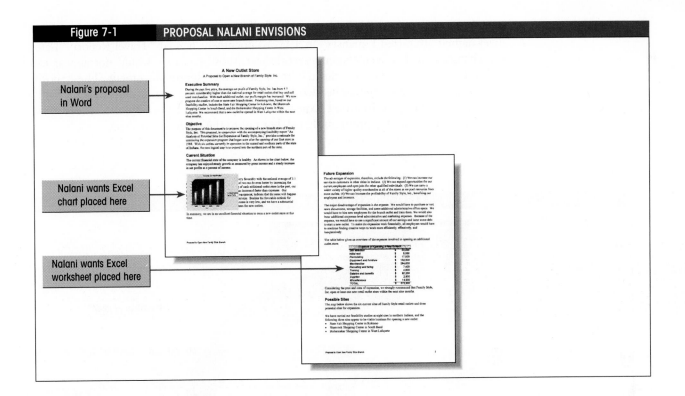

Figure 7-1   PROPOSAL NALANI ENVISIONS

Integrating **Objects from Other Programs**

Every software program is designed to accomplish a set of specific tasks. As you've seen with Microsoft Word, you can use a word-processing program to create, edit, and format documents such as letters, reports, newsletters, and proposals. A **spreadsheet program**, on the other hand, allows you to organize, calculate, and analyze numerical data. A spreadsheet created in Microsoft Excel is known as a **worksheet.** For example, one of Family Style's managers used a Microsoft Excel worksheet to prepare a breakdown of expenses involved in opening a new branch. The Accounting department created an Excel chart that provides a visual representation of income and profit data.

Both the worksheet and the chart are Excel objects. An **object** is an item such as a graphic image, clip art, a WordArt image, a chart, or a section of text, that you can modify and move from one document to another. Nalani asks you to place the worksheet and chart objects into her proposal, but she also wants to be able to modify the Excel objects after they are inserted into the document. A technology called **object linking and embedding**, or **OLE** (pronounced "oh-lay"), allows you to integrate information created in one program into a document created in another and then to modify the object using the tools originally used to create it.

The program used to create the original version of the object is called the **source program** (in this case, Excel). The program into which the object is integrated is called the **destination program** (in this case, Word). Similarly, the original file is called the **source file** and the file into which you insert the object is called the **destination file**.

The next two sections describe two options for transferring data between source files and destination files: embedding and linking.

Embedding

Embedding is a technique that allows you to insert a copy of an existing object into a destination document and edit the object by double-clicking it to bring up the tools of the source program. Because the embedded object is a copy, any changes you make to it are not reflected in the original source file, and vice versa. For instance, you could embed a worksheet named "Itemized Expenses" in a Word document named "Travel Report." Later, if you changed the Itemized Expenses worksheet, those revisions would not appear in the embedded version of the worksheet, within the Travel Report document. The opposite is also true. If you edited the embedded version of the worksheet, those changes would not show up in the original Itemized Expenses worksheet. The embedded worksheet retains a connection to the source program, Excel, but not to the source worksheet.

Figure 7-2 illustrates how you can use embedding to place the Excel worksheet in Nalani's Word proposal.

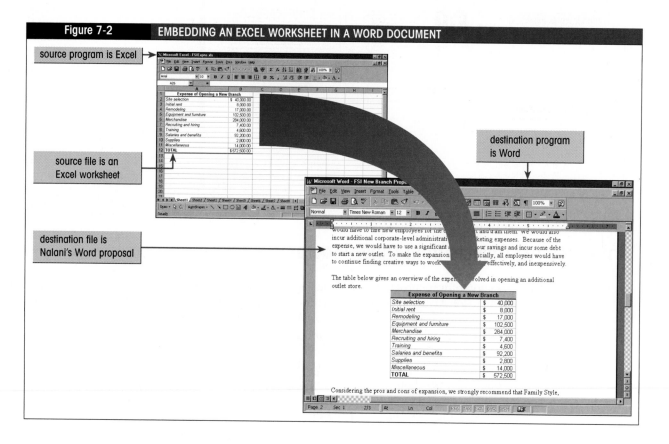

Figure 7-2   EMBEDDING AN EXCEL WORKSHEET IN A WORD DOCUMENT

Once an object is embedded, you can edit it using the source program's editing tools. You simply double-click the embedded Excel chart, and the Excel menus and toolbars appear without your having to leave Word. Excel must be installed on the computer you are using if you want to edit the Excel worksheet while you are still in Word.

Linking

Linking is similar to embedding, except that the linked object maintains a two-way connection between the source file and destination file. If you want to edit the linked object, you can open the source program from within the destination program and make changes that will also appear in the original source file. Likewise, if you edit the original file in the source program, the changes will appear in the linked object. The linked object you see in the destination document is not a copy; it is only a representation of the original object in the source file. As a result, a document that contains a linked object usually takes up less space on a disk than a document containing an embedded version of the same object. Figure 7-3 illustrates how you can use linking to place the Excel chart into Nalani's Word document proposal.

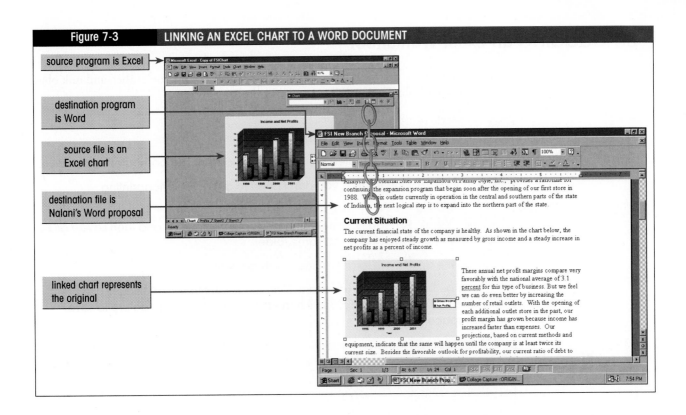

Figure 7-3   **LINKING AN EXCEL CHART TO A WORD DOCUMENT**

Keep in mind that not all software programs allow you to embed or link objects. Only those programs that support OLE let you embed or link objects from one program to another. Office 2000 programs such as Word, Excel, and PowerPoint, are OLE-enabled programs and fully support object linking and embedding.

Choosing between Embedding and Linking

If you need to make changes to an object after inserting it in a Word document, and you know that you have the source program installed on your computer, then you can use either embedding or linking. Of these two options, embedding is best when you know the information in the source file is not likely to change often. For example, if you want to integrate an Excel worksheet into your Word document, you should embed the worksheet so you can access Excel commands occasionally to modify formatting or data. The original Excel worksheet (the source file) remains unchanged, and you could even delete it from your disk without affecting the copy embedded in your Word document.

Link a file whenever you have data that is likely to change over time. For example, suppose you created a Word document called "Refinancing Options" into which you want to insert an Excel worksheet containing the latest interest rates for home mortgages. Suppose also that your assistant updates the Excel worksheet daily to make sure it contains the latest information. By linking the worksheet to the Refinancing Options document, you can be certain that the mortgage rates will be updated every time your assistant updates the Excel worksheet. The advantage to linking is that the data in both the Excel worksheet and the Word document can reflect the latest revisions. The disadvantages to linking are that you must have access to both Excel and the linked file on your computer.

Keep in mind that files containing embedded and linked objects can be very large. Because of this (and because of the many Web page files you will create later in this tutorial) you will need to copy the Tutorial.07 folder to your computer's hard drive before proceeding with the steps in the next section.

Embedding an Excel Worksheet

Nalani prepared the new branch proposal using Word. Before you embed and link objects, you'll first open Nalani's Word document (the destination file).

To open the destination file:

1. Verify that you have copied the Tutorial.07 folder to your computer's hard drive.

2. Start Word. For this tutorial, you don't need to display the nonprinting characters.

3. Open the file **FSIProp** from the Tutorial folder for Tutorial 7, and then save it as **FSI New Branch Proposal** in the same folder.

4. Read the document to get an idea of its content.

   Because this tutorial will use many files, you'll want to make efficient use of your available disk space. You'll turn off the Word Fast Save feature to save disk space.

5. Click **Tools** on the menu bar, click **Options**, click the **Save** tab, if necessary remove the check mark from the Allow fast saves check box and click the **OK** button.

The proposal begins with an Executive Summary that quickly summarizes the main points of the document. Notice that in the "Current Situation" section, there is the placeholder "[insert chart]" where you'll insert the Excel chart that illustrates the company's growth in income and profits. In the "Future Expansion" section, there is the placeholder "[insert spreadsheet]" where you'll insert the worksheet outlining the expenses involved in opening a new retail outlet. Under Possible Sites, there is a map, originally created in Microsoft Paint (a graphics program included with Microsoft Windows), that has been inserted into the document via linking. At the end of the proposal, Nalani has also inserted a photograph of Virgil Jackson, the proposed manager for the new location.

You'll start by embedding the Excel worksheet into the "Future Expansion" section of the proposal, in place of the "[insert spreadsheet]" placeholder. By embedding the worksheet, you can maintain a one-way connection between Excel and the worksheet in Word. You'll use the Object command on the Insert menu to embed the existing Excel worksheet in the proposal.

REFERENCE WINDOW   **RW**

Embedding An Existing File

- Move the insertion point to the location in your document where you want the embedded file to appear.
- Click Insert on the menu bar, and then click Object to open the Object dialog box.
- Click the Create from File tab.
- Click the Browse button, select the file you want to embed, click Insert, and then click the OK button.

Once the expense worksheet is embedded in the proposal document, you'll be able to modify its contents and appearance using Excel commands from within Word, as long as Excel is installed on your computer.

To embed the Excel worksheet:

1. Scroll until you see the bracketed phrase "(insert spreadsheet)" a few lines above the "Possible Sites" heading.

2. Select the entire line, and then delete the placeholder (insert spreadsheet) and the line on which it was located. The insertion point should appear on the blank line between the two paragraphs. This is where you want to embed the Excel worksheet.

   TROUBLE? If the insertion point is not on a blank line, or if two blank lines appear between the paragraphs, edit the proposal so that only one blank line appears between the paragraphs and that the insertion point blinks on that line.

3. Click **Insert** on the menu bar, and then click **Object** to open the Object dialog box, which has two tabs—Create New and Create from File.

4. Click the **Create from File** tab. You'll use the Browse feature to find the Excel worksheet file on your Data Disk.

5. Click the **Browse** button. The Browse dialog box opens.

6. Select the **FSIExpns** file in the Tutorial folder for Tutorial 7.

7. Click the **Insert** button. The Browse dialog box closes and the filename FSIExpns.xls appears in the File name text box in the Object dialog box. See Figure 7-4. Make sure the Link to file check box is not selected. You don't want to link the worksheet—only embed it.

Figure 7-4	OBJECT DIALOG BOX

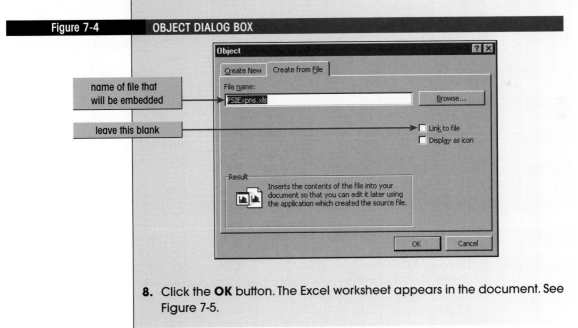

name of file that will be embedded

leave this blank

8. Click the **OK** button. The Excel worksheet appears in the document. See Figure 7-5.

| Figure 7-5 | **DOCUMENT WITH EMBEDDED EXCEL WORKSHEET** |

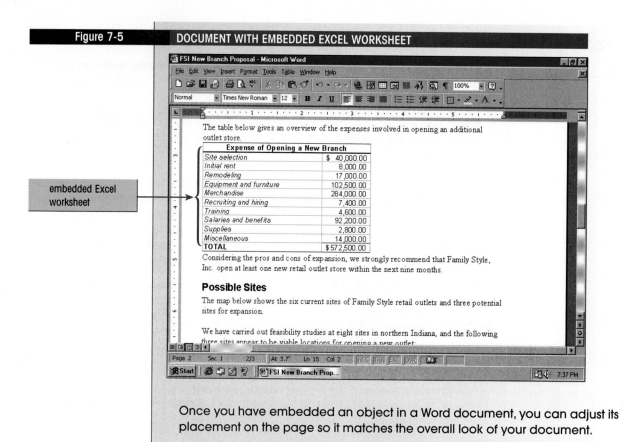

embedded Excel
worksheet

Once you have embedded an object in a Word document, you can adjust its placement on the page so it matches the overall look of your document.

TROUBLE? If you don't see the worksheet, close the document without saving changes, open FSI New Branch Proposal again, switch to Normal view, and begin again with Step 1.

Centering the Embedded Worksheet

You have embedded the worksheet in the proposal. It would look better, however, if it were centered between the left and right margins rather than positioned at the left margin.

To center the worksheet:

1. Click the worksheet to select it. Black resize handles appear around the outside of the worksheet.

2. Click the **Center** button ▤ on the Formatting toolbar. The Excel worksheet is centered horizontally in Nalani's proposal document. See Figure 7-6.

| Figure 7-6 | EMBEDDED EXCEL WORKSHEET CENTERED HORIZONTALLY |

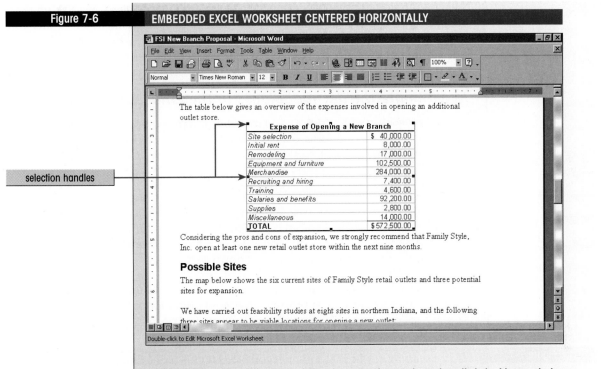

selection handles

TROUBLE? If the worksheet if not properly centered, switch to Normal view.

Once you have embedded an object, you might want to change the information it contains. It would be inconvenient to go back to the original Excel spreadsheet, make changes, and then embed it in your document again. Because the spreadsheet object is embedded, you can make changes to the object from within Word, which you'll do in the next section.

Modifying the Embedded Worksheet

Because the worksheet is embedded, and as long as the source program (Excel) is installed on your computer, you can edit the worksheet by double-clicking it and using Excel commands and tools. After you modify the worksheet, you can click anywhere else in the Word document to deselect the worksheet and re-display the usual Word editing commands and tools. Any changes that you make in the embedded worksheet will affect only the copy in Word and will not affect the original FSIExpns file.

| REFERENCE WINDOW | RW |

Modifying An Embedded Object
- Double-click the object. The commands and tools from the source program become available.
- Using the commands and tools from the source program, modify the object.
- Click anywhere outside the object in the document window to deselect the object and close the source program.

Nalani wants you to make two changes to the embedded worksheet. Because all the cost figures are large and are all rounded to the nearest $100 increment, she wants you to remove the decimal points and trailing zeroes. She also asks you to format the table heading to make it more prominent.

To eliminate the decimal places in the embedded worksheet:

1. Double-click the worksheet. After a moment, the menu bar and toolbars display Excel commands and tools, although the title bar retains the title of the Word program and document. See Figure 7-7. Depending on how your computer is set up, the Excel toolbars may appear one on top of the other, as in Figure 7-7, or they may appear side by side on one row.

   Notice that an Excel worksheet is arranged in rows and columns, just like a Word table. The intersection between a particular row and column is called a **cell** and takes its name from its column letter and the row number. For example, the intersection of column B and row 2 is known as "cell B2."

   TROUBLE? If the Excel commands and toolbar don't appear or a message tells you it can't find the source program, ask your instructor or technical support person for assistance. Excel might not be installed on your computer.

Figure 7-7	EDITING THE WORKSHEET IN WORD USING EXCEL COMMANDS AND TOOLS

Word title bar

Excel menu bar and toolbars

frame indicates worksheet is active

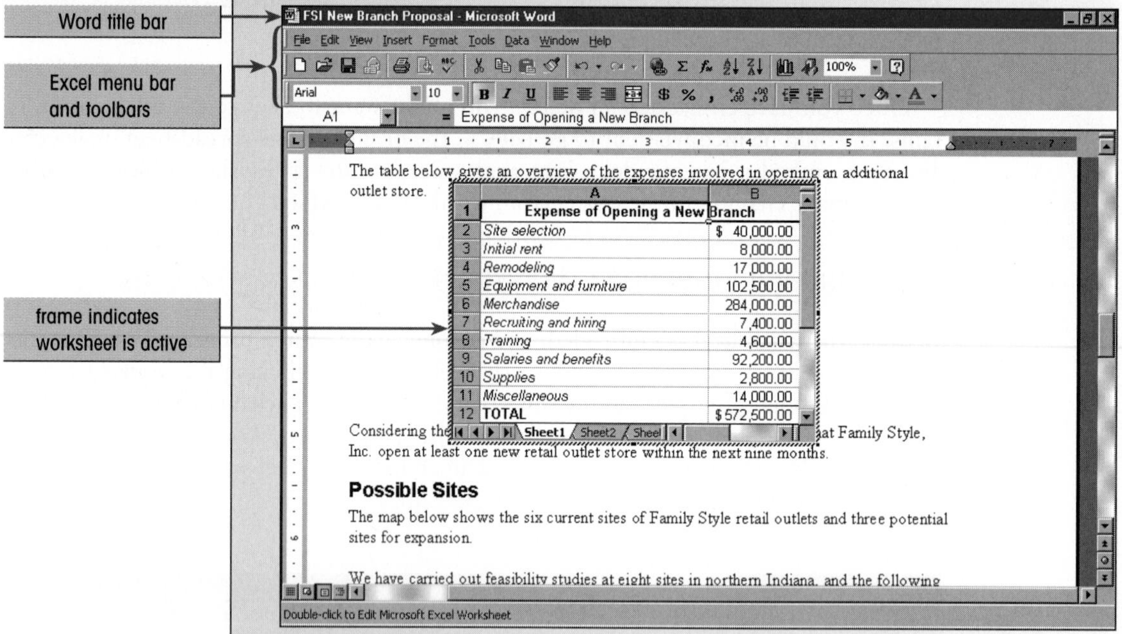

2. Click cell **B2**, which currently contains the figure $40,000.00, hold down the mouse button, and drag downward to highlight all the cells from B2 through B12. The column of cost figures should be highlighted.

3. Click the **Decrease Decimal** button [image] on the Excel Formatting toolbar twice. The numbers in the worksheet change to whole dollar amounts.

TROUBLE? If you don't see the Decrease Decimal button on your screen, click Format on the menu bar, then click Cells. The Format Cells dialog box opens. Click the Number tab, if necessary, click Number in the Category list box, change the setting in the Decimal places box to 0, and then click the OK button.

Now you'll use the Excel tools to format the heading row of the worksheet with a shade of gray, to make it more prominent.

To add shading to the heading row of the embedded worksheet:

1. Click cell **A1** and drag to the right to cell B1 to select the worksheet heading in cells A1 and B1, "Expense of Opening a New Branch."

2. Click the Fill Color list arrow [icon] on the Excel Formatting toolbar, and on the fill color palette click the Gray - 25% color tile (4th row down, far right column). The heading row is now shaded with the gray color you selected.

   TROUBLE? If you don't see the Fill Color list arrow on your screen, click Format on the menu bar, and then click Cells. The Format Cells dialog box opens. Click the Patterns tab. In the palette of colors click the gray square in the fourth row down (on the far right side) and then click the OK button.

3. Click anywhere on the proposal document outside the embedded worksheet. The Excel commands and toolbars are replaced by the Word commands and toolbars, and the embedded worksheet displays the newly formatted figures and heading row. See Figure 7-8.

Figure 7-8	EDITED AND FORMATTED WORKSHEET EMBEDDED IN THE PROPOSAL

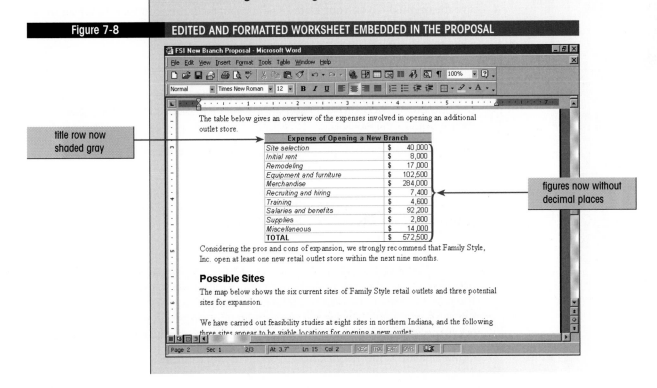

title row now shaded gray

figures now without decimal places

The original Excel worksheet, FSIExps, remains in its original form on your disk, with the two decimal places and the unshaded heading row. You have only modified the embedded copy in Nalani's proposal.

Linking an Excel Chart

Nalani wants you to incorporate the financial chart that shows the increase in gross income and net profit of Family Styles for the previous four years because she thinks this information will help convince others to open a new outlet. However, the Accounting department is currently auditing the sales and profit figures and might have to modify the chart they have given her. Because the source document might change over time, and Nalani wants her proposal to display the most current information at the time it is printed or viewed online, she recommends that you link the chart to the proposal.

REFERENCE WINDOW   **RW**

Linking an Object
- Move the insertion point to the location in your document where you want the file to appear.
- Click Insert on the menu bar, and then click Object to open the Object dialog box.
- Click the Create from File tab on the dialog box.
- Click the Browse button, select the file you want to link, and then click the OK button.
- Click the Link to File check box, and then click the OK button.

You'll link your proposal document to the FSIChart file on your Data Disk. Because you'll make changes to the chart after you link it, you'll make a copy of the chart as you link it. Leave the original file on your Data Disk unchanged in case you want to repeat the tutorial steps later.

To link an Excel chart to the proposal document:

1. Scroll up to the middle of page 1, until you see the "Current Situation" heading and the bracketed phrase "(insert chart)" one line above the second paragraph under the heading.

2. Delete the placeholder "(insert chart)". Make sure the insertion point is positioned on the second blank line between the two paragraphs.

3. Click **Insert** on the menu bar, and then click **Object** to open the Object dialog box. You used this same dialog box earlier to embed the Excel worksheet in the proposal. This time, you'll use it to link to a file.

4. Click the **Create from File** tab.

5. Click the **Browse** button to open the Browse dialog box, and then, if necessary, use the Look in list arrow to open the Tutorial folder within the Tutorial.07 folder. The Browse dialog box displays a list of files in the Tutorial folder for Tutorial 7. Because you want to leave the original file unchanged in your Tutorial folder, you'll make a copy of it now. That way you can use the file again if necessary.

6. Right-click the filename **FSIChart**. A shortcut menu opens.

7. Click **Copy**, and then press **Ctrl + V**. A new file, Copy of FSI Chart, appears in the file list.

8. Make sure the filename Copy of FSIChart is selected, and click the **Insert** button. The chart name appears in the File name text box. Now, you need to specify that you want the chart file to be linked, not embedded, in the proposal document.

9. Click the **Link to file** check box to select it. See Figure 7-9.

Figure 7-9	COMPLETED CREATE FROM FILE TAB IN THE OBJECT DIALOG BOX

copy being linked to keep original intact

select this check box to link a file

Object

Create New | Create from File

File name:
"Copy of FSIChart.xls"   Browse...

☑ Link to file
☐ Display as icon

Result
Inserts the contents of the file into your document and creates a shortcut to the source file. Changes to the source file will be reflected in your document.

OK | Cancel

10. Click the OK button. After a moment, the chart image appears in the proposal, displaying income and profit numbers for the last four years.

The figure is far too large for the document, but you can change its size easily.

To resize the chart and wrap text around it:

1. Click the chart. Black resize handles appear around its border.

2. Click **Format** on the menu bar, and then click **Object**.

3. Click the **Size** tab, and in the Scale section, use the **Height** down arrow to decrease the Height and Width settings to 30%. Both the height and width of the selected object will be reduced by 30%, because the Lock aspect option is selected. (If it is not selected, select it now.) Click the **OK** button.

4. Scroll up, if necessary, to display the chart. After a pause, the chart appears in the Word document in a smaller size. Next, you'll wrap text around the chart.

TROUBLE? If the chart is no longer located below the first paragraph after the heading "Current Situation," just continue with the steps. You will have a chance to adjust its position later.

TROUBLE? Don't be concerned if it takes a few moments for the chart to appear. Some computers need extra time to display graphics on screen. You may notice similar delays through this tutorial. You also may observe that the colors of your graphics change slightly after you have scrolled through the document.

5. Click the chart to select it, if necessary, click **Format** on the menu bar, and then click **Object**.

6. Click the **Layout** tab, and then click the **Advanced** button. The Advanced Layout dialog box opens.

7. Click the **Tight** icon, click the **Right only** option button, click the **OK** button, and then click the **OK** button again. The document text now wraps to the right of the chart.

8. If necessary, drag the chart to the left margin, so that it is positioned after the first paragraph under the "Current Situation" heading. See Figure 7-10.

Figure 7-10   **LINKED EXCEL CHART IN WORD PROPOSAL**

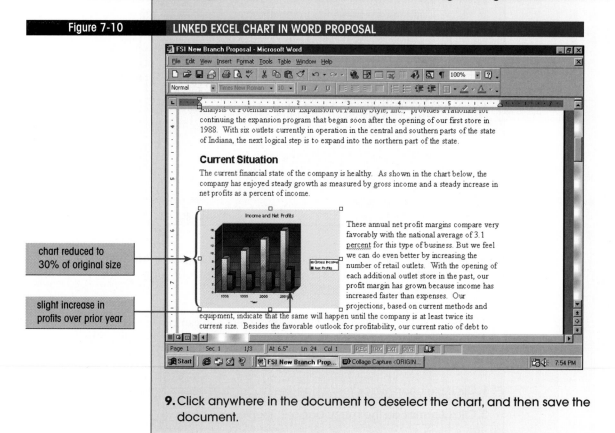

chart reduced to 30% of original size

slight increase in profits over prior year

9. Click anywhere in the document to deselect the chart, and then save the document.

Because you have linked the file, you have not inserted a copy of the file in the proposal but merely a visual reference to the original. The size of the proposal file on disk has not increased significantly as a result of the link. If you double-clicked the chart, Excel would start and display the original source file. Instead of seeing the Word title bar at the top of the screen, you would see the Excel title bar. Because Nalani wants to leave Accounting's chart intact, she will not modify it now. However, when Accounting updates the figures, the changes will be reflected in the linked chart in the proposal. You'll see how this works in the next section.

Modifying the Linked Chart

The advantage of linking a file over embedding it is that the destination file is updated whenever you modify the source file. Furthermore, you can update the source file either from within the source program or from within the destination program. In the following steps, you'll simulate what would happen if the Accounting department modified the file in

Excel. You'll open the chart in Excel, the source program, change some figures, and then view the updated information in the Word proposal.

To modify the chart in the source program:

1. Click the **Start** button on the taskbar, point to **Programs**, and then click **Microsoft Excel**. The Excel program window opens.

   TROUBLE? You must have the Microsoft Excel 2000 program installed to complete this section. If you do not see Microsoft Excel on your Programs menu, see your instructor or technical support person.

   TROUBLE? If the Office Assistant opens asking if you want help, click the Start Using Excel button.

2. Click the **Open** button [icon] on the Standard toolbar to display the Open dialog box.

3. Use the Look in list arrow to open the Tutorial folder for Tutorial 7.

4. Double-click **Copy of FSIChart**. The chart showing Family Style's income and profits opens. The profit figure for 2001 is somewhat higher than for 2000, indicating a modest growth in profit. See Figure 7-11.

| Figure 7-11 | CHART IN SOURCE PROGRAM, EXCEL |

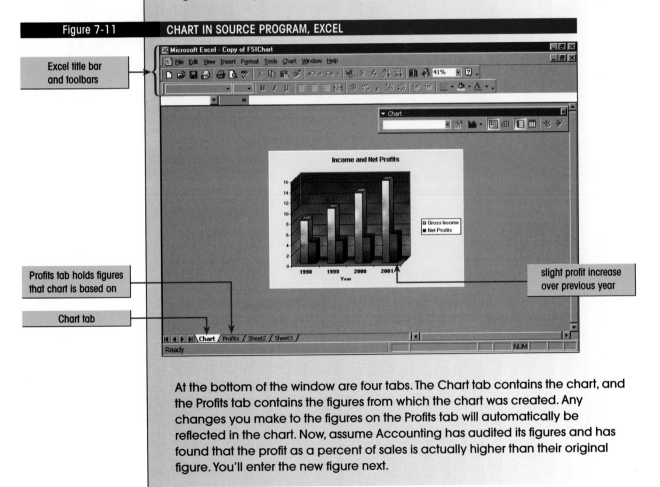

Excel title bar and toolbars

Profits tab holds figures that chart is based on

Chart tab

slight profit increase over previous year

At the bottom of the window are four tabs. The Chart tab contains the chart, and the Profits tab contains the figures from which the chart was created. Any changes you make to the figures on the Profits tab will automatically be reflected in the chart. Now, assume Accounting has audited its figures and has found that the profit as a percent of sales is actually higher than their original figure. You'll enter the new figure next.

5. Click the **Profits** tab. The worksheet containing the profits information appears. You'll change the Net profit figure for 2001. Click cell **E4**, which currently contains the value "5.5".

6. Type **7.5**, and press the **Enter** key. Now you'll look at the chart in Excel and see the effect of the change.

7. Click the Chart tab, and see that the Net Profits bar for 2001 is now higher, reflecting the new figure you entered. See Figure 7-12.

Figure 7-12 | **EXCEL CHART REFLECTING HIGHER PROFIT MARGIN**

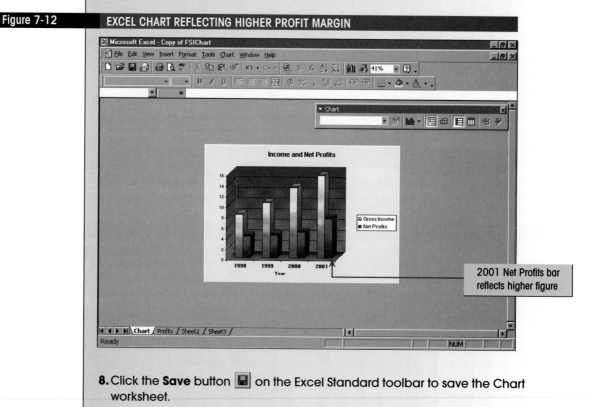

2001 Net Profits bar reflects higher figure

8. Click the **Save** button 🖫 on the Excel Standard toolbar to save the Chart worksheet.

Now, you'll return to the proposal and view the linked version.

To view the linked chart in the proposal:

1. Close Excel. The Word program window redisplays, with the linked version of the chart displayed in the FSI New Branch Proposal file.

You notice that the linked version of the chart still has the 2001 Net Profits bar that represents the older figure. Why doesn't it reflect the change you made in the source program? You must perform one more step to make sure the changes are carried to the linked version: updating the link.

Updating the Link

When you **update** a link, you ensure that the linked object in the destination file reflects the latest version of the source file. If you modify a linked object in the source program and the Word document to which it's linked is closed, Word will automatically update the link the next time you open the document. (Alternatively, it might ask if you want to update the link.) But if you modify a linked object in the source program and the Word document is still open, you'll have to tell Word to update the link.

REFERENCE WINDOW   **RW**

<u>Updating A Link</u>
- From within Word, click Edit on the menu bar, and then click Links.
- Select the filename of the linked file, and then click the Update Now button.
- Click the OK button.

Once the linked chart is updated, it will reflect the change you made in Excel.

To update a linked file:

1. Make sure Microsoft Word appears in the title bar and that you still see the linked chart in the document window. You should be looking at the original version of the chart, not the one with the higher profits bar.

2. Click anywhere in the Microsoft Word window to activate it if necessary.

3. Click **Edit** on the menu bar, and then click **Links** to open the Links dialog box. See Figure 7-13. Two linked files are listed, Copy of FSI Chart and Indiana.bmp, the graphic image of the state of Indiana, although the file names are probably truncated.

Figure 7-13	LINKS DIALOG BOX

the two source files linked to this document

filenames may be truncated

click to display modified chart in Word version

4. Click **COPY OF FS...**, and then click the **Update Now** button. Word momentarily switches back to the document window, retrieves the latest version of the linked file, and then returns to the Links dialog box.

5. Click the **Close** button in the Links dialog box to close it.

6. If necessary, deselect the chart. The updated version of the chart appears in Word; the maroon bar representing Net Profits for 2001 reflects the higher number (7.5) you entered in Excel. See Figure 7-14.

| Figure 7-14 | LINKED COPY OF CHART REFLECTING HIGHER NET PROFITS FIGURE |

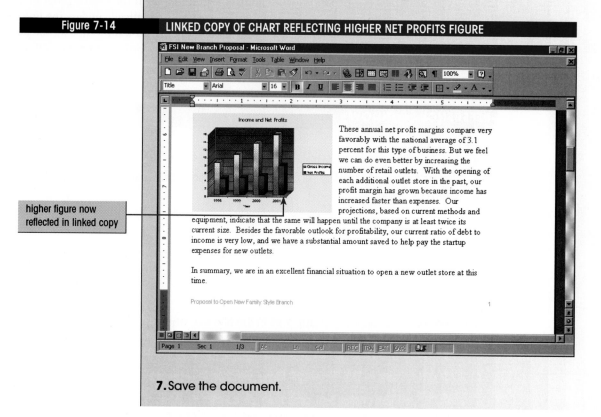

higher figure now reflected in linked copy

7. Save the document.

Now, you can be assured that any updates that Accounting makes to the chart will be reflected whenever the proposal is opened.

Keep in mind that although you just edited the source file by opening it in the source program (Excel), you could just as easily edit the source file in the destination program. You would double-click the linked object in the destination document window. The source program would start, and the source file would open. After editing the source file, you would simply close the source program. The linked object in the destination file would update automatically.

Your document is finished. You are ready to print it for distribution to the owners and stockholders of Family Style.

To print and then close the document:

1. Preview the document. If necessary, change the bottom margin to 1.5" so that the map falls on the third page.

2. Print the document. Your three-page document should look similar to Figure 7-15, although the exact layout of the text and graphics may differ.

Figure 7-15	PRINTED DOCUMENT READY FOR DISTRIBUTION TO OWNERS AND STOCKHOLDERS

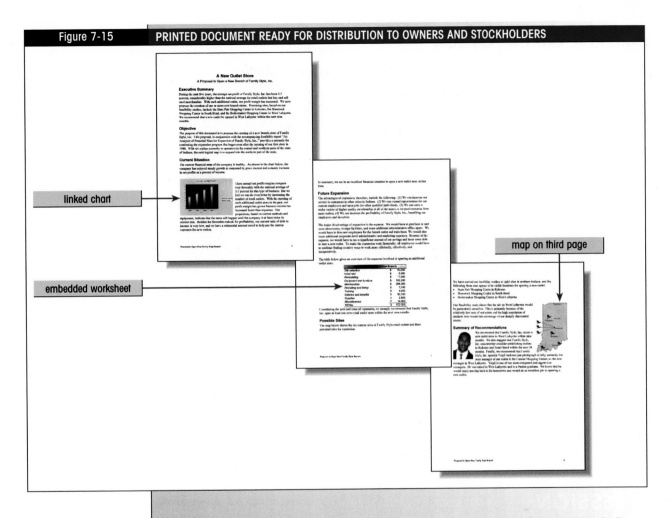

linked chart

embedded worksheet

map on third page

3. Close the FSI New Branch Proposal document. If you did not save changes to it earlier, do so now. You will not save the document with a new name at this point because doing so might interfere with the link between the proposal and the Excel chart.

You give the completed proposal to Nalani, who is pleased with your work. She distributes the proposal to the owners and stockholders who are considering the proposed expansion. Now, she wants you to focus on the task of distributing the document electronically, which you'll do in the next session.

Session 7.1 QUICK CHECK

1. Define the following in your own words:
   a. source file
   b. object
   c. source program
   d. destination file

2. What is the difference between embedding and linking?

3. In what situations would you choose linking over embedding?

4. What does OLE stand for? What is an OLE-enabled program?

5. How do you embed an Excel worksheet into a Word document? How do you link an Excel chart to a Word document?

6. Explain how to create a copy of a file from within the Browse dialog box.

7. How do you modify an embedded object from the destination program?

8. True or False: When you modify an embedded object, your changes are also made to the source file.

You've learned how to combine information created in different source programs into a single document. The OLE technology that makes this integration of information possible allows users of ordinary word-processing programs to create highly informative, interesting, and well-illustrated documents. In the next session, you'll create the electronic document that Nalani will distribute to company employees.

SESSION 7.2

In this session, you'll modify the proposal so that it is better suited to online viewing by Family Style management, who will access it over the company's network. You'll begin by creating hyperlinks that allow users to navigate through the document more easily and to access additional information. Then, you'll see how the document looks in Web Layout view. Finally, you'll modify the document's appearance to make it more interesting for online viewers.

Creating and Navigating Hyperlinks

In addition to printing the proposal for company owners and investors, Nalani wants to place her proposal in a shared folder on the company's network so that other company employees will be able to read it. She wants you to modify the document so people can read it **online**, which means they will read it on the computer screen rather than on a printed page. Because people can't efficiently "flip through pages" when they read online, you should add navigational aids to the online document.

One such navigational aid is a **hyperlink** (short for "hypertext link" and also called a "hot link" or just "link"), which is a word, phrase, or graphic image that users click to "jump to" (or display) another location, called the **target**. Text hyperlinks are usually underlined and appear in a different color from the rest of the document. The target of a hyperlink can be a location within the document, a different document, or a page on the World Wide Web. Figure 7-16 shows a hyperlink pointing to a different document, a resume.

| Figure 7-16 | EXAMPLE OF HYPERLINK POINTING TO A TARGET (IN THIS CASE, A DIFFERENT DOCUMENT) |

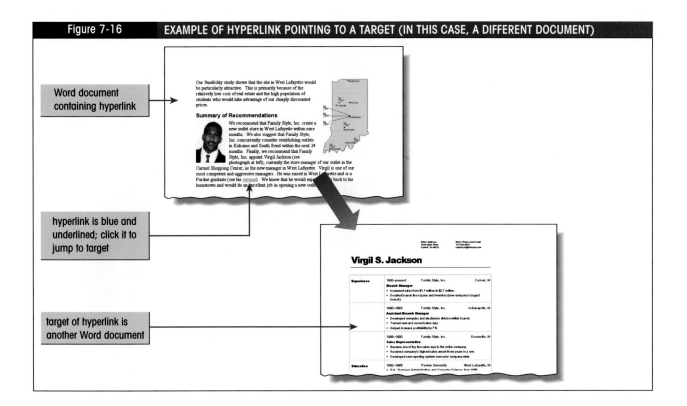

All Office 2000 programs support hyperlinking. If you have many Office 2000 documents that are related to each other, you can create a useful hyperlink system that allows users to retrieve and view related material. Nalani wants you to add two hyperlinks to the proposal document—one that targets a location within the proposal and one that targets a different document.

Inserting a Hyperlink to a Bookmark in the Same Document

Nalani wants users to be able to jump directly to the proposal's conclusions without having to scroll through topics sequentially. You can add a hyperlink at the beginning of the proposal that users can click to jump to the summary of recommendations at the end of the document. Creating a hyperlink to a location in the same document requires two steps. First, you insert an electronic marker called a bookmark at the location you want Word to target. Second, you enter the text that you want users to click and format it as a hyperlink. Figure 7-17 illustrates this process.

Figure 7-17	HYPERLINK THAT TARGETS A BOOKMARK

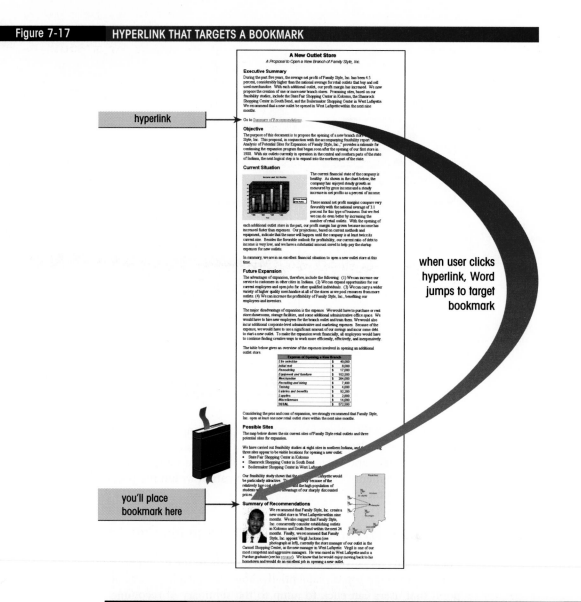

hyperlink

when user clicks
hyperlink, Word
jumps to target
bookmark

you'll place
bookmark here

REFERENCE WINDOW — RW

Inserting a Hyperlink to a Target in the Same Document

- Insert a bookmark at the target location.
- Select the text or graphic image you want to use as the hyperlink.
- Click the Insert Hyperlink button.
- Under Link to, click the Place in This Document option.
- Click the bookmark you want to link to, and then click the OK button.
- Click the OK button.

First, you'll open the document you saved at the end of the previous session. Then you'll insert the hyperlink to the Summary of Recommendations just below the Executive Summary.

To insert a hyperlink to a location within the same document:

1. If you took a break after the last session, make sure Word is running, and then open the **FSI New Branch Proposal** document.

2. Move the insertion point to the beginning of the heading "Summary of Recommendations," near the end of the document. This is where you'll insert a bookmark required for the hypertext link.

3. Click **Insert** on the menu bar, and then click **Bookmark**. The Bookmark dialog box opens. You can now type the bookmark name, which must be one word, without spaces.

4. Type **Recommendations**, and click the **Add** button. Although you can't see it, a bookmark has been inserted before the heading. This bookmark will be the target of the hyperlink. In other words, when you click the hyperlink (which you will create next), the insertion point will jump to this bookmark.

5. Move the insertion point to the end of the "Executive Summary" paragraph, near the beginning of the document. The insertion point should immediately follow the phrase, "within the next nine months."

6. Press the **Enter** key twice to insert two new blank lines into your document, and type **Go to Summary of Recommendations**. Now, you'll create the hyperlink in this line of text.

7. Select the phrase **Summary of Recommendations** that you just typed, and then click the **Insert Hyperlink** button 🖼 on the Standard toolbar. The Insert Hyperlink dialog box opens.

8. Under Link to, click the **Place in this Document** option, if necessary. The right side of the dialog box now displays a list of headings and bookmarks in the document. See Figure 7-18.

Figure 7-18	INSERT HYPERLINK DIALOG BOX

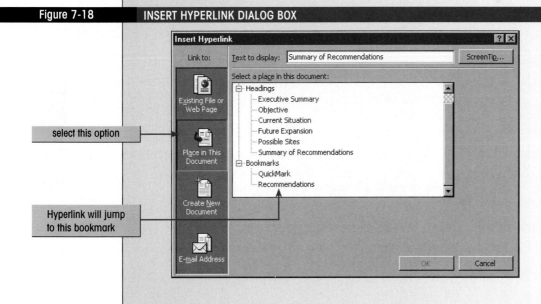

TROUBLE? If you only see three items in the right side of the dialog box, click the plus signs next to "Headings" and "Bookmarks".

9. Click **Recommendations**, and then click the **OK** button. Word formats the hyperlink as underlined blue text. The hyperlink now targets the Recommendations bookmark. See Figure 7-19.

TROUBLE? If you formatted the wrong text as a hyperlink (such as the words "Go to"), click the Undo button ⟲ and begin again with Step 7.

Figure 7-19	DOCUMENT WINDOW WITH HYPERLINK

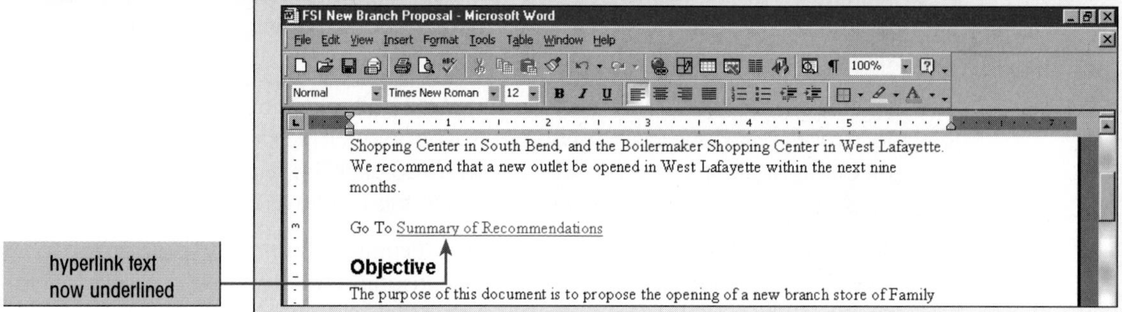

hyperlink text now underlined

Your proposal now features a hyperlink that points to the proposal summary of recommendations.

Navigating Hyperlinks and the Web Toolbar

Now that you have inserted a hyperlink into the document, you should test it to make sure that it targets the correct location. When you click a hyperlink in a document, Word automatically displays the **Web toolbar**, a toolbar with buttons that let you access and navigate your document and the World Wide Web, a global information-sharing system you'll learn about in the next session.

To test the hyperlink in your document:

1. Move the insertion point to the blue underlined text (the hyperlink). Notice that the pointer changes to 🖑. If you leave the pointer on the hyperlink for a moment, Word displays a ScreenTip (yellow rectangle) with the name of the bookmark.

2. Click the hyperlink. The insertion point jumps to the Recommendations bookmark, and the "Summary of Recommendations" section appears. The Web toolbar appears above the document. See Figure 7-20. You'll use one of the Web toolbar buttons to return to the beginning of the document.

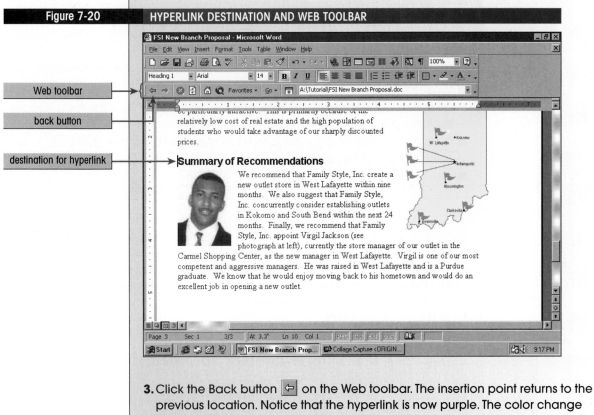

| Figure 7-20 | HYPERLINK DESTINATION AND WEB TOOLBAR |

3. Click the Back button ⇐ on the Web toolbar. The insertion point returns to the previous location. Notice that the hyperlink is now purple. The color change indicates that you have already used, or followed, the hyperlink.

4. Save the document.

The fact that the hyperlink changes color after you use it doesn't have much importance in this document. However, hyperlinks can also point to other documents, including Web documents on the World Wide Web. In that environment, it's helpful to know which links you've already tried. If you were to close and then reopen the document, the hyperlink would be blue again until you clicked it.

Creating Hyperlinks to Other Documents

The greatest power of hyperlinks lies not in jumping to another location within the same document, but in jumping to other documents. These documents can be located on the World Wide Web, on your computer's hard drive, or on your company's network server. When you add a hyperlink to another document, you don't necessarily target a bookmark as you do for hyperlinks pointing to a location within the same document. Instead, you target either a Web document address, called a **URL**, or a path and filename of a file on your computer or network.

REFERENCE WINDOW   RW

Creating a Hyperlink to Another Document

- Move the insertion point to the desired location for the hyperlink.
- Click the Insert Hyperlink button.
- Under Link to, click the Existing File or Web Page option.
- To target a specific file, click the File button, and then use the Link to File dialog box to select the file you want to link to.
- To target a Web page, open your browser, connect to the Internet, and then click the Web Page button to go to the Web page you want to link to.
- Click the OK button.

Nalani's proposal recommends Virgil Jackson as the manager for the new Family Style branch. She has a Word file containing his résumé, VJResume.doc, and she would like to make it available to interested Family Style employees so they can evaluate his skills. You can add a hyperlink that targets Virgil's resume. Because this hyperlink will take users to a different document, you don't need to insert a bookmark as the target. Instead, you use the name of the target document.

To create a hyperlink to another document:

1. Move the insertion point to the next-to-the-last sentence of the last paragraph of the document, after the period following the phrase "a Purdue graduate." This is where you'll insert text, some of which will become the hyperlink.

2. Press the **spacebar**, and type **(See his resume.)** making sure to include the parentheses.

3. Select the word "resume" in the text you just typed. See Figure 7-21.

Figure 7-21   SELECTED WORD IN NEW TEXT

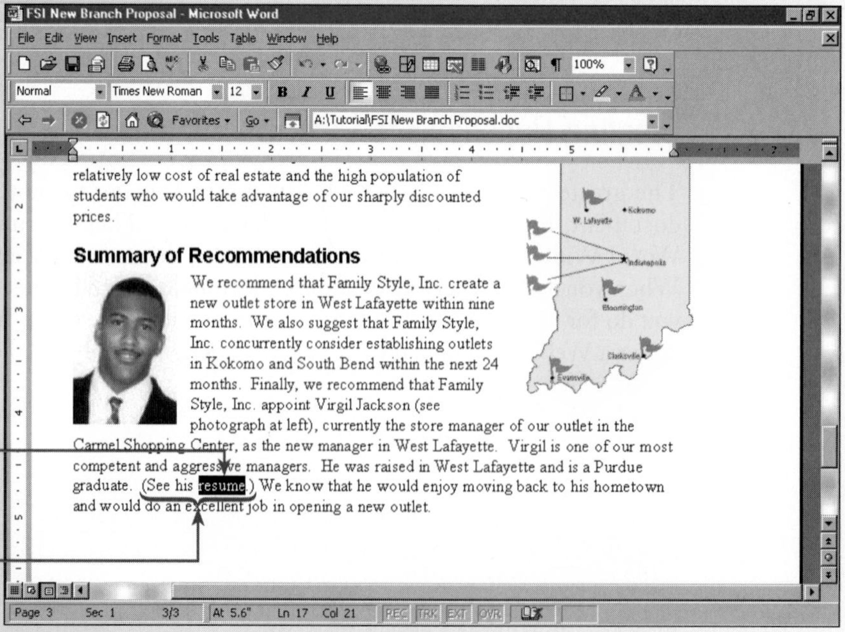

this word will become the hyperlink

new text

4. Click the **Insert Hyperlink** button 🖼 on the Standard toolbar. The Insert Hyperlink dialog box opens.

5. Under Link to, click the **Existing File or Web Page** option. The right side of the dialog box displays options related to selecting a file or a Web page.

6. Click the **File** button. The Link to File dialog box opens.

7. Select the file **VJResume** in the Tutorial folder for Tutorial 7, and then click the **OK** button.

8. Click the **OK** button. The word "resume" now appears as a hyperlink. It looks the same as the first hyperlink you created, even though the target is another file, not a location within the same document.

When your documents include hyperlinks to other documents, you need to pay special attention to where you store those target documents. If you move a target document to a different location, any hyperlinks to it contained in other documents may not function properly. In this case, you created a hyperlink in the proposal document that links to the résumé document. Both documents are stored in the Tutorial subfolder within the Tutorial.07 folder, which is most likely located on a hard disk. To ensure that the hyperlink in the proposal document will continue to function, you must keep the two documents in the same folder.

Now, you're ready to test the hyperlink you just created.

To use a hyperlink to jump to another file:

1. Move the pointer to the hyperlink "resume." Again, the pointer changes to 👆.

2. Click the hyperlink. Word opens the file VJResume.

3. Read through the resume, and then click the **Back** button ⬅ on the Web toolbar to return to the Proposal document. Notice that the hyperlink color is now purple, indicating that you have used the hyperlink.

4. Save the proposal.

Viewing a Document in Web Layout View

Because the version of the proposal you are working on now is intended for an online audience, Nalani suggests that you place it in Web Layout view. **Web Layout view** offers several advantages for online viewers:

■ Text appears larger in Web Layout view.

■ Text wraps to the window, not to the printed page.

■ Documents can be displayed with different background effects.

■ Page setup elements, such as footers, headers, and breaks, are not displayed. Because users don't view the document as printed pages, these page elements aren't necessary.

Web Layout view is useful when you need to format a document for online viewing. Text wrapping doesn't always survive the conversion from a Word document to a Web page, which means that graphics will often shift position when you save a document as a Web page. Web Layout view prepares you for this by showing you what the graphics will look like in their new positions.

But keep in mind that, despite its name, Web Layout view does not show you exactly how a document will look when saved as a Web page. Some of the features that are visible in Web Page view (such the animation you will add in the next section) will disappear when you save the document as a Web page. (You will learn more about saving a document as a Web page later in this tutorial.)

If you switch to Web Layout view and then save the document in that view, it will open that way automatically. Within Web Layout view, you might want to use the Document Map, a list of the headings in your document that you can use as a navigational aid. If you want to move immediately to a certain section of your document, you click its heading in the Document Map. For this reason, the Document Map is an especially useful tool for online viewers, who might not want to scroll through an entire document. They can simply jump to the sections they are interested in.

To display a document in Web Layout view:

1. Click the **Web Layout View** button (next to the Normal View button, just above the status bar) 🔲. Notice that the text now wraps to the width of the right window pane—not to the printed page boundaries.

2. Click the **Document Map** button 🔲 on the Standard toolbar. The document appears on the right, with the Document Map on the left. The text and graphics shift position again to accommodate the Document Map. See Figure 7-22.

   TROUBLE? If you don't see the Document Map button, click View, and then click Document Map.

| Figure 7-22 | WEB LAYOUT VIEW AND DOCUMENT MAP |

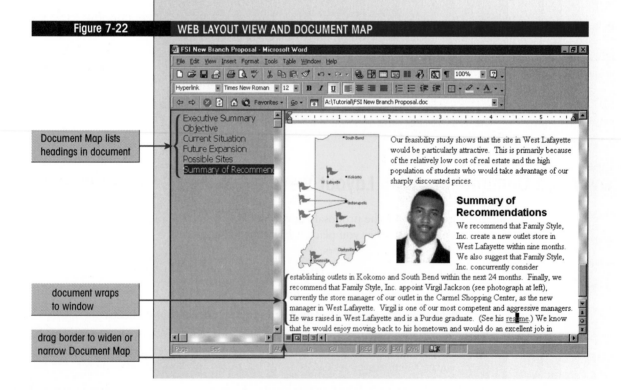

Document Map lists headings in document

document wraps to window

drag border to widen or narrow Document Map

3. Click the **Future Expansion** heading in the Document Map. You jump to that heading.

4. Click the **Executive Summary** heading in the Document Map. You jump back to the beginning of the document.

5. Click 🔍 to close the Document Map.

Although the Document Map is especially useful in Web Layout view, you can display it in any view. You can also change the width of the Document Map by dragging its right border to the left or to the right. Now that you have inserted a hyperlink, and have seen how to navigate the document with the document map, you'll improve its appearance for online viewing.

Improving the Appearance of an Online Document

Nalani suggests you use two features to make the online version of the proposal more visually interesting for online viewers—animated text and a textured background. Keep in mind that some features that are visible in Web Layout view are not visible when you convert the document to a Web page. (You will learn more about converting a document to a Web page in the next session.)

Animating Text

Animated text is text that "comes alive," like a cartoon animation, because the text blinks, sparkles, shimmers, or displays a moving border. Word offers several animation formats. Nalani suggests you try animating the subtitle of the proposal, "A Proposal to Open a New Branch of Family Style, Inc.," with a moving border.

To animate the subtitle of the proposal:

1. Scroll to the beginning of the document.

2. Select the subtitle text **A Proposal to Open a New Branch of Family Style, Inc.**

3. Click **Format** on the menu bar, click **Font**, and then click the **Text Effects** tab.

4. Click **Marching Black Ants**. Notice the Preview box displays the sample text with a moving black border. See Figure 7-23.

Figure 7-23   **PREVIEWING ANIMATED TEXT**

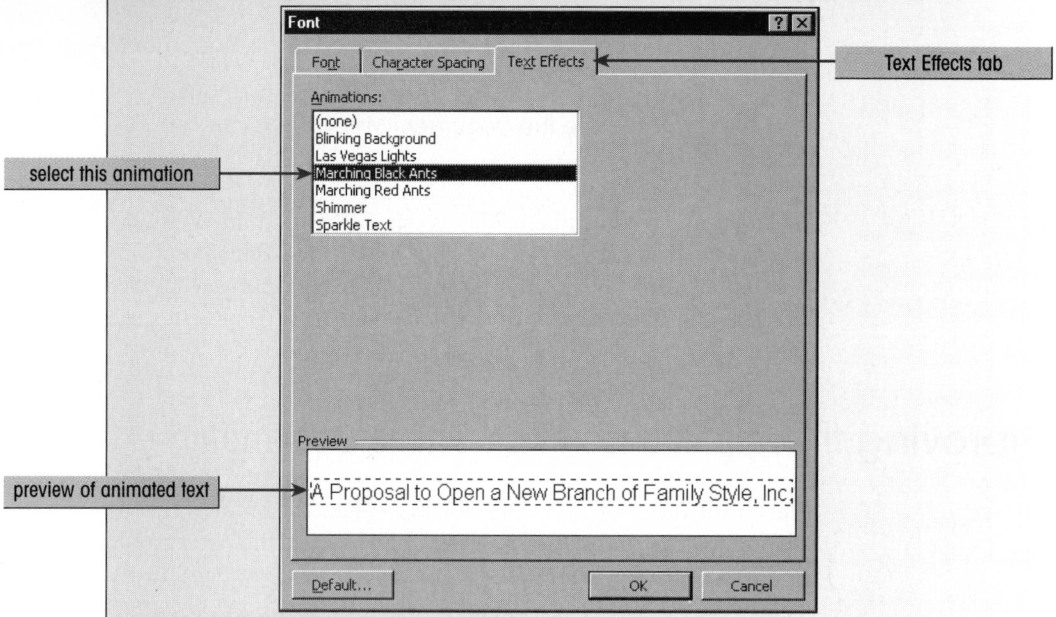

Text Effects tab

Font

Font | Character Spacing | Text Effects

Animations:

(none)
Blinking Background
Las Vegas Lights
Marching Black Ants
Marching Red Ants
Shimmer
Sparkle Text

select this animation

Preview

preview of animated text

A Proposal to Open a New Branch of Family Style, Inc.

Default...   OK   Cancel

5. Click the **OK** button, and then click anywhere outside the subtitle to deselect it. The subtitle now has a moving border.

Animation draws an online viewer's eyes immediately to the animated text, so use this feature only for your most important words or phrases. Overusing animated text makes your document difficult to view. Also, keep in mind that animation effects don't appear in printed documents.

Applying a Textured Background

You can make an online document more visually appealing by applying background effects. As with animated text, backgrounds do not appear in printed documents. You can apply one of the following background effects:

- Solid color
- Gradient—a color or combination of colors that fades from one side of the screen to the other
- Texture—choose from a collection of textures
- Pattern—choose from a collection of interesting patterns; you designate the colors in the pattern
- Picture—a graphic image

In choosing a background color or texture, make sure your text is still readable. In poorly designed online documents, the background might be so dark or the pattern so obtrusive that the text is illegible. In addition, a background that contains a complicated background pattern will increase the file size and take longer to appear on a user's screen. Nalani suggests you use a parchment texture to give the background a professional, but not distracting, appearance.

To apply a texture to a document:

1. Click **Format** on the menu bar, point to **Background**, click **Fill Effects**, and then click the **Texture** tab. A selection of textures appears.

2. Click the third box on the left in the top row. The name of this texture, "Parchment," appears below the texture options. See Figure 7-24.

Figure 7-24	SELECTING A TEXTURED BACKGROUND

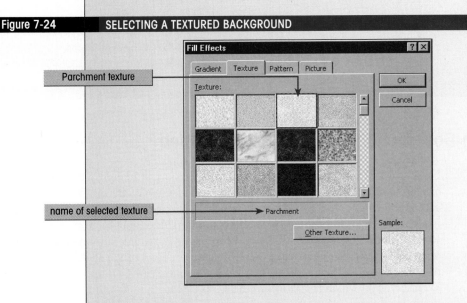

Parchment texture

name of selected texture

3. Click the **OK** button. The texture fills the background of your document.

4. Save the document in Web Layout view, and close it.

5. Close the VJResume document, which opened earlier when you clicked the hyperlink in the proposal document.

The background texture is light in color and attractive and leaves the black text easy to read. Nalani agrees that the Parchment background enhances the look of the online document.

Session 7.2 QUICK CHECK

1. What is a hyperlink?

2. True or False: A hyperlink can only take a user to a location within the current document.

3. Explain how to create a bookmark.

4. Which name is an invalid bookmark name? a) Recommendations, b) Executive Summary, c) README

5. What does a change in the color of a hyperlink indicate?

6. True or False: Web Layout view shows you exactly what your document will look like when saved as a Web page.

7. What is the purpose of the Document Map?

You have finished preparing the proposal document for online viewing. Nalani places the document and its linked files in a shared folder on the company network and e-mails her colleagues that it is available for viewing. Any employee who opens it in Word has the immediate benefit of easy viewing in Web Layout view. The hyperlink you added, as well as the Document Map, make it easy to navigate, and your visual enhancements make it a pleasure to view.

SESSION 7.3

In this session, you'll convert Nalani's proposal into a Web page for placement on the World Wide Web and then format the Web page to make it easier to read in a Web browser. Finally, you'll insert and edit hyperlinks that link the proposal and résumé documents, and then preview your Web page in a browser.

Publishing Documents on the World Wide Web

Nalani now wants you to prepare the final version of her proposal, which she will make available on the World Wide Web (also called the "Web" or "WWW"). The Web is a global information-sharing system, which is part of the **Internet**, a worldwide network made up of millions of interconnected computers. Information is stored on the Web in the form of electronic documents, called **Web pages**. Organizations and individuals make their Web pages available by storing them on special computers called Web servers. Each Web page is assigned a Web address (or **URL**) which indicates, among other things, the specific Web server on which it is stored. URLs can be long and complicated or fairly simple. One example of a simple URL is: *http://www.course.com*. To access a Web page, you need to open a special program called a **browser**, such as Netscape Navigator or Microsoft Internet Explorer. Once you open your browser, you need to enter the page's URL. The browser then retrieves the page and displays it on your computer screen.

A collection of interrelated Web pages is known as a **Web site**. Most companies and many private computer users operate their own Web sites. Keep in mind that Web sites may not be designed for public access on the World Wide Web. Increasingly, companies use Web sites to make information available to their own employees, within the company's private network.

Most Web sites include a **home page**, a Web page that contains general information about the site. Home pages are like "home base"—a starting point for online viewers. They usually contain hyperlinks targeting other documents or Web pages that online viewers can click to locate the information they need. Nalani wants to include a hyperlink on the Family Style home page that targets her proposal. Potential investors can click that hyperlink to view the proposal.

The hyperlinks the document already contains will remain intact after the conversion to HTML. You also may want to create additional hyperlinks, such as one to the company's home page. You can add these links before or after you convert the document.

Saving a Word Document as a Web Page

Web browsers only read documents formatted in **HTML** (HyperText Markup Language), a special programming language that tells a Web browser how the page should look on the screen. So to distribute a Word document on the World Wide Web, you have to convert it to HTML by saving the document as a Web page. The HTML codes in a file tell the browser exactly how to format the text. Fortunately, you don't have to learn the Hypertext Markup Language to create HTML documents; Word does this work for you when you save the document as a Web page. When you save the document as a Web page, Word creates the necessary HTML codes (called markings, or tags) for the desired format. This process is transparent to you, which means you won't actually see the HTML tags in your new Web pages.

The relatively small size of Web pages makes them easy to share on the Internet. For example, a Word document containing a moderate amount of formatting and a few graphics, might be 500 kilobytes in size. The same document saved as a Web page might be only 20 kilobytes in size, along with about 50 kilobytes of graphics files. To help keep your Web-page file small, Word automatically puts any graphics it might contain into a separate folder. This folder also contains other small files that your Web browser needs in order to display the Web page correctly. By default, this folder has the same name as your Web page, plus an underscore and the word "files." For instance, a Web page saved as "Finance Summary" would be accompanied by a folder named "Finance Summary_files."

Although saving a Word document as a Web page is easy, it's not foolproof, particularly when it comes to formatting. Some Word formatting features (such as special borders, or certain font effects) will not "translate" into HTML. This means that when you save your document as a Web page, document formatting might be lost, or it will look different. Also, keep in mind that the formatting that does translate into HTML might not look as nice on screen as it does on the printed page. So after translating the document to a Web page, you might want to adjust the formatting to make it more suitable for online viewing. At the same time, you might want to add some special formatting features that are not always available in printed documents, such as color and animation. (In some cases, the original document might contain special features, such as animation, that don't survive the translation to HTML. In that case, you may need to reapply the feature once the document has been saved as a Web page.) As a general rule, once you save a document as a Web page, you'll probably want to modify it to make it more attractive for users of the World Wide Web. At the very least, you will probably need to reposition graphics.

Keep in mind that to create really sophisticated Web pages, you'll probably want to use a dedicated HTML editor, such as Microsoft Front Page. You can also use a Word Web Page Wizard, as explained in the case projects at the end of this tutorial, to create a Web page from scratch. But to share an existing Word document as a Web page, you must convert it to HTML.

REFERENCE WINDOW   **RW**

Converting a Word Document to a Web Page

- Click File on the menu bar, and then click Save as Web Page.
- If desired, give the file a new filename. Word will automatically add the file extension .html at the end of the document, although this extension probably won't be visible in the Save As dialog box.
- Click the Save button.
- If Word warns you that the document has formatting not supported by Web browsers, click the Continue button.

To prepare Nalani's proposal for viewing on the Web, you'll begin by saving the current document as an HTML file.

To save a document as a Web page:

1. If you took a break after the last session, make sure Word is running. Close any Internet-related programs, such as e-mail editors or browsers.

2. Open the **FSI New Branch Proposal** document.

3. Click **File** on the menu bar, and then click **Save as Web Page**. The Save As dialog box, with which you are already familiar, opens. The only difference between this dialog box and the one you used earlier to save the proposal document with a new name, is that the Save as type text box indicates that the document will be saved as a Web page.

4. Change the filename so it reads **FSI New Branch Proposal Web Page**.

5. Click the **Save** button. Word displays a warning message indicating that animated text and text wrapping around pictures are not supported by Web browsers. These features will appear differently in the Web page. See Figure 7-25.

Figure 7-25	WARNING MESSAGE

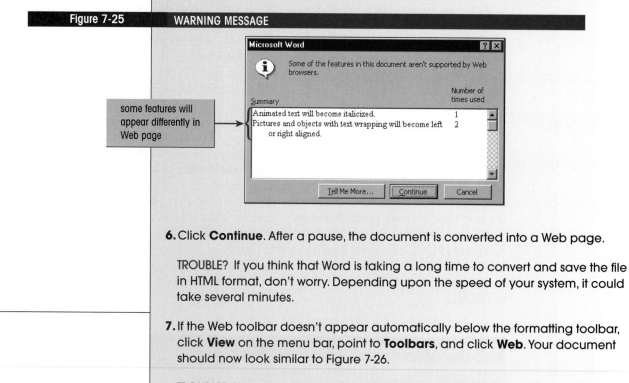

some features will appear differently in Web page

6. Click **Continue**. After a pause, the document is converted into a Web page.

TROUBLE? If you think that Word is taking a long time to convert and save the file in HTML format, don't worry. Depending upon the speed of your system, it could take several minutes.

7. If the Web toolbar doesn't appear automatically below the formatting toolbar, click **View** on the menu bar, point to **Toolbars**, and click **Web**. Your document should now look similar to Figure 7-26.

TROUBLE? If you see a dialog box saying that the dimensions after resizing are too small or too large, click the OK button.

Figure 7-26	DOCUMENT FORMATTED AS A WEB PAGE

Web toolbar

animated border replaced with italics

margins no longer visible

your filename and location may differ

A New Outlet Store

A Proposal to Open a New Branch of Family Style, Inc.

Executive Summary

During the past five years, the average net profit of Family Style, Inc. has been 4.5 percent, considerably higher than the national average for retail outlets that buy and sell used merchandise. With each additional outlet, our profit margin has increased. We now propose the creation of one or more new branch stores. Promising sites, based on our feasibility studies, include the State Fair Shopping Center in Kokomo, the Shamrock Shopping Center in South Bend, and the Boilermaker Shopping Center in West Lafayette. We recommend that a new outlet be opened in West Lafayette within the next nine months.

Go To Summary of Recommendations

Objective

The purpose of this document is to propose the opening of a new branch store of Family Style, Inc. This proposal, in conjunction with the accompanying feasibility report "An Analysis of Potential Sites for Expansion of Family Style, Inc.," provides a rationale for continuing the expansion program that began soon after the opening of our first store in 1988. With six outlets currently in operation in the central and southern parts of the state of Indiana, the next logical step is to expand into the

As you look through the document, you'll notice two differences between the Web page and the original document:

- The margin settings are no longer the same. In fact, Web pages don't have margin settings. The lines of text wrap so that the text fits within the width of the browser (or in this case, the document window), whatever size it might be.

- The graphic images (that is, the map and the photograph) may have shifted position.

- The animated border around the subtitle no longer appears. Instead, the subtitle is italicized.

You might notice other differences as well. One of the major differences, in fact, is not apparent by viewing the document: The file size has decreased from about 500 KB to only about 19 KB (plus about 65–70 KB of graphics files). This reduced size is a tremendous advantage for Web pages that must be transferred electronically over long distances and often through slow modems. The smaller file size allows them to display more quickly in Web browsers.

Formatting a Web Page

You're now ready to format the Web page to give it the look and feel of a typical Web page and to correct some of the problems that occur when you convert a file from a normal Word document to a Web page. You'll begin by correcting the text formatting.

Moving and Editing Text and Graphics

You can edit and format a Web page the same way you would edit and format a normal Word document. Now, you'll change the text wrapping around the last two graphic images to adjust for changes that occurred in the document when you saved it as a Web page.

To change the text wrapping around graphics:

1. Scroll so you can see the map of Indiana. It might have shifted on the page and increased in size, so that it is now positioned to the left of the photograph, as in Figure 7-27. (Your map could have shifted somewhat differently, so that it is positioned below the bulleted list, or elsewhere on the page. Your map may also have decreased in size.) You could adjust the position of the map by adjusting settings in the Format Picture dialog box. But it's often easier simply to drag the graphic to the correct location.

Figure 7-27   MAP AND PHOTOGRAPH IN WRONG POSITION

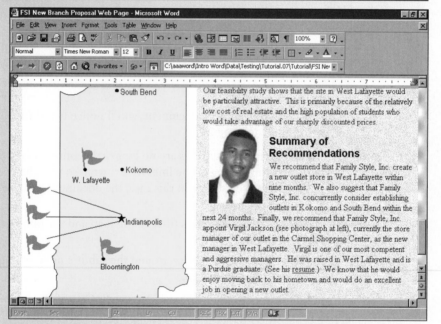

2. If necessary, click the map to select it, and then drag it up so that it is positioned under the sentence that begins "The map below shows the six current....".

3. Click **Format** on the menu bar, click **Picture**, click the **Size** tab, verify that the Lock aspect ratio check box is selected, change the Height setting to 50% and click the **OK** button.

4. Verify that the sentence that begins "We have carried out..." and the bulleted list wrap to the right of the map. The top of the map should be just slightly above the top of the "W" in "We." If the text does not wrap correctly, adjust the position or size of the map. Next, you need to adjust the position of the photograph, which you will do by adding more space between before the "Summary of Recommendations" heading.

5. Click to the left of the "S" in the heading "Summary of Recommendations," and then press **Enter** three times. The heading moves down below the map, and the photograph moves along with it.

6. If necessary, drag the photograph down to position it below the "Summary of Recommendations" heading. The text wraps to the right of the photograph.

7. To verify that the map and the photograph are positioned correctly, click **View** on the menu bar, and then click **Full Screen**. The map and the photograph should now be positioned as in Figure 7-28.

| Figure 7-28 | MAP AND PHOTOGRAPH IN NEW POSITION |

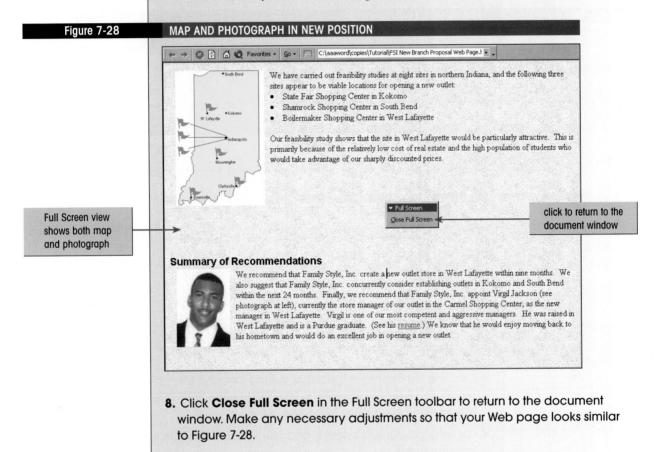

Full Screen view shows both map and photograph

click to return to the document window

8. Click **Close Full Screen** in the Full Screen toolbar to return to the document window. Make any necessary adjustments so that your Web page looks similar to Figure 7-28.

Now that you've corrected the placement of the text and graphics in Nalani's proposal, you'll add some rules (horizontal lines) to the online document.

Inserting Horizontal Lines

Many Web pages have horizontal lines that separate sections of a document to make it easier to read and navigate. You'll add a horizontal line below the subtitle of the proposal Web page and at the end of the Web page.

To insert horizontal lines into the Web page:

1. Move the insertion point to the left of the "E" in "Executive Summary" near the beginning of the document.

2. Click **Format** on the menu bar, click **Borders and Shading**, click the **Borders** tab in the Borders and Shading dialog box, and then click the **Horizontal Line** button. The Horizontal Line dialog box opens, where you can select from a number of horizontal lines. See Figure 7-29.

| Figure 7-29 | HORIZONTAL LINE DIALOG BOX |

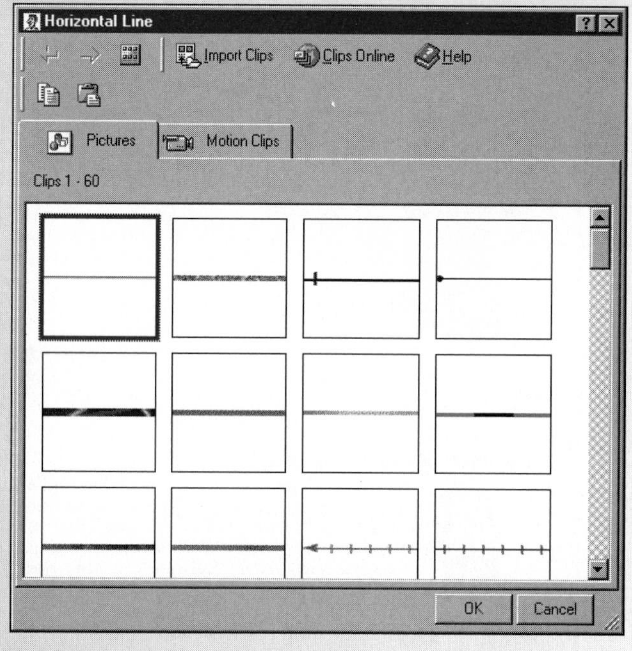

3. Click the first option on the left, in the top row, and then click the **Insert clip** button . A simple gray line is inserted into the Web page, below the subtitle. Nalani wants something with more color.

4. Click the gray line to select it, and then press the **Delete** key. The line is removed from the page.

5. Repeat Steps 2 through 4, but select the horizontal line with shades of blue and green (third row down, second from left). Your Web page should look similar to Figure 7-30.

| Figure 7-30 | WEB PAGE AFTER INSERTING HORIZONTAL LINE |

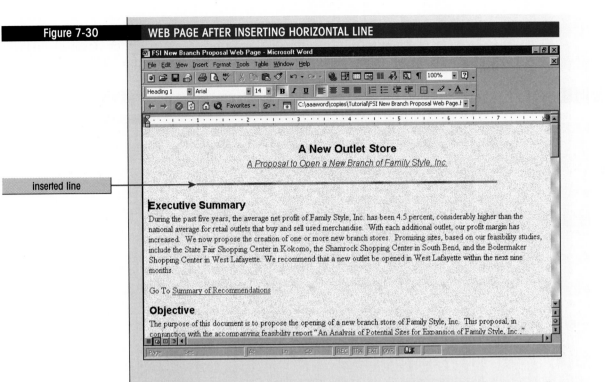

inserted line

TROUBLE? Don't be concerned if your horizontal line changes color after you scroll or perform some other action. Your computer may not have enough memory to display graphics correctly.

6. Move the insertion point to the end of the document, if necessary press **Enter** to move the insertion point to a new blank line, and then insert another horizontal blue line.

7. Scroll back to the top of the document.

Now that you've given shape to the document with horizontal lines, you decide to improve the appearance of the document's text.

Modifying Text Size and Color

Web pages use colored text to enhance the appearance of the page and to call attention to important information. You also can adjust font sizes on a Web page just as you would on a printed document. To improve the proposal's readability and appearance, Nalani wants you to increase the font size of the title text and to change its color to teal, to match the horizontal lines.

To change the size and color of text:

1. Select the title **A New Outlet Store** at the beginning of the Web page.

2. Use the **Font Size** list arrow on the Formatting toolbar to change the font size from 16-point to 24-point.

3. Click the **Font Color** list arrow [A ▾] on the Formatting toolbar, click the teal tile (second row from the top, fifth column from the left), and then deselect the text. The title matches the color of the horizontal line. See Figure 7-31.

| Figure 7-31 | TITLE WITH FONT CHANGES |

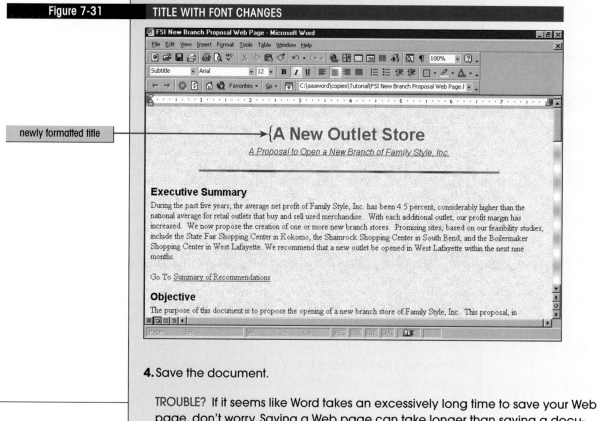

newly formatted title

4. Save the document.

TROUBLE? If it seems like Word takes an excessively long time to save your Web page, don't worry. Saving a Web page can take longer than saving a document in Word format.

You've now formatted Nalani's proposal document so that it will be visually appealing on screen. Next, you'll create some additional hypertext links and edit one of the existing links.

Creating and Editing Hyperlinks in a Web Page

As you looked through the HTML version of the proposal, you probably noticed that the blue underlined hyperlink text is still present. Most likely, any Web browser could successfully display the target of the first hyperlink (that is, the Summary of Recommendations at the end of the page), but, depending on the browser, it might not be able to display the Virgil Jackson resume (VJResume.doc) unless you save it as a Web page, too. In the following steps, you will convert the resume to a Web page, create a new link from the resume back to the proposal, and then modify the hyperlink in the proposal so that browsers can easily jump between the two documents.

To convert the resume to a Web page:

1. Open the file **VJResume** from the Tutorial folder for Tutorial 7, and save it (in the same folder) as a Web page using the filename **VJResume Web Page**. While you have the Open dialog box displayed, notice that Word has created a new folder, named "FSI New Branch Proposal Web Page_files," in which to store the files related to the proposal Web page. Note that you should never save any other documents to this folder.

Now, you'll make some minor formatting changes so that the résumé Web page has the same look as the proposal Web page. You'll use the procedures you learned earlier.

To format the VJResume Web Page:

1. Apply the Parchment background texture to the Web page.

2. Select the text **Virgil S. Jackson** at the top of the page, and format it in teal.

3. Click the **Spelling and Grammar** button ![abc check icon] on the Standard toolbar, click the **Ignore All** button to remove any red or green underlinings, and click the **OK** button.

4. If necessary, switch back to Web Page layout.

5. Change the font color of "Experience," to teal. Note that the headings "Education" and "Interest" change color as well.

6. Move the insertion point to the end of the document and insert the same horizontal line you used in the proposal.

7. Save the document.

The resume and the proposal now have a similar appearance.

Inserting a Hyperlink to a Web Page

Users who read Virgil's resume will most likely want to return to the proposal, so you decide to insert a hyperlink that targets the proposal. You insert hyperlinks into Web pages in the same way you do Word documents.

To insert a hyperlink:

1. Make sure the insertion point is below the horizontal line at the end of the document, and then type **Return to FSI New Branch Proposal**.

2. Select the text "FSI New Branch Proposal" in the phrase you just typed, click the **Insert Hyperlink** button ![hyperlink icon] on the Standard toolbar, under Link to click **Existing File or Web Page**, click the **File** button, locate and select **FSI New Branch Proposal Web Page**, and click the **OK** button twice. Word inserts the hyperlink to the proposal.

3. Save, and close the resume document. You return to the proposal.

The resume now contains a hyperlink that takes users back to the proposal.

Editing a Hyperlink

Recall that the proposal itself still contains the hyperlink that targets the resume in its Word document format. You need to edit the hyperlink so that it targets the resume with its new Web page name. Rather than deleting the hyperlink and reinserting a new one, you can edit the existing hyperlink and indicate the new target path. You want to target the file named VJResume Web page.

To edit a hyperlink:

1. Scroll to the end of the proposal, and right-click the resume hyperlink. Word displays a shortcut menu.

   TROUBLE? If the original resume document opens, you clicked the link with the left mouse button by mistake. Close the document, and repeat Step 1.

2. Point to **Hyperlink**, and then click **Edit Hyperlink**. The Edit Hyperlink dialog box opens.

3. Verify that the Existing File or Web Page option is selected under "Link to".

4. Click the **File** button, and the Link to File dialog box opens.

5. Delete the filename "VJResume" from the Filename text box.

6. Click the **Files of type** list arrow, and select **All Files**.

7. Select **VJResume Web Page** in the Tutorial folder for Tutorial 7, and then click the OK button. You return to the Edit Hyperlink dialog box. Note that you could type the correct filename in the Type the file or Web page name text box, but if you made even a small typing error, the link would not work. Selecting the correct file using the File button is a less error-prone method.

8. Click **OK**. You return to the proposal Web page.

9. Save the document.

The edited hyperlink in the proposal Web page correctly targets the resume Web page. You're now ready to view the finished Web pages in a Web browser and to test the hyperlinks.

Viewing the Web Page in a Web Browser

While you're editing a Web page in Word, the document window shows how the document will look when viewed from a Web browser. But it's always a good idea to view your Web pages with a Web browser to see exactly how they will look and to test the hyperlinks. Before attempting to display your document in a browser, however, make sure you save any changes first. Also, if your browser is open at the time you make and save changes, you might need to update or reload the document in your browser to display the latest updates to the HTML file.

To view the Web pages in a Web browser:

1. Click **File** on the menu bar, and then click **Web Page Preview**. Word opens your default Web browser and displays the FSI New Branch Proposal in its document window. See Figure 7-32. Your browser might be Netscape Navigator or some other browser, but the view of the FSI New Branch Proposal should be similar. Maximize the browser window, if necessary.

| Figure 7-32 | VIEWING THE WEB PAGE IN INTERNET EXPLORER |

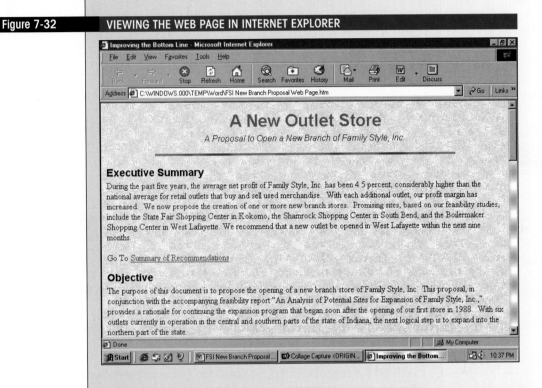

TROUBLE? If a message appears informing you that you have to save the document first, click the Yes button to save the document and display it in the Web browser.

TROUBLE? If you see a message informing you that Internet Explorer is not your default browser and asking you if you want to make it your browser, click the No button.

2. Scroll through the document so you can see how it looks in the browser.

3. Move the insertion point to the beginning of the document, and click the Summary of Recommendations hyperlink. The heading "Summary of Recommendations" is displayed in the browser window.

4. Click the resume hyperlink in the last paragraph of the document. The browser opens the Resume Web page. See Figure 7-33.

Figure 7-33   **BROWSER SHOWING RESUME DOCUMENT**

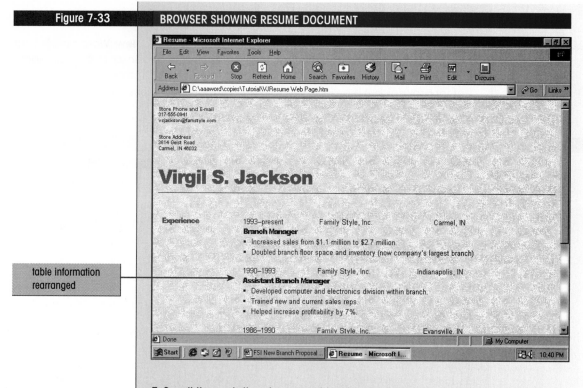

table information rearranged

5. Scroll through the document to view it. Notice that when you view the resume in the browser, the table format disappears. But in this case, the format is still acceptable.

6. Click the **Return to FSI New Branch Proposal** hyperlink. The Browser now returns to the proposal Web page.

   TROUBLE? If any of these hyperlinks don't work properly, edit them so they link to the proper document.

7. Close the browser window. You return to the proposal document in the Word window.

8. Scroll to the bottom of the Web page and insert the text **Prepared by** followed by your first and last name.

9. Print the document, and save and close the proposal. The printed Web page looks similar, but not identical, to the printed Word document.

You have now finished preparing two Web pages, the proposal and the resume, for online viewing.

Session 7.3 QUICK CHECK

1. Define the following terms:
   a. Web browser
   b. Web site
   c. HTML
   d. Web page

2. Name two types of formatting that cannot be translated into HTML.

3. True or False: After you convert a Word document to a Web page, you need to re-create all hypertext links.

4. Explain how to insert a horizontal line into a Web page. What is the purpose of such a line?

5. List the various tasks you should perform after converting a Word document into a Web page.

6. Describe the steps necessary to preview a Web page in your default Web browser.

You show your documents to Nalani, who tests them and sends them to the company's Internet service provider (ISP), which manages the Family Style Web site. The ISP will make the documents available on the World Wide Web by storing them on its Web server. At that point, anyone with Internet access and a Web browser can view the documents. Nalani hopes that posting the proposal on the World Wide Web will attract new investors for the Family Style expansion.

REVIEW ASSIGNMENTS

Marina Leavitt is the director of sales for Family Style, Inc. She is preparing a quarterly sales report to give to each of the company's sales representatives. The main purpose of the short report is to show sales, income, and expenses over the last three months, but it will also include new policies for purchasing used merchandise. Marina has written the body of the report in Word and wants you to embed a spreadsheet of sales figures in the report and then modify one of the figures. She also asks you to link a Paint graphics file showing the quarterly profits for each branch outlet, and then modify the file. Finally, she requests that you save the report as a Web page for publication on the World Wide Web, and create appropriate hyperlinks to related documents, including a URL for a Web page that contains additional information on Family Style procedures.

1. Make sure that Word is running, open the file **Salesrep** from the Review folder for Tutorial 7 on your Data Disk, and save it as **Family Style Sales Report**.

2. Below the subheading "2nd Quarter 2001 Sales Report," insert the text "Prepared by" and then type your first and last name. Center this new text below the subheading.

3. Delete the "[insert worksheet here]" placeholder, and in its place, insert a linked copy of the worksheet 2QSales from the Review folder for Tutorial 7 on your Data Disk. So that you can repeat the review assignments later, be sure to create a duplicate of the worksheet from within the Browse dialog box, and name the duplicate "Copy of 2Qsales." Remember to select the Link to file check box in order to link the worksheet to the Word document.

4. Center the worksheet using the Center button on the Formatting toolbar.

5. Save, and close the Word document.

6. Open Excel and modify the Copy of 2QSales worksheet by changing the June sales figure to 1.42.

7. Click the Save button on the Excel Standard toolbar, and then close Excel.

8. Open the Family Style Sales Report document, and verify that the change you made in Step 6 appears in the linked copy of the worksheet.

Explore

9. Double-click the worksheet within the Word document, and then use the Excel tools to format the column titles (April, May, and June) with a bright yellow fill and format the type in bold. Format the Expenses and Sales cells with boldface type only. Close the Excel window, and click Yes when asked if you want to save your changes to the Copy of 2Qsales.xls workbook. Verify that your changes to the worksheet appear in the Word document.

10. Locate and delete the line containing the phrase "[embed figure here],"and in its place insert the graphic file Brnchsls from the Review folder for Tutorial 7 on your Data Disk.

11. Click the graphic to select it, and verify that the Picture toolbar is displayed. Click the Format Object button on the Picture toolbar, and use the Size tab to reduce the graphic's height to 70% of its original size. (Make sure the Lock aspect ratio is selected so that the picture's proportions remain constant.) Click the Text Wrapping button on the Picture toolbar, and select the Tight option. The text wraps around the graphic.

12. Verify that the top of the graphic is level with the sentence beginning "The figure shows…." If it is not, drag the figure to position it properly.

13. Click outside the graphic to deselect it.

Explore

14. Change the color of the star at Indianapolis to red as follows: Double-click the graphic to display the tools of the Paint program. If necessary, scroll to display the Indianapolis star. Click the Magnifier button on the Paint toolbar, and then click the Indianapolis star to zoom in on it. Click the Fill with Color button on the Paint toolbar, click the red tile in the color palette in the bottom-left corner of the Paint window, and then click the Indianapolis star. The star fills with the bright red color. Click outside the graphic to return to the Word tools and menus.

15. Save the Word document.

16. Create a bookmark at the beginning of the document's title. At the end of the document, insert a hyperlink to that bookmark that reads "Return to Sales Report." Save the document.

17. View the document in Web Layout view.

18. Format the background with the Parchment texture.

19. Format the subtitle with the Las Vegas Lights animation. Remove any Spelling and Grammar markings, and save the document.

20. Save the report as Web page under the name Family Style Sales Report Web Page.

21. Review the information regarding the document features that are not supported by Web browsers and click Continue.

Explore

22. In the tutorials, you repositioned a graphic by dragging it. Now you can try using the Format Picture dialog box to position the map so the text wraps to its left. Click the map graphic to select it, click the Format Picture button on the Picture toolbar, click the Layout tab, click the Advanced button, click the Picture Position tab, click the Alignment option button in the Horizontal section (if necessary) to select it, and then click the Alignment list arrow and click Right. Click the OK button twice. Make sure the text "The figure shows…" is placed so the map is to its right.

23. Add or delete return characters to improve the layout of the document.

24. Enlarge the title, bold format the subtitle, and apply the color blue to the title, subtitle, and the "New Policies" heading.

25. Insert a horizontal separator line below the subtitle and another line at the end of the document. Save the document, and leave it open.

26. Open the file FSIAds in the Review folder for Tutorial 7 of your Data Disk, and save it as a Web page with the name FSIAds Web Page.

27. Format the FSIAds Web Page with the Parchment texture, enlarge the "Family Styles Inc." title, and color the title blue. Enlarge the "Advertising Summary" subhead. Put a horizontal line under Q1 2001, and delete the extra return character above the line. Put another horizontal line at the end of the document. Save the document.

28. In the sales report document, locate the text in the first paragraph that reads "advertising efforts in the first quarter," and format it as a hyperlink that jumps to the FSIAds Web page. Test the hyperlink.

29. At the end of the FSIAds Web page, insert the text "Return to Sales Report," and enlarge it. Format this new text as a hyperlink that jumps to the Family Style Sales Report Web page, and test the link.

Explore

30. Now, create the hyperlink to the URL for a related Family Style Web page. Scroll to the bottom of the Family Style Sales Report Web page document, press the Enter key twice to add two new blank lines, and then type "Click to see more information on Family Style purchasing procedures for new merchandise." Highlight the line you just typed. Open the Insert Hyperlink dialog box, click the Existing File or Web Page option under Link to, click the Type the file or Web page name text box, and then type the following URL: *http://www.course.com/cti/NewPerspectives/office2000/famstyle.html*

31. Click the OK button. Save the document, and then use the Web Page Preview command to view it in your Web browser. Test the hyperlinks you added, including the one at the bottom of the document. (*Hint:* To test the hyperlink at the bottom of the document, your computer must have access to the Internet.)

Explore

32. Right-click the Start button, click Explore, and then use the Windows Explorer to display the contents of the Family Style Sales Report Web Page_files folder (which you'll find within the Review folder for Tutorial 7 on your data disk). How many files does this folder contain? What is their total size? What size is the Family Style Sales Report Web Page file, in the Review folder?

33. Close the Windows Explorer.

Explore

34. Save the Family Style Sales Report Web Page as a Word document, using the name "Family Style Sales Report Word Document." Remember to select "Word Document" as the file type in the Save As dialog box. Do you notice any changes to the document now that it is a Word document again, rather than a Web page?

35. Save, and close your documents.

Explore ▸

36. Use your e-mail program to send the Family Style Sales Report Word Document file to a fellow student. In most e-mail programs, you need to create a new message, and then attach the file to the message. Ask the recipient of the file to open it, display it in Web Layout view, and test the various links. Can he or she access the source file for the Excel workbook? Why or why not? Do the other links in the document work? Why or why not?

37. Close all open files.

CASE PROBLEMS

Case 1. Office Location for Vista Insurance Company Steven Woodhouse works for the Vista Insurance Company, a new, rapidly growing company. Emma Knightly, vice president of operations for the company, has proposed that Vista open a new downtown office and has assigned Steven the responsibility of finding a good location. Steven has contacted local real estate agencies through the World Wide Web, and he has located an available office building that seems satisfactory. He has downloaded an image of the office building and asks you to prepare a memo to Emma describing the office site. He'd like you to include the image in the memo. When you've finished, he requests that you e-mail the memo to Emma for online viewing. Emma won't be viewing the memo in her browser; she'll just open it directly in Word.

1. If necessary, start Word. Open the file **NewOffic** from the Cases folder for Tutorial 7 and then save it to the same folder as **New Office Memo**.

2. In the From: section of the memo heading, replace "Steve Woodhouse" with your name.

3. At the end of the third paragraph, delete the bracketed phrase "[insert chart]," and embed the chart called Rent from the Cases folder for Tutorial 7.

4. Double-click the chart to display the Excel tools. Click the chart title, click after the "e" in "Average," press the spacebar, and then type "monthly" so that the title reads "Average monthly rent ($)."

5. Reduce the size of the chart to 30% of its original size, and center it between the left and right margins.

6. Link a copy of the Logo file (located in the Cases folder for Tutorial 7) to the top-left margin of the document. (Be sure to make a copy of the file from within the Browse dialog box before you link it.)

7. Save and close the Word document, open the Paint program from the Start menu, and then open the Copy of Logo file. Change the red bar at the bottom of the logo to a light turquoise, save the file, and exit Paint.

8. Reopen the New Office Memo document, and make sure the color change was automatically made to the linked version of the logo.

9. Animate the "Interoffice Memorandum" heading with Las Vegas Lights.

Explore ▸

10. Format the document with a solid tan background. (*Hint:* Click Format on the menu bar, point to Background, then click the Tan tile on the color palette.) Preview the New Office Memo document in Web Layout view. Notice how Word switched automatically to Web Layout view when you added the tan background.

11. In the second paragraph, just after the sentence that ends with "…downtown business district," insert text that reads "See Recent Downtown Developments" for a listing of recent renovations in the area." Make "Recent Downtown Developments" a hyperlink, targeting a copy of the Devel file in the Cases folder for Tutorial 7 on your Data Disk. Be sure to make a copy of the Devel file in the Link to File dialog box, and then link the copy to the New Office Memo document.

12. Open your copy of the Devel file by clicking the hyperlink to it, insert a hyperlink at the end that takes users back to the New Office Memo, add a tan background, and save the file.

13. Return to the memo and save it. Test all the links in the two documents one last time, and then close the copy of the Devel file.

14. Print the New Office Memo document while it is displayed in Web Layout view. Close the document.

Explore ▶ 15. Use your e-mail program to send the New Office Memo document to a fellow student. (If you prefer, send the file to yourself.) In most e-mail programs, you need to create a new message, and then attach the file to the message. Ask the recipient of the file to open it, display it in Web Layout view, and test the various links. Can he or she access the source file for the logo? Why or why not? Do the other links in the document work? Why or why not?

Case 2. *Pacific Views Brochure* Leah Bakula is a sales representative for Pacific Views, a company that offers guided tours to many of the popular tourist sites in the western United States. She is preparing a flyer describing upcoming tours to selected western National Parks. She asks you to help finish the project and then convert it to a Web page so she can post it on the company's home page and make it available to prospective tourists.

1. If necessary, start Word. Open the file **Natbroch** from the Cases folder for Tutorial 7 and then save it as **National Parks Tours** in the same folder.

2. Position the photograph of the arch against the left margin, wrap text around it, and enlarge it so that the entire second paragraph wraps to the right of the photo.

Explore ▶ 3. In the tutorial you learned how to link and embed objects using the Object command on the insert menu. If you prefer, you can also link or embed an object by copying it to the Clipboard, and then pasting it into the destination file using the Paste Special command on the Edit menu. To experiment using Paste Special now, move the insertion point to the last line of the document, start Excel and open the worksheet PacTours from the Cases folder for Tutorial 7. Click cell A1, and then drag down and to the right to cell E7. The worksheet data should now be selected. Click the Copy button on the Excel toolbar, click the Microsoft Word button on the taskbar, click Edit on the menu bar, and then click Paste Special. The Paste Special dialog box allows you to paste objects from the Clipboard in a variety of formats, including HTML, unformatted text and formatted text. To embed the worksheet data as a worksheet, you could select the Microsoft Excel Worksheet Object option. To simply embed a worksheet, you can select the Paste option button. To link a worksheet, you can select the Paste link option button. In this case, you will experiment with pasting the worksheet data as formatted text. Click the Formatted Text (RTF) option in the As list box, verify that the Paste option button is selected, and then click OK. The worksheet is inserted into the document as a Word table.

4. Format the new table as necessary to make it attractive and easy to read.

Explore

5. Design a logo of your own at the top of the document. Open the Paint program from the Start menu. Click Image in the menu bar, click Attributes, and change the Width settings to 200 and the height setting to 50. Use the text tool to draw a text box the same size as the image, and then create a logo using the words "Pacific Tours." Format the text in the style and size of your choice, using the Text toolbar, which you can display, if necessary, by selecting it on the View menu. Use the Rectangle tool to draw a rectangle the same size as the image, and then use the Fill tool to fill the rectangle with a blue color. You may need to click inside some of the letters to fill them with the blue color, too. (*Hint:* Use the Undo command on the Edit menu to reverse any mistakes. Use the Magnifier tool to zoom in on the image, if necessary, to make it easier to edit.) Save the logo as a 256-color bitmap file named **Tours Logo** in the Cases folder for Tutorial 7. (Click Yes if you see a Paint Warning dialog box.) Link a copy of the logo at the top of the National Parks Tours flyer. After saving the flyer, double-click the logo and edit it any way you want to improve its appearance.

6. At the bottom of the document type "Prepared by:" followed by your fist and last name.

Explore

7. Preview the document. Because this document does not fill the entire page, it would look better formatted horizontally on the page, in landscape orientation. Click File, click Page Setup, click the Paper Size tab, in the Orientation section click the Landscape option button, and then click OK. Review the newly formatted document in the preview window. Note that landscape orientation is also useful for tables containing many columns, or large, embedded Excel worksheets, save your changes, print the document, and then close the Preview window.

8. Save the flyer as a Web page with the name **National Parks Tours Web Page**. Adjust the placement of text and graphics as necessary. Give it an appropriate background color or pattern, and add one or two lines. Adjust the size and color of the text headings so they go well with the background.

9. Place a hyperlink at the bottom of the document that reads "Click here to see a photo of last year's tour!," and have the hyperlink display a copy of the file PacPhoto in the Cases folder for Tutorial 7 on your Data Disk. Be sure to make a copy of the PacPhoto file in the Link to File dialog box and then link the copy to the National Parks Tours document.

10. Place a hyperlink at the bottom of the PacPhoto page that takes the user back to the flyer.

11. Save both files, view them in a browser, and test the links. Print the files from your browser.

Case 3. Maple Tree Sports Sales Report Nicholas Paulsen is vice president of marketing for Maple Tree Sports, a national sporting goods distributor headquartered in Birmingham, Alabama. Because of the enormous volume of sales in California, Nicholas has decided to reorganize the sales regions. To lessen the load on the western region, he has decided to enlarge the southeast region to include Texas. He will explain this change in a report to all regional sales representatives. He asks you to create an integrated document that includes an Excel chart and a Paint image file of a map. He wants you to prepare the file for online viewing because he plans to post it on his company's network. Then he wants you to save and format the file for posting on the Web.

1. If necessary, start Word. Open the file **MapleRep** from the Cases folder for Tutorial 7, and save it to the same file as **Maple Sales Org**.

2. Between the first and second paragraphs, embed the Excel chart Maple, and reduce it to 30% of its original size.

3. Center the chart between the left and right margins.

Explore

4. Double-click the chart to display the Excel tools, click any bar, and select the fill color of your choice using the Fill Color button on the Formatting toolbar. Then, click the background and choose a contrasting color.

5. At the end of the document, link a copy of the Paint image file Salesreg, naming the copy Sales Regions Map. Center the map between the left and right margins with no text wrapping.

6. Edit the linked Paint image from within Word: Fill the state of Texas with the blue color that matches the other southern states. Save the image, and close Paint.

7. Save, preview, and print the document.

8. Switch to Web Layout view, and apply an appropriate background. Animate text with an animation of your choice. Save the Word document.

9. Save the report as a Web page. Adjust the placement of text and graphics. Change the font sizes and colors to make the on-screen document more visually appealing. Print the file from within your browser.

10. Create another Word document containing additional information that readers of this report might want to see. It might contain text, a chart, or graphics; avoid using Word tables. (If you are using floppy disks to save your files, be aware that graphics files can be quite large. You might want to use only text.) Save it as a Web page, and format it so it is compatible with the report. Create hyperlinks to move the user back and forth between the two documents. Save and preview the documents in a browser, and then test the links. Print the file from your browser.

Case 4. Educational Expenses Your local community education program is hosting a seminar for adults who want to return to college. The program coordinator has asked you to create a Web page providing information about the current cost of going to college. You will create the Web page using Word's Web Page Wizard, which leads you through the steps of creating a Web site:

1. Open a new Word document, and then, in several paragraphs, explain the various types of expenses that a student faces.

Explore

2. Use Microsoft Graph to create a chart detailing three major expenses, as follows: Click Insert on the menu bar, point to Picture, and then click Chart. In the Datasheet window, replace the row labels "East," "West," and "North" with your three major expenses. Replace the existing numbers with expense data for four quarters, and then click your report document to embed the completed chart.

3. Save the report as a Web page using the name **School Expenses**.

Explore

4. Notice that the New Blank Document button in the Standard toolbar has been replaced with a New Web Page button. Click the New Web Page button, and begin creating a new Web page.

5. At the top of the document add the title "Additional Data," and then link a picture or diagram that would enhance your report's content. For example, if you have access to a scanner, you could scan a picture of a campus building or your own picture. You can use Paint to modify the map of the United States in the graphics file SalesReg, showing the location of selected educational institutions.

Explore

6. If you have access to the World Wide Web, use a search engine to find relevant information about college costs and incorporate the information into the Additional Data document. Credit the source with a footnote, or create a hyperlink to the Web address in your report.

7. Save the new Web page as **Additional Information.**

8. Format both Web pages attractively, using the techniques you learned in the tutorial. Remember to make the pages look similar.

Explore

9. Close all open documents. Now you can use the Web Page Wizard to create a sophisticated Web site containing the two pages. Click File on the menu bar, and then click New. In the New dialog box, click the Web Pages tab, and double-click the Web Page Wizard icon. The first Web Page Wizard dialog box opens.

10. Read the dialog box, and then click Next. Type an appropriate title for your Web site, such as "School Expense Information." In the Web site location text box, verify that the file path in the Web site location text box indicates a folder within the Cases folder for Tutorial 7. Word assigns a default name, such as "New Web" to this folder.

11. Click Next, and read the information in the next dialog box.

12. Verify that the Vertical frame option is selected, and then click Next.

13. In the Current pages in Web site list box, select Personal Web Page, and then click the Remove Page button. Repeat for Blank Page 2, and Blank Page 1. Click the Add Existing File button, and select the School Expenses Web page. Repeat to select the Additional Information page, and then click Next.

14. Review the information regarding organizing links, and then click Next.

15. Click the Browse Themes button, select a formatting scheme (called a "theme") in the Choose a Theme list box, preview your scheme in the Sample of theme window, and then click OK. If a theme is not installed on your computer, click Install. (You may need to insert the Office 2000 installation CD in order to install a theme.) Click OK, and then click Next.

16. Click Finish. After a pause, Word creates your Web site, including a home page with links to the pages you created earlier. If the Frames toolbar opens, close it. Click a link in the left pane to display the relevant page on the right. Note that Word has assigned the filename "default" to the home page. All the files related to the Web site are stored in a new folder whose name is the same as the Web Site name you specified earlier.

17. Preview the new home page in your Web browser. Print the page once with the School Expenses link selected and once with the Additional Data link selected.

18. Close your browser, and then close the home page in Word.

LAB ASSIGNMENTS

The Internet: World Wide Web

These Lab Assignments are designed to accompany the interactive Course Lab called Internet World Wide Web. To start the Lab, click the Start button on the taskbar, point to Programs, point to Course Labs, point to New Perspectives Applications, and click Internet World Wide Web. If you do not see Course Labs on your Programs menu, see your instructor or technical support person.

The Internet: World Wide Web   One of the most popular services on the Internet is the World Wide Web. This Lab is a Web simulator that teaches you how to use Web browser software to find information. You can use this Lab whether or not your school provides you with Internet access.

1. Click the Steps button to learn how to use Web browser software. As you proceed through the steps, answer all of the Quick Check questions that appear. After you complete the steps, you'll see a Quick Check summary report. Follow the instructions on the screen to print this report.

2. Click the Explore button. Use the Web browser to locate a weather map of the Caribbean Virgin Islands. What is its URL?

3. Enter the URL http://www.atour.com. A SCUBA diver named Wadson Lachouffe has been searching for the fabled treasure of Greybeard the pirate. A link from the Adventure Travel Web site leads to Wadson's Web page called "Hidden Treasure." Locate the Hidden Treasure page, and answer the following questions:

   a. What was the name of Greybeard's ship?
   b. What was Greybeard's favorite food?
   c. What does Wadson think happened to Greybeard's ship?

4. In the steps, you found a graphic of Jupiter from the photo archives of the Jet Propulsion Laboratory. In the Explore section of the Lab, you can also find a graphic of Saturn. Suppose one of your friends wants a picture of Saturn for an astronomy report. Make a list of the blue underlined links your friend must click to find the Saturn graphic. Assume that your friend begins at the Web Trainer home page.

5. Jump back to the Adventure Travel Web site. Write a one-page description of the information at the site, including the number of pages the site contains, and diagram the links it contains.

6. Chris Thomson, a student at UVI, has his own Web page. In Explore, look at the information Chris included on his page. Suppose you could create your own Web page. What would you include? Use word-processing software to design your own Web page. Make sure to indicate the graphics and links you would use.

QUICK | CHECK ANSWERS

Session 7.1

1. **a.** A source file is the file containing the original object.

    b. An object is an item such as a graphic image, clip art, a WordArt image, a chart, or a section of text that you can modify and move from one document to another.

    c. The source program is the program in which an object was originally created.

    d. A destination file is the file into which you want to insert an object.

2. With embedding, you place an object into a document and retain the ability to use the tools of the source program. With linking, you place a representation of an object into a document. With embedding, there is no connection maintained between the source file and the destination file; with linking there is.

3. Linking is the best choice for data that might change over time.

4. "OLE" is short for "object linking and embedding". An OLE-enabled program is one whose objects can be integrated into other documents using OLE technology.

5. To embed an existing worksheet, click Insert on the menu bar, click Object, click the Create from File tab, select the file, click Insert, and then click OK without selecting the Link to file check box. To link an Excel chart, follow the same procedure but select the Link to file check box.

6. To copy a file, right-click it, click Copy, and then press Ctrl+V.

7. To modify an embedded object from within the destination program, double-click the object and then use the tools and menus of the source program.

8. False

Session 7.2

1. A hyperlink is a word, phrase, or graphic image that you can click to move to another location.

2. False

3. Click where you want to insert the bookmark, click Insert on the menu bar, click Bookmark, type the bookmark name, and then click Add.

4. "Executive Summary" (b) is an invalid bookmark name because it has a space.

5. A change in the color of hyperlink text indicates that the link has been used, or followed.

6. False

7. The Document Map is a navigational aid that you can use to move quickly from one heading to the next in a document.

Session 7.3

1. **a.** A program used to download and display Web pages.

   b. A Web site is a collection of inter-related Web pages.

   c. "HTML" is short for "Hypertext Markup Language," a special programming language that tells a Web browser how a Web page should look on the screen.

   d. A Web page is an electronic document. Organizations and individuals make their Web pages available on the World Wide Web by storing them on special computers called Web servers.

2. Text wrapping around graphics and animated text cannot be translated into HTML.

3. False

4. Click Format on the menu bar, click Borders and Shading, click the Borders tab, click the Horizontal Line button, and then click the Insert clip button. A horizontal line separates sections of a document to make it easier to read and navigate.

5. After converting a Word document to a Web page, you should adjust the formatting to make it more suitable for online viewing and possibly add some special formatting features that are not always available in printed documents, such as color and animation. In some cases, the original document might already contain special features such as animation that don't survive the translation to HTML. In that case, you may need to reapply the feature once the document has been saved as a Web page. At the very least, you will probably need to reposition graphics.

6. To preview a Web page in the default Web browser, click File on the menu bar, and then click Web Page Preview.

TASK REFERENCE

TASK	PAGE #	RECOMMENDED METHOD
Action, redo	WD 2.11	Click ⟳
Action, undo	WD 2.11	Click ↺
Background, apply textured	WD 7.30	Change to Web layout view, open document, click Format, point to Background, click Fill Effects, click Texture tab, click texture, click OK
Bookmark, create	WD 7.23	Move insertion point to desired location, click Insert, click Bookmark, type bookmark name, click Add
Border, draw around page	WD 4.25	Click Format, click Borders and Shading, click Page Border tab, click Box, apply to Whole Document
Bullets, add to paragraphs	WD 2.25	Select paragraphs, click 📋
Catalog, create	WD 6.36	See "Telephone list, create"
Character spacing, expand or condense	WD 5.34	Select text, click Format, click Font, click the Character Spacing tab, click the Spacing list arrow, click Expanded or Condensed, click OK
Click and Type, enable	WD 5.31	Click Tools, click Options, click Edit tab, select the Enable click and type check box, click OK
Clip art, insert	WD 4.15	Click 🖼 on Drawing toolbar, click Pictures tab, click the category you want, click the image you want, click 📥
Clipboard, erase contents of	WD 2.15	Click 🗑
Column break, insert	WD 4.25	Click Insert, click Break, click Column Break, click OK
Columns, balance	WD 4.24	Insert column break or click the end of the column, click Insert, click Break, click Continuous, click OK
Columns, format text in	WD 4.11	Select the text, click Format, click Columns, select the column style you want in the Presets section, click OK
Data source, attach	WD 6.09	Open Mail Merge Helper, click Get Data, click Create Data Source, remove and add field names as necessary, click OK, save the data source document
Data Source, create	WD 6.08	Click Tools, click Mail Merge, create or select main document, click Get Data, click Create Data Source, add or delete fields, click OK, and save source document
Data Source, filter	WD 6.29	Open main document, click 📑 on Mail Merge toolbar, click Query Options, click Filter Records tab, select field and comparison operator, type text to compare, click OK, click Close or Merge
Data Source, sort	WD 6.26	Open data source document, click in header row of desired sort column, click ↑A or ↓Z on Database toolbar
Date field, insert	WD 6.18	Click Insert, click Date and Time, click a format, select the Update automatically check box, click OK
Date, insert current	WD 5.32	Click Insert, click Date and Time, click desired format, click OK

TASK	PAGE #	RECOMMENDED METHOD
Document, browse by heading	WD 5.40	Click ⬚, click ⬚, click ⬚ or ⬚
Document, close	WD 1.30	If more than one document is open, click ✕ on title bar; if only one document is open, click ✕ on menu bar
Document, create new	WD 1.13	Click ⬚
Document map, view	WD 7.28	Click ⬚
Document, open	WD 2.02	Click ⬚, select drive and folder, click the filename, click OK
Document, preview	WD 1.26	Click ⬚
Document, print	WD 1.27	Click ⬚, or click File, click Print, specify pages or number of copies, click OK
Document, save	WD 1.17	Click ⬚
Document, save with new name	WD 2.05	Click File, click Save As, select drive and folder, enter new filename, click Save
Drop cap, insert	WD 4.20	Position insertion point in paragraph, click Format, click Drop Cap, select desired features, click OK
Embedded object, modify	WD 7.09	Double-click object, use commands and tools of source program to modify object, click outside embedded object
Envelope, print	WD 1.29	Click Tools, click Envelopes and Labels, click Envelopes tab, type delivery and return addresses, click Print
File Properties, add	WD 1.19	Click File, click Properties, click Summary tab, add desired information, click OK
Folder, create new	WD 5.04	Click File, click Save As, click ⬚, type folder name, click OK
Font size, change	WD 2.27	Select text, click Font Size list arrow, click new font size
Font style, change	WD 2.29	Select text, click **B**, *I*, or U̲
Font, change	WD 2.27	Select text, click Font list arrow, click new font
Footer, insert	WD 3.10	Click View, click Header and Footer, click ⬚, type footer text, click Close
Footnote, add	WD 5.27	Switch to Normal view, click footnote reference location, click Insert, click Footnote, select note type and numbering method, click OK
Format Painter, use	WD 2.24	Select text with desired format, double-click ⬚, click paragraphs you want to format, click ⬚
Graphic, crop	WD 4.18	Click graphic, click ⬚ on Picture toolbar, drag resize handle
Graphic, resize	WD 4.17	Click graphic, drag resize handle
Graphic, wrap text around	WD 4.19	Select graphic, then click ⬚ on Picture toolbar and select option or click ⬚ on Picture toolbar, click Layout tab, click Advanced, click Text Wrapping tab, select Wrapping style option, set Distance from text, click OK twice

TASK	PAGE #	RECOMMENDED METHOD
Header, insert	WD 3.10	Click View, click Header and Footer, type header text, click Close
Help, get	WD 1.28	Click 🔲 and type a question, click Search, click topic
Horizontal line, insert	WD 7.37	Click Format, click Borders and Shading, click Borders tab, click Horizontal Line, click a line style, click Insert clip button
Hyperlink, edit	WD 7.40	Right-click hyperlink text, point to Hyperlink, click Edit Hyperlink, edit filename or select a new file, click OK
Hyperlink, use	WD 7.24	Click blue underlined hyperlink; click ⬅ to return to original location
Hyperlink to another document, create	WD 7.25	Select hyperlink text, click 🔲, click Existing File or Web Page, locate target document, click OK
Hyperlink to same document, insert	WD 7.21	Insert bookmark at target location, select hyperlink text or graphic, click 🔲, click Place in This Document, click bookmark name, click OK twice
Hyphenation, change	WD 5.25	Click Tools, point to Language, click Hyphenation, enter size of Hyphenation Zone, set limit for consecutive hyphens, click Automatically hyphenate document, click OK
Insertion point, move with Click and Type	WD 5.30	Move pointer to location where you want to insert text, a table or a graphic; double-click
Line spacing, change	WD 2.20	Select the text you want to change, then press CTRL+1 for single spacing, CTRL+5 for 1.5 line spacing, or CTRL+2 for double spacing
Link, update	WD 7.17	Open destination file, click Edit, click Links, select filename, click Update Now, click OK
Mail Merge, create	WD 6.23	Create main document with merge fields, create data source, attach data source to main document, click 🔲 or 🔲
Mailing Labels, create	WD 6.31	Click 🔲, click Tools, click Mail Merge, click Create, click Mailing Labels, click Active Window, click Get Data, click Open Data Source, select source file, click Set Up Main Document, select label options, click OK, insert merge fields, click OK, click Merge twice
Main Document, create	WD 6.06	Click 🔲, click Tools, click Mail Merge, under Main Document, click Create, click Form Letters, click Active window, under Data Source, click Get Data, and create or open Data Source, click Close, add text and merge fields
Margins, change	WD 2.18	Click File, click Page Setup, click Margins tab, enter margin values, click OK
Merge fields, insert in main document	WD 6.19	Click at field location in main document, click Insert Merge Field button on the Mail Merge toolbar, click a field name
Merged data, view in main document	WD 6.22	Click 🔲 on the Mail Merge toolbar
Nonprinting characters,	WD 1.10	Click 🔲
Normal view, change to	WD 1.07	Click 🔲

TASK	PAGE #	RECOMMENDED METHOD
Numbering, add to paragraphs	WD 2.25	Select paragraphs, click ▤
Object, embed	WD 7.06	Click destination location, click Insert, click Object, click Create from File tab, click Browse, select file, click Insert, click OK
Object, insert with Paste Special command	WD 7.49	Copy object, click Edit, click Paste Special, select desired format in As list box, select the Paste link option button to link object to its source, click OK
Object, link	WD 7.12	Click destination location, click Insert, click Object, click Create from File tab, click Browse, select file, click Insert, click Link to File check box, click OK
Object, modify linked	WD 7.14	Double-click linked object, use source program tools to modify object, click outside linked object; or open object in source program, modify, save, open destination program, and update links
Office Assistant, close	WD 1.28	Click Help, click Hide Office Assistant
Office Assistant, open	WD 1.28	Click ▣
Outline, create	WD 5.21	Click ▤ on horizontal scroll bar, enter or edit headings, click number of head levels to show
Outline, edit	WD 5.23	Click ▤, click in line of text, click ⬆ or ⬇ to move line; click ⬅ or ➡ to promote or demote heading
Outline numbered list, create	WD 5.49	Click ▤, type first heading, press Enter, type next heading; to demote a heading, click ▤; to promote a heading, click ▤; press Enter twice to end list
Page, move to top of next	WD 3.12	Click ▼
Page, move to top of previous	WD 3.12	Click ▲
Page orientation, change	WD 7.50	Click File, click Page Setup, click Page Size tab, click Portrait or Landscape, click OK
Page, view whole	WD 4.13	Click Zoom list arrow, click Whole Page
Page break, insert	WD 3.15	Position insertion point at break location, press Ctrl+Enter
Page number, insert	WD 3.12	Switch to header or footer, click ▦ on Header and Footer toolbar
Paragraph, change indent	WD 2.23	Select paragraph, drag left or first-line indent marker on ruler; click ▤ or ▤
Paragraph spacing, adjust	WD 5.36	Move the insertion point to the paragraph, click Format, click Paragraph, click Indents and Spacing tab, use Before box to specify amount of space above the selected paragraph, use After box to specify amount of space to insert below the selected paragraph, click OK
Print layout view, change to	WD 3.12	Click ▣
Ruler, display	WD 1.09	Click View, click Ruler

TASK	PAGE #	RECOMMENDED METHOD	NOTES
Section break, create	WD 3.06	Position insertion point at break location, click Insert, click Break, click Section break types option button, click OK	
Section, vertically align	WD 3.07	Move insertion point into section, click File, click Page Setup, click Layout tab, click Apply to list arrow, click This section, click Vertical alignment list arrow, click desired option, click OK	
Shading, insert	WD 4.30	Click Format, click Borders and Shading, click Shading tab, select Fill and Pattern options, click OK	
Spelling, correct	WD 1.23	Right-click misspelled word (as indicated by red wavy underline), click correctly spelled word	
Spelling and grammar, correct	WD 2.05	Click at the beginning of the document, click ![ABC], review any errors, accept suggestions or ignore errors as desired; to type corrections directly in the document, click outside the Spelling and Grammar dialog box, make the desired correction, and then click Resume in the Spelling and Grammar dialog box	
Style, apply	WD 5.09	Select text, click Style list arrow, click style name	
Style, define by example	WD 5.14	Format text as desired, select text, type new style name in the Style list box	
Style, define new with style command	WD 5.14	Select text you want to format, click Format, click style, click New, type name of new style, click Format, click Paragraph or Character, specify formatting options, click OK twice, click Apply or Close	
Style, modify	WD 5.12	Click in paragraph formatted with style, click Format, click Style, verify Style name is selected, click Modify, click Format, click Font or Paragraph, select new style characteristics; click OK twice, click Apply or Close	
Symbol, insert	WD 4.22	Click Insert, click Symbol, click desired symbol, click Insert, click Close	
Tabs, set	WD 3.04	Select text, click tab alignment selector to display ![L], ![⊥], ![⅃], or ![⊥] at left of ruler, click ruler to place tab; click in text and press Tab	
Table cells, merge	WD 3.23	Select cells you want to merge, click ![icon] on Tables and Borders toolbar	
Table cells, split	WD 3.23	Select cells you want to split, click ![icon] on Tables and Borders toolbar, specify the number of cells or rows into which you want to divide the cell, click OK	
Table column width, change	WD 3.24	Position pointer over column's right border, press and hold down ALT and mouse button, drag to adjust column width to desired measurement as indicated in horizontal ruler	
Table gridlines, display	WD 3.29	Select table, click Table, click Show Gridlines	
Table, sum cells of	WD 3.23	Click cell where you want sum, click ![Σ] on Tables and Borders toolbar	
Table row, align text horizontally in	WD 3.27	Select a cell or range, click ![icon], ![icon], ![icon], or ![icon]	
Table row, align text vertically in	WD 3.27	Select row, click alignment list arrow on Tables and Borders toolbar, click desired alignment	

TASK	PAGE #	RECOMMENDED METHOD	NOTES
Table row, add or delete border	WD 3.28	Select line weight and style on Table and Borders toolbar, click ✏, click ✏ on cell borders; to delete, select No Border as line style	
Table row, delete	WD 3.21	Select row, click Table, point to Delete, click Rows	
Table row height, change	WD 3.24	Position pointer over row's bottom border, press and hold down ALT and mouse button, drag to adjust row height to desired measurement as indicated in vertical ruler	
Table row, insert at end of table	WD 3.21	Position insertion point in lower-right cell at end of table, press Tab	
Table row, insert within table	WD 3.21	Select row below, then click ⊟ᶜ or click Table, point to Insert, and click Rows Above	
Table text, rotate	WD 3.31	Select cells, click ‖₁ on the Tables and Borders toolbar	
Table, center on page	WD 3.32	Click in table, click Table, click Table Properties, click Table tab, click Center Alignment option, click OK	
Table, create	WD 3.13	Click ▦▾, drag pointer to select desired number of columns and rows; or click ✏ on Tables and Borders toolbar, draw desired number of columns and rows	
Table, shade	WD 3.29	Select table area, click 🪣 on Tables and Borders toolbar, and click a shading option	
Table, sort	WD 3.19	Click within column you want to sort by, click ⬇ or ⬇ on Tables and Borders toolbar	
Tables and Borders toolbar, display	WD 3.20	Click ▦	
Table of Contents, create	WD 5.38	Apply heading styles to document, click Insert, click Index and Tables, click Table of Contents tab, select desired format, select number of headings to include, click OK	
Telephone List, create	WD 6.36	Click 🗋, click Tools, click Mail Merge, click Create, click Catalog, click Active Window, click Get Data, click Open Data Source, select source file, click Open, click Edit Main Document, insert merge fields, click 🔳	
Template, create new	WD 5.19	Create a new document with styles, save as Word document, delete all text from the document, click File, click Save As, click the Save As type list arrow, click Document Template, verify that the Templates folder is displayed in the Save in list box or choose another location, click Save	
Template, saved in any location, open	WD 5.19	Click Tools, click Templates and Add-ins, click Attach, select template, click Open, select the Automatically update document styles check box, click OK	
Template, saved in Template folder, open	WD 5.19	Click File on the menu bar, click New, click the icon for your template in the General tab, and then click OK, type document text, apply styles, save as a Word document	

TASK	PAGE #	RECOMMENDED METHOD	NOTES
Template (Word predefined), attach	WD 5.10	Click Format, click Themes, click Style Gallery, click template name, click OK	
Text, align	WD 2.22	Select text, click ▤, ▤, ▤, or ▤	
Text, animate	WD 7.29	Select text, click Format, click Font, click Text Effects tab, click animation style, click OK	
Text, copy by copy and paste	WD 2.13	Select text, click 📄, move pointer to target location; then either click 📋 or, if Clipboard opens, click item to paste in Clipboard	
Text, copy by drag and drop	WD 2.12	Select text, press and hold down Ctrl and drag pointer to target location, release mouse button and Ctrl key	
Text, delete	WD 2.09	Press Backspace key to delete character to left of insertion point; press the Delete key to delete character to right; press Ctrl + Backspace to delete to beginning of word; press Ctrl + Delete to delete to end of word	
Text, find	WD 2.15	Click 🔘, click 🔍, type search text, click Find Next	
Text, find and replace	WD 2.15	Click 🔘, click 🔍, click Replace tab, type search text, press Tab, type replacement text, click Find Next	
Text, format	WD 2.29	See "Font Style, change"	
Text, highlight	WD 5.33	Select text, click 🖊	
Text, move by cut and paste	WD 2.13	Select text, click ✂, move to target location, click 📋	
Text, move by drag and drop	WD 2.12	Select text, drag pointer to target location, release mouse button	
Text, select a block of	WD 2.09	Click at beginning of block, press and hold down Shift and click at end of block	
Text, select a paragraph of	WD 2.09	Double-click in selection bar next to paragraph	
Text, select a sentence of	WD 2.09	Press Ctrl and click within sentence	
Text, select entire document of	WD 2.09	Press Ctrl and click in selection bar	
Text, select multiple lines of	WD 2.09	Click and drag in selection bar	
Text, select multiple paragraphs of	WD 2.09	Double-click and drag in selection bar	
Thesaurus, use	WD 7.05	Select word, click Tools, point to Language, click Thesaurus, click appropriate meaning and synonym, click Replace	
Toolbar, display	WD 1.08	Right-click any visible toolbar, click name of desired toolbar	

TASK	PAGE #	RECOMMENDED METHOD	NOTES
Web layout view, change to	WD 7.27	Open document, click	
Web page, create	WD 7.32	Create and save document, click File, click Save as Web page, click Save, click Yes, modify formatting as necessary	
Web page, view in Web browser	WD 7.42	Open Web page document, click File, click Web Page Preview	
Word, exit	WD 1.30	Close all open documents, then click on the title bar	
Word, start	WD 1.05	Click Start, point to Programs, click Microsoft Word	
WordArt object, create	WD 4.04	Click , click desired WordArt style, type WordArt text, select font, size, and style, click OK	

Standardized Coding Number	Certification Skill Activity Activity	Tutorial Pages	End-of-Tutorial		
			End–of–Tutorial Pages	Exercise	Step Number
W2000.1	**Working with text**				
W2000.1.1	Use the Undo, Redo, and Repeat command	2.10–2.11 (undo, redo) 4.22 (repeat)	2.38 2.39 2.40 2.41	CP1 CP2 CP3 CP4	4 3 4 5
W2000.1.2	Apply font formats (Bold, Italic and Underline)	2.29–2.31	2.35, 2.36 2.38, 2.39 2.39, 2.40 2.40, 2.41 2.41	RA CP1 CP2 CP3 CP4	4, 8 6, 10, 13, 14 4, 14, 15 6, 13, 15, 16 8, 10
W2000.1.3	Use the SPELLING feature	1.22–1.24 2.05–2.07	1.33 1.35 1.36 2.35 2.38 2.40 2.41	RA CP1 CP2 RA CP1 CP3 CP4	12 11 10 3 3 3 2
W2000.1.4	Use the THESAURUS feature	5.05–5.06	5.44 5.46 5.47 5.48	RA CP1 CP2 CP3	5 10 8 6
W2000.1.5	Use the GRAMMAR feature	2.05–2.07	2.35 2.38 2.40 2.41	RA CP1 CP3 CP4	3 3 3 2
W2000.1.6	Insert page breaks	3.06–3.07 3.15	3.34, 3.35 3.37 3.38	RA CP1 CP2	5, 13, 20 3, 8 4
W2000.1.7	Highlight text in document	2.09 (select text) 5.33–5.34 (highlighter)	2.37–2.38 2.40 5.45 5.47 5.48	RA CP3 RA CP2 CP3	10, 11 10, 11 16 11 11
W2000.1.8	Insert and move text	1.16–1.17 (insert) 2.12–2.15 (move)	1.32–1.33 1.34 1.35–1.36 1.37 2.35, 2.36 2.38, 2.39 2.39 2.40 2.41	RA CP1 CP2 CP4 RA CP1 CP2 CP3 CP4	3–9, 13 3–8 4–6, 9, 11, 12 4–8 4, 8 6, 15 9, 10 5, 8 5

Standardized Coding Number	Certification Skill Activity — Activity	Tutorial Pages	End-of-Tutorial Pages	End-of-Tutorial — Exercise	End-of-Tutorial — Step Number
W2000.1.9	Cut, Copy, Paste, and Paste Special using the Office Clipboard	2.12–2.15	2.35, 2.36, 2.38 2.40 2.41	RA CP3 CP4	4, 8, 11 6, 8 5
		7.03–7.05	7.49	CP2	Step 3
W2000.1.10	Copy formats using the Format Painter	2.24–2.25	2.39	CP1	9
W2000.1.11	Select and change font and font size	1.09–1.10			
		2.27–2.29	2.35, 2.36 2.39 2.39 2.40, 2.41	RA CP1 CP2 CP3	4, 8 12 3 6, 13, 14
W2000.1.12	Find and replace text	2.15–2.18	2.35, 2.36 2.39 2.39 2.40	RA CP1 CP2 CP3	4, 8 10 11 12
W2000.1.13	Apply character effects (superscript, subscript, strikethrough, small caps and outline)	5.08	5.44 5.46	RA CP1	9 9
W2000.1.14	Insert date and time	1.14–1.15 (AutoCmplt)	1.32 1.34 1.35	RA CP1 CP2	8 3 3
		5.32–5.33	5.45 5.47 5.48	RA CP2 CP3	15 10 11
W2000.1.15	Insert symbols	4.22–4.24	4.28, 4.29 4.30 4.32	RA CP1 CP3	22, 26 16 14
W2000.1.16	Create and apply frequently used text with AutoCorrect		5.49	CP1	17
W2000.2	**Working with paragraphs**				
W2000.2.1	Align text in paragraphs (Center, Left, Right and Justified)	2.22–2.23	2.35, 2.36 2.39 2.39 2.40 2.41	RA CP1 CP2 CP3 CP4	4, 8 9, 13 4 11 8, 9
W2000.2.2	Add bullets and numbering	2.25–2.27	2.36 2.39 2.39 2.40	RA CP1 CP2 CP3	8 11 6 7, 8

Standardized Coding Number	Certification Skill Activity — Activity	Tutorial Pages	End-of-Tutorial — End-of-Tutorial Pages	End-of-Tutorial — Exercise	End-of-Tutorial — Step Number
W2000.2.3	Set character, line, and paragraph spacing options	2.20–2.21 (line)	2.37	RA	10
		5.16, 5.34–5.38 (char, para)	5.44	RA	8, 10
			5.46	CP1	9, 13
			5.48	CP3	9
W2000.2.4	Apply borders and shading to paragraphs		4.30	CP1	11
			4.33	CP4	11
		5.17	5.48	CP3	9
W2000.2.5	Use indentation options (Left, Right, First Line and Hanging Indent)	2.23–2.24	2.39	CP1	11
			2.39	CP2	6
			2.40	CP3	10
W2000.2.6	Use TABS command (Center, Decimal, Left and Right)	3.04–3.06	3.34, 3.35	RA	3, 11
			3.37	CP1	6
			3.38	CP2	6
W2000.2.7	Create an outline style numbered list	5.21–5.24	5.49	CP4	4, 5
W2000.2.8	Set tabs with leaders	6.36–6.37	6.41	RA	28
			6.42	CP1	18
W2000.3	**Working with documents**				
W2000.3.1	Print a document	1.26–1.27	1.33	RA	16, 18
			1.35	CP1	13
			1.36	CP2	15
			1.36	CP3	5
			1.37	CP4	9
		2.31	2.38	RA	13
W2000.3.2	Use print preview	1.26–1.27	1.33	RA	16
			1.35	CP1	13
			1.36	CP2	14
			1.36	CP3	5
W2000.3.3	Use Web Page Preview	7.42–7.44	7.47	RA	31
			7.51	CP3	10
			7.52	CP4	17
W2000.3.4	Navigate through a document	2.07–2.08	2.35, 2.36, 2.38	RA	4, 8, 11
			2.38–2.39	CP1	4, 5, 6, 7
			2.39, 2.40	CP2	5, 7, 9, 15
			2.40, 2.41	CP3	4, 5, 8, 16
W2000.3.5	Insert page numbers	3.11–3.12	3.3.35	RA	8, 15, 18
W2000.3.6	Set page orientation		7.50	CP2	7

Standardized Coding Number	Certification Skill Activity / Activity	Tutorial Pages	End-of-Tutorial Pages	End-of-Tutorial Exercise	End-of-Tutorial Step Number
W2000.3.7	Set margins	2.18–2.20	2.36–2.37 2.39 2.39–2.40 2.41	RA CP1 CP2 CP4	8, 9 8 12, 13 6, 7
W2000.3.8	Use GoTo to locate specific elements in a document	5.40	5.45	RA	20
W2000.3.9	Create and modify page numbers	3.11–3.12	3.35	RA	8, 15, 18
W2000.3.10	Create and modify headers and footers	3.10–3.13	3.35 3.37 3.38	RA CP1 CP2	7, 8,15–18 5 6, 7
W2000.3.11	Align text vertically	3.07–3.09 (title page) 3.27–3.28 (table cells)	3.34,3.35,3.36 3.37, 3.38 3.38	RA CP1 CP2	6, 14, 40 4, 12 5, 8
W2000.3.12	Create and use newspaper columns	4.11–4.13	4.28, 4.29 4.30 4.31 4.32 4.33	RA CP1 CP2 CP3 CP4	13, 23, 24 12, 19 7, 8 13, 15 8
W2000.3.13	Revise column structure		4.31	CP2	8
W2000.3.14	Prepare and print envelopes and labels	1.29 (envlps) 6.33–6.35	1.33 6.40–6.41 6.42 6.43 6.44 6.45	RA RA CP1 CP2 CP3 CP4	18 20–26 14–16 13–16 14–18 11–14
W2000.3.15	Apply styles	5.09–5.12	5.44 5.47 5.48 5.49	RA CP2 CP3 CP4	7, 10 4 9 5
W2000.3.16	Create sections with formatting that differs from other sections	3.06–3.09	3.34–3.35 3.37 3.38	RA CP1 CP2	5–8,12,14–16 3–5 4–7
W2000.3.17	Use click & type	5.30–5.33	5.45 5.47	RA RA	15 9
W2000.4	**Managing files**				
W2000.4.1	Use save	1.17–1.19, 1.25–1.26	1.33 1.35 1.35, 1.36 1.36 1.37	RA CP1 CP2 CP3 CP4	10 9, 12 7, 13 3 9

Standardized Coding Number	Certification Skill Activity — Activity	Tutorial Pages	End–of–Tutorial Pages	Exercise	Step Number
W2000.4.2	Locate and open an existing document	2.02–2.04	2.35, 2.36	RA	2, 7
			2.38	CP1	2
			2.39	CP2	2
			2.40	CP3	2
W2000.4.3	Use Save As (different name, location or format)	2.05	2.35, 2.36	RA	2, 7
			2.38	CP1	2
			2.39	CP2	2
			2.40	CP3	2
			2.41	CP4	11
		7.32–7.35	7.46, 7.47	RA	21, 35
			7.50	CP2	6
			7.51	CP3	9, 10
			7.51	CP4	3, 7
W2000.4.4	Create a folder	5.04–5.05	5.43	RA	3
			5.49	CP3	2
W2000.4.5	Create a new document using a Wizard		5.48	RA	24
			7.52	CP4	9–16
W2000.4.6	Save as Web Page	7.32–7.35	7.46, 7.47	RA	21, 26
			7.50	CP2	8
			7.51	CP3	9, 10
			7.51, 7.52	CP4	3, 7
W2000.4.7	Use templates to create a new document		1.36–1.37	CP4	2–9
		5.10–5.11	5.44, 5.45	RA	6, 22, 23, 24
		5.18–5.21	5.47	CP2	3
W2000.4.8	Create Hyperlinks	7.20–7.27	7.46, 7.47	RA	16, 28–30
		7.40–7.42	7.49	CP1	11, 12
			7.50	CP2	9, 10
			7.51	CP3	10
			7.52	CP4	14
W2000.4.9	Use the Office Assistant	1.28–1.30	1.32, 1.33–1.34	RA	2, 17–19
			1.35	CP2	9
W2000.4.10	Send a Word document via e–mail		7.52	RA	37
			7.55	CP1	15
W2000.5	**Using tables**				
W2000.5.1	Create and format tables	3.13–3.18	3.35, 3.37	RA	21–25, 42–45
			3.37–3.38	CP1	9–15
			3.38	CP2	8–12
			3.39	CP3	2–11
			3.40–3.41	CP4	3–10

Standardized Coding Number	Certification Skill Activity — Activity	Tutorial Pages	End-of-Tutorial Pages	End-of-Tutorial Exercise	End-of-Tutorial Step Number
W2000.5.2	Add borders and shading to tables	3.28–3.31	3.36, 3.37 3.38 3.38 3.39 3.40, 3.40	RA CP1 CP2 CP3 CP4	38, 39, 44 14, 15 11, 12 11 3, 4, 8, 10
W2000.5.3	Revise tables (insert & delete rows and columns, change cell formats)	3.21–3.23, 3.27–3.28	3.35, 3.36 3.38 3.38 3.39 3.40, 3.40	RA CP1 CP2 CP3 CP4	27–29,31,35, 37, 40 12, 13 8, 10 3, 5, 7, 8 3, 4, 6, 10
W2000.5.4	Modify table structure (merge cells, change height and width)	3.23, 3.24–3.26	3.36, 3.37 3.38 3.38 3.39 3.40, 3.41	RA CP1 CP2 CP3 CP4	29, 34, 36, 40, 45 11, 12 9 8, 9, 10 4, 5, 9
W2000.5.5	Rotate text in a table	3.31	3.38 3.40	CP2 CP4	8 5
W2000.6	**Working with pictures and charts**				
W2000.6.1	Use the drawing toolbar		3.41	CP4	7
		4.05, 4.15	4.28, 4.29 4.29 4.32	RA CP1 CP3	4, 16, 25 3 7
W2000.6.2	Insert graphics into a document (WordArt, ClipArt, Images)	4.04–4.11 4.14–4.17	4.28 4.29–4.30 4.31 4.32 4.33	RA CP1 CP2 CP3 CP4	4–6, 16–17 3–7, 13, 14 4, 9 4 4, 9

File Finder

Location in Tutorial	Name and Location of Data File	Student Saves File As...	Student Creates New File
WORD, LEVEL I			
Tutorial 1			
Session 1.2			Tutorial.01\Tutorial\Tacoma Job Fair Letter.doc
Review Assignments			Tutorial.01\Review\Job Fair Reminder.doc
Case Problem 1			Tutorial.01\Cases\Confirmation Letter.doc
Case Problem 2			Tutorial.01\Cases\Rock Climbing Request Letter.doc
Case Problem 3			Tutorial.01\Cases\Awards Memo.doc
Case Problem 4			Tutorial.01\Cases\My Template Letter.doc
Tutorial 2			
Session 2.1	Tutorial.02\Tutorial\Annuity.doc	Tutorial.02\Tutorial\RHS Annuity Plan.doc	
Session 2.2	Tutorial.02\Tutorial\RHS\Annuity Plan.doc (Saved from Session 2.1)	Tutorial.02\Tutorial\RHS Annuity Plan Copy 2.doc Tutorial.02\Tutorial\RHS Annuity Plan Final Copy.doc	
Review Assignments	Tutorial.02\Review\RHSQuart.doc Tutorial.02\Review\RHSPort.doc	Tutorial.02\Review\RHSQuarterly Report.doc Tutorial.02\Review\RHS Portfolio Changes	
Case Problem 1	Tutorial.02\Cases\Store.doc	Tutorial.02\Cases\Store-It-All Policies.doc	
Case Problem 2	Tutorial.02\Cases\UpTime.doc	Tutorial.02\Cases\UpTime Training Summary.doc	
Case Problem 3	Tutorial.02\Cases\Ridge	Tutorial.02\Cases\Ridge Top Guide.doc	
Case Problem 4			Tutorial.02\Cases\Restaurant Review.doc Tutorial.02\Cases\Edited Restaurant Review.doc
Tutorial 3			
Session 3.1	Tutorial.03\Tutorial\EverRipe.doc	Tutorial.03\Tutorial\EverRipe Report.doc Tutorial.03\Tutorial\EverRipe Report Copy 2.doc	
Session 3.2	Tutorial.03\Tutorial\EverRipe Report Copy 2.doc (Saved from Session 3.1)	Tutorial.03\Tutorial\EverRipe Report Final Copy.doc	
Review Assignments	Tutorial.03\Review\StatRep.doc Tutorial.03\Review\ZonReq.doc Tutorial.03\Review\Members.doc	Tutorial.03\Review\AgTech Status Report.doc Tutorial.03\Review\Zoning Request.doc Tutorial.03\Review\Zoning Board Members.doc	
Case Problem 1	Tutorial.03\Cases\OceanRep.doc	Tutorial.03\Cases\Ocean Breeze Report.doc	
Case Problem 2	Tutorial.03\Cases\Europe.doc	Tutorial.03\Cases\Europe Tour Report.doc	
Case Problem 3	Tutorial.03\Cases\Classics.doc	Tutorial.03\Cases\Classical Music CDs.doc	
Case Problem 4			Tutorial.03\Cases\Bright Star Training.doc
Tutorial 4			
Session 4.1	Tutorial.04\Tutorial\MiniInfo.doc	Tutorial.04\Tutorial\FastFad Newsletter.doc	
Session 4.2	Tutorial.04\Tutorial\FastFad Newsletter.doc (Saved from Session 4.1)	Tutorial.04\Tutorial\FastFad Newsletter Final Copy.doc	
Review Assignments	Tutorial.04\Review\FigSpecs.doc	Tutorial.04\Review\Action Pros.doc	
Case Problem 1	Tutorial.04\Cases\CityComp.doc Tutorial.04\Cases\Knight.bmp	Tutorial.04\Cases\Computer.doc	

File Finder

Location in Tutorial	Name and Location of Data File	Student Saves File As...	Student Creates New File
Case Problem 2	Tutorial.04\Cases\MSM_NEWS.doc	Tutorial.04\Cases\MSM Newsletter.doc	
Case Problem 3	Tutorial.04\Cases\Wellness.doc	Tutorial.04\Cases\Wellness Newsletter.doc	
Case Problem 4			Tutorial.04\Cases\New Home.doc
WORD, LEVEL II			
Tutorial 5			
Session 5.1	Tutorial.05\Tutorial\Industry.doc	Tutorial.05\Tutorial\Chapter 2\Industry Analysis.doc	Tutorial.05\Tutorial\ Chapter 2\Business Plan Template.dot
Session 5.2	(Continued from Session 5.1)		Tutorial.05\Tutorial\ Chapter 2\Industry Analysis Copy 2.doc
Session 5.3	(Continued from Session 5.2)	Tutorial.05\Tutorial\Chapter 2\Industry Analysis Final Copy.doc	
Review Assignment	Tutorial.05\Review\Training.doc	Tutorial.05\Review\Policies\Training Courses.doc	Tutorial.05\Review\ Policies\Policy Template.dot Tutorial.05\Review\New Policy.doc
Case Problem 1	Tutorial.05\Cases\Flowers.doc	Tutorial.05\Cases\Mountainland Flowers.doc	
Case Problem 2	Tutorial.05\Cases\Catering.doc	Tutorial.05\Cases\Classic Catering.doc	
Case Problem 3	Tutorial.05\Cases\Business.doc	Tutorial.05\Cases\Writing Project\Business of Basketball.doc	
Case Problem 4	Tutorial.05\Cases\Income.doc		Tutorial.05\Cases\Median Family Income.doc
Tutorial 6			
Session 6.1	Tutorial.06\Tutorial\PetShopp.doc Tutorial.06\Tutorial\Shopdat	Tutorial.06\Tutorial\Pet Shoppe Form Letter.doc	Tutorial.06\Tutorial\Pet Shoppe Data Tutorial.06\Tutorial\Pet Shoppe Phone List
Session 6.2	(Continued from Session 6.1)		Tutorial.06\Tutorial\Pet Shoppe Form Letters1 Tutorial.06\Tutorial\Pet Shoppe Form Letters2 Tutorial.06\Tutorial\Pet Shoppe Form Letters3
Session 6.3	(Continued from Session 6.2)		Tutorial.06\Tutorial\Pet Shoppe Labels Tutorial.06\Tutorial\Pet Shoppe Labels Form Tutorial.06\Tutorial\Pet Shoppe Phone Form
Review Assignment	Tutorial.06\Review\Vaccines.doc Tutorial.06\Review\Payroll.doc	Tutorial.06\Review\Pet Shoppe Vaccines.doc Tutorial.06\Review\Pet Shoppe Payroll Memo.doc	Tutorial.06\Review\Pet Vaccine Data Tutorial.06\Review\Pet Shoppe Payroll Memo 2 Tutorial.06\Review\Payroll Envelope Form Tutorial.06\Review\Payroll Envelopes Tutorial.06\Review\Employee Phone List Form Tutorial.06\Review\Employee Phone List

File Finder

Location in Tutorial	Name and Location of Data File	Student Saves File As...	Student Creates New File
Case Problem 1	Tutorial.06\Cases\Campaign.doc	Tutorial.06\Cases\Campaign Form Letter	Tutorial.06\Cases\Supporters Data Tutorial.06\Cases\Campaign Letters Tutorial.06\Cases\Campaign Envelope Form Tutorial.06\Cases\Campaign Envelopes Tutorial.06\Cases\Campaign Phone Form Tutorial.06\Cases\Campaign Phone List
Case Problem 2	Tutorial.06\Cases\Gems	Tutorial.06\Cases\Gems Form Letter	Tutorial.06\Cases\Gems Data Tutorial.06\Cases\Gems Letters Tutorial.06\Cases\Gems Labels Form Tutorial.06\Cases\Gems Labels Tutorial.06\Cases\Gems Customer List Form Tutorial.06\Cases\Gems Customer List
Case Problem 3	Tutorial.06\Cases\AutoSale	Tutorial.06\Cases\Auto Sale Form Letter	Tutorial.06\Cases\Auto Sale Data Tutorial.06\Cases\Auto Letters Tutorial.06\Cases\Auto Envelopes Form Tutorial.06\Cases\Auto Envelopes
Case Problem 4			Tutorial.06\Cases\Graduation Guest Data Tutorial.06\Cases\Graduation Form Letter Tutorial.06\Cases\Graduation Merge Tutorial.06\Cases\Graduation Labels Form Tutorial.06\Cases\Graduation Labels
Tutorial 7 Session 7.1	Tutorial.07\Tutorial\FSIProp.doc Tutorial.07\Tutorial\FSIExpns.xls Tutorial.07\Tutorial\FSIChart Tutorial.07\Tutorial\Indiana.bmp	Tutorial.07\Tutorial\FSI New Branch Proposal.doc Tutorial.07\Tutorial\Copy of FSIChart.xls	
Session 7.2	*(Continued from Session 7.1)* Tutorial.07\Tutorial\VJResume.doc		Tutorial.07\Tutorial\VJResume Web Page
Session 7.3	*(Continued from Session 7.2)*		Tutorial.07\Tutorial\FSI New Branch Proposal Web Page Tutorial.07\Tutorial\VJResume Web Page
Review Assignment	Tutorial.07\Review\SalesRep.doc Tutorial.07\Review\2Qsales.xls Tutorial.07\Review\BrnchSls Tutorial.07\Review\FSIAds	Tutorial.07\Review\Family Style Sales Report.doc Tutorial.07\Review\Copy of 2Qsales.xls Tutorial.07\Review\Family Styles Sales Report Word Document.doc	Tutorial.07\Review\Family Style Sales Report Web Page Tutorial.07\Review\FSIAds Web Page

File Finder

Location in Tutorial	Name and Location of Data File	Student Saves File As...	Student Creates New File
Case Problem 1	Tutorial.07\Cases\NewOffic.doc Tutorial.07\Cases\Rent.xls Tutorial.07\Cases\Logo.bmp Tutorial.07\Cases\Devel.doc	Tutorial.07\Cases\New Office Memo.doc	
Case Problem 2	Tutorial.07\Cases\NatBroh.doc Tutorial.07\Cases\PacTours.xls Tutorial.07\Cases\PacPhoto.html	Tutorial.07\Cases\National Parks Tours	Tutorial.07\Cases\Tours Logo.bmp Tutorial.07\Cases\National Parks Tours Web Page
Case Problem 3	Tutorial.07\Cases\MapleRep Tutorial.07\Cases\Maple.xls Tutorial.07\Cases\SalesReg	Tutorial.07\Cases\Maple Sales Org Tutorial.07\Cases\Sales Regions Map	
Case Problem 4			Tutorial.07\Cases\School Expenses Web Page Tutorial.07\Cases\Additional Information Web Page

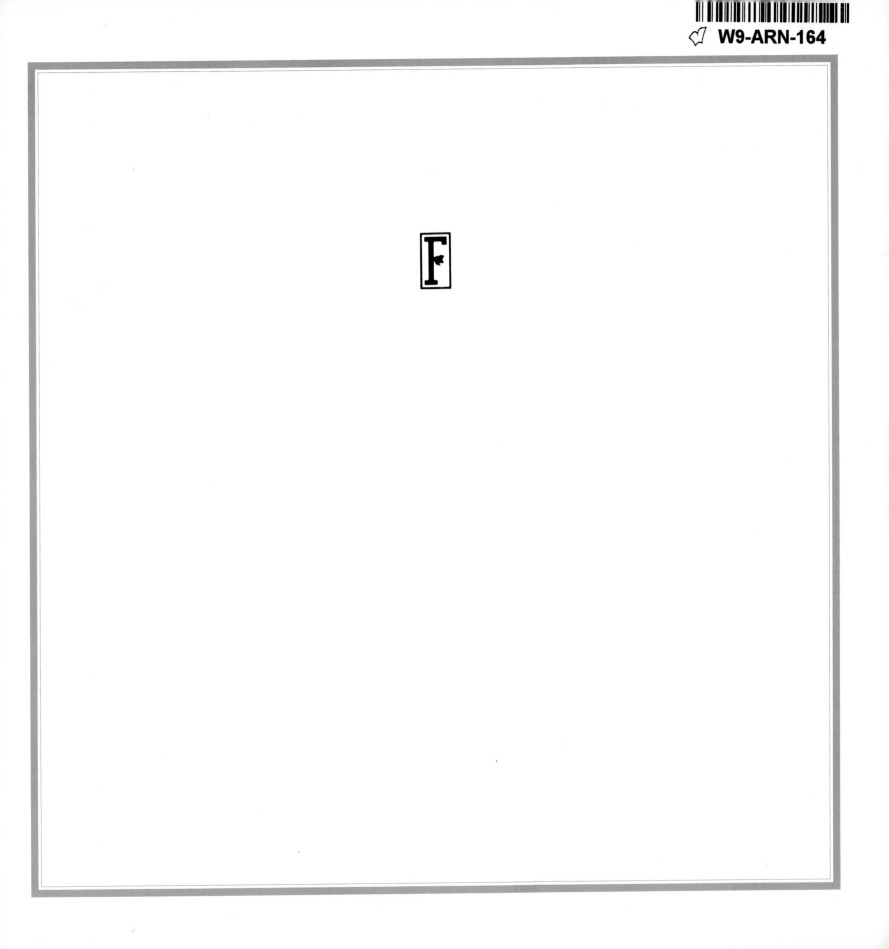

CITY GARDENING

PLANTING, MAINTAINING, AND DESIGNING THE URBAN GARDEN

DEIRDRE COLBY

KEN DRUSE, CONSULTING EDITOR
MARIA C. GLEASON, CONTRIBUTING EDITOR
HANS VAN ZELST, SPECIAL CONSULTANT

PRINCIPAL PHOTOGRAPHER
KEN DRUSE

A Fireside Book
Published by Simon & Schuster, Inc.
New York   London   Toronto   Sydney   Tokyo

A FRIEDMAN GROUP BOOK

Copyright © 1987 by Michael Friedman Publishing Group, Inc.

Simon and Schuster/Fireside Books,
Published by Simon & Schuster, Inc.
Simon & Schuster Building
Rockefeller Center
1230 Avenue of the Americas
New York, New York 10020

SIMON AND SCHUSTER, FIRESIDE and colophons are registered trademarks of
Simon & Schuster, Inc.

CITY GARDENING: Planting, Maintaining, and Designing the Urban Garden
was prepared and produced by
Michael Friedman Publishing Group, Inc.
15 West 26th Street
New York, New York 10010

Editor: Louise Quayle
Copy Editor: Mary Forsell
Art Director: Mary Moriarty
Designer: Robert W. Kosturko
Photo Editor: Philip Hawthorne
Production Manager: Karen L. Greenberg

Typeset by BPE Graphics, Inc.
Color separations by Hong Kong Scanner Craft Company Ltd.
Printed and bound in Hong Kong by Leefung-Asco Printers Ltd.

1 3 5 7 9 10 8 6 4 2
1 3 5 7 9 10 8 6 4 2 Pbk.

Library of Congress Cataloging in Publication Data

Colby, Deirdre.
    City gardening.

    ''Fireside book.''
    Bibliography: p.
    Includes index.
    1. Gardening.   2. Gardens—Design.   I. Druse,
Kenneth.   II. Gleason, Maria.   III. Van Zelst, Hans.
IV. Title.
SB453.C618 1987b   635.9   87-14866
ISBN 0-671-63697-9
ISBN 0-671-63698-7 (pbk.)

DEDICATION

From Pliny the Elder, to the present, this book is dedicated to the literary tradition of garden writing. Thank you for the inspiration and imagery that keep vibrant my visions of paradise.

ACKNOWLEDGMENTS

My grateful thanks for their time and expertise are due to: Bonnie Billet, Bonnie Billet Horticulturists; Jane Brennan, Assistant Librarian, New York Botanical Garden; Dimitri's Gardens Ltd.; Josh Edgerly, New York Planter Co.; Susan Rademacher Frey, Editor-in-Chief, Landscape Architecture & Garden Design; Charlotte Frieze Jones, Springland Associates; Lothian Lynas, Head Reference Librarian, New York Botanical Garden; Cindy Olson, C.O.R.E. Contracting; Leo Plofker, structural engineer; Pam Wilkinson, Managing Editor, *American Gardens of the Nineteenth Century,* The University of Massachusetts Press.

Thanks are also due to Roz Bernstein, Robert Colby, Kavid Koosis, Susan Littlefield, Timothy Mawson, Edwin T. Morris, Linda Reville, Marge Ternes, David Winn, and Linda Yang for their encouragement and support. Thank you to Louise Quayle, Philip Hawthorne, Sharon Kalman, Bob Kosturko, and Karla Olson for invaluable advice, assistance, and support. And a special thanks to Flora Stuart, whose magical garden in Ocho Rios, Jamaica, West Indies, continues to be an enduring source of enlightenment.

CONTENTS

CONTENTS

INTRODUCTION

No one would contest that the allure of trade and commerce has been one of the primary motivations for people around the world to leave their rural lifestyles for urban centers. Yet, increased commercial activity has never, and will never, replace the human need, for both aesthetic and health reasons, to be surrounded by beauty and nature. This is evidenced by the incorporation of public and private parks and gardens in even the most crowded spaces throughout the world.

For example, Paris, often called the most beautiful city in the world, was designed after the revolution to be a work of art, with its connecting grand boulevards lined with trees. However, its aesthetic design was inspired by the requirement of the people for refuge from the city—escape they found in lush growth and nature. Two game parks originally owned by the aristocracy were maintained, literally, for the kings of the people. They became the two infamous public parks flanking the city—Bois de Bologne in the east, and Parc Vincennes in the west.

Meanwhile, in North America, city squares were well shaded and many streets were tree lined. In New York, the first public park, Bowling Green, was opened in 1733. However, the city was also filled with private gardens, usually in backyards.

In nineteenth-century America, a new movement inspired by Andrew Jackson Downing encouraged the development of naturalistic, "picturesque" gardens. As a result, the large urban park designed without an emphasis on formal design emerged as a new phenomenon. One such park is Central Park in New York City, designed by Olmsted and Vaux. The idea of the public park was pushed through by reformers for the therapeutic benefit of the increasing hordes of workers pouring into the cities. In this same spirit of adding nature to the urban landscape, the New York Botanical Garden was established in 1899.

Concerned that cities might spread haphazardly or harbor disease and infection, reformers instituted the City Beautiful Movement. The movement focused on integrating city functions with the beauty of nature. The reconstruction of San Francisco after the great earthquake, for example, incorporated many of these ideals with its grand Golden Gate Park.

By the nineteenth century in Europe, apartment living had become traditional in Paris, Vienna, Berlin, Prague, Warsaw, St. Petersburg, and Dresden. In London, Mr. & Mrs. John C. Louden began a journal to address a new interest in plantings for small spaces of an acre or less.

The invention of the electric motor and, subsequently the elevator, made tall apartment buildings possible. In the 1920's in New York, after the Park Avenue railroad tracks were covered, it was chic for society members to move into apartment buildings along both sides of the avenue. As a result, penthouses became part of sophisticated city living. Additionally, from the 1950's through the present, the terrace has come into its own as a way of giving some sense of the outdoors to apartment dwellers.

These developments, rather than diminishing the city garden, altered its specifications by moving the site upward. Since that time, urban gardens have continued to be adjusted to scale and perspective; however, their original purpose of providing aesthetic and physical respite has been maintained.

"The best way to survive life in the city," garden expert Ken Druse says, "is to have a way to get away from it: a bit of green, a patch of blue sky—contact with growing things. In order to experience the true benefit of a garden to soothe and restore the spirit, you don't need to have a rambling country house or to book a villa on the Mediterranean for three months in the summer. The power of nature is legion. A simple window box can remind you of beauty, growth, and the continuity of life on earth. There's nothing like it!"

Susan Rademacher Frey, editor-in-chief of *Landscape Architecture* and *Garden Design* magazines which are published by the American Society of Landscape Architects, suggests that the urban gardener should capitalize on the small garden space by making it very personal and expressive. "Spark an experience that mingles the intrinsic qualities of you and the place," she advises. "Look for something to respond to, even in the most desolate places. For instance, the view of a water tank might evoke country memories.... Garden design operates on two levels. Physically, it is total sensual engagement. Symbolically, it tells your story as it lives in that place. We want to be more fully alive. One way to recreate and reproduce ourselves is in a private garden. Metaphorically, in this same way, gardens can recreate the city.''

French landscape architect, Gilles Clement, agrees that a successful urban garden will not thrive unless its attendant is passionate and personal. ''A garden can't live unless it is loved by its owner,'' he says. ''You have to ask yourself, 'What is this plant? What is its significance?' Every plant has a soul.''

Yet, a great number of would-be city gardeners are intimidated by what they interpret as a new and unfamiliar set of cultivation rules. They do not recognize that the true basis for successful urban gardening is the same as for any kind of gardening. As Reginald Farrar, the late nineteenth century plant collector and rock-gardener defines it in *A Yorkshire Garden*, a successful gardener must be '' . . . a lover of his flowers, not a critic of them. I think the true gardener is the reverant servant of nature, not her truculent wife-beating master. I think the true gardener, the older he grows, should more and more develop a humble, grateful and un-

certain spirit, cocksure of nothing except the universality of beauty.''

Yet, this is not to say that special knowledge and skills are not necessary and should not be investigated before cultivating an urban garden. Frey stresses that a wealth of horticultural information on city gardening is available not only through horticultural societies, but also through other gardeners. She would like to see more linkage within the vast network of public, community, and private gardening and encourages the revitalization of public gardens. Ms. Frey emphasizes the differences between public parks and public gardens, saying, ''Public gardens express the soul of the community.'' Together, these garden spaces help define a city, and each garden adds a new and individual dimension.

Carrie Maher of the landscape architecture firm Maher & Greenwald, is responsible for some of New York's most impressive community garden efforts. The public garden at the Cathedral of St. John the Divine, for example, symbolically pays tribute to a number of religions. In doing so, it represents the diverse cultural identity of New York and successfully carries out Ms. Frey's requirement that a public space should reflect its community. A brick garden path is in the shape of a Celtic cross. Some of the plantings are arranged in a menorah-like design. The garden also makes visual references to the Tibetan Buddhist tradition and contains plantings revered in both North and South American sacred rituals.

Fruits and vegetables grown in this garden are used in meals for the needy and homeless. There is also a corps of underprivileged neighborhood kids for whom it is a badge of honor to belong to this great garden. They make it grow and often enjoy its fresh vegetables and fruits. The garden, therefore, not only represents, but also serves the community.

Classes for area school children who wish to learn more about how plants grow are conducted in nearby solar greenhouses. Outside, a variety of ancient flowers grow, laden with religious and mythical significance.

Many believe, as I do, that there should be legislation that designates spaces throughout cities as public or communal gardening plots. While free ground space is at a premium, a multitude of unused space exists above the ground, atop garages, and other relatively low buildings as well as on roofs of apartment houses. The low-weight-bearing capacity of some residential buildings is perhaps the single greatest obstacle to creating private city gardens. However, technological breakthroughs can compensate for this hindrance.

The artistic challenge for the urban gardener is to create a flourishing plot in very little space. Therefore, a city garden should have in quality what it lacks in quantity. This book adheres to this philosophy. Disheartened by the losing battle city dwellers often wage with vandalism and the inconsiderate public, I have chosen not to address front-yard city gardens and to concentrate on backyard, roof, penthouse, and terrace garden design. Principles for these gardens can be applied to frontyard spaces, however. Wherever your garden may be, you will succeed if you follow Ms. Maher's advice: "Let the garden be your teacher. Remember, the seeds you hold in the palm of your hand already know what to do."

CHAPTER ONE

THE URBAN ENVIRONMENT

CLIMATE AND HARDINESS ZONES

SOIL

CITY CODES AND WEIGHT RESTRICTIONS

BUDGETING

"Half the interest of a garden is the constant exercise of the imagination," wrote Mrs. C.W. Earle in 1897 in *Pot-Pourri from a Surrey Garden*. A creative art, designing and planning a garden should afford its owner as much pleasure as the final result. In fact, the more carefully you plan and design beforehand, the more successful your city garden will be.

Even though a terrace, a balcony, or an atrium can become another living room, gardening is more complicated than interior decorating; choosing plants, making beds, and maintaining soil conditions requires more effort than, for example, picking out a chair. Making a city garden is a creative, resourceful process of trial and error. Trees, shrubs, flowers, and vegetables are living creatures, and these "greenlings," like children and pets, need time and care. City living can be even more stressful for them than it is for us, and that's saying something! Aside from the obvious specter of pollution, one reason for this difficulty in adjusting is that they must adapt to an artificial habitat. Many of the more beloved popular selections for city gardens are not necessarily native to

© Michael Selig

Seeming to grow naturally and effortlessly, this informal Washington, D.C., garden is the product of careful planning.

Rhododendrons, peonies, and irises thrive in the full sun on this exposed rooftop.

nearby suburban or rural areas. It is useful to learn which trees and shrubs are indigenous to the immediate region, and a good atlas will provide a natural vegetation map of North America.

In alleys behind apartment buildings, and most especially on the balconies, terraces, and rooftops, a growing environment has to be simulated. One approach is to force a planting scheme on the garden—not an approach I would advocate, unless you want to work against nature. Such a process usually involves inordinate doctoring and altering to keep plants alive that are not native to or compatible with a particular region. This folly will demand time-consuming maintenance from either you or the expensive landscape-maintenance service you will need to hire. This is not to say that making adjustments and soliciting professional care won't be necessary. The recommended approach, however, is to design your garden based on the plants that will thrive on the strengths, weaknesses, and idiosyncracies of your particular growing conditions. If a plant is in an environment that won't support it, it will die.

CLIMATE AND HARDINESS ZONES

The amount of precipitation and the temperature range in your area constitute your local climate. The most important component that lets you know what you can grow in your area is *temperature*. *Hardiness* describes the lowest winter temperature at which a tree, shrub, or flower can survive. There are ten zones in the United States and Canada. The U.S.D.A. hardiness zone map (see right) shows the lowest average winter temperature in your zone. When choosing plants, use this chart as a guide to be sure you get the right plants for your climate. If you live in Louisville, Kentucky, for example, you live in Zone 6, and you may choose plant materials that are hardy to, or can survive, a minimum winter temperature of −10°F to 0°F (−23°C to −18°C). The last spring frost is between March 30 and April 30, and the first fall frost usually occurs between September 30 and October 30. Therefore, the average growing season in Louisville is 225 days.

Factors other than just latitude and longitude, however, affect hardiness. Cities that are along the same general latitude north, for example, may have milder or more severe climates than their counterparts. For example, Fargo, North Dakota, has an inland climate with hot summers and cold winters. On approximately the same latitude, Fargo's counterpart Vancouver, British Columbia, is a coastal city with a mild climate because of its location. Cities around the Great Lakes, on the other hand, are affected by lake-effect precipitation, while those along the Gulf Coast are subject to seasonable stormy weather. In a city such as Denver, Colorado, the high altitude also will have a bearing on what can be grown there. Wind-swept prairie states, on the other hand, have their own special climate, while in the American Southwest aridity is a factor. While climatic conditions vary widely, city gardens are thriving all over North America.

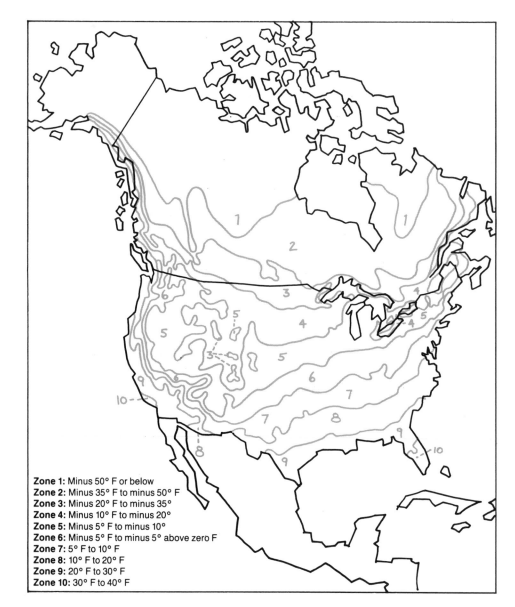

Zone 1: Minus 50° F or below
Zone 2: Minus 35° F to minus 50° F
Zone 3: Minus 20° F to minus 35°
Zone 4: Minus 10° F to minus 20°
Zone 5: Minus 5° F to minus 10°
Zone 6: Minus 5° F to minus 5° above zero F
Zone 7: 5° F to 10° F
Zone 8: 10° F to 20° F
Zone 9: 20° F to 30° F
Zone 10: 30° F to 40° F

Plant Hardiness Zone Map

Different types of plants and trees are only able to withstand a certain mean low temperature. Every city in North America belongs to one of ten growing zones; your garden selections must include only those plants that are suited to your city's zone.

Miniclimates

In addition to your regional climatic conditions, your garden space has its very own *miniclimate*, which includes the variables of sun, shade, moisture, and wind exposure. Together, these factors determine the optimum growing conditions for your city garden. Experienced urban gardeners know that they have to juggle what they want with what they can have.

If you have a sheltered backyard garden, low light levels will probably affect plant selection more than anything else. You might have only two to six hours of sun per day, which is considered partial shade. If you have less than two hours of sun you have full shade. In either case, you have a variety of plants to choose from that like shady growing conditions, such as flame azalea, periwinkle, and Canadian hemlock.

Garden walls that are painted or finished in light colors will reflect more light and warmth into your sheltered garden. Sheltered gardens can be warmer than surrounding areas in winter if they are protected from wind with a fence or hedge of evergreens or yews. Under these conditions, city gardeners could try some plants from one hardiness zone to the south of their own. For a different effect, if there are trees already on the property, you can "create" more light by removing some of the branches. This has an added bonus of increasing air circulation so that fungal problems can be prevented. Poor air circu-

This small, shady courtyard has been designed to make the most of what sunlight it does get and of its horizontal growing space.

lation in the sheltered garden will tend to keep soils damp and even boggy. There is, however, a range of plants, including tamarack trees, wintergreen shrubs, and marsh marigolds, that like very moist conditions. If the drainage is so poor that you practically have a swimming hole, there is much that a landscape contractor can do to improve the site.

Exposed sites, such as rooftops, penthouses, terraces, and balconies, often receive six to twelve hours of direct sunlight daily and perhaps additional indirect light as well. This seems to be the best of all possible situations; the range of flowering and vegetable-producing plants that can grow in these conditions is virtually unlimited. Too much sun and wind can be a problem, however. Plants bake in intense summer heat; excessive wind pulls moisture out of plants' leaves, causing them to wilt; and containers often freeze solid in winter. If your exposed site is windy, containers may have a tendency to topple if not weighted properly.

In exposed sites, most plants welcome a little shade from broiling sun, so that such overhead structural amenities as trellises, pergolas, slatted lathe houses, and shade trees are desirable additions. Fences and other vertical structures may help diminish the drying effects of wind. Awnings, canopies, and umbrellas are easily destroyed by strong rooftop winds, unless they are secured or located in a protected spot.

Depending on which way they face (north, south, east, or west), terraces, balconies, and penthouses generally are exposed some of the time and shaded part of the time. A south-facing terrace usually gets sunlight practically all day long and offers the widest growing selection of fruits, vegetables, and flowers. East- and west-facing terraces receive about six hours of sunshine, but in the morning and afternoon, respectively. Because of cooler morning sun, hydrangeas, daylilies, impatiens, and azaleas are good plants for east-facing balconies. West-facing balconies, which receive warmer afternoon light, can sport privet,

A rose collection surrounds a breakfast nook on a wraparound terrace. Designed by Lisa Stamm.

geraniums, coreopsis, roses, and herbs. A north-facing exposure receives the least sunlight, perhaps as little as two hours a day. Although the city gardener with a north-facing exposure might face a greater challenge in plant cultivation, a magnificent garden can be created with a broad variety of plant materials to choose from, such as begonias, hostas, ferns, and some forms of the colorful rhododendron.

Within your site, too, plantings may vary due to the influences of light and shade. A penthouse terrace may wrap around two or three sides of a building. In fact, neighboring buildings can affect sun and shade patterns by cutting off sunshine or reflecting more of it to you from light-colored walls and windows. Heat, too,

can be reflected from neighboring buildings, and in some cases it is absorbed during the day and radiated back to the garden at night. This can be a boon to the cool north-facing exposure and a bane to a sultry southern one.

If it is very windy on one or both sides of your garden in the sky, you may have to provide shelter by erecting latticed partitions on which vines like honeysuckle can be grown to create a windbreak. Dense shrubs such as yew also can act as protective screens and windbreaks. Many landscape experts advise city gardeners to select plants from one or two hardiness zones north of their own because of adverse windy conditions on roofs, balconies, and terraces.

This little garden has an eastern exposure, therefore it gets cooler morning sun.

Depending on your climate and miniclimate, you may have a perfect spot for a tiny lily pond stocked with goldfish.

Zeroing in on Your Miniclimate

Whenever you have a chance—spring, summer, fall, or even winter—the key to discovering your miniclimate is observation. Draw a simple diagram of your garden and note where the sun hits it at various points in the day, how precipitation drains, and other important natural features as outlined.

1. Note which direction your site faces and whether you receive partial shade, full shade, direct sunlight, or some form of indirect sunlight. Determine where it is sunniest and for how long. Note whether it is morning or afternoon sun. Observe when, and for how long, shadows fall.

2. When it rains, note how precipitation is distributed. You may see some areas getting soaking wet, other spots receiving less water, and some places—such as a fully sheltered corner—remaining almost completely dry.

3. Observe the direction and strength of the wind patterns. Garden photographer and writer Ken Druse suggests walking around on a windy day with a child's pinwheel to help figure it out. Find out where the wind is strongest and where it is calmest. Note how nearby buildings and such architectural elements as chimneys, buttresses, walls, and fences on and around your location affect the wind flow onto the site. Determine if there are changes in wind direction from summer to winter. You want to ensure that wind will not unexpectedly blow rain under awnings and into other sheltered spots. On the other hand, perhaps you will discover that your garden has almost no wind circulation.

Your diagram should serve as a general guideline based on your observation. Have some fun—exact knowledge of earth science isn't necessary! Your garden is unique and there's no better way to learn about your growing conditions than by firsthand experience. The reward is well worth the initial investment of your time and observation. By creating a garden that can live with you, you'll be making a garden you can live with: a permanent inspiration.

The United States Department of Agriculture's Extension Service and in Canada your provincial office of Agriculture Canada (see "Sources and Useful Addresses") offers a wealth of horticultural information. They are very comprehensive sources of information about the most pollution-tolerant and best-suited plantings for your city. Search out horticultural societies and garden clubs in your area. Quiz the person at the nursery. Most urban gardeners share information generously.

SOIL

For gardens on the ground, you will need to know the pH level, drainage capacity, nutrient and trace-element levels, and the balance between organic and inorganic matter in the soil. Most soil is composed of three substances: clay, sand, and organic matter. Any soil that has too much or too little of these ingredients has an imbalance.

Clay is made up of tiny, densely packed particles. It provides a secure foundation for plants, but if used alone, holds too much water and drowns plants. *Sand* is made up of relatively large particles. It provides excellent drainage and air circulation. But sandy soil has so many air spaces that water and nutrients run through too quickly. Roots therefore cannot absorb enough moisture and food. *Humus* is decayed material, such as leaf mold, dehydrated manure, or sphagnum peat moss. Humus helps soil retain water and nutrients. However, humus by itself retains too much moisture. When soil has a good balance of clay, sand, and humus, it is called *loam*—the gardener's best friend.

The acidity or alkalinity of soil also has to be in balance. The *pH acidity/alkalinity scale* ranges from 0 (most acid) to 14 (most alkaline). A pH of 7 is neutral. For most plants, 6.5 to 7 is optimum. However, many plants like a slightly acidic soil of 5.5 to 6.5 pH. Some plants, such as colorful azaleas and rhododendrons, thrive in acidic conditions. Others, like clematis, like it slightly alkaline.

There are two ways to learn something about the drainage on your property. Dig a hole one foot deep, fill it with water, and watch how quickly it drains away. If it drains too slowly, you may have too much clay. If the water disappears almost immediately, you may have sandy soil. A second way is to watch where the water goes during a heavy rainstorm. Does it run onto your neighbor's property or into your basement? Are there some areas that stay wet while others drain quickly? If there is a

severe problem, you may need a landscape contractor to assess the situation—he can determine if the problem is one of slope, poor soil, or both.

Soil testing is necessary to determine pH levels, as well as quantities of nutrients, trace elements, and organic and inorganic matter in your soil. There are home-testing kits. However, the best way to ascertain soil makeup is to have it analyzed by a county extension agency, usually affiliated with a state university, or local office of Agriculture Canada.

"Soil testing is nothing more than an inventory of what is in the soil at the time the sample is taken," writes Ralph Snodsmith in his helpful *Tips from the Garden Hotline*. For a composite sample, gather about four cupfuls from all over the property. Remove any noticeable trash or rubble, then dig down 6 to 8 inches (15 to 20 centimeters) for the specimen. Place the soil in an airtight, sturdy container and attach a five-item note to the sample with the following information and requests:

1. Write down anything you know about what grew on the site before.
2. Request a trace-element test.
3. Briefly outline what you would like to grow, and ask whether or not your scheme is viable.
4. Ask how you can correct or amend the soil.
5. Ask what would grow best in the soil.

Mail the sample off in a sturdy container or airtight plastic bag in a padded envelope to your county extension agency or in Canada to the University of Guelph, Ontario or the Oric Garden Centre in Toronto (see "Sources" for addresses).

The charges for soil testing vary, but it is not expensive and worth every penny. The soil-testing service will tell you just about everything there is to know about your soil. You'll find out which nutrients it has or lacks, its composition and texture, and if

Sparkling clematis prefers alkaline soil and some shade.

Colorful rhododendron, perhaps the quintessential city shrub, requires slightly acidic soil.

Above left: *Brightly colored, fragrant Iceland poppies thrive in sunny spots throughout North America.* **Above right:** *This garden, consisting entirely of raised beds, includes one full of herbs and leafy green vegetables.*

any diseases or fungi are present.

Contingent upon the test results, you may be able to improve the quality of your old soil. Soils that have a high clay content can be loosened by the addition of gypsum or coarse builder's sand. Sandy soils improve when mixed with topsoil. Soil amendment also involves adding nutrients and fertilizers (see page 29). However, all soils improve with the addition of humus. Sphagnum peat moss is a good choice of humus. This coarse-textured organic material comes from bogs in Canada.

Acidic soils are commonly found in woodland and rainy areas. Overly acidic soil conditions can be corrected by adding ground limestone. Alkaline soils occur in arid areas and parts of the continent where surface limestone is present. Alkalinity may be adjusted a bit by adding humus. You may need something stronger if you live in the arid Southwest. If so, add sulfur according to the manufacturer's directions.

Sand, topsoil, sphagnum peat moss, ground limestone, and sulfur are available at garden centers. Ask the staff's opinion on how much of these additives to use and which tools you'll need. Generally, soil is best amended in the fall so that nutrients and additives have a chance to become integrated over the winter. Also, you'll have more time without being distracted by spring and summer chores.

If your soil is in very bad shape (filled with construction rubble, for example), you may have to prepare a raised bed of entirely new soil. A raised bed is simply a contained area for planting. Landscape, lighting, and irrigation designer Hans Van Zelst suggests the following raised bed construction:

1. Contain the bed with sturdy retaining walls of bricks, or tiles, railroad ties, or preserved wood about 20 inches (50 centimeters) high. Ultimately, the size of the bed depends on the size of your garden. An arrangement of stones reminiscent of New England's rock walls with violas poking out of the crevices would look lovely. You can frame the bed with anything, as long as the construction can contain the weight of the soil and the pressure of spreading root systems. If you encase the bed with stout redwood or cedar, you might think about planing its surface off with a bench for grandstand garden seating.

2. Put 2 to 3 inches (5 to 7.5 centimeters) of gravel on the bottom.

3. Cover the gravel with thin hairlike fiberglass netting (Dupont's Landscape Fabric or DeWitt's Weed Barrier, for example), which are easily found at a good nursery.

4. On top of the netting, lay 18 inches (45 centimeters) of topsoil mixed with 6 inches (15 centimeters) of sphagnum peat moss, or three parts topsoil to one part moss.

5. Add fertilizer suited to what you will be growing (see page 31).

A raised bed is just a giant container for soil. It gives you a fresh start and lets you influence the destiny of your plants.

CITY CODES AND WEIGHT RESTRICTIONS

Before you begin any kind of city garden, inquire about your city's building and zoning codes. Generally, these are available from your city's building department. Obtain a written copy to be able to refer to as necessary. Make sure that you can recognize fire hazards and that you understand weight restrictions. Follow them exactly.

The weight restriction on roofs, penthouses, terraces, and balconies in older buildings in New York City, for example, is 40 pounds (18 kilograms) per square foot (0.09 square meter). In newer buildings, the weight restriction is reduced to 30 pounds (13 kilograms) per square foot. In cities where snowfall amounts are larger, the weight allowance may be 50 pounds (22 kilograms) per square foot, while in more southern cities it is not uncommon to find restrictions of as little as 20 (9 kilograms) or even 10 pounds (4.5 kilograms) per square foot.

When planning a large elevated city garden it is always advisable to contact a structural engineer. An engineer can best counsel you on a surface's structural soundness, alert you to which areas can tolerate the greatest and least amount of weight, and tell you what measures can be taken to distribute weight evenly. If surface conditions are poor, dunnage, or a deck, may have to be constructed to distribute the weight of a container garden. Many larger apartment buildings retain a structural engineer. If yours does not, call or write the local Association of Consulting Engineers or the group's headquarters in Washington, D.C., or Ottawa, Ontario. They may be able to answer your questions.

Drainage requirements and provisions should be provided by your landlord or building management company. In many places, building permits are required. In any case, speak to your landlord before assembling any container-supporting system on a roof, penthouse, or terrace. If the landlord or tenants' association offers resistance to your plans, point out that a well-landscaped terrace apartment can command a higher rental or selling price. And show them this book. Let them see how gorgeous and trouble-free a carefully constructed city garden can be.

BUDGETING

Depending on your resources, a sensible strategy is to think big but start small, expanding every year. Substantial city gardening is seldom inexpensive. City rents for garden-supply centers are high. Consequently, their prices are high, and their space and resources could be limited. In addition, the services of landscape professionals are not cheap. Start your garden with a small selection of plants, particularly trees and evergreen shrubs. Quality, rather than quantity, is the key. It is preferable to add to your design every year rather than to buy everything all at once if it means establishing a big, flashy garden with shoddy workmanship and inferior materials. Second-rate gardens inevitably have to be replaced.

Setting up a garden can involve lifting, stooping, and moving around some heavy materials. Think about whether you'll need help. It can be a good investment in your health—as well as in your garden—to hire a landscaping service to help out.

Before this lush roof garden was designed, weight restrictions and drainage requirements were carefully studied.

© Ken Druse

Basic Gardening Tools

If you're new to gardening, or just want to update your supplies, this list of tools covers the essential items necessary for maintaining a garden.

1. A **hose** with a spray attachment is a must for watering plants and also can be used to spray debris off paved surfaces.

2. A **rake** will facilitate clearing uprooted weeds, fallen leaves, and other unwanted waste in your garden.

3. A **pail** can be used for anything from carting weeds out of the garden to transporting fertilizer and soil.

4. A **hand-spading fork** is a good tool for turning soil and lifting a plant out of its growing spot for transplanting.

5. A **trowel** with a short or long handle is a gardener's staple used for light digging, transplanting smaller plants, and weeding.

6. **Pruning shears** facilitate clipping unwanted tree branches and cutting flowers. A heavy duty electric **hedge trimmer,** however, should be used for shaping and pruning larger bushes and trees.

7. **Gardening gloves** will protect your hands from injury and dirt, and a broad brimmed **hat** is ideal for keeping the hot sun out of your eyes and off of your head and neck.

8. A reversible **garden stool and kneeling pad,** which folds for easy storage, will save your body from some unnecessary aches and pains.

9. A small **hand truck or dolly** (available from larger hardware stores) is indispensable for transporting soil, weeds, or whatever to the street for disposal or from one part of your garden to another.

10. A small **shovel** will make heavy digging jobs easier.

Begin with a few tools and garden supplies, adding new ones as you need them. Storage space, too, is probably at a premium, so think about where you're going to stash something before you order or buy it.

© Ken Druse

CHAPTER TWO

PLANTING, PROCEDURES, AND MAINTENANCE

PLANTING

TROUBLE-SHOOTING

GARDEN CARE

CONTAINER GARDENING

DRIP IRRIGATION SYSTEMS

© Ken Druse

Once you have assessed the needs and condition of your site, you will need to decide on a planting scheme and plan a timetable of garden care, from ordering plants to winterizing beds. You must also determine what kind of garden will grow best for you, one that grows in a container or window box, one that blossoms from a soil bed, or any combination of these growing methods.

Additionally, a thorough understanding of the possible pitfalls you will face as an urban gardener is necessary to ensure long-term success. A consultation with a local expert, such as a horticulturist or your county or provincial agricultural agent will also help you determine which plants and garden-care methods will work best for you. Whatever planting scheme you choose for your garden, the basic procedures outlined in this chapter will help you get started.

Above right: The planting scheme for this corner of annuals can be changed every year. Red salvia, impatiens, marigolds, gladioli, and pink, flowering tobacco adorn the spot here. Below right: Every bit of horizontal growing space is being utilized on this colorful, narrow terrace, but there is no sense of overcrowding because of the even spaces between each planting.

PLANTING

A planting scheme can be scaled to a large or a small garden.

Ready for transplanting, this tree has just arrived from the nursery. Choose trees with root balls that are about as wide as the tree branches extend.

Trees, shrubs, flowers, fruits, and vegetables come ready to plant in several forms. Trees and shrubs tend to survive the best when they have been *balled and burlapped*. This simply means that their root balls are surrounded by soil that is wrapped up in burlap and tied with cord near the crown, where the trunk and roots meet. It's the least traumatic way for a middle-size tree or shrub to make the transition from the nursery to your city garden. Middle-size trees and shrubs measure between five and seven feet tall and have had a good start, even before you plant them. Planting instructions are usually included with your purchase. Also keep in mind that some trees have to be staked at first until they are strong enough to grow on their own.

Another planting method for smaller shrubs, dwarfed trees, and perennials from 2 to 6 feet high (1.9 to 5.4 meters) is *bare root*. Your selection arrives in a dormant state with its roots bare. Bare-root plants take longer to establish themselves than the balled-and-burlapped variety and can be harmed by windy terrace conditions. Follow the planting directions accompanying the selection. If you can't put the plant into the ground or a container right away, moisten the roots frequently to keep them from drying out.

Bulbs, such as crocuses, daffodils, and other annuals and many kinds of vegetables, fruits, and herbs can be grown from seedlings and carefully transplanted into your garden. Many herbs and vegetables can also be grown from seed. A lot of seeds come in one tiny packet. In small-space gardens, it is always better to use lesser amounts than the package directions suggest. If you want to get an early start, buy a seed-starter kit and germinate them indoors before planting them outdoors in the spring.

Generally, when you live in a cold climate, it is preferable to plant your garden in spring right after the last frost. This way, plant roots will be well established by winter. In areas with shorter, less severe winters, you can plant in the spring or in the fall before the ground freezes. Additionally, spring-flowering bulbs like tulips and hyacinths have to be planted in fall. Most herbaceous perennials like spring planting, but there are exceptions, as with peonies and Oriental poppies. In warm climates you can generally plant throughout the year, but no plants should be planted at the height of summer's heat.

Above: City nurseries may offer only a limited selection of plants and supplies because they lack space. If you cannot find what you are looking for, try a nearby suburban nursery.

It is a good policy to place your orders early because mail-order nurseries do run out of stock. Reputable suppliers send orders at the appropriate time for planting in your area, though you may be allowed to request a specific delivery date. If your order arrives while the ground is still frozen, well in advance of the planting date, send it back. Don't be too surprised if the shrub you have ordered isn't quite as pretty as the one pictured in the catalog. Catalogs usually depict perfect specimens photographed at maturity. However, if the plant has obviously been damaged in transit, refuse delivery and send it back.

An advantage in using catalogs is that they supply common names of plants along with their Latin botanical names. Common names vary from place to place, but Latin names are the same worldwide so you will always be able to identify the plant you want. Catalog descriptions often include information about hardiness zones, types of soil in which to plant, and sunlight requirements, which is generally all the information you need. A disadvantage when you order by mail, however, is that you have no choice in the appearance of what is being shipped to you. Trees and shrubs form the backbone of your garden: Their woody stems or evergreen boughs must complement your garden's design through every season. Therefore, I recommend that you pick them out from the local nursery. If you don't like its selection, or if it doesn't carry a particular item you're searching for, find a friend with a car, or rent one for the day, and drive out to a suburban nursery. Before you go, call ahead to make sure the one you visit has what you're looking for and can deliver larger orders to you in the city. Measure doors and elevators to make sure your new garden trees and shrubs won't be too tall or wide to squeeze through with a little bit of coaxing.

Be fussy and use your artist's eye. Van Gogh was inspired by the cypress tree. In his diary, the painter wrote that the tree "is as beautiful in line and proportion as an Egyptian obelisk" (Van Gogh at St. Rémy and Auvers. Metropolitan Museum of Art: New York, 1986). Select trees and shrubs for their interesting shapes, beautiful forms, or perfect symmetry. Look for richness and variation in the color of the bark and a pleasing configuration of branches.

Planting Vegetables

Cabbage, spinach, onions, cauliflower, beets, peas, lettuce, and asparagus are cool-season vegetables. They require an outdoor growing temperature of 48°F to 70°F (8°C to 21°C). Parsley, chicory, and chives also enjoy early planting. (Consult package directions for each plant's specific sowing timetable, and the frost date map for your growing season.)

Such warm-season vegetables as beans, eggplant, peppers, tomatoes, and summer squash need day and nighttime temperatures between 55°F and 90°F (12°C and 32°C). They should be planted when all danger of frost has passed, about two weeks after leaves have appeared on the trees. In spring, if your garden is threatened by a late frost, insulate budding plants by covering them with heavy-duty plastic garbage bags. Warm-season herbs—which are mostly annuals and include basil, caraway, chervil, coriander, sweet marjoram, and arugula—should also be planted when all possibility of frost has passed.

Ordering Plants

On a cold January evening, seed catalogs are a thrilling reminder that spring is just around the corner. It's impossible to plant in winter, but it's a wonderful time to plan. Our imaginations have more space than our city gardens, so think about your design as you read through, and try to resist the temptation to send away for everything you see.

Succulent tomatoes and green peppers allowed to ripen until they are red and sweet are but two of the rewards of an urban vegetable garden.

TROUBLE ⋈ SHOOTING

Regular watering is the number one priority for the maintenance of a flourishing city garden.

Here is a nice fat tomato horn worm, hard at work destroying tomatoes.

Despite your noblest intentions, it is inevitable that a plant that is supposed to flourish in your growing conditions just won't do so. It may have been a weak or unhealthy specimen in the first place. If you wish to replant the specimen in the same spot, try investigating the possible reasons why the plant did not grow. Perhaps the soil has been drying out too quickly or staying too wet. The amount of sunlight may have been too little or too much. In these cases, try replanting in another spot. If you still don't get good results, this just may not be the right plant for the site.

While there are fewer pests in city gardens than in rural sites, you will undoubtedly encounter a few. The indomitable red spider is said to have been seen crawling up the Empire State Building in New York City in January! Aphids, caterpillars, and white flies are the most common garden pests. When insects or diseases are responsible for a plant's demise, there are recognizable signs. Curled, dry leaves, holes, and ragged edges usually indicate that a plant is under siege. Some insect is definitely responsible for any sticky substance above leaves or silvery webs below. Vegetables tend to be more susceptible to pests. Usually, a thorough spraying with insecticidal soap (read the label and follow directions) will get rid of common pests. Western Publishing Company's illustrated *Golden Guide to Insect Pests* is a handy reference book for identification. Other signs that a plant is sick include leaf rust (a disease resembling the familiar oxidant), leaf spot, and a thin coating of white, powdery mildew. Signs of root rot or water mold are more difficult to detect but manifest themselves in dry, wilting leaves, even though the soil is moist.

The best way to fight trouble is to identify the enemy. Pick off a few leaves, twigs, or dead bugs, stick them in a plastic bag, and show them to your nurseryman. If powerful insecticides are called for, read the label and follow directions. Insecticides are poisonous, so handle them with care and keep them away from children and pets. Personally, I would hire a certified insecticide applicator to do the job. Call your local botanical garden or horticultural society for references.

Finally, it is absolutely crucial that the garden is watered regularly during the growing season. A drip irrigation system (see page 37) is the most effective means of preventing over- or underwatering. Every so often, spray leaves to rid them of accumulated soot and grime or pests trying to get a foothold. If you are fortunate enough to have an area of lawn in your city garden, use a sprinkler system when needed from early spring to late fall.

GARDEN CARE

Feeding

City gardens, which grow in all kinds of soil mixtures, are particularly vulnerable to damage from an imbalance or lack of nutrients. Of all the nutrients required, nitrogen, phosphorous, and potassium are the most important. These elements are abbreviated on fertilizer bags as N, P, and K respectively. Nitrogen promotes vigorous green-foliage growth and overall vigor. Phosphorous stimulates flower production. Potassium—also called potash—is essential for sturdy stem and root growth and enhances both winter hardiness and immunity to diseases.

Chemical, inorganic fertilizers list the ingredients in order of nitrogen, phosphorous, and potassium. A good general N-P-K ratio is 5 percent, 10 percent, and 5 percent, respectively, which is written as 5-10-5. However, garden-center shelves are filled with fertilizers formulated just for evergreens, roses, azaleas, bulbs, vegetables, and many other kinds of plants. They are available in liquid, tablet, and granular forms.

Calcium, which strengthens cell walls, and magnesium, which aids in the process of photosynthesis, are also important. Additionally, there are seven less important elements that are known to be essential to plants' biochemical processes: boron, copper, iron, manganese, molybdenum, sulfur, and zinc. They are most readily found in organic fertilizers such as fish emulsion, bone meal, and dehydrated manure.

In New York City, the Bronx Zoo has kindly dehydrated and packaged animal manure, selling it as Zoo Doo. The Metro Toronto Zoo also packages the manure. It is available in nurseries in metropolitan areas. Check your local nursery to see if there is a similar initiative in your area.

Opinions vary on how frequently to fertilize. Landscape experts agree that plant food must be applied at least once in spring and then again in fall. One of the best guides is simply how healthy and green the plants are looking. Mr. Van Zelst recommends adding small, weekly doses of fish emulsion in a 5-1-1 ratio of N, P, and K all summer long. It seems to intensify flower colors and won't burn roots like the overuse of chemical fertilizers can. Whenever you are going to apply fertilizer, make sure you read the label and follow directions. However, many gardeners suggest erring on the conservative side.

Grass clippings (above) and wood chips (below) are two of the many possible types of mulch.

Mulching

A mulch is a layer of added material that covers the top of the growing medium in beds and containers. Mulching performs several vital functions. It helps to retard moisture evaporation from the soil—always a concern in container gardening. Mulching also smothers weeds by denying them access to sunlight. At the same time, mulch insulates the soil so that it maintains an even temperature, which is especially important in colder weather. By stabilizing soil temperature, the damage plants undergo from thawing and freezing in late winter is reduced.

Balsam boughs are a good choice for a supplemental mulch when laid over the autumn mulch about January 1 (a perfect use for the Christmas tree). Good choices for spring city garden mulches are aged minichips of bark. Straw is excellent for vegetable gardens. Mulches are usually applied twice a year. Apply them first in spring and then again in autumn after weeds and debris have been cleared away.

Carefully consider each cut before you prune anything; a mistake will be very obvious to you for a long time.

Weeding

If something is growing that you don't recognize, it could be a weed. However, do not be too quick to eliminate the plant. It may bloom into an attractive specimen. Ken Druse says, "A weed is an unwanted plant in an undesirable place. One person's weed is another's wildflower." Confirmed weeds should be eradicated as quickly as possible, however, because their growth can damage other plants. When the soil is wet, digging them out is easier. At the end of the growing season, it is always a good idea to thoroughly inspect the garden for any intruders. Western Publishing's illustrated *Golden Guide to Weeds* can help identify common culprits. If you are still uncertain about what a plant is or how to best get rid of it, bag a sample and take it to your local nursery for identification and advice on elimination.

Pruning

Pruning is the process of cutting something back. It could be the new growth at the top of a plant or the roots below the soil. Form and silhouette should be considered when pruning. Nothing in the garden is sorrier looking than a wretchedly hacked tree. Since special tools and a light touch are needed to properly perform this job, it might be best to hire a landscaping service to do it. However, you should be able to take care of the smaller plants and shrubs.

Root pruning is advisable when you suspect that a larger plant's roots are outgrowing its container home. A simple method involves plunging a spade directly into the growing medium, about two inches from the planter's edge, and scraping once or twice all the way around. A trowel works well for plants in small containers.

It is a good practice to remove flowers from plants as soon as they begin to fade. *Deadheading,* as this technique is called, promotes a longer flowering time, and keeps your garden looking neat and vibrant.

Winterizing

To prepare your garden for winter, pull weeds, throw out annuals, and eliminate sick or weak plants. Do a general cleanup. If your terrace is very windy, tuck lighter containers out of the wind. Plants in heavier tubs that are difficult to move may have to be staked with a cylindrical windscreen of burlap. Do this also with broadleaved evergreens such as holly and rhododendron if they are in very exposed sites. Furthermore, the leaves of all evergreens and conifers would do well to be protected with an antidessicant spray. Spray the plants again in midwinter to make sure they survive the winter.

With diligent pruning, espaliered shrubs and trees can be the most interesting features of a city garden and can soften an unornamented wall.

CONTAINER GARDENING

When you create a garden on a rooftop, terrace, or balcony, all your plantings will have to be in containers. Rather than being a limitation, however, container gardening offers you the opportunity to exercise your imagination. From a colorful African pot to an ornate sarcophagus, a container can be almost anything you choose, providing it conforms to certain criteria. Anything you select has to be light enough to satisfy weight restrictions on roofs, terraces, and balconies. (Never use soil alone—1 inch (2.5 centimeters) of topsoil weighs 100 pounds (45 kilograms) on a roof.) On older roofs, use lightweight containers. Containers have to be roomy enough for the roots of your chosen plants to grow. They have to be able to last through the coldest days of winter and the hottest days of summer. They also have to be able to tolerate being in contact with the constant moisture and must have holes in the bottom for drainage.

No container should ever lie directly on a surface. Elevate it 2 to 3 inches (5 to 7.5 centimeters) on bricks, pressure-treated wood blocks, or rollers, for adequate drainage. Be sure, too, not to push plants directly against a parapet wall. This could have the effect of making the plant grow in one direction. Leave about 3 inches (7.6 centimeters) between the plant and the wall for this reason, and so you can sweep away debris from behind the containers.

The larger the plant and the longer it lives, the more expansive its root system will be. A container must be matched with a plant's size. Trees, of course, need the largest containers. Shrubs (roses, taxus, and forsythia) and herbaceous perennials (asters, chrysanthemums, and daylilies) bloom every year, and their roots hibernate during the cold season. They require roomy, sturdy boxes and tubs. Planters for trees and shrubs also have to be rugged enough to withstand pressure from expanding roots without cracking. Trees and shrubs are long lived, so they need stalwart containers that can last for many winters. Because they bloom and die within one growing season, annuals (mari-

A colorful grouping of richly toned terra-cotta pots filled with a profusion of blooming flowers and small trees demonstrates the endless variations that can be created using containers.

Pots and tubs transform this rooftop into a lush retreat. Their positioning along the roof's edges and walls both defines the garden room and masks weatherworn sufaces. Additionally, their portability allows for easy seasonal changes and rearrangements.

golds, petunias, and snapdragons) can be grown in less durable containers.

Because the tannic acid in the wood keeps them from rotting, the most permanent containers are boxes and tubs made of redwood, cedar, teak, and mahogany. (If you want to use another kind of wood, such as yellow pine, make sure it has been pressure-treated with a preservative that is not toxic to plants.) If well constructed and properly maintained, containers can last for more than ten years. Ideally, the boxes should be reinforced along the exterior corners with aluminum, copper, or brass

brackets bolted in place. Anything larger than four or five feet long by two feet wide tends to be unwieldly. Sagging in the middle of a long trough can be alleviated by adding interior bracing to stabilize the construction. To prevent drooping, planters have to be supported from underneath with bricks or blocks.

A very durable and less expensive container is the ubiquitous whiskey half-barrel made of oak. For best results, it should be treated with copper or zinc napthanate, which is nontoxic to plants but should be used with caution nonetheless (read the

label and follow directions). Also, the metal hoops should be coated with Rust-oleum™.

Elegant carved stone urns—Georgian, Regency, and Adamesque planting troughs—once found in stately European gardens are now being replicated in lighter weight materials such as fiberglass. Fiberglass copies of the dignified Versailles planting box—standing on four legs with finials atop each corner—are available through mail-order suppliers (see "Sources and Useful Addresses") Victorian cast-iron garden furniture and other classic lead forms—now hard to locate and unsuitably heavy for elevated gardens—are being realistically duplicated in aluminum. Old-fashioned planters decorated with garlands, leaf patterns, scrolls, and mythological creatures are expertly reproduced in weatherproof, lightweight materials. For rooftop rock gardens, rough-hewn pumice and simulated-stone alpine boxes are available.

Undeniably, planters and containers can provide interest in and of themselves. There are many exquisite Oriental urns and pots that can grace the city garden. You can look for something special at an auction house or in an art gallery. To protect your treasure, pot the plant first in an inexpensive container. For adequate drainage, the inner pot should sit on a few inches of gravel.

There are several styles of lightweight, imitation terra-cotta containers made of plastic that resemble their heavier counterparts (see page 33). Many, adorned with friezes and fluted mouldings, can fool even the most discerning eye. Make sure that terra-cotta pots, real or simulated, are frostproof.

Unattractive plastic containers can be covered with trailing plants and are perfect when used for cascades of flowering plants. In Italy, some inventive city gardeners wrap their containers in colorfast fabrics that complement their design schemes. Imagine pots of bushy, blue hydrangeas draped in a subtle pink and cream cotton design gracing the perimeter of a Florentine terrace. Use your imagination to invent other decorative motifs for containers, such as stenciling your own designs on your more unattractive pots.

Because of windy conditions on rooftops, hanging baskets are only appropriate in sheltered, backyard gardens. There are, however, many pretty and unusual receptacles that fasten securely to exterior walls of condominium and cooperative apartments. Annuals can be placed in virtually any container for a season, no matter how frivolous. As long as there are drainage holes, even a ceramic chamber pot or a conch shell will do.

© Ken Druse

Tulips and pansies in a classically French, square, Versailles-style planter set in front of a trellis, lend a formal appearance to a garden.

Window Gardening

In the summertime, there is nothing lovelier in the city than a town house whose windows are overflowing with colorful blossoms and herbs. Most container requirements such as weather resistance and drainage holes apply to window boxes. Because of hazardous windy conditions, window boxes are prohibited on high-rise buildings. In most cities, having window boxes is against the law. Some permit window boxes only as high up as four to six stories and only if there is no pedestrian traffic underneath. It would be a good idea to check your city's ordinances. Lizzie Boyd's outstanding book *Window Gardens* includes many interesting and innovative ideas for safe, yet attractive, window adornments.

Here is a cross-section of a mix suitable for ground-floor window boxes. A layer of perlite is covered with a layer of charcoal, then several inches of a soil-free mix.

A variety of colors, shapes, and textures grace a box outside this basement window.

Planting Mediums

Topsoil by itself is seldom used in elevated gardens because it is so heavy. Landscape designer Bonnie Billet, of Bonnie Billet Horticulturists, recommends a good, lighter mixture made by combining two parts of topsoil and eight parts of any soil-free mix, which contains peat moss for moisture retention and lightweight mica (instead of sand) for good drainage. Billet's formula calls for lining the bottom of a container with porous fiberglass netting before filling it with her soil-free recipe. This way, you ensure adequate drainage for your plants.

Ken Druse has had good results with a soil-free mix consisting of three parts sphagnum peat moss combined with one part coarse (horticultural-grade) perlite. Perlite is a silica derivative that is only a fraction of the weight of sand. Perhaps the only drawback to a soil-free mix is that it contains no nutrition. But as Druse points out, "The inherent nutrition in topsoil would be depleted after two months in a container. You'll have to add fertilizer in any event. So the lighter-weight medium might be advantageous." Garden centers and nurseries sell prepackaged brands of topsoil and also carry a wide variety of soil-free mixtures.

First discovered in the 1860s, *hydroponics* is a system of gardening in which plants grow aquarium style in an all-nutrient solution that the roots absorb by osmosis. In the United States, it is primarily used as a farming technique for growing vegetables and herbs. The National Aeronautics and Space Administration of the United States is developing hydroponics for its proposed space stations. Although somewhat futuristic, this method could offer exciting possibilities for city gardeners. Israel's abundance of fruits and flowers is largely due to the country's extensive use of hydroponics. Those interested in pursuing hydroponics should consult Richard E. Nicholls's *Hydroponics Soilless Gardening*.

DRIP IRRIGATION SYSTEMS

The one constant need in your city garden is adequate watering. Rain water tends to fall off a plant's leaves, spill over the sides of the container, and never penetrate the planting mix. In our busy, hectic city lives, we can't always count on hand watering. Even if you live and work at home, there is always a chance that you might have to rush out unexpectedly. And if you forget to water the plants, it spells trouble for the garden. For these reasons, installing a drip irrigation system in your container or ground-level garden can make your life easier and, perhaps, save the life of your garden.

Such a device works like the human circulatory system. Like arteries, inconspicuous hoses carry water to the containers. Like capillaries, skinny little "invisible" tubes called hydroinoculators go directly into the soil. Drip irrigation systems work by timers so that every individual container automatically gets watered. The cost of a drip irrigation system varies greatly. Mr. Van Zelst estimates that it can range from five to thirty percent of the total landscape project's cost, depending on the size of the garden and the system used. However, experienced city gardeners attest to its indispensability.

Elevated city gardens grow better with drip irrigation systems. Without them, soil is more likely to dry out in the summer, and roots are more likely to sustain damage in winter. Because the moisture level in the soil is maintained at the proper level, the survival rate of the garden is increased immeasurably. Additionally, since each container gets only the precise amount of moisture it needs, drip irrigation systems actually conserve water.

For a ground-level garden in a courtyard, a drip irrigation system also saves you time with the garden hose. Installing the system here may be a little more complicated, however, as the pipes must be installed underground, both for aesthetics and to preserve the life of the system.

Before you begin an extensive planting scheme, consult your local nursery and irrigation specialist to be sure your system will suit your needs.

You should be able to locate an irrigation designer-installer in the telephone book, or ask your nursery to recommend someone. An irrigation specialist will service your system and adjust it seasonally, even in periods of water shortage. In late fall, the irrigation specialist turns off and blows air out of the system. This helps create an equilibrium between the amount of moisture in the soil and the amount of moisture in the roots. It also helps reduce one of the leading garden killers—winter root damage. On a smaller, less expensive scale, fine drip-irrigation kits produced by Gardena System of West Germany can be purchased. They are available at larger garden centers, from good gardening-supply sources like Smith & Hawken (catalog), and sometimes at botanical garden shops.

© Derek Fell

This is a close up of one of the hydroinoculators or "capillaries" in a drip-irrigation system. Working on a timer, the indispensable system makes sure everything automatically gets watered.

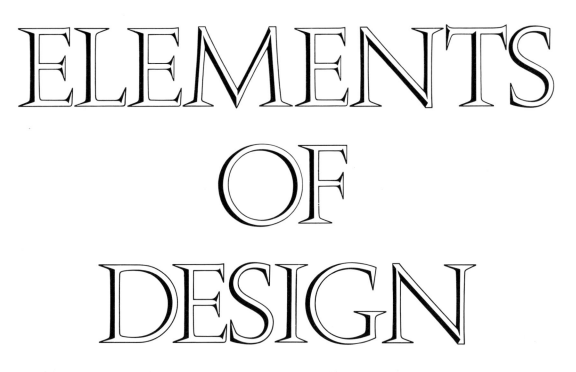

CHAPTER THREE

ELEMENTS OF DESIGN

THE VIEW FROM YOUR WINDOW

SCALE, COMPOSITION, AND PERSPECTIVE

COLOR, SHAPE, AND TEXTURE

SURFACES, LAWNS, AND GROUNDCOVERS

DESIGNING FOR YEAR-ROUND INTEREST

LIGHTING AND NIGHT GARDENS

© Ken Druse

The preeminent twentieth-century landscape architect Thomas D. Church theorized in his well-known work *Gardens Are For People* (McGraw-Hill: New York, 1983), "No definite style of garden from the past answers all the needs of today's small garden.... Even the term garden has changed its meaning.... The new kind of garden is still supposed to be looked at. But that is no longer its only function. It is designed primarily for living. ...How well it provides for the many types of living that can be carried on outdoors is the new standard by which we judge a garden." In other words, once you've determined how you're going to *use* your garden, you can get to work and start designing.

In our heart of hearts, most of us hope to create a dazzling display of horticultural beauty and ornamentation. Even when there is very little elbowroom outside, there is no exultation that compares to showing off your garden to an appreciative audience. When you start thinking about the design of your city garden, allow yourself the freedom to experiment. There are so many suggestions, formulas, and how-tos in garden design that most should only be used as guidelines rather than taken as mandates. Yes, you can recreate what you have admired in the pages of a magazine or in someone else's garden. As in life, however, even if you follow every dictate, there is no guarantee things will turn out exactly as you plan. Most importantly, you must ensure that after the garden has been constructed, its design will contain your own unique imprint. Establish a theme; anchor the design with a pleasing diversity that also incorporates unbroken harmony. By doing so, you

Above: *A formal design has been chosen for the garden gracing the front of this brownstone. The window boxes and planters are identical, as are the vines and plant materials in each.*
Below: *Graceful boughs, water, and statuary lend a subtle Oriental influence to this serene, Washington, D.C., town house garden.*

will have reaffirmed an affinity with nature.

Space permitting, there is no greater joy than entertaining outside in the warm seasons. A minimum of soft lighting is necessary if you are planning to make the most of your garden at night (see page 52), and if there's room to do so, allow space for seating, an end table, or—if your garden is spacious enough—a small dining or buffet table. Guests, of course, are one thing, but insects are another. Insects are drawn to light, so try to keep lighting subdued.

Some form of shelter from hot sun and sudden showers would be appreciated by friends and family alike. Canvas awnings can be both pretty and practical and are easy to roll up and put away. One family who lives in Zurich, Switzerland, has a beloved old rose pergola. For three generations, at dusk, covered in dense foliage with roses cascading down its sides, it has been a scented summer dining room.

Should you wish only to grow a food garden, you can still make it pretty. There are many ornamental vegetables that are as decorative as they are delicious (see page 67). There are some flowers, like marigolds, which naturally repel pests. They can be grown simultaneously with vegetables. Vegetables welcome some shade in the summertime, so consider planting a fruit tree or two.

However you plan to use your garden, following a few simple design guidelines will save you the headache and expense of replacing plants or features that just don't work. Before you do anything, draw a rough plan of your garden, or consult a professional garden designer, so that the execution of the plan is as spectacular as your original concept.

© Mark Ross 1987

Cale Roberts' fantastic atrium design of plants, lights, and varying textures is beautiful both day and night.

THE VIEW FROM YOUR WINDOW

© Richard Mandelkorn

Parisians have mastered the art of creating small courtyard gardens that are beautiful when viewed from above. Summer flowers cover the outside walls. An evergreen parterre poised between cobblestones adds interest throughout the year. Looking down at it in winter, its lacy pattern glistens like the frosting on a snowy white cake.

Attention should be directed to some intriguing feature in the distance so that the garden seems to become a part of the magical skyscape. Take advantage of anything interesting or beautiful that lies beyond your garden. Does your apartment face the mountains or rise above a lake or a river? Can you see the Empire State Building or the John Hancock Building? Is the Golden Gate Bridge or the Brooklyn Bridge visible from your terrace? Does your apartment overlook a park or other natural view? If there is a beautiful picture out there, you can "frame" it. Plant tall Italian cypress trees on the left and right of the view. Place dwarf evergreens beside them and "underline" the vista with a low row of evergreen shrubs. If you're fortunate enough to have a view of someone else's beautifully designed garden, try to incorporate this scenery into your garden.

All too often, however, our apartments adjoin garbage-strewn roofs, abut dead-end walls, and confront laundry rooms. (And those are some of the nicer "views.") Undaunted city gardeners cleverly screen out unsightly views with trees, foliage-covered trellises, or rows of tall potted plants. If you have a rooftop, ter-

Opposite: Container plants frame a magnificent Charles River view in Boston. Lightweight, portable furniture is easily brought indoors during bad weather. *Below:* A brightly colored and reliable plant, forsythia can camouflage necessary but unsightly features like this chain-link fence. *Right:* Circular, rhythmically repeated shrubbery effectively softens the narrow outlines of this city garden. Flowering trees planted against the back wall draw the eye into the garden and provide the illusion of spaciousness.

race, or penthouse garden, parapet walls often are required by city ordinance to be a permanent construction of no less than 43 inches (1.2 meters) high. Even though walls should enhance or detract from the view as you wish, make certain your parapet walls comply with local regulations. A painted facade of an attractive eighteenth-century English architectural folly or other garden-house structure can be transposed onto wallboard and attached to an opposite wall (with the owner's consent, of course.)

SCALE, COMPOSITION, AND PERSPECTIVE

Perhaps no other garden on earth is as symbiotically integrated with architecture as is the city garden. The city's very soul seems expressed in city garden design. Often, form and design follow the urban contour. Like skyscrapers, rooftop and ground-floor city garden designs extend upward. The vertical plane of tree and trellis reflect the city's own expansion heavenward to conserve space. Container plantings and espaliers (trained trees on fences) reflect the city's intent to employ its precious horizontal space advantageously. Yet, the city garden is ultimately an urban refuge, a place to reaffirm our affinity with nature.

Scale, how one part of the design relates to another, is the fundamental design element that makes the plants and objects in your garden a cohesive whole. With proper scale, the relationship and size of each element to the other is proportionate—no part of the garden detracts from another unless you want it to. Scale also concerns how the garden relates to the environment around it and vice versa. One should feel gently compelled to enter the garden and just as pleased to reenter the apartment. Pay close attention to what is placed just outside the entryway to the garden as the transition from inside to outside is as important as what's in your garden. Plants and ornaments at the entryway should serve to introduce one to the garden's *composition.*

Within the garden, oversize plants may upset the scale of a small garden. Yet, large flowers like peonies can attract attention inward and away from an unattractive view. Too many plants, too many colors, and too many ornaments are distracting and unsettling. Create a rhythm and movement as in a watercolor painting. For relaxation of the senses and easier maintenance, keep things simple.

The arrangement of a container garden depends upon three factors. You have to counterbalance growing conditions, weight restrictions, and available space. Refer to the written plan you've made. Linda Yang, in her excellent book *The Terrace Gardener's Handbook*—a helpful guide for all city gardeners—suggests that you use chalk to begin marking out spots on the terrace's surface where you're considering placing trees, shrubs, and flowers. This way you'll have a good idea of how all the pieces will work together.

Many landscapers suggest grouping smaller and larger containers together. On

Left: *A translucent glass wall broadens the perspective of this small courtyard by diffusing the boundaries of the space without obstructing available light.* **Right:** *Terra-cotta containers of geraniums dramatically adorn the entrance of a Charleston, South Carolina, town house.*

© Ken Druse

The technique of trompe l'oeil has been used in this garden to suggest that it extends well beyond the brick wall.

a penthouse or large terrace, a wooden platform, or dunnage may have to be erected for them to rest on so that the weight is distributed evenly. Long, thin terraces can be broken up by curvilinear arrangements of planters of multiple heights to disguise the narrowness.

How the backyard city garden is arranged, however, depends entirely on growing conditions and how much space you have. If you're planning to make a raised bed, consider first how large or small it should be in relation to the rest of the garden. Existing trees and shrubs are usually a bonus. Even fallen trees, so long as they are not rotting, can add an unusual acadian influence to the city garden. When ivies and other trailing plants are grown over them, a backyard can be transformed into a sylvan setting.

There may be a tree growing somewhat intrusively right in the middle of your small plot. But before you chop it down, consider pruning away some top growth so shade-loving flowers can grow around it. Or, you could encircle it with a Victorian cast-iron or rustic wooden tree bench.

Perspective in garden design deals with the spatial relationship of objects as they ultimately appear to the eye. This differs from scale in that perspective concerns how elements work together to draw the eye into or around the garden. Trompe l'oeil, for example, is a technique that literally "fools the eye" into believing that a painted wall is actually an extension of the garden. Latticework, painted murals, and sometimes even mirrors are combined to make the garden appear longer or larger. Using perspective, the designer can create optical illusions that create space in a small garden or enclose space in a garden with, for example, an unsightly view.

Another method of suggesting length and space is to make a path from the apartment that gets thinner as it stretches from the doorway. Tall plantings on either side of a small statue or gate at the path's end complete the illusion of depth.

COLOR, SHAPE, AND TEXTURE

An artistic approach to garden *color* resembles that of the nineteenth-century impressionist painters. With a light and subtle blending of colors, you can draw the eye around the garden. Dark objects, such as brown-stained wooden trellises, make the garden recede, while light-colored structures attract attention.

Color variety, however, is somewhat a matter of taste. What is dignified and harmonious to one person can seem boring and lifeless to another. Although many landscape designers advocate limiting color within a narrowly defined range, make a color arrangement that is ultimately going to please you. At first, beginners should limit extensive color experimentation to using fast-blooming annuals; if you're unhappy with the color scheme, something new can be tried the following year.

On the whole, pale colors are the easiest to work with. Soft, creamy whites and ivory are pretty with just about every color, and pale yellows mix nicely with mauve, lilac, and blue. Underplantings of the gray-foliaged Artemisia species and the *Senecio cineraria* (identical to dusty miller) show roses off to great advantage. When using stronger colors, always consider their intensity and the hue. Bright reds, oranges, and very strong flower colors can be used to lead the eye around the composition. Strong purples blend well with delicate mauves and pale lavenders. Scarlet and crimson look good with true white or rosy pink. Many designers advocate using strong colors in the foreground followed by a subtle fading through the spectrum in the center, finally blending to buttery pinks and soft white hues in the background.

Tropical climates offer the most luxuriant palette of brilliant colors. A big, bushy, bold magenta bougainvillea may stand beside canary-yellow allemandas and salmon-colored hibiscus flowers. Part of the magic of these gardens is that nothing

Green euonymus, reddish barberry, and golden daylilies planted below a smooth, white stone wall sculpture exemplify how color, shape, and texture combine in the well-designed garden.

© Sandra Dos Passos

seems to clash. It sometimes appears that the more variety there is in these gardens, the better they look!

However, even in those paradisiacal climates, it isn't color alone that makes the garden beautiful. In every hardiness zone, there are varieties of plants whose leaf colorations, shapes, patterns, forms, and textures can be used decoratively. My favorite variegated leafy plants are green-and-yellow hostas, glossy green-and-white hollies, and splotchy, multicolored crotons. Many gray plants like lamb's ear

are also noteworthy for their felty textures, while others, like yucca leaves, which are long and swordlike, contribute form.

The most prominent features in the garden design are trees and shrubs. Designers use the *shape* of these plants to add decorative effects to the garden. There are many wonderful shapes to work with: horizontal and somewhat rectangular like honey locust; round or flat topped and umbrella shaped like an almond; graceful weeping forms, such as cherries and willows; wedge-shaped or conical varieties

© Ken Druse

The variety of color, shape, and texture in this small corner of Victor Nelson's garden is lovely.

such as a Bradford pear; fastigiate or vertical trees, which include the majestic ginkgo; and curving and spiraling trees like crab apples, which are particularly lovely forms in the city garden.

Although they require much pruning and take time to be completed, *espaliered,* or trained trees, seem particularly appropriate in city gardens. *The Oxford Companion to Gardens* defines an espalier as "a line of fruit trees whose branches are pruned and trained into formal patterns against a wall or fence, so as to make the most of sunshine and warmth. The wall itself against which they lean can also be called an espalier." A popular use of this technique is an espalier of fruit trees on a very sunny west- or south-facing wall. But you can espalier just about anything: Espaliered camellias are particularly sophisticated, while elegant designs along an open wire or wood fence can be braided, fanned, oblique, or tiered. The Verrier espalier, named for Louis Verrier, a nineteenth-century French gardener, resembles the noble menorah. Espaliers can also be made into geometric forms—diamonds, squares, or wavy lines expressive of art nouveau.

Shadowy areas in a garden suspend uniformity and add *texture* and depth to the composition. Trees are the best natural means of achieving shade in the garden. Trellises, arbors, pergolas, and lath houses are garden structures that can add height and shape as well as shade to a design. They can be built against a wall or, as in roof gardens, placed apart in a carefully chosen position. Made of redwood, cedar, bamboo, and other treated woods or even from fiberglass, such structures can be covered with sweet peas, morning glories, wisteria, pyracantha, moonvine, and any other vine or climbing plant.

Another technique of creating shade on exposed roofs is to plant a row of hedges to cast afternoon shade. This can provide limited morning or afternoon shade for plants, such as variegated dogwood and coleus, which are less tolerant of full, all-day sunshine.

SURFACES, LAWNS, AND GROUNDCOVERS

Slate, tile, brick, stone, and wood surfacing should harmonize with a garden's planting scheme. Surfacing can play a particularly important part in covered porches. Exquisitely tiled, a floor can become a focal point in itself.

Surfaces of washed pebbles and pea gravel are recommended by many city garden designers. On small high-rise balconies, weight restrictions prohibit adding any surfacing other than what is already there. If you decide to add tile or slate to your penthouse, in most places the law dictates that the material cannot be thicker than 1 inch (2.5 centimeters). The roof should be prepared properly to avoid leakage problems later on. Mr. Van Zelst

says, "To prepare a roof properly, copper flashing all around the perimeter is necessary. If it already exists, check for holes. Old seams should be resoldered. Roof surfaces should be primed and then layered with hot tar, tar paper, and fiberglass netting. A reputable roofing company will be acquainted with these practices. Ask for a minimum of a fifteen-year guarantee."

Wooden decks are best constructed of a number of small-sized pieces of lumber for access to a roof's surface. Each plank should be light enough to be lifted by one or two people. The construction should allow for expansion of the wood. Durable woods such as redwood and cedar are

Above left: *The curving redwood deck of this San Francisco garden helps unify the design and complements a plum tree's coppery leaves in the background.*

Above right: *Tile, wood, and a dense groundcover of English ivy blend to create this roof garden by Halstead Welles.*

often used as they are most resistant to the effects of weathering. But a good carpenter can suggest just the right wood for your location.

An uneven backyard surface can be regraded, but a slope may require a raised platform. Slate can be applied to a foundation of either concrete or sand, and tiles can be used only with a concrete foundation. Bricks and cobblestones, on the other hand, require a sand base. When drainage is poor, surfaces tend to deteriorate, and a drainage pipe should be placed underneath beforehand.

Backyard walkways can be constructed of slate or flagstone in rectangular, oval, or naturally formed shapes. Particularly attractive walkways are those that are constructed of natural flagstones with moss, clover, periwinkle, or fragrant thyme protruding from the spaces in between. If there's enough direct sunlight for three hours a day, and if you have enough space for one, you might want to consider a lawn. Everything you've heard about them is true. They can be difficult to grow

and maintain, but it's such a thrill to have your own little plot of green grass just outside the back door. For small city greenswards, it is best and easiest to use purchased sod. You'll need a planed-off surface with 6 inches (15 centimeters) of topsoil to put on it. Underneath the topsoil, if necessary, place a 3-inch (7.5-centimeter) diameter drainage pipe in 3 inches of gravel.

In most sheltered gardens, however, too much shade makes growing a lawn impossible. Although many cannot be walked on, there are several groundcovers that make pretty substitutes. An excellent source for suggestions is Ortho Books's *All About Ground Covers.*

Astroturf™ is an option for those too-shady areas, but you'll be better off with the more attractive, natural groundcovers. Astroturf is impractical as it does not dry, and, as a result, it grows a fungus that can grow unprotected and turn the *faux* turf black within two years. Stay away from this artificial cover unless you are prepared to replace it after it rots.

English ivies are particularly pretty when located near city brick walls. This variety is called **Hedera helix** *'Erecta'.*

Above left: *Pots of bushy orange lantana on a flagstone terrace create a visual transition into a grassy lawn, the most prized of all ground covers. Designed by Oehme, van Sweden & Associates.* ***Above right:*** *The groundcover between city row houses can be attractively paved with flagstones.*

DESIGNING FOR YEAR ⋈ ROUND INTEREST

Many gardeners become bored and restless with what seems to be the never-ending green of midsummer. In small-space gardens, one should avoid planting flowers whose blooms will fade very quickly. Lovely as they are, lilacs, cabbage, and moss roses bloom for a very short time. Actually, there is no reason, other than poor planning, why there cannot be something flowering from early spring to late fall. Look at nature's own growing cycle: white snowdrops, pussy willows, pale yellow-green weeping willows, bright yellow forsythia, brilliant pink and red tulips, vibrant green grass, and violet-blue Jacob's ladder of spring. Melon-toned daylilies, multicolored zinnias, and a host of other annuals carry the color through the summer. Quietly colorful chrysanthemums and luminescent dahlias give way to fall's blazing red, orange, and gold, eventually fading into the rich and varied browns and grays of winter. Carefully choose your plants for their shape, color, fragrance, and timing.

When the flowers are gone and the last autumn leaves are strewn about the garden, there can be something to look forward to if you have planted for year-round interest. Autumn- and winter-flowering witch hazels (*Hamamelis* spp.) are cherished by many city gardeners. Some trees are covered in magnificently colored and patterned barks. Silvery birches and aspen, the Zelkova (*Zelkova sinica*), mottled in a plethora of green shades, white-and-gray snow gum (*Eucalyptus niphophila*), and foamy green and pink-brown lacebark pine (*Pinus bungeana*) are a few examples. The bark of the evergreen *P. nigra* looks like an opaque, brown, stained-glass window.

There are shrubs with colorful twigs in winter, such as red-twig dogwood. The leaves of andromeda (*Andromeda glaucophylla*) turn purple in winter, as do some species of juniper. The leaves of evergreens of the genus *Arctostaphylus* turn bronze in winter. Heaths and heathers will also add color to the winter landscape. Many holly plants (*Ilex* spp.) bear red and yellow berries in fall and winter.

A beautifully shaped tree is a lovely living sculpture. Some especially graceful bare winter trees are magnolias, crape myrtles, and willows. Among willows, *Salix matsudana* is recommended for its evocative, twisting shape. Like beautifully shaped bare trees and evergreens, statuary and weatherproofed ornaments add interest to a garden's design throughout the year. Looking out the window on a bleak winter night, when dramatic lighting emphasizes tree shapes, evergreens, and ornamentation, the garden will be as interesting and attractive as it is in summer.

© Sandra Dos Passos

Left: Marigolds, coleus, and other annuals can only be grown in the spring and summer. **Opposite page, above left:** *Trees and shrubs with bare branches look especially beautiful coated with ice or sparkling snow.* **Above right:** *Anemones and tulips are just a few of spring's dazzling array.* **Below right:** *Autumn's blazing leaf colors can be enjoyed just as easily in the city.* **Below left:** *Lush vines are a sure sign of summer's presence in the city.*

© Derek Fell

© Kate Bader

© Alex Roy

© Alex Roy

LIGHTING AND NIGHT GARDENS

Looking up at a clear, moonlit night sky through the bare branches of a tree, it is easy to visualize what Van Gogh painted on some of his canvases. But even when there is a full moon, does it bathe your garden in its special light? Artificial lighting can complement the soothing, tranquil nature of the nightscape and be a gentle guide to explore the mysteries of a different dimension—the night garden. Lighting shouldn't compete with the glittering city skyline, but rather, be a gracious, if not exciting, extension of it. Lighting may not be as important to your garden as it is to more decorative ones, but some outdoor lighting would make it possible for you to do garden work at night, to entertain in the garden, or to simply enjoy looking at it.

Subtlety is the key to effective lighting. You want to see what is being lit without the source of the light being visible. One has, in essence, the ability to recreate an entirely new garden out of the darkness. There are many features that are not always visible during the day, and these can be played up to full advantage at night. Night lighting is best used to create and accentuate garden aspects such as the shadow of a beautiful tree, a curious configuration of twigs, a tiny statue, or a neoclassical pillar overflowing with sparkling white clematis. The right lighting can turn a weeping willow into a shimmering fountain of light. Arbors and other garden structures are strong features to highlight. Additionally, illuminating gargoyles, chimneys, eaves, gables, dormer windows, columns, and architectural features like decorative friezes, capitals, and tympanums on neighboring buildings can add a spectacular dimension to the night garden. Just as you can use light to bring out shape and form, you can use darkness to block out what you don't want to see.

Electric wiring should be concealed for aesthetics as well as safety, and it must be impervious to water. There are lighting kits available, but do not compromise quality

© Balthazar Korab/Design: Dan Kiley Landscape Architecture

Lit from below, this bosk of little-leaf linden trees in the Hamilton Garden of Columbus, Indiana, is very alluring. Even in daylight, the silhouettes of the tree branches stand out like living sculptures. Designed by Dan Kiley.

for cost. Gardeners are cautioned not to attempt installation without professional advice—an electrician is mandatory. Electricians, however, are not designers. It is better to consult a professional landscape-illumination specialist to achieve the results you want.

Lighting systems can be manually or automatically controlled by timers or photocells, which are solar-powered devices that turn lights on at dusk, off at daybreak. There are also some computer software programs being developed for automatic operation of garden lighting. Remote-control switches can be conveniently located inside the apartment so you can enjoy night views from inside, and dimmers offer flexibility.

Tiny, low-voltage lights very often are used to illuminate trees. Landscape-lighting designers prefer incandescent white light. These masters of illumination have innumerable filters for capturing the romance of the night garden. While one filter attempts to duplicate the color of moonlight, another can create flesh-flattering tones for down-lighting a dining table.

Other popular garden lighting fixtures include Japanese lanterns, the Mexican tin *lampion* with pinpoint holes for light filtration, and antique and other lighting fixtures, which can be mounted on the outside wall of your apartment. For the sole enjoyment of them after night falls, landscape architect Charlotte Frieze of New York City suggests adding plants with iridescent and evening-fragrant flowers. Dogwoods, birches, white-flowered periwinkles, lilies, impatiens, caladiums, azaleas, and rhododendrons show up well at night. I recommend the exotic smell of night-blooming jasmine, night-blooming cactus, creeping rosemary, or evening primrose. There are some fragrant, night-blooming orchids that grow in tropical gardens. Other flowers with heavenly scents include nicotiana, petunias, stephanotis, wisteria, freesia, hyacinth, and many other trumpet-shaped flowers.

The Lure of Fragrance

And because the breath of flowers is far sweeter in the air (where it comes and goes like the warbling of music) than in the hand, therefore nothing is more fit for that delight, than to know what be the flowers and plants that do best perfume the air.

—Francis Bacon, *Of Gardens*

By all means, locate a few fragrant plants near seating areas to enhance the appeal of your garden. Like most herbs, many plants have aromatic leaves. Use this list to select the most fragrant plants.

Common Name	Latin Name	Description
Angel's Trumpet*	*Datura* spp.	Heavy musk
Bachelor's button	*Centaurea imperialis*	Light and airy
Carnation	*Dianthus* spp.	
Creeping Rosemary*	*Rosmarinus officinalis*	Herbaceous
Freesia*	*Freesia x Kewensis*	Delicate
Gardenia	*Gardenia jasminoide*	Sweet and heavy
Geranium (scented)*	*Pelargonium*	Lemon or rose
Globe thistle*	*Eclrinops exaltatus*	
Hyacinth	*Muscari* bulbs	
Jasmine	*Jasminium* spp.	Springtime perfume
Lavender	*Lavandula* spp.	Sweet and heavy
Orange and lemon trees	*Citrus* spp.	
Pot Marigold	*Calendula*	Earthy
Rose*	*Rose* varieties	
Stephanotis	*Stephanotis floribunda*	Fresh and flowery
True Sweet Bay Laurel	*Laurus nobilis*	Herbaceous
Wisteria	*Wisteria sinensis*	Light and sweet

*Use for fragrance at night

Grape Hyacinth

Bachelor's Button

CHAPTER FOUR

CITY STYLES

FORMAL

INFORMAL

MINIMALIST

ORIENTAL

SHADE GARDENS

FRUIT AND VEGETABLE GARDENS

SCULPTURE GARDENS

COMMUNITY GARDENS

© Ken Druse

In the classic book *The Principles of Gardening* (Simon & Schuster: New York, 1984), Hugh Johnson equates straight edges and architecture with formal gardens and flowing and naturalistic forms with informal gardens. He writes that "modern . . . and small gardens frequently have no straight lines or traditional formality, yet their flowing forms are definitely not of nature's making. Their spiritual ancestors are the works of Mondrian, Picasso or [Henry] Moore."

Johnson recognizes that a garden's style takes its cues from painting and sculpture and emphasizes the need for the design to take these artistic techniques into account in a garden's plan. Therefore, a garden's style can reflect the artistic tenets of a particular era or culture. Additionally, Johnson's comparison of a garden to architecture is particularly applicable to the city garden. Because your garden is located amid buildings, it is appropriate for you to relate its style to that of its surroundings. You can also choose to juxtapose the garden's style with the look of the city, further highlighting its unique qualities.

Whether you are starting from scratch in the backyard or working with an old, or neglected garden, begin thinking about your garden in one of two ways: as a means of recreating the outdoor landscape of a bygone era or as something completely new. If your site is new, you might want to model your garden on historic gardens in the area. If you are adapting an existing garden, consider what residents may have done with the space before. Some roof and terrace gardens, for example, have existed since the 1920s. However, the weight of masonry construction, soil, and water damage are forcing these lovely old gardens, one by one, out of existence. Because of more stringent building codes and ordinances, owners are being compelled to grow plants only in containers.

If you happen to be one of these romantic souls who prefers the lovely antique appearance of a rooftop garden, but is being forced to comply to building codes

This is an outstanding example of dignified city terrace design that relates the garden to its surroudings. The superimposed balustrade acts on a nexus; the eye is then led outward to the city's architecture.

Courtesy Morgan Wheelock Inc. Landscape Architects

In this outdoor space, a variety of structural forms and gravel surfaces establish the modern design scheme. Evocative neon lighting is an exciting and appropriate alternative to traditional lamps.

A nineteenth century limestone bust, a period bench, brick, marble, and terra-cotta surfaces, and a profusion of cascading ivy, tulips, daisies, foxgloves, and hyacinths lend an old-fashioned richness to this restored period garden.

(see page 22), there is good news. At a symposium on landscape architecture trends in 1987, Diane Kostial McGuire, renowned landscape architect and garden adviser to Dumbarton Oaks in Washington, D.C., said, "One doesn't have to wipe the blackboard clean—the garden isn't just one more place where our culture and heritage have to be sacrificed." Fortunately, there is now a great surge in preserving the appearance of these old city gardens.

Those converting their old penthouses to container gardens might easily be able to conserve the original design by duplicating the masonry or brick in fiberglass façades and attaching them to new, wooden containers. Weatherproof, simulated brick and mortar wallboard can be erected (with weep holes for drainage) to resemble the original masonry walls, behind which new containers can be placed.

If you have a ground-level garden and live near a landmark or in an area of historic preservation, you might also want to consider a period restoration design. If alterations have been made to the original home site over the centuries, you may even wish to recreate a period garden that previous occupants might have enjoyed. Botanical garden libraries and historical societies can be good sources from which to learn more about garden history.

If you want or need a completely new garden, however, chances are you'll have to develop slowly from old to new. Starting entirely from scratch can be prohibitively expensive—combine the old containers with the new to get started. Over time, you can do away with the elements of the garden that don't suit you.

For best results, I recommend contacting a landscape architect. You can find one through the local chapter of the Society of Landscape Architects. In conjunction with a landscape professional, you can create a container garden using lightweight soil mixtures and containers with façades resembling the old, heavy masonry. In this way, historical flavor can be preserved.

FORMAL

Perhaps the truest forerunner of today's formal urban garden is the walled Persian *pardes*, or paradise garden. In the scorching heat, a highly controlled, rectangular space was created, which was crisscrossed with four water courses that met in the center. The entire space was walled in. Within the confines of these very elegant gardens, royalty lounged in the soothing shade of porticoes and surrounding trees.

In the Italian Renaissance villa landscape tradition, the connection between architecture and garden was integral and apparent. The garden's contours followed the geometric lines of the architecture. Viewed from any angle, a garden's symmetrical visual field dominated the composition. At Versailles, the French extended and expanded on the concept by transforming a great expanse of land into a masterfully planned garden that exemplifies the extent to which nature can be artfully manipulated.

Even in the modern urban garden, the tenets of formality—geometry, order, structure, and control—are evident. In admiring such well-executed designs, one senses the presence of the clarity, logic, and philosophy of Rene Descartes, mathematician and cofounder of analytical geometry. Borders of boxwood and yew, clipped hedges, trained plants, and topiary— the epitome of control — are common in the formal garden. Sleek, elegant, or period-inspired furniture and ornamentation complement the design.

In introducing symmetry to create a formal garden, you will have to arrange all garden elements so that they are proportionately situated. For example, if you have a clipped hedge of Korean box, a nearby bench must be placed parallel to the hedge. Additionally, the bench should be perfectly centered along the length of the hedge. Paths must be perfectly straight and should be constructed of uniformly spaced and shaped paving materials.

Sculptural and other decorative features must also conform to the basic formal plan. For example, if there is a sculpture of Venus to the right of the path, there should be one of Adonis situated equidistant from the path to the left. If there are three ornate terra-cotta planters, each should be identical and they should be geometrically aligned; if they are arranged in a straight line, they should be evenly spaced. Each planter should contain the same color combinations and be of the same design. For instance, each planter could contain pink verbenas growing in the center, edged by red verbenas.

Formal designs also demand that flowers be planted in rows or neatly defined areas. The beds are rigorously, geometrically patterned. Begonias, salvias, geraniums, ageratum, zinnias, chrysanthemums, and dusty miller are commonly used, because they provide a reliable block of color that continues to bloom all season long. Borders should be clipped and contoured to contribute to the overall symmetry. For instance, if you plant a bed of tall pink begonias on one side of a path, there should be an identically colored bed of begonias of the same height on the other side of the path.

During the process of planning a formal garden, always think in terms of harmonic proportions. If you feel you need more tangible inspiration, you could visit an exemplary formal garden in your region. Your local horticultural society or botanical garden library can provide you with more information.

© Sandra Dos Passos

The lines throughout this small formal garden located in Savannah, Georgia, follow the rectangular, architectural shape. Beds are uniformly shaped and evenly spaced apart.

INFORMAL

*T*he eighteenth-century philosopher and writer Jean Jacques Rousseau believed that the human being and the garden alike should be allowed to develop free of limiting intervention. Building on the momentum of such a philosophy, the romantic period of the nineteenth century was attracted to and fueled by a deep reverence for the informal, untamed beauty of nature. Ironically, however, it was in a London garden and not in the pastoral English countryside that John Keats wrote his famous "Ode to a Nightingale."

During the eighteenth and early nineteenth centuries in Europe, people came to believe that garden formality itself should be restrained. Plants were allowed to grow out. There was a new feeling for natural meandering and undulating forms. The popularity of this style has given rise to a variety of informal designs from the rustic style populated with simple yet appealing wooden furniture to the wild garden, a self-sustaining native-plant environment first proposed by William Robinson in 1870 in his book *The Wild Garden*.

The asymmetry of an informal garden is the essence of its design. "Your planning should expose the inherent forms of nature," says garden writer Edwin T. Morris. The purpose is to expose and highlight the natural growth patterns of plants. Therefore, the informal urban garden takes on a more free-form look and allows nature to create an ever-changing array of shapes. Patterns are more organic than the square, triangle, or rectangle forms found in the formal garden, and the natural shapes of plants create spatial, and even symbolic, relationships. For example, a clump of silvery artemesia resembling the shape of a drop of water can create natural garden symbolism. Despite the free use of shapes, colors, and textures, even an informal garden has to be planned. Unlike a formal garden, however, the plan is harder to detect. The gardener must draw up a planting plan to achieve a pleasing variety

Victor Nelson's informal Manhattan roof garden has been entirely created from a clever arrangement of containers. One contains a willow, a dogwood, and a birch tree. Others feature azaleas, lilies, hostas, violets, and ferns.

of textures, heights, and shapes. You may have apricot roses growing in front of a wall of ivy with creamy foxgloves, shell-pink phlox, and silvery, fernlike *centaurea gymnocarpa* in the foreground.

To begin planning, decide where plants should be raised and where they should be left at ground level. Colors should be artfully blended with one another. Warm colors should be kept together. A good warm-color balance, for instance, is a container of red and magenta geraniums combined with orange-red zinnias and coralbells. Similarly, cool colors should be combined. Clematis, hollyhocks, lavender, and delphiniums blend for a cool blue look. Gardens landscaped with flowers of only one color say, white, are considered informal. But it takes a lot of skill to effectively achieve this look.

Wild gardens are informal, but their plants are selected for interesting shapes, colors, and contours. A mix of plant types is emphasized, and subtle masses of color are encouraged. The wild-garden plan involves using native plants because they are well suited to a region's climate and require less cultivation. In this environment, plants' shapes and hues interact to create subtly beautiful vignettes. In general, the wild garden is a more relaxed outdoor space that brings a spot of nature into the urban setting.

In informal schemes, paths undulate and plantings such as Virginia creeper or ivy trail casually across paths. Oak chips or varying types of fieldstones can create pathways. The furniture and ornamentation in informal gardens shouldn't interfere with the plantings or natural elements and should blend in as much as possible. Trees, rather than elaborate structures, are used for shade.

Furnishings can range from the intentionally rustic to simple and unpretentious selections, which are placed in naturally occurring hollows or where a weeping tree arches. Ornamentation is kept to a minimum. You might decoratively display large natural rocks to show their grain, striation, or naturally occurring crystalline forms, such as quartz or calcite. Birdfeeders and sundials—garden accessories that relate directly to nature—are also appropriate ornaments for the informal garden. Ornamentation can also include tree stumps fringed with delicately colored lichen, fungi, and mushrooms. There are several that resemble underwater algae, sea coral, and lacy aquatic plants. Some exquisite examples include the aptly named coral fungus (Clavicorona pyxidata) and the speckled, rubbery Dryad's saddle, (Polyporus squamosus).

Beds and containers should be filled (but not overcrowded) with shrubs and perennials and underplanted with groundcovers. By adhering to a relaxed garden plan that incorporates a few rustic touches, it is possible to capture the feeling of being out in the country.

© Ken Druse

This lush rooftop wild garden features purple loose strife and perky black-eyed Susans.

MINIMALIST

A single palm tree leaps out as the only natural element, when featured against blocks of primary colors.

Perfectly embodying the principles of minimalist garden design, this Mondrian-esque garden uses plantings as a focal point, juxtaposes diverse textures, and delineates crisp lines.

The roots of minimalist landscaping probably extend as far back as Stonehenge. However, the contemporary applications of minimalist landscape design grew out of the 1960s minimalist movement in painting and sculpture. Evocative of the later works of Mondrian, minimalist design stresses line, shape, color, and contrast.

Expressed in stone and tile, a minimalist garden is like architecture without a ceiling. With the emphasis on the use of walls and water, planting is restricted in deference to the visual importance of the sharp architectural line of a brightly colored wall. Water is used for its mirroring quality. A long trough, for example, can be used to reflect surrounding buildings or moving clouds. The overall effect is one of conscious serenity. Luis Barragan, architect and minimalist garden designer, says, "In my fountains, silence sings."

The manipulation of space through color and form is also an objective of the minimalist garden. Walls are painted vibrant coral, purple, pink, and lemon hues, which interact to enlarge and shrink space in interesting ways. Sculpturally formed plants like trees with twisted trunks, cacti, and spears of agaves and phormiums can be silhouetted against walls to create contrasts of color and shape.

Interpreting Barragan's ideas for city gardens, landscape architect Charlotte Frieze says, "In a small space you can have a great deal of interest without having too many elements in that space. There is usually just one focal point in the garden, perhaps a trickling fountain. A solitary cherry tree or Japanese maple against a plain background is fabulous. Dense groundcovers such as pachysandra and myrtle can be grown in masses. And the way edges of the stone pavement and the plant material meet is important." Texture can be introduced by mixing differing clumps or tufts of ornamental grasses. For instance, you could mix buff-colored cloud grass (*Agrostis nebulosa*) with green-flowering pearl grass, (*Briza maxima*). Shimmering feather grass (*Stipa pennata*) makes a nice contrast with richly structured, dark lavender statice (*Limonium* spp.).

ORIENTAL

Familiar elements of Oriental garden design are evergreens, azaleas, pines, and rocks and gravel. If space permits, a stone lantern and a pool of goldfish can also be included.

A practical and aesthetic solution to the limited space of city gardens is to create an Oriental-inspired design. Chinese and Japanese garden arts imbue each element with symbolic association. Therefore, even a small space can have great significance and beauty. Says landscape architect Charlotte Frieze, "These gardens are very spiritual. They are meant to offer an experience of transcending everyday life." Oriental gardens were admired by Western visitors and then copied in Europe and North America. One such example is the Japanese garden in Golden Gate Park in San Francisco. And small Japanese gardens began to be added to big estate gardens in the early twentieth century such as those built in Newport, Rhode Island.

Oriental gardens are meant to be sanctuaries of nature, associated with old, refined ways of life and traditions, such as those practiced by Chinese rulers and Buddhist monks. According to Edwin T. Morris, who leads yearly garden tours to China and is the author of *The Gardens of China: History, Art and Meanings,* "Walking into an Oriental garden should be like walking into an Oriental painting. They avoid symmetry, as should the garden designer."

Each of the four seasons is meant to be represented in the Oriental garden. This results in extensive use of evergreens and rocks so that there is year-round color. The garden is used almost like an outdoor room, where such events in nature as moonrises and the blossoming of flowers can be observed and contemplated.

Japanese

A woman once asked a Japanese gardener what gardening meant to him. He smiled and held up his pruning shears! Contrary to what many believe, a Japanese garden can require high maintenance. Such gardens are not formal in the geometric sense, but everything is pruned and very tightly controlled. Although highly contrived, the relative positioning of elements reflects their natural counterparts. For example, in a dry rock garden, rocks, gravel, and sand are positioned to mirror the proportions of a water-bordered landscape.

In addition to each component in the garden having symbolic value—as a mirror of an element in nature—there are four different kinds of garden styles: the dry rock garden, the literary men's garden, the water garden, and the tea garden. The dry rock garden is designed for meditation and the only plants used are mosses. The literary men's garden is generally small and is planned for quiet thought. In the water garden, rocks and plants are placed to lead the viewer through a progression around and over the water. The tea garden serves as an entrance path for the tea ceremony.

Traditionally, paths in Japanese gardens are fraught with significance and are used in all arrangements. In the days when Japan was divided up by feuding warlords and their samurai, the garden path leading up to the teahouse was called "the dewy path." Made of carefully chosen

© Kate Bader

If designed for meditation, Japanese dry rock gardens require only gravel, rock arrangements, and mosses.

rocks and stones and sprinkled with water, the path was said to cause all who walked on it to forget the animosity of the times by concentrating on the dewiness of the approach to the teahouse. The path represents the virtues of restraint, politeness, sensibility, and modesty. Weapons, were mandatorily left at the garden's entrance, and no political conversations were allowed in the garden or teahouse. A squat granite lantern usually lit the path.

Other common elements are fine, smooth-edged white gravel, broken shells, or river stone used among the plantings. They can be laid in a curving manner to highlight plant material. If the element of water is missing, rocks are sometimes arranged to imitate a meandering river bed of dry stone, or the gravel combed to suggest ripples of water. Randomly imbedded granite rocks symbolize a feeling of depth and strength held in reserve.

A predominance of green plants are used in Japanese gardens because color variations are kept to a minimum. Even the much-used azalea is pruned to appear marbleized. Dwarf pines, junipers, conifers, and smaller bamboos suit the Japanese-style city garden perfectly. Groundcovers include grass and mosses, which the Japanese like to use because of their rich coloration and patina. Flowering plants are used sparingly. Those most often chosen are chrysanthemums, gardenias, and water lilies. Although they must fit the scale of your particular site, flowering cherry, plum, peach, and crab-apple trees, whose spreading boughs remain green throughout most of the year, are appropriate in Japanese designs.

© Ken Druse

Water lilies are often planted in Japanese gardens. If you do not have room for a pool, try growing water lilies that are hardy to your area in insulated half-whiskey barrels.

Chinese

Chinese gardening style is relatively rare in North American cities, which is unfortunate. Such gardens are easier to maintain than Japanese gardens, and in many ways suit the city life-style better. Though similar to Japanese gardens in that both glorify nature, the Chinese prefer more color, both in plant materials and furnishings. Plantings are looser and allowed to grow out more freely. The irregular form of the azalea shrub is considered interesting, and the plant is allowed to grow freely, unlike in Japanese gardens.

The composition of Chinese designs is asymmetrical. One often sees pairs of high and low trees or big and small stones situated together, reflecting the design principle of the "guest-host" relationship. Paths are often paved with river stones, which, according to the Chinese, should look as if a bolt of brocade has been unraveled across the garden. An "ocean" of terra-cotta paving or tiling is also used as a hard surface so that is swirls around rock and plant materials.

Typically, seating is a sturdy, hollow, barrellike ceramic. Ming blue, turquoise, canary yellow, and Chinese red are the preferred colors, which are then glazed for a luminous finish. Four holes on top of the seat allow puddles to drain off the surface after a rain shower.

Symbolism in Chinese gardens is manifested in the use of rocks to evoke the nine sacred peaks of China. Groups of rocks

Opposite left: A carefully positioned rock becomes the focal point of a Chinese garden scheme. Trees frame this irregularly shaped feature. Opposite right: In a variation on penjing, *a ceramic container holds a vignette representing towering mountain peaks surrounded by trees.*

Right: The understated quality of Oriental schemes is exemplified by this richly textured paving. A variety of shapes and sizes of stones are interlocked on both horizontal and vertical axes. Far right: An "ocean" of complexly patterned paving, an evocative tree, and a simple bench create a meditative setting. Below: An evergreen loquat tree is the perfect ornamental touch in a Chinese design.

are often placed together and used to evoke a hilly and mountainous landscape. Sometimes a "landscape" of jutting rocks is set on a marble tray. Such a composition is called a *penjing*. Additionally, tiny sprigs or dwarf pine seedlings might be stuck into rock crevices on the tray. Circular lattice-work and rounded ornamental grilles can be used in Chinese city garden design to create the classic moongate.

Aside from their beauty, plants are valued for their symbolism in Chinese gardens. Bamboo, for example, represents resiliency. There are many very hardy bamboos. Two that are grown successfully in cities are golden bamboo (*Phylostachys aurea*) and hard-running bamboo (*Phylostachys nuda*). Additionally, peach tree flowers, which bloom on naked wood in early spring before the leaves appear, are a symbol of rebirth. Chrysanthemums evoke a Mandarin poet, Tao Yuan-ming, who chose to leave a civil service position to live close to nature. He had to survive in adversity just as chrysanthemums have to bloom in cool weather. Perhaps the most beloved of all flowers is the lotus, which is the embodiment of purity. An eleventh-century poem states that the lotus "rises from foul mud and is not defiled."

Appropriate trees for a Chinese city garden are dwarf pines, juniper cypress, small willows, magnolias, and wintersweet (*Chimonanthus praecox*), which smells like jasmine and blooms in late winter or early spring. The Chinese also love fruit trees. Choices include plum (their national flower), evergreen loquat, litchi (*Nephelium litchi*), orange, peach, and brilliant, red-berried pomegranate trees. Among flowers and shrubs, rosy azaleas, rhododendrons, gardenias, carnations, narcissus, camellias, forsythia, daphne, lilacs, crape myrtle, and the climbing rose (*Rosa banksiae*) are used in profusion. Other popular flowers are peonies, daylilies, irises, morning glories, poppies, dwarf water lilies, and China asters.

SHADE GARDENS

This shady garden incorporates diverse elements including cherry blossoms, yellow flowering broom, and basket of gold. Sun and shade patterns were studied to ensure that each plant receives an appropriate amount of light.

Strangely enough, shady city backyards are sometimes more bosklike than their sunny suburban counterparts. A lack of sunlight doesn't necessarily prevent plants from flourishing. Look at the underbrush in the Amazon!

Designing a shade garden depends on what sort of trees or obstacles are creating the shadow. During spring and summer, scrutinize the overshadowing to determine how the amount of sunlight differs during the day and how it shifts from spot to spot. Some shade-loving plants require more light than others do, and your design will need to conform to the patterns of filtered light and dense shading to accommodate the plants you want to grow. Moreover, you might notice dry, shady conditions on a windswept roof but damp shade in the backyard. While some sites have enough sunlight to grow flowers and ground-covers, other sites are so dark that little more than ferns and decorative mosses will grow.

After assessing conditions, plantings should be selected to suit the mood of the location, which is influenced by the tracery of tree branches and the shape and height of the tree canopy. So much has been written lately on shade plantings that your best bet is to look in the local botanical garden and horticultural society book shops for any publications written about suggested shade plantings specifically for your region.

Plants that thrive in damp, shady conditions are ferns, mosses, blue or white gentians, primroses, marsh marigolds, camellias, and hydrangea quercifolia. For dry, shady conditions, try euphorbias, the foam flower (*Tiarella cordifolia*), foxgloves, the aucuba (*Aucuba japonica*), butchers broom, and pachysandra. Vincas and hostas are good choices for both situations.

FRUIT AND VEGETABLE GARDENS

Space is so tight in city gardens that if you're seriously interested in growing a large variety of vegetables, your best bet is to join an urban community vegetable garden (see page 69). It's also a great way to learn. However, there's no reason you can't create a pretty little snippet of fruits and vegetables on a roof or sunny south-facing terrace.

Increasingly, fruits and vegetables are being bred especially for small-scale gardens. The Bushstar hybrid is a small variety of cantaloupe, while Burpee offers a Missouri midget. There are also many dwarf fruit trees. Among vegetables, cute dwarf carrots (with feathery tops that look like Queen Anne's lace) and cherry tomatoes are very suitable for the urban produce plot.

You probably have more vertical than horizontal space for growing vegetables and fruits. Walls, fences, arbors, poles, and pergolas can be covered with peas, string beans, lima beans, cucumbers, and grapes. Strawberries and raspberries are popular city growers. Sunflowers, corn, red rhubarb, tomatoes, and asparagus are some taller candidates that can do double duty to shade less light-tolerant herbs, flowers, and vegetables growing beneath them.

With excellent results, Cindy Olson, a veteran city vegetable grower, horticulturist, and owner of C.O.R.E. Landscape Contracting, has been disobeying the old rule of planting rows a foot (30.48 centimeters) or more apart. She is able to grow food plants closely together, because her site has very good air circulation. But, Ms. Olson admits that she is very attentive. She constantly inspects for pests or any signs of disease and regularly sprays the undersides of leaves and cleans debris away. "A nice, healthy garden will attract fewer pests and diseases. Be observant!" she advises. One sure way to avoid overcrowding is by planting only a few seedlings. If you are starting from seed, plant no more than half a dozen of them. Or, plant half the packet and thin out weaker plants as they begin to sprout. Ms. Olson has grown zucchini and violets, curly parsley, basil, upright onions, lettuces, tomatoes, nasturtiums, glorious red cabbages, and a companion planting of marigolds (to ward off pests) all in the same small lot.

An efficient approach in small city spaces is to add vegetables for their decorative as well as edible attributes. Most leafy vegetables are beautifully shaped and colored. Many edible flowers and plants are quite lovely. Among the prettiest are pea, bean, okra, and squash blossoms. Some have very lovely fragrances. Spark the design with brightly colored chili, cherry, and bell peppers.

Children can have a lot of fun growing vegetables with you. They enjoy planting things and watching them come up soon afterward; having their own small garden gives them a special feeling of pride when it does produce. Cucumbers, lettuces, beans, and herbs grow very quickly. Test your fruits and vegetables for ripeness as you would in a produce market. They should smell ripe and be firm but not hard. Ms. Olson recommends twisting off, rather than wrenching or pulling, fruits and vegetables from the top of the stem. She uses scissors or pinches off fresh herbs between her thumb and forefinger. *The Beautiful Food Garden: Encyclopedia of Attractive Food Plants* by Kate Rogers Gessert, suggests landscape uses for food plants.

© Derek Fell

Fruit trees grow very well in containers. You can grow a fruit tree that isn't hardy in your area by leaving it outside only in the summer. To keep it thriving all year, however, you should position it at a window exposure that allows for exactly as much light as the plant needs.

SCULPTURE GARDENS

Above left: In a Georgetown, Washington, D.C., garden, a Chagall is framed in lush greenery and contrasted with a gravel-covered seating area.
Above right: Highlighted by a backdrop of single-form red oleanders, Max Ernst's In the Streets of Athens *decorates Peggy Guggenheim's sculpture garden in Venice, Italy.*

Early seventeenth-century gardens in Holland consisted mainly of stonework, sculpture, and urns, with perhaps a single tree for greenery. Having flowers in the garden was even frowned upon. Later on, of course, the Dutch fell in love with flowering bulbs. The seventeenth-century Italian island garden of Isola Bella was originally designed to resemble a floating geometric, stone galleon, with few plantings, drifting across Lake Maggiore. The Bomarzo sculpture garden at Villa Orsini in Lazio, Italy, is a collection of grotesque stone figures and fantastical beasts. Not merely a repository for sculpture, the garden was meant to be interpreted as a series of cryptic allusions to sixteenth-century and classical literature.

Possibly the best example of a modern sculpture garden attached to a city residence can be seen at the Palazzo Venier di Leoni, which belonged to Peggy Guggenheim. Located along the Grand Canal in Venice, Italy, the house is now a museum, filled with her astonishing collection of modern art. In 1982, Italian architect Giorgio Bellavitis designed the adjoining garden to display works of art, including pieces by Max Ernst, Alberto Giacometti, and Claire Falkenstein. Made of masonry and Belgian block, the garden has trees, shrubs, and stone and marble seating.

One doesn't have to have art works of modern or old-master craftsmanship as a reason to create a sculpture garden. Antique shops, galleries, and art schools are a good source for creations. Carvings and constructions of stone, wood, bronze, copper, metal, and even found objects can be used. Sculpture gardens require a minimum of maintenance. The most challenging aspect is selecting the right piece or pieces to fit the sense of place and, most importantly, to fit the scale of the site and to place them decorously.

Most sculpture gardens have hard surfaces. Contrasts can be created by juxtaposing cobbles, pebbles, and gravel with concrete, brick, or tile designs. Unless the seat itself is a specially carved work of art, unobtrusive seating is suggested. Plantings, of course, are optional. A groundcover or a wall overrun with an evergreen vine can be handsome focal points.

COMMUNITY GARDENS

In much of early Western culture, gardens were created and tended communally. Medieval monks and nuns healed and fed themselves with the herbs and edibles that grew in their cloistered gardens. During World War II, civilians worked together to create the celebrated victory garden.

"It can be important for people who move into a neighborhood to become part of the community," says Carrie Maher, director of the Lotus Community Garden in New York City. One way to get to know your neighbors and to meet new people is by joining in the fun of an urban community garden. "In this case, people are sharing in something of beauty. Gardens are social places that seem to form their own 'families.' After all, Adam and Eve, the first couple, met in a garden," says Maher.

In 1982, The Trust for Public Land and luxury condominium developer, Bill Zeckendorf with Ms. Maher created the concept of the 7,000-square-foot (2,130-square meter) Lotus Garden. Residents overlook the garden that sits over the condominium's garage. More than thirty volunteers actively garden there. Open from 8 A.M. to nightfall, access is free to garden participants and building residents.

The garden is a lush oasis in the concrete canyons of Upper Manhattan. There are forty-two trees, shrubs, and vines and more than one hundred perennials growing. There is an herb garden, a rock garden, and a berry patch. A native plant and woodland area has recently been added with shade-loving flowers and ferns. Pathways of oak chips meander throughout the garden, which is decorated with rock ornaments, moss and fungi-covered tree stumps. Several benches provide resting places to contemplate the garden. There are even two ponds, graced with water lilies and lotuses and filled with exotic fish. The diversity of such a community garden illustrates the virtually unlimited design and plant possibilities for the urban setting.

Joining a community garden is a great way to learn gardening, and to meet people.

One of the oldest community gardens in Manhattan, this little slice of Eden is located in Greenwich Village. Although the residents of the area do not tend this garden themselves, they arrange for its design and ongoing maintenance.

CHAPTER FIVE

FINISHING TOUCHES

ORNAMENTS

FURNISHINGS

WATER FEATURES

GARDENING ARTS

THE URBAN WILDLIFE GARDEN

© Ken Druse

ORNAMENTS

Ornamentation can be used either as a focal point or as an accent. The sundial depicted here acts as an eye-catching yet integral focal point in this quaint herb and vegetable garden.

In his book *Room Outside: A New Approach to Garden Design* (Thames Hudson Books: London, 1985), the British landscape architect John Brookes writes, ''Ornamentation should be integrated with the design of the garden, and the accents it provides should not look as if they were applied as an afterthought. . . . Both the scale and the colour of the ornamentation should fit the character of the setting.'' Unless you are deliberately planning an architectural, sculpture garden where plants take second place, ornamentation should be used selectively and

sparingly. Ornaments are most effective when they don't dominate the plantings, but rather, are used as focal points. Small-scale ornaments, for example, belong in small gardens, while a well-planned combination of large and small pieces belong in larger spaces.

In elevated gardens, where weight is always a primary consideration, avoid heavy materials such as stone and lead when choosing large statuary and containers. There are a great variety of light-weight replicas that are much more suitable for your conditions. In backyard

gardens, where any material can be supported, don't get carried away and choose ornaments that will be out of scale with your garden's design.

Garden-ornament sellers have many items from which to choose. If there aren't any bona-fide garden ornament merchants in your city, many major dealers ship by mail order (see ''Sources and Useful Addresses''). Appropriate selections for city gardens can include small urns and obelisks. There are finials in pineapple, pinecone, and ball shapes as well as carved stone bowls, baskets, and vases of

This wall niche holding a brass vase of hyacinths illustrates one of the many ways that space for special garden ornamentation can be built into a garden's design.

A cobalt-blue urn provides a bright accent in this garden space.

fruits and flowers. Small busts can be placed atop pedestals, while pedestals themselves make very attractive garden ornaments. You can find copies from virtually every period: ancient, Greek, Gothic, Renaissance, baroque, Victorian, art nouveau, Bauhaus, modern, and postmodern.

Mythical creatures such as gods and beasts also are popular items—a baby unicorn, for example, would enchant children. Turtles, frogs, birds, and armadillos are available in wood, fiberglass, and stone, while an Oriental foo dog comes in various materials. There are many lovely hand-painted ceramics from Italy, Spain, and Portugal (which would have to be brought indoors in cold climates). Lion heads and fox heads fashioned out of stone, rosette- and vegetal-patterned plaques, sun dials, and faces of the sun or moon can be mounted on exterior walls.

To please your artistic sensibilities, create a landscaped corner for a special sculpture, or search for just the right piece to ornament a planting area. Modern sculpture can be commissioned or purchased in an art gallery. Period garden sculptures are often sold at auction houses, and with a little imagination, one can find an endless array of objects at flea markets, country auctions, and antiques shops.

Your garden should delight all the senses, and the value of sound shouldn't be ignored. To take advantage of every aspect of nature in adding ornamentation, hang wind chimes or copper or bronze Chinese bells, which will provide soothing music at all times of day. Wall fountains, too, with recirculating pumps powered by electricity produce the tranquil resonance of gurgling water.

FURNISHINGS

This unfinished bench contributes an orderly yet informal feeling to this urban garden corner.

Evoking the charm of the Old South, recreations of antique wrought-iron furniture are particularly suitable for city gardens in that region.

Above : *It is difficult to believe that this lush, comfortable garden, whose style hints at Mexico and the Caribbean, exists on a city terrace in a northern city.*

Garden furnishings include chairs, benches, stools, and tables. Furnishings should harmonize with the design scheme, rather than glaringly stand out. Woody, natural colors blend in while white furniture attracts attention to itself. To avoid letting the furniture become the centerpiece of the garden, place it near trees, which also provide welcome shade on a hot, sunny day.

Garden furniture can be formal or informal. The formal sort looks rather like traditional interior furnishings. The lines are crisp and elegant, with backs, arms, and legs which are carved or decorative. Benches are often modeled after the classical designs of the ancient world. Informal furniture has a relaxed, country feeling to it. Old chairs can be hand painted in the country style with hearts and ducks. Wooden garden furniture is available in an array of regional and rustic designs—rough-hewn and bent-willow seats are particularly attractive and contribute to the garden theme. Another long-forgotten "seat," is the old-fashioned wooden swing, secured with ropes hanging from a sturdy tree branch and located over a soft carpet of greenery.

Wicker furniture is a common choice, but is good only in warm, dry climates. Painted and rust-proofed wrought-iron pieces are a good choice for city gardens as they are durable and easy to care for. These furnishings are often crafted with lacelike patternings that make them fine decorative features for a city garden. Because they can be left outside all year long, weather-treated redwood, cedar, oak, teak, and mahogany, however, are your best choices for materials. If you choose wooden tables and chairs, cover the chair bottoms with comfortable, waterproof chintz-covered cushions that can be tied on and removed in winter. For elevated gardens, furniture must be heavy enough to withstand winds; it should have an open, slatted design so that wind blows through it. Additionally, outdoor furniture must be easy to clean.

WATER FEATURES

Perhaps more so than in any other type of garden, the use of water in urban gardens has a far-reaching design impact. Water adds an authentic touch of nature to the city environment by nurturing the life that grows within it, whether it is plants, animals, or both. In the same way that contrasting paving, groundcovers, plant forms, and color are used to introduce variety and interest in a small space, water can be used to amplify a garden's effect by introducing diversity. Additionally, the sound of flowing water is very soothing, so you might want to consider installing a fountain. Water's reflective properties, meanwhile, can amplify the effects of greenery and outdoor lighting and mirror the changing face of the sky.

A water feature, therefore, provides great interest in the garden. There are several ways to approach this element. If you have a backyard garden, you may wish to create a small pool. To do so, you can either use a butyl pond liner as a water container if the feature will be small, or, if you prefer a larger feature, you can create a depression of waterproof concrete. Deeper ponds must be reinforced with extra base material, such as steel mesh. Prefabricated fiberglass growing pools are also available; they require sturdy PVC liners. Pools can be put into the ground and surrounded with stone or set into a lightweight wooden frame on your terrace.

Whatever method you choose, aquatic plants can be grown in open baskets filled with potting mix, and bog plants can be planted directly into a mixture of peat and soil, layered onto the pond base. A pump can also be installed to circulate water. Before undertaking such a project, however, make sure that you are not violating any city codes. A landscape architect could also provide sound advice and guidance.

There are a variety of stunning plants that can add charm to your water garden.

Above left: This formal lily pond accentuates a view of Boston Harbor. Notice that the aquatic flowers are white, in keeping with the overall color scheme of the design. Designed by Morgan Wheelock. *Above right:* A modern water feature acts as both fountain and sculpture. Even its color blends richly with the purple and lavendar cineraria and campanula behind it.

Water lilies, lotuses, and bog plants, which require three to five hours of sunshine a day, add immeasurably to the appeal of a small pool. In the evening, some species of night-blooming water lilies can be indirectly lit for a spectacular effect. Water lilies need 10 to 18 inches (25 to 50 centimeters) of still water to grow. The leaves of water lilies help prevent the growth of algae. Bog plants, including dwarf papyrus, Chinese water chestnuts, and bog lilies, require extremely moist soil. Marginal aquatics need about 3 inches (7.5 centimeters) of water, while submerged aquatics thrive on about 12 inches (30 centimeters) of water. Marginal aquatics include the water forget-me-not (*Myosotis scorpioides*), which boasts delicate flowers, and brooklime (*Veronica bec-*

cabunga), whose flowers and foliage are equally delightful. A pond or small pool needs to be oxygenated to sustain life, and you should include plants that perform this function. Among them are the submerged aquatics waterweed (*Egeria densa*) and curled pondweed (*Potamogeton crispus*).

If your backyard space is simply too small, or if your urban garden is on a terrace or rooftop, another option is to use a whiskey half-barrel lined with durable PVC covering as a miniature water garden. You can fit two small water lilies, two bog plants, or one of each in the barrel. Other possibilites include birdbaths, oversized urns filled with aquatic plants, and small-scale waterfall systems of water jets and skillfully placed rocks.

GARDENING ARTS

© Alex Roy

© R.W. Kosturko

Bonsai

Bonsai ranks among the most demanding of garden arts requiring a skillful hand and a full understanding of the technique. Bonsai, derived from the ancient Chinese art of dwarfing trees and shurbs in containers, was adapted several hundred years ago by the Japanese. In the Western world, however, where many native species have been found suitable for bonsai, the technique has an enthusiastic following. Horticultural societies often host lectures on the art, and botanical gardens periodically offer hands-on-classes.

Plants grown in true bonsai manner are usually classified into two specific groups—trees or grasses. The larger group, trees, consists of pines and oaks, foliage trees (such as the Japanese ma-

ple), fruit trees (like persimmon or crabapple), and flowering trees (such as cherry or plum). Grass bonsai consists of shrubs, mosses, and bamboo.

Bonsai is an art form and its cultivator a bonsai artist. These dwarfed container-grown plants must be "trained" first, perhaps for decades, by regular pruning, feeding, and watering, and by applying wire coils, which are used to restrict the plant's growth, to the plant's branches. Once coaxed into the desired shape, the plant is then maintained and cared for—sometimes for generations.

The bonsai's shape may be intentionally contorted or allowed to assume the natural shape of its larger counterpart. As a container plant, it works well as a meaningful architectural feature when placed by a door or at the corner of a terrace or garden walk. The bonsai is undoubtedly a revered, living work of art that should be

valued for its development, composition, and beauty.

Topiary

While the technique of restricting a plant's size by pruning and potting is an art form that originated in the Orient, topiary—the art of geometrically designing plants to change their natural shape—is essentially a Western practice. Topiary is particularly well-suited to formal city gardens. One should be careful, however, not to turn a beautifully designed garden into an overdone menagerie of sculpted animals.

THE URBAN WILDLIFE GARDEN

*Far left: The art of bonsai requires great skill and knowledge on the part of the gardener; it is an expensive but rewarding hobby. **Left:** This topiary display is obviously on a scale that is much too large for an urban garden. Nevertheless, smaller topiary can lend dignity and grace to a formal city garden.*

Imagine a garden for meditating surrounded by monarch butterflies fluttering around gaillardia (*Gaillardia* spp.) or chickadees refreshing themselves in a Victorian birdbath on your terrace. Picture the curious child's amazement at first sight of a spring wren or his or her excitement over caterpillars and adult swallowtails in July. Wildlife provides a wonderful educational experience, helps your garden grow, and enhances the appeal of it to visitors.

By providing the proper devices for wildlife, you can attract fascinating creatures to your city garden. You'll soon discover that red flowers attract hummingbirds, bellflowers attract bumblebees, and bright orange and pink flowers attract butterflies—it's easy to become an amateur naturalist in your own urban space. According to Violet Stevenson in her book *The Wild Garden* (Viking: New York, 1985), one advantage to attracting wildlife to your garden is the automatic ecosystem of nature. If your garden attracts one kind of animal, it will inevitably attract another. For example, if your garden plants are attacked by *aphids,* which suck valuable juices from plants, visiting birds or ladybugs and other insects will consume the problems for their nourishment. *Syrphids,* banded yellow-and-black insects, whose larvae love to gorge on aphids, can be welcome guests.

Water is the most important ingredient in a wildlife garden. Any size container will do—a saucer sunk into a flower border, a traditional birdbath, or a garden pond filled with radiant water lilies. While water brings birds and other beautiful wildlife to your garden, it also attracts insects. This same water will, in turn, bring delicate dragonflies in summer to lunch on the more bothersome insects in your pond. One of these undesirable visitors is the mosquito. In as little as two weeks, it can have laid eggs, which will have grown to mature adults. By frequently replacing the water in your pool, you can halt the life cycle

Primarily used in landscape gardening, topiary is usually composed from thick, slow-growing evergreens such as box and yew, arborvitae and privet. The sculptures themselves can be as elaborate or as simple as you please. Some trees and shrubs are designed to resemble statuary (such as birds, nymphs, or urns) and intricate mazes, while others are clipped into simple cubes and obelisks. Parents looking forward to playing outside with their children might consider some small-scale topiaries. Little rabbits, ducks, and elephants shaped out of green leaves can be grown on wire forms specifically designed for the purpose. Topiary should be set off on its own or it can be planted against a simple background where it can be appreciated and enjoyed. The center of a lawn, near an entrance or pathway, or by a fence or wall, are all ideal spots for garden topiary.

Select plants, such as crocuses, will attract beneficial insects like the bumblebee.

before completion. In John V. Denniss's *The Wildlife Gardener* (Knopf, 1985), he suggests introducing the mosquito fish (*Gambusia affinis*) in larger reflecting pools to combat this problem.

There is no reason a terrace gardener cannot lure the common Eastern Phoebe, among others, with the proper birdfeeder. Most birds require these basic needs: food, water, and shelter. Birdhouses can make up for the lack of old oak trees for nesting birds on rooftop gardens. Bird watchers can view early morning feeders from a safe distance at their carefully chosen sitting area. Feeders filled with a combination of wild bird feed and suet will provide your flock with their basic dietary needs. Oranges are an inexpensive food source for birds. Don't leave food uneaten for long, however, or it will attract night stalkers such as racoons, oppossums, and rats. This can cause disease within your bird population.

Plants with berries, such as elderberries, attract birds by providing a source of food. The honeysuckle vine feeds birds in autumn and calls hummingbirds with trumpet blooms in summer.

The common gray squirrel will be the most predominant form of wildlife to appear. Squirrels actually favor mushrooms, oranges, apples, and grapes for their diets. Recycle your leftover scraps for them—the more decayed the better. Squirrels will not eat suet and will stay away from a bird's nest, but take care with how you place your seed because the gray squirrel will find a way to it. Suspending the container on a limb or extension 8 to 10 feet (2.4 to 3 meters) from a wall or tree will convince them to keep off. Cats, as well, can be prevented from climbing post feeders by attaching an inverted funnel-shaped metal collar at the base. This should be placed 3 to 4 feet (.9 to 1.2 meters) from the ground to deter any further scampering upward. Also, your feline should wear a bell around the neck to warn the birds of the approaching predator. Domestic pets may try to nibble on your carefully chosen plants. You can try spraying hot salsa as a remedy against their discriminating palate. Or plant your cat's own crop of oat grass to chew upon.

A window box (see page 36) can provide a rest stop for butterflies. Butterflies, and the flowers they land upon, will need at least four to six hours of sunlight to flourish. These beautiful winged creatures are attracted to warm colors: oranges, pinks, reds, and yellows. Butterflies are a sign of tranquility in nature—floating along softly from flower to flower. Plant your garden spot along a protected hedge, fence, or corner wall away from wind swirls to encourage butterflies to linger. Nectar is a source of energy for the butterfly. The plants listed on page 79 are full of this sweet sap and convince butterflies to return often. The Mexican sunflower (*Tithonia rotundifolia*) is a favorite of the monarch. A tall, heat-resistant red daisy, it will bloom all summer long. Wildflowers, such as milkweed, sweet clover, and chicory are bringing butterflies back to urban centers. As new trends are incorporated into contemporary garden designs, these splendid creatures of nature increasingly appear.

© Ken Druse

Plants like joe-pye-weed can attract the beautiful swallowtail butterfly to your sanctuary in the city.

Butterfly Plants

Plant	Butterfly
Aster (*Aster* 'Ostrich Plume')	Tortoiseshell
Bachelor's Button (*Centaurea* spp.)	Red Admiral
Butterfly bush (*Buddleia* spp.)	Fritillary
Butterfly weed (*Asclepias tuberosa*)	Edward's hairstreak
Globe amaranth (*Gomphrena* spp.)	Snout
Globe thistle (*Echinops* spp.)	Painted lady
Milkweed (*Aslepias* spp.)	Monarch
Nasturtium (*Tropaeolum* spp.)	Common sulphur
Snapdragon (*Antirrhinum* spp.)	Buckeye
Queen Anne's lace (*Daucus carota*)	Black swallowtail
Violet (*Viola* spp.)	Great-spangled fritillary
Zinnia (*Zinnia* spp.)	Yellow-tiger swallowtail

Other Butterfly Plants

Annuals	Perennials
Cosmos (*Cosmos* spp.)	Coral bell (*Hevchera sanguinea*)
Gaillardia (*Gaillardia* spp.)	Coreopsis (*Coreopsis* spp.)
Lantana (*Lantana* spp.)	Dahlia (*Dahlia* spp.)
	Daylily (*Hemerocallis* spp.)
	Liatris (*Liatris* spp.)
	Phlox (*Phlox* spp.)

Container Plants for Birds

Latin Name	Common Name
Nadina var. 'Nana Purpurea'	Boston ivy
Pyracantha var. 'Tiny Tim'	Compact inkbery
Ilex crenata var. 'Helleri'	Chinese sacred bamboo
Ilex glabra compacta	Firethorn
Ilex opaca var. 'Maryland Dwarf'	Maryland American holly
Parthenocissus tricuspidata	Heller Japanese holly

Bird Feed

Bird	Feed
Blue Jay	Sunflower
Cardinal	Safflower seeds
Catbird	Chopped fruit
Chickadee	Sunflower hearts
Finch	Black oil sunflower
Mockingbird	Suet (beef or mutton fat)
Morning dove	Finely chopped corn
Robin	Chopped fruit
Sparrow	Millet (white)
Woodpecker	Suet

Hummingbird Plants

Common Name	Latin Name
Annual delphinium	*Delphinium* spp.
Balloon flower	*Platycodon*
Beard-tongue	*Penstemon* spp.
Beebalm	*Monarda* 'Cambridge Scarlet'
Red cardinal flower	*Lobelia cardinalis*
Russell hybrids	*Lupinus* spp.
Salvia 'Rodeo'	*Salvia* spp.
Snapdragon	*Antirrhinum* spp.
Spider flower	*Cleome*
Tobacco plant	*Nicotiana* spp.

Bumblebee Plants

Common Name	Latin Name
Apple blossom	*Malus* spp.
Canadian goldenrod	*Solidago canadensis*
Foxglove	*Digitalis purpurea*
Live Forever	*Sedum* 'Autumn Joy'
Sage	*Salvia officinalis*
Virginia bluebells	*Mertensia virginica*
Yarrow	*Achillea millefolium*

PLANT GROWTH CHARTS

N O R T H E A S T

	NAME	ZONE	MAXIMUM HEIGHT	OPTIMUM SUN EXPOSURE	COMMENTS
	SHELTERED				
TREES	Flowering Dogwood *Cornus florida* 'New Hampshire'	5	20 ft	all	deciduous; full burst of flowers in spring; brilliant scarlet color in autumn; berries attract birds
	Japanese Crabapple *Malus floribunda*	5	20 ft	all	deciduous; pyramidal shape; excellent for small spaces
	Weeping Japanese Pagoda *Sophora japonica* 'Pendula'	5	20-30 ft	E, S	deciduous; long bloom period; tolerates wind and ice
	Scarlet Japanese Maple *Acer palmatum* 'Sanguineum'	5	20 ft	all	deciduous; use in shade gardens and Oriental designs
SHRUBS	Lily-of-the-Valley *Pieris japonica* 'Valley Valentine'	6	9 ft	all	evergreen; use in Oriental designs; shade gardens
	Dwarf Fothergilla *Fothergilla gardenii* 'Blue Mist'	5	3 ft	S, W	native to Northeast; white spring flowers; mixes well with conifers
	Fountain Bush *Buddleia altenifolia*	5	12 ft	S, W	deciduous; prune after bloom period; purple flowers
	Summersweet *Clethra alnifolia* 'Pink Spire'	5	10 ft	S, W	native to Northeast; suited to dry areas and seashore
PERENNIALS	Astilbe *Astilbe x arendsii* 'Fanal'	5	2-4 ft	N, E	hardy; use in woodland shade gardens; fertilize every summer
	Bellflower *Campanula glomerata*	3	1-3 ft	N, E	hardy; use in rock garden borders and shade gardens
	Foxglove *Digitalis purpurea* 'Foxy'	5	4 ft	E, S	use in cutting and wild gardens; attracts bumblebees
	Garden Phlox *Phlox paniculata* 'Mount Fujiyama'	4	3 ft	E, S	hardy; large pink, white and scarlet flowers; excellent in borders
	Giant Snowdrops *Galanthus elwesii*	4	4-11 in	**E, S**	bulb; white flowers in earliest spring; does well in containers
	Plantain lily *Hosta decorata*	4	2 ft	**N, E**	hardy; white flower spikes provide contrast in dark corners
ANNUALS	Blue Laceflower *Trachymene coerulea*		2-3 ft	E, S, W	hardy; grows best in well-drained soil
	Busy Lizzy *Impatiens wallerana* 'New Guinea'		2 ft	S, W	tender; use in borders, containers, and small boxes or pots
	Tuberous Begonia *Begonia x tuberhybrida*		2 ft	E, S	tender; use in containers and small patio or terrace pots

TERRACE				
NAME	ZONE	MAXIMUM HEIGHT	OPTIMUM SUN EXPOSURE	COMMENTS
TREES				
Japanese Maple *Acer palmatum* 'Atropurpureum'	3	20 ft	E, S, W	deciduous; use in Oriental and woodland designs
Sargent Crabapple *Malus sargentii*	3	8 ft	all	deciduous; rose-colored spring flowers
Siberian Dogwood *Cornus alba* 'Sibirica'	3	9 ft	E, S, W	deciduous; bright coral-red spring flowers
Silvery Blue Spruce *Picea pungens* 'Glauca Globosa'	3	2 ft	all	evergreen; use as accent with conifers; good container plant
Spreading Euonymus *Euonymus kiautschovica* 'Manhattan'	6	9 ft	all	deciduous; pollution tolerant; flaming red autumn color
SHRUBS				
Cranberry Cotoneaster *Cotoneaster apiculatus*	5	3 ft	E, S, W	evergreen; use for espaliers and low ledges, and in rock gardens
European Cranberrybush *Viburnum opulus* 'Compactum'	5	4-5 ft	S, W	deciduous; pollution tolerant; berries attract birds
Korean Boxwood *Buxus koreana*	6	5 ft	all	evergreen; excellent for formal gardens or topiary
PERENNIALS				
Bearded Iris *Iris* hybrids	3	2 ft	S, W	hardy; use in containers and borders
Black-Eyed Susan *Rudbeckia fulgida* 'Goldsturm'	4	2½ ft	S, W	hardy; native to North America; good container plant; use for wild-garden or meadow designs
Chinese Wisteria *Wisteria sinensis*	5	4-5 ft	E, S, W	deciduous; perfect for trellises and pergolas; makes an attractive weeping tree
Leather Flower *Clematis jackamnii*	4	15 ft	N, E	deciduous vine; flat, open, purple, white, and rose flowers in summer; roots need cool shade; prune in late winter
ANNUALS				
Purple Loosestrife *Lythrum Salicaria*		3-5 ft	all	hardy; spreads rapidly, so use in containers only or to edge garden pools
Dusty Miller *Senecio cineraria*		2-3 ft	E, S, W	tender; lovely grey-tinged foliage; use for edging or borders
Feverfew *Chrysantemum parthenium* 'Golden Feather'		3 ft	E, S, W	daisy-like flowers; use in beds, borders, and small containers
Floss Flower *Ageratum houstonianum*		1 ft	S, W	tender; small, blueish-purple summer flowers; use as edging, walkways, and borders or in containers
Lobelia *Lobelia erinus*		3-8 in	S, W	hardy; lovely cascading form; use in rock gardens and containers

EXPOSED				
NAME	ZONE	MAXIMUM HEIGHT	OPTIMUM SUN EXPOSURE	COMMENTS
TREES				
Callerya Pear *Pyrus calleryana* 'Faureri'	5	20 ft	all	deciduous; heat, wind, and pollution tolerant
English Hawthorne *Crategus monogyna* 'Crimson Cloud'	5	20 ft	all	deciduous; thrives in city conditions; berries attract birds
Service Berry *Amerlanchier canadensis*	4	20-30 ft	all	deciduous; early spring flowers; berries attract birds
SHRUBS				
American Arborvitae *Thuja occidentalis*	3	8 ft	all	evergreen; creates columnar or pyramidal windscreen
Bush Cinquefoil *Potentilla fructicosa* 'Goldfinger'	2	4 ft	S, W	deciduous; low grower; golden summer flowers; tolerates dryness and extreme cold
Fringetree *Chionanthus retusus*	6	15 ft	S, W	deciduous; early flowering shrub
Japanese Barberry *Berberis thunbergii* 'Atropurpurea'	4	2 ft	S, W	deciduous; reddish leaves in winter; drought tolerant
Bridal Wreath *Spiraea x japonica* 'Little Princess'	6	3-4 ft	S, W	deciduous; small crimson summer flowers
Witch Hazel *Hamamelis x intermedia* 'Arnold Promise'	4	8 ft	E, S, W	deciduous; yellow blooms in late winter; tolerates moderate pollution
PERENNIALS				
Allium *Allium roseum*	5	2 ft	S, W	bulb; rose-pink blooms in late spring
Lily *Lilium rubrum*	5	4-5 ft	S, W	bulb; pink summer trumpet-shaped flowers
Queen-Anne's-Lace *Daucus carota*	5	1-3 ft	all	hardy; good choice for wild gardens; attracts bees and butterflies
Trumpet Honeysuckle *Lonicera sempervirens* 'Dropmore Scarlet'	3	50 ft	S, W	deciduous; winter-hardy into Canada
ANNUALS				
Martha Washington Geranium *Pelargonium x domesticum*		1½ ft	E, S, W	tender; pink, red, and white flowers; provides long-lasting summer color; use in borders, containers, and window boxes
Morning Glory *Ipomoea purpurea*		10 ft	S, W	vine; tolerates hot, summer sun; white, red, and purple flowers
Nasturtium *Tropaeolum majus*		12 ft	all	tender vine; easily grown from seed; tolerates dry soil; orange edible flowers
Verbena *Lantana camera* 'Sanguinea'		2 ft	S, W	tender; white and deep-red pompom flowers; use small, decorative pots

S O U T H E A S T

SHELTERED

	NAME	ZONE	MAXIMUM HEIGHT	OPTIMUM SUN EXPOSURE	COMMENTS
TREES	Japanese Dogwood *Cornus florida*	5-9	20 ft	E	deciduous; scarlet summer flowers; use in Oriental designs; berries attract birds
	Japanese Maple *Acer palmatum*	6-9	20 ft	S	deciduous; red autumn color; use in woodland and Oriental designs
	Saucer Magnolia *Magnolia soulangiana*	6-9	20 ft	S	deciduous; mauve spring flowers; likes cool, moist spots
SHRUBS	Chinese Holly *Ilex cornuta* 'Rotunda'	6-10	3 ft	N, E, S	evergreen; compact spreading habit; use as windscreen; berries attract birds
	India Hawthorn *Raphiolepis indica* 'Rosea'	7-10	3 ft	E, S	evergreen; use as windscreen; pink flowers
	Japanese Privet *Ligustrum japonicum*	8-10	6-15 ft	all	evergreen; use as hedge or topiary in formal or Oriental designs
PERENNIALS	Aaron's Beard *Hypericum calycinum*	5-8	1-1½ ft	E, S	hardy groundcover; yellow summer flowers; thrives near garden pools
	Fern *Athyrium spp.*	4-9	6 in-2 ft	N, E	native to North America; use in shade and woodland gardens; many varieties
	Mondo Grass *Ophiopogon japonicus*	6-10	6 in-1 ft	N, E, S	evergreen groundcover; tropical, grassy look; lawn substitute
ANNUALS	Fairy Primrose *Primula malacoides*		1½ ft	E, S	tender; pink and white summer flowers; use in moist, soggy areas
	Forget-me-not *Myosotis sylvatica*		1 ft	E, S	hardy wildflower; use under trees
	Spider Flower *Cleome hasslerna*		4-5 ft	E, S	tender; plant under trees in filtered light

TERRACE

	NAME	ZONE	MAXIMUM HEIGHT	OPTIMUM SUN EXPOSURE	COMMENTS
TREES	Bradford Pear *Pyrus calleryana* 'Bradford'	6	30 ft	E, S, W	deciduous; flaming red autumn color; can use for espalier or topiary
	European Fan Palm *Chamaerops humilis*	9	6 in-1 ft	all	palm; large container plant; tolerates hot, dry conditions
	Pigmy Date Palm *Phoenix roebelenii*	9-10	6 in-1 ft	N, E	palm; container or patio plant; has feathery, light green leaves
SHRUBS	Common Camellia *Camellia japonica*	8	3-5 ft	E, S, W	evergreen; use in Oriental designs or for espaliers; many varieties
	Sweet Viburnum *Viburnum odoratissimum* 'Nanum'	8	6-10 ft	E, S	evergreen; white fragrant spring flowers; year-round foliage color; berries attract birds
	Twisted Juniper *Juniperus chinensis* 'Torulosa'	5-9	10 ft	E, S, W	evergreen; use in isolated space so twisted branches are visible

	NAME	ZONE	MAXIMUM HEIGHT	OPTIMUM SUN EXPOSURE	COMMENTS
PERENNIALS	Confederate Jasmine *Trachelospermunium jasminoides*	9	30 ft	E, S	vine; fragrant; requires a structure for support
	Coral Vine *Antigonon leptopus*	8-10	30 ft	E, S, W	tender tendrils grow on fences, trellises, and trees
	Nippon Lily *Rohdea japonica*	6-10	1-1½ ft	N, E	evergreen; short spike of pale-yellow flowers; container plant; use in shade gardens
ANNUALS	English Daisy *Bellis perennis*		6 in	S, W	tender; white to rose daisy flowers in early summer; use in containers, and as borders
	White Sage *Lantana camara* 'Alba'		4 ft	all	tender; container plant; use in all-white gardens; good container plant; shrub-like plant form
	Sweet Pea *Lathyrus odoratus* 'Mammoth Mixed'		6 ft	E, S, W	tender creeper; very fragrant, color varies in flowers; use as border plant

EXPOSED

	NAME	ZONE	MAXIMUM HEIGHT	OPTIMUM SUN EXPOSURE	COMMENTS
TREES	Cherry Laurel *Prunus caroliniana*	7	10-20 ft	E, S, W	evergreen; pink blooms in spring; prune into compact shape
	Crape Myrtle *Lagerstroemia indica*	7-10	10-20 ft	S, W	deciduous; rosy summer flowers; drought tolerant
	Fringe Tree *Chionanthus virginicus*	5-9	10-20 ft	S, W	deciduous; native to North America; white, late-spring flowers
SHRUBS	Golden Bamboo *Phyllostachya aurea*	8	10 ft	E, S, W	evergreen; use in Oriental designs and near water pools; tolerates moist soils
	Flame-of-the-woods *Ixora coccinea*	10	5-10 ft	E, S	evergreen; tropical; brilliant orange flower; use as container plant, hedge, or windscreen
	Japanese Boxwood *Buxus microphylla japonica*	7-10	3 ft	all	evergreen; use in formal gardens, as a hedge, border plant, or as topiary
	Spiraea *Spiraea x vanhouttei*	5	2-3 ft	E, S, W	deciduous; white summer flowers; can be used as hedge or alone
	Goucher Abelia *Abelia x grandeflora* 'Edward Goucher'	3-9	3-5 ft	E, S, W	semi-deciduous; small pink trumpet-shaped summer flowers
PERENNIALS	Lawn leaf *Dichondra carolinensus*	8-10	6 in	all	groundcover; lawn substitute; very invasive
	Poet's Jasmine *Jasminium officinale*	7-10	30 ft	E, S	evergreen vine; fragrant white flowers; use on arbors and trellises
	Lily-of-the-Nile *Agapanthus africanus*	8-9	1-3 ft	S, W	tender bulb; use as container plant, and in rock gardens
ANNUALS	Black-eyed Susan *Thunbergia alata*		6 ft	S, W	vine; likes heat; good container plant; can be grown in wildflower border
	Morning Glory *Ipomoea alba*		50 ft	S, W	vine; white or violet-blue flowers; likes containers; climbs along walls, trellises, fences
	Lily Turf *Liliope muscari*		1-1½ ft	N, E, S	evergreen; use as a groundcover or border; provides contrasting foliage
	Zephyr Lily *Zephyranthes grandiflora*		1 ft	S, W	tender bulb; use in rock gardens, borders, and containers
	Ten-weeks Stock *Matthiola incana* 'Annua'		2 ft	E, S, W	hardy; mix with foxglove, and larkspur in English cottage flower designs

N O R T H W E S T

	NAME	ZONE	MAXIMUM HEIGHT	OPTIMUM SUN EXPOSURE	COMMENTS
	SHELTERED				
TREES	Amur Maple *Acer ginnala*	5	20 ft	all	deciduous; vibrant scarlet autumn foliage
	Mountain Stewartia *Stewartia ovata*	7	15 ft	E, S	deciduous; white blooms in summer; likes moist acidic soil
	Saucer Magnolia *Magnolia x soulangiana*	2	25 ft	all	deciduous; white flowers in early spring; use in a corner or as a focal point
SHRUBS	Flowering Fuchsia *Fuchsia x hybrida*	4	4-12 ft	N, E, S	deciduous; use as topiary, in a container, or as a hanging plant
	Golden Chaintree *Laburnum x watereri* 'Vossii'	2	25 ft	N, E, S	deciduous; long golden flower clusters in midspring; requires moist soil; good espalier plant
	Red-flowering Currant *Ribes sanguineum*	6	12 ft	E, S, W	deciduous; yields lovely red flowers in spring; berries attract birds
	Tartarian Honeysuckle *Lonicera tatarica* 'Arnold Red'	1	9 ft	all	deciduous; tolerates shade; use as windbreak; thrives in Rocky Mountain region
	Arrowwood *Viburnum davidii*	7	3 ft	N, E, S	evergreen; use as groundcover or grow under Azaleas and Rhododendrons
PERENNIALS	Lily-of-the-field *Anemone coronaria*	5	6 in-1½ ft	N, E	bulb; blooms in early spring; open flower form with red and purple petals
	Lupine *Lupinus polyphyllus*	4	2 ft	all	hardy wildflower; native to North America; best in moist areas; use in wild-garden designs
	Peach-leafed Bells 'Alba' *Campanula persicifolia*	2	3 ft	N, E, W	hardy; use in borders and to lighten dark areas
ANNUALS	Beard-tongue *Penstemon gloxinoides* 'Scarlet and White'		2-3 ft	E, S	half-hardy; prefers cool weather; use in beds or borders; good cutting flower
	Prairie Gentian *Eustoma grandiflorum*		2-3 ft	E, S, W	half-hardy; use in moist soils; good choice for wild gardens
	Blue Wings *Torenia fournieri*		1 ft	E, S	tender; use in moist soils; good for rock gardens
	TERRACE				
	NAME	ZONE	MAXIMUM HEIGHT	OPTIMUM SUN EXPOSURE	COMMENTS
TREES	European White Birch *Betula pendula* 'Dwarf'	2	3 ft	all	deciduous; striking white peeling bark with weeping branch form
	Fragrant Snowball *Styrax obassia*	5	25 ft	E, S, W	deciduous; fragrant white flowers; use in Oriental designs
	Vine Maple *Acer circinatum*	6	5-30 ft	all	deciduous; fire-red autumn foliage; likes shade; good espalier plant; grows well in British Columbia
	Western Redbud *Cercis occidentalis*	2	1½ ft	E, S, W	deciduous; drought tolerant; brilliant-rose spring flowers

	NAME	ZONE	MAXIMUM HEIGHT	OPTIMUM SUN EXPOSURE	COMMENTS
SHRUBS	Oregon Holly-grape *Mahonia Aquifolium* 'Moseri'	5	3 ft	all	evergreen; fragrant yellow flowers; tolerates wind and sun exposure
	Noble Fir *Abies procera* 'Prostrata'	5	3 ft	all	evergreen; foliage is blue-gray in color; contributes winter beauty with graceful, spreading form
	Scotch Broom *Cytisus scoparius*	4	5-10 ft	E, S, W	evergreen; grow in containers to keep plant from spreading; prune after blooming
PERENNIALS	Pineapple Lily *Eucomis comosa*	7	1-2 ft	all	bulb; blooms in summer; tall greenish-white flower; good for cutting
	Spring Heath *Erica carnea* 'Spring Wood'	2	8 in	E, S	groundcover; blooms in spring; flower color varies; rock garden plant
	Red-Hot Poker *Kniphofia Uvaria*	7	3 ft	S, W	plant in sheltered spot; avoid windy, northern exposures; orange-yellow flowers on tall spikes
ANNUALS	Farewell-to-Spring *Clarkia amoena*		3 ft	S, W	annual; grows well in British Columbia; thrives in crowded conditions
	Sweet Pea *Lathyrus* spp.		3 ft	E, S, W	hardy; use in containers or small terrace boxes
	Tricolor Chrysanthemums *Chrysanthemum carinatum*		3 ft	E, S, W	hardy; use in beds and borders; flowers are bronze, yellow, or crimson

				EXPOSED	

	NAME	ZONE	MAXIMUM HEIGHT	OPTIMUM SUN EXPOSURE	COMMENTS
TREES	Flowering Plum *Prunus x blireiana*	2	25 ft	E, S, W	deciduous; vibrant pink spring flowers; tolerates city climates
	Japanese Flowering Crabapple *Malus floribunda* 'Profusion'	2	25 ft	all	deciduous; resistant to rust disease; fruit attracts birds
	Russian Hawthorn *Crataegus ambigua*	2	20 ft	S, W	deciduous; extremely hardy; berries attract birds
SHRUBS	Chinese Witch Hazel *Hammamelis mollis*	4	10 ft	all	deciduous; fragrant yellow late-winter flowers
	Common Lilac *Syringa vulgaris*	1	15 ft	all	deciduous; fragrant purple blooms; thrives in Rocky Mountain region
	Flowering Quince *Chaenomeles japonica*	1	2-6 ft	S, W	deciduous; thrives in Rocky Mountain region; excellent as windscreen or hedge; flowers attract hummingbirds
PERENNIALS	Butterfly Weed *Asclepias tuberosa*	4	3 ft	S, W	hardy; orange blooms in summer; mix with grasses and use in wild-garden designs; attracts bees and butterflies
	Pacific Coast Iris *Iris tenax*	4	1 ft	E, S, W	use in rock gardens and borders
	Purple Cornflower *Echinacea purpurea*	all	4 ft	all	mix with daisy forms or with matching colors; has noninvasive root system
ANNUALS	Blue Marguerite *Felicia amelloides*		3 ft	E, S, W	half-hardy; use in well-drained soils; good for borders or for cutting
	Garden Verbena *Verbena x hybrida* 'Pink Bouquet'		1 ft	E, S, W	tender; use in beds and borders or small individual decorative pots

S O U T H W E S T

	SHELTERED			
NAME	ZONE	MAXIMUM HEIGHT	OPTIMUM SUN EXPOSURE	COMMENTS
TREES				
Citrus Trees *Citrus spp.*	8	varies	E	evergreen; fragrant flowers and fruit; good container, espalier, and topiary plant
Mexican Redbud *Cercis canadensis* 'Mexicana'	5	10 ft	N, E	deciduous; bursting, pink, spring flowers
Juniper *Juniperus scopulorum* 'Tolleson's Weeping'	4	15 ft	E, S	evergreen; blue foliage; use in Oriental designs
SHRUBS				
Agave *Agave spp.*	9	4 ft	S, W	evergreen; succulent; use in rock gardens or desert designs
Bamboo *Bambusa glancescens Riviereorum*	9-10	10 ft	E, S, E	evergreen; use in Oriental and water-garden designs; grassy leaf form
Japanese Aralia *Fatsia japonica*	9-10	15 ft	N, E	tropical evergreen; use in containers or as filler at tree base
Mexican Stone Pine *Pinus cembroides*	7	25 ft	all	evergreen; use in Japanese designs
Persian Lilac *Syringa x persia*	5	5 ft	S, W	deciduous; fragrant purple flowers
Chinese Wax-leaf Privet *Ligustrum lucidum*	8	6-25 ft	E	evergreen; use as hedge, windscreen, or topiary
Arrowwood *Viburnum x burkwoodii*	5-7	4-6 ft	N, E	evergreen; fragrant pinkish-white, tubular spring flowers
PERENNIALS				
Aralia Ivy *Fatshedera lizei*	7	8 ft	N, E	evergreen vine; lush greenery creates attractive espalier and wallclimbing designs
Creeping Fig *Ficus pumila*	8	varies	N, E	evergreen vine; has invasive root system; use for espalier
Daylily *Hemerocallis spp.*	all	2-3 ft	E, S	hardy; summer blooms; varied colors; fragrant cutting plant; edible flowers
Umbrella Sedge *Cyperus alternifolius*	7	3 ft	E	tropical evergreen; use in Oriental designs; grows well near water in moist soil
ANNUALS				
Calendula Marigold *Calendula officinalis* 'Orange Coronet'		1½ ft	E, S, W	hardy; prefers cool areas; provides long-lasting, bright-orange flowers
Cape Marigold *Dimorphotheca pluvialis*		1½ ft	S, W	tender; showy blooms; use in well-drained soil
Carnation *Dianthus barbatus* 'Sweet William'		2 ft	N, E, S	hardy; thrives in sun and shade; good choice for borders and English-cottage designs
Rocket Larkspur *Consolida ambigua*		2 ft	N, E, S	hardy; excellent bedding plant; can also be supported against ornamental fence

TERRACE

	NAME	ZONE	MAXIMUM HEIGHT	OPTIMUM SUN EXPOSURE	COMMENTS
TREES	Mock Orange *Prunus caroliniana*	7	20 ft	E, S	evergreen; use in formal designs and as hedge, windscreen, or espalier
	Peach Tree *Prunus persica*	5	15 ft	S, W	deciduous; provides bright mass of color in spring; pink, puffy flowers
	Weeping Fig *Ficus benjamina*	9	20 ft	S	evergreen; prune into topiary or natural weeping form
SHRUBS	Gardenia *Gardenia jasminoides*	9-10	6 ft	E, S	evergreen; fragrant, white flowers; use as windscreen
	Chinese Hibiscus *Hibiscus rosa-sinensis*	9	5 ft	S, W	evergreen; use as hedge, espalier, or windscreen; attracts hummingbirds
	Willow Pittosporum *Pittosporum phillyraeoides*	8	15 ft	all	evergreen; adapts to small spaces; provides grassy effect
	Cape Leadwort *Plumbago auriculata*	9	3-4 ft	S, W	evergreen; blue flowers; use as container, espalier, trellis, or pergola plant
	Sago Palm *Cycas revoluta*	9	10 ft	E	tropical evergreen; requires no maintenance
PERENNIALS	Confederate Jasmine *Trachelospermum jasminoides*	8	30 ft	E, S	vine; requires support; fragrant blooms; grow hanging over ledge
	Ground Morning Glory *Convolvulus mauritanicus*	7	1 ft	all	evergreen groundcover; blue-gray foliage and flowers; use in rock garden or in baskets
	Rosemary *Rosemarinus officinalis*	6	2 ft	S, W	evergreen groundcover; berries attract birds
ANNUALS	Star Phlox *Phlox drummondii* 'Twinkle'		1½ ft	E, S, W	hardy; use in borders or containers
	Garden Petunia *Petunia x hybrida* 'Flash Series'		1½ ft	E, S, W	half-hardy; use in containers or borders
	Mexican Zinnia *Zinnia haageana*		1½ ft	E, S	tender; excellent cutting flower, but strip off leaves first
	Sweet Alyssum *Lobularia maritima* 'Rosie O'Day'		9 in-1 ft	E	hardy; good edging plant; use in rock gardens

EXPOSED

	NAME	ZONE	MAXIMUM HEIGHT	OPTIMUM SUN EXPOSURE	COMMENTS
TREES	Crape Myrtle *Lagerstroemia indica*	7	10-20 ft	S, W	deciduous; magenta summer flowers; drought tolerant
	Fringe Tree *Chionanthus virginicus*	5	10-20 ft	S, W	deciduous; native to North America; late-spring, white flowers
	Italian Cypress *Cypressus arizonica* 'Glauca'	7	40 ft	all	evergreen; silvery-gray foliage; columnar form; use in formal designs or as windbreak
SHRUBS	Crimson Bottlebrush *Callistemon citrinus* 'Jeffers'	8	6 ft	W	evergreen; use for topiary; spectacular spring red brush blooms
	Prickly Pear *Opuntia spp.*	6-10	2-20 ft	S, W	cactus; excellent for erosion control, as windscreen, or in desert designs

	Plant	Zone	Height	Exposure	Description
SHRUBS	Fan Palm *Chamaerops humilis*	8-10	6 ft	S, W	tropical evergreen; use in narrow areas or as bold accent plant
	Oleander *Nerium oleander*	7	5 ft	S, W	evergreen; likes heat; use as hedge or windscreen
	Red Grassy Yucca *Hesperaloe parviflora*	8	3-4 ft	S, W	evergreen; succulent; has tall red spike blooms; use in rock gardens or borders; thrives in desert conditions
	Spanish Bayonet *Yucca spp.*	6-10	4-25 ft	all	evergreen; succulent; dramatic form; container or border plant
PERENNIALS	Bougainvillea *Bougainvillea spp.*	9-10	varies	S, W	vine; purple, red, and white flowers; use on trellis or pergola or as espalier
	Tickseed *Coreopsis grandiflora* 'Goldfink'	7	2 ft	S, W	hardy wildflower; has yellow blooms; blooms from spring through autumn; use as border or in wild-garden designs
	Gaillardia *Gaillardia grandiflora*	6	1-2 ft	S, W	hardy; red and yellow flowers in spring through summer; tolerates heat; attracts butterflies
	Mexican Primrose *Oenothera berlandieri*	7-10	6 in	all	hardy wildflower; pink and white flowers from April through May; use in rock gardens or for lining walkways
	Pampas Grass *Cortaderia selloana*	8	4 ft	S, W	hardy grass; plant along water creates seaside effect; drought tolerant
ANNUALS	Cosmos *Cosmos sulphureus*		3 ft	S, W	tender; orange, pink, and yellow flowers from July through October; attracts butterflies
	Globe Amaranth *Gomphrena globosa*		2 ft	S, W	hardy; pink and purple flowers from June through October; use as cutting flower; also good for drying
	California Poppy *Eschschozia californica*		1 ft	S, W	wildflower; yellow and orange cup-shaped flowers from spring through summer; use for wild-garden designs or borders

NORTHEAST	ZONES
Portland, Maine	4
Boston, Massachusetts	5
New York, New York	6
Philadelphia, Pennsylvania	6
Detroit, Michigan	4

SOUTHEAST	ZONES
Washington, District of Columbia	7
Nashville, Tennessee	7
Atlanta, Georgia	8
New Orleans, Louisiana	9
Miami, Florida	10
Houston, Texas	9
Dallas, Texas	8

NORTHWEST	ZONES
Portland, Oregon	7
Seattle, Washington	8
Denver, Colorado	4
Salt Lake City, Utah	4
Billings, Montana	3

SOUTHWEST	ZONES
San Francisco, California	9
Los Angeles, California	9
San Diego, California	9
Phoenix, Arizona	8
Tucson, Arizona	9
Albuquerque, New Mexico	6
Tulsa, Oklahoma	6

MIDWEST	ZONES
Omaha, Nebraska	4
Milwaukee, Wisconsin	4
Chicago, Illinois	4
Minneapolis, Minnesota	3

CANADA	ZONES
St. John's, Newfoundland	5
Halifax, Nova Scotia	4
St. John, New Brunswick	3
Montreal, Quebec	3
Toronto, Ontario	3
Winnipeg, Manitoba	2
Regina, Saskatchewan	3
Calgary, Alberta	3
Vancouver, British Columbia	8

SOURCES

DESIGNERS

Ascot Designs
286 Congress Street
Boston, Massachusetts 02210

Grass Roots Garden
75 University Place
New York, New York 10003

Hans Van Zelst
Hans Van Zelst Associates
5 East 73rd Street
New York, New York 10021
—lighting and irrigation design

Maher and Greenwald
Designers of Fine Gardens
241 West 97th Street, PH 2
New York, New York 10025

Morgan Wheelock Inc.
286 Congress Street
Boston, Massachusetts 02210

Nightscaping
A Division of Loran, Inc.
1705 East Colton Avenue
Redlands, California 92373

Reed Brothers
6006 Gravenstein Highway
Cotati, California 94928

Janet Rosenberg and Associates
Landscape Architects, Inc.
28 Cecil Street
Toronto, Ontario M5T 1N3

GARDEN SUPPLIERS AND NURSERIES

W. Atlee Burpee Co.
Warminster, Pennsylvania 18974

Bear Creek Nursery
P.O. Box 411
Bear Creek Road
Northport, Washington 99157

Kurt Bluemel
2543 Hess Road
Tallston, Maryland 21047
—bamboo, grasses

Bountiful Gardens
5798 Ridgewood Road
Willits, California 95490
—organic heirloom seeds, herbs,
grains, flowers

Chesnut Corporation
622 Airport Road
Menasha, Wisconsin 54942
—garden tools

Clyde Robin Seed Company
P.O. Box 2366
Castro Valley, California 94556

The Cook's Garden
P.O. Box 65
Londonderry, Vermont 05148
—culinary vegetable and herb
seeds

The Country Garden
Box 455A
Route 2
Crivitz, Wisconsin 54114
—cutting flowers

De Giorgi Co., Inc.
Box 413
1409 Third Street
Council Buffs, Iowa 51502
—rare seeds

Florentine Craftsmen
46-24 28th Street
Long Island City, New York 11101
—ornamental sculptures

G.M. Nurseries, Inc.
P.O. Box 824
Holland, Michigan 49423

Gale Nurseries, Inc.
Box 264
1716 School House Road
Gwynedd, Pennsylvania 19436
—period and native plants

Gardena, Inc.
6031 Culligan Way
Minnetonka, Minnesota 55345
—tools

Gilbertie's Herb Gardens
Sylvan Lane
Westport, Connecticut 06880

Girard Nurseries
Box 428
Route 20 East
Geneva, Ohio 44041
—rhododendrons, azaleas

Green Gardens
1280 Good Pasture Island Road
Eugene, Oregon 97401
—rhododendrons, azaleas

Harris Seeds
3670 Buffalo Road
Rochester, New York 14624
and
1155 Harkins Road
Salinas, California 93901

Heath Manufacturing
P.O. Box 125
Coopersville, Michigan 49404
—redwood planters

High Altitude Gardens
Ketchum, Idaho 83340
—seeds for alpine gardens

Hilltop Herb Farm
P.O. Box 1734
Cleveland, Texas 77327
—hard-to-find plants

Japan Nurseries
Box 60 M
RD #1
Dey Grove Road
Englishtown, New Jersey 07726
—Japanese garden materials

Lilypons Water Gardens
P.O. Box 10
6800 Lilypons Road
Lilypons, Maryland 21717

Logee's Greenhouses
55 North Street
Danielson, Connecticut 06239
—scented geraniums

Maclin Designs
652 Glenbrook Road
Stamford, Connecticut 06906
—conservatories

Marcolina Brothers, Inc.
Masonry Contractors
133 East Mermaid Lane
Chestnut Hill, Pennsylvania 19118
—lily ponds, waterfalls

McClure and Zimmerman
1422 West Thorndale
Chicago, Illinois 60660
—bulbs

McLaughlin's Seeds
P.O. Box 550
Mead, Washington 99201

Mellinger's, Inc.
3210 W. South Range Road
North Lima, Ohio 44452
—trees

Midwest Wildflower
Box 64
Rockton, Illinois 61072

Milaeger's Gardens
4838 Douglas Avenue
Racine, Wisconsin 53402
—perennials

Moon Mountain
P.O. Box 34
Morro Bay, California 93442

Musser Forests
Box 21RS
Indiana, Pennsylvania 15701
—evergreens, shrubs, azaleas

Natural Gardens
113 Jasper Lane
Oak Ridge, Tennessee 37830

Nature's Garden
Box 488
Route 1
Beaverton, Oregon 47007

Nichols Garden Nursery
1190 North Pacific Highway
Albany, Oregon 97321
—herbs, rare seeds

Nor'East Miniature Roses, Inc.
58 Hammond Street
Rowley, Massachusetts 01969
or
P.O. Box 473
Ontario, California 91762

Oliver Nurseries
1159 Bronson Road
Fairfield, Connecticut 06430
—conifers

Park Seed Co.
Highway 254 North
Greenwood, South Carolina 29647
—flowers, vegetables

Peter's
1320 Route 309
Quakertown, Pennsylvania
—fountains, sundials, planters

Pinetree Garden Seeds
New Gloucester, Maine 04260

Plants of the Southwest
1570 Pacheco Street
Santa Fe, New Mexico 87501

Rhapsis Gardens
Gregory, Texas 78359

Santa Barbara Designs
P.O. Box 90610
Santa Barbara, California 93190

Sculpture Design Imports, Ltd.
416 South Robertson Boulevard
Los Angeles, California 90048

John Scheepers, Inc.
63 Wall Street
New York, New York 10005
—bulbs, perennials

Seed Savers Exchange
P.O. Box 70
Decorah, Iowa 52101

Shanti Bithi Nursery
3047 High Ridge Road
Stamford, Connecticut 06903
—bonsai

Shady Hill Gardens
821 Walnut Street
Batavia, Illinois 60510
—geraniums

Shepherd's Garden Seeds
7389 West Zayante Road
Felton, California 95018
—hard-to-find vegetables, edible
flowers

Smith and Hawken
25 Corte Madera
Mill Valley, California 94941
—garden tools

Sprain Brook Nursery, Inc.
448 Underhill Road
Scarsdale, New York 10583
—shrubs, trees, perennials,
woodland plants

Stark Brothers Nurseries and
   Orchards
Louisiana, Missouri 63353
—fruit and berry trees

Thompson and Morgan
P.O. Box 1308
Jackson, New Jersey 08527
—vegetables and flower seeds

William Tricker, Inc.
P.O. Box 398
74 Allendale Avenue
Saddle River, New Jersey 07458
   and
P.O. Box 7843
7125 Tanglewood Drive
Independence, Ohio 44131
—specializes in water gardens

Vick's Wildgardens, Inc.
Box 11
Conshohocken State Road
Gladwyne, Pennsylvania 19035
—wildflowers, native plants, ferns

Andre Viette
Box 16
Route 1
Fisherville, Virginia 22939
—numerous varieties of hosta

Wayside Gardens
Hodges, South Carolina 29695
—bulbs, perennials

We-Du Nurseries
Box 724
Route 5
Marion, North Carolina 28752
—wildflowers, native plants

White Flower Farm
Litchfield, Connecticut 06759
—perennials, begonias

Williams-Sonoma
P.O. Box 7301
San Francisco, California 94120

Wildginger Woodlands
P.O. Box 1091
Webster, New York 14580
—shrubs, ferns, wild and native
plants

Woodlanders
1128 Colleton Avenue
Aiken, South Carolina 29801

A World Seed Service
P.O. Box 1058
Redwood City, California 94064

Wyatt-Quarles Seed Company
P.O. Box 2131
Raleigh, North Carolina 27602
—herbs

SOURCES FOR FURTHER INFORMATION

Administrative Council
Extension Service
United States Department of
   Agriculture
Washington, D.C. 20250

American Horticultural Society
Department N
PO Box 0105
Mt. Vernon, Virginia 22121

American Rhododendron Society
RD #1 Kresson-Gibbsboro Road
Marlton, New Jersey 08053

American Rock Garden Society
413 Little Egypt Road
Elkton, Maryland 21921

American Rose Society
PO Box 30000
Shreveport, Louisiana 71130

The Herb Society of America
2 Independence Court
Concord, Massachusetts 01742

National Wildflower Research
   Center
2600 FM 973 North
Austin, Texas 78725

New England Wildflower Research
   Society
Garden-in-the-Woods
Hemenway Road
Framingham, Massachusetts 01701

RECOMMENDED READING

Allen, Oliver E. *Gardening with the New Small Plants: The Complete Guide to Growing Dwarf & Miniature Shrubs, Flowers, Trees & Vegetables.* Boston, MA: Houghton Mifflin Company, 1987.

Balston, Michael. *The Well Furnished Garden.* New York: Simon and Schuster, 1986.

Barton, Barbara J. *Gardening By Mail: A Sourcebook.* San Francisco: Tusker Press, 1986.

Bird, Rain. *The Gardener's Palette, The Ultimate Garden Plant Planner.* Garden City, New York: Doubleday and Company, Inc., 1987.

Boyd, Lizzie. *Window Gardens: How to Create Beautiful Windows Indoors and Out.* New York: Clarkson N. Potter, Inc./Publishers, 1985.

Bush, James and Louise Brown. *America's Garden Book.* New York: Charles Scribner's Sons, 1980.

Chamberlin, Susan. *Hedges, Screens and Espaliers.* Tucson: HP Books, 1982.

Ferguson, Nicola. *Right Plant, Right Place.* New York: Summit Books, 1984.

Gessert, Kate Rogers. *The Beautiful Food Garden Encyclopedia of Attractive Food Plants.* New York: Van Nostrand Reinhold Company, 1983.

Harper, Pamela and Frederick McGourty. *Perennials: How to Select, Grow & Enjoy.* Tucson: HP Books, 1985.

Johnson, Hugh. *The Principles of Gardening.* New York: Simon & Schuster, Inc., 1979.

Kinahan, Sonia. *The Overlook Guide to Winter Gardens.* Woodstock, New York: The Overlook Press, 1985.

Lerner, Joel M. *101 Townhouse Garden Designs to Fit Your Personality.* Tucson: HP Books, 1987.

Llewellyn, Roddy. *Little English Backyards.* Topsfield, Mass: Salem House, 1985.

McNelan, Ray and Micheline Ronningen. *Pacific Northwest Guide to Home Gardening.* Portland, OR: Timber Press, 1983.

Moon, Douglas. *Gardening for People (Who Think They Don't Know How).* Sante Fe: John Muir Publications, 1975.

Morris, Edwin T. *The Gardens of China: History, Art and Meanings.* New York: Charles Scribner's Sons, 1983.

Nicholls, Richard E. *Hydroponics Soilless Gardening: The Beginner's Guide to Growing Vegetables, Houseplants, Flowers and Herbs Without Soil.* Philadelphia: Running Press, 1977.

Puma, Joan. *The Complete Urban Gardener.* New York: Harper & Row, Inc., 1985.

Saville, Diana. *The Illustrated Garden Planter.* Harmondsworth, Middlesex, England: Penguin Books, 1986.

Seike, Kiyoshi, Masanoba Kudo, and David H. Engel. *A Japanese Touch for Your Garden.* Tokyo: Kodansha International, Ltd., 1980.

Snodsmith, Ralph. *Tips from the Garden Hotline.* Dallas: Taylor Publishing Company, 1984.

Strong, Roy. *Creating Small Gardens.* New York: Villard Books, 1987.

Wilkinson, Elizabeth and Marjorie Henderson. *The House of Boughs: A Sourcebook of Garden Designs, Structures, and Suppliers.* New York: Viking Penguin, Inc., 1985.

Wyman, Donald. *Wyman's Gardening Encyclopedia.* New York: MacMillan Publishing Company, 1986.

Yang, Linda. *The Terrace Gardener's Handbook.* Beaverton, Oregon: Timber Press, 1982.

INDEX